Strategy

The Harvard Business Review Book Series

Strategy
Seeking and Securing
Competitive Advantage

Edited with
an Introduction by
**Cynthia A. Montgomery and
Michael E. Porter**

A Harvard Business Review Book

Library of Congress Cataloging-in-Publication Data

Strategy : seeking and securing competitive advantage / edited and with an
    introduction by Cynthia A. Montgomery and Michael E. Porter.
        p.   cm. — (The Harvard business review book series)
    Includes bibliographical references and index.
    ISBN 0-87584-243-7 (hardcover : alk. paper) :
    1. Strategic planning.   I. Montgomery, Cynthia A., 1952–   .
II. Porter, Michael E., 1947–   .   III. Series.
HD30.28.S7292   1991
658.4'012—dc20   91-12193
                                                                   CIP

The *Harvard Business Review* articles in this collection are available individually. Discounts apply to quantity purchases. For information and order-
ing contact Operations Department, Harvard Business School Publishing
Division, Boston, MA 02163. Telephone: (617) 495-6192. Fax: (617) 495-
6985.

99 98 97   9 8 7

Contents

v

Introduction

Cynthia A. Montgomery and Michael E. Porter

The 1980s were the decade during which strategy became a full-fledged management discipline. Many of the early tools and techniques of strategic planning were replaced by more sophisticated, more appropriate, and more actionable approaches. Strategic planning evolved from an art practiced by specialists to an accepted and integral part of the job of all line managers. The result has been a downsizing of planning staffs, but an upsizing of the significance of strategic planning in many organizations.

The advances in strategic planning could not have come at a better time. Companies all over the world face growing competition, both at home and abroad, as trade barriers fall and government intrusion in competition recedes. Today, as never before, the need for sound strategies is no longer a luxury but a necessity. To cope with a more competitive environment, more sophisticated analysis is necessary, as is a more rapid translation of plans into action.

This collection of articles from the *Harvard Business Review* mirrors, in many ways, the progress of the strategy field in recent decades. With hindsight, we now have some perspective on how individual pieces fit together and which of the ideas have emerged as truly important advances.

Here we have endeavored to select articles that are timeless in the sense that they are not tied to fads or trends that pass quickly. We have also looked for ideas that have significantly influenced management practice or have had the potential to do so. Although space constraints prohibited the inclusion of every valuable article, we offer this collection as representative of the best of them.

We have organized the articles into the major areas of the strategy field. We will comment briefly on each area, highlighting what has been learned and the contribution of individual articles. There is still much to be learned, however, and we will also comment on some of the challenges that we believe lie ahead.

The Concept of Strategy

The articles in this collection are best seen against the backdrop of the pioneering work on which many modern strategy ideas rest. That work took place at the Harvard Business School in the early 1960s, led by Kenneth R. Andrews and C. Roland Christensen. At a time when management thinking was oriented toward individual functions such as marketing, production, and finance, Andrews and Christensen identified a pressing need for a holistic way of thinking about an enterprise. They articulated the concept of strategy as a tool for doing so.

Andrews and Christensen saw strategy as the unifying idea that linked together the functional areas in a company and related its activities to its external environment. Formulating strategy in this approach involved a juxtaposition of the company's strengths and weaknesses and the opportunities and threats presented by its environment (see Exhibit I).

The central concept in this early work was the notion of *fit* between the unique capabilities of a company and the competitive requirements of an industry that distinguished it from others. The challenge for management was to choose or create an environmental context where the company's distinctive competence and resources could produce a relative competitive advantage. This strategy then would be actualized through a consistent effort that coordinated the firm's goals, policies, and functional plans.

The work of Andrews and Christensen, along with that of others such as Igor Ansoff, Alfred D. Chandler, Jr., and Peter F. Drucker, propelled the notion of strategy into the forefront of management practice. Since that time, there have been many advances and refinements in both the practice and theory of strategy. It is a tribute to the soundness of this original work that it can comfortably encompass, and indeed has spawned, many of these developments.

Exhibit I.   Schematic Development of Economic Strategy

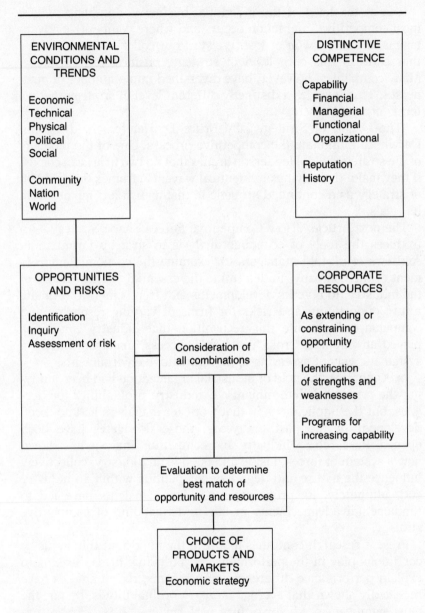

ENVIRONMENTAL
CONDITIONS AND
TRENDS

Economic
Technical
Physical
Political
Social

Community
Nation
World

DISTINCTIVE
COMPETENCE

Capability
   Financial
   Managerial
   Functional
   Organizational

Reputation
History

OPPORTUNITIES
AND RISKS

Identification
Inquiry
Assessment of risk

Consideration of
all combinations

CORPORATE
RESOURCES

As extending or
constraining
opportunity

Identification
of strengths and
weaknesses

Programs for
increasing capability

Evaluation to determine
best match of
opportunity and resources

CHOICE OF
PRODUCTS AND
MARKETS
Economic strategy

Source: Kenneth R. Andrews, The Concept of Corporate Strategy, 3d ed. (Homewood, IL: Dow Jones Irwin, 1978), p. 50. Reprinted with permission.

Business Strategy

It is at the level of the individual business or industry where most competitive interaction occurs and where competitive advantage is ultimately won or lost. We start our collection with articles that address this core level of strategy, *business-level* strategy. Many companies, however, have diversified into a number of businesses. This involves a distinctly different level of strategy that we term *corporate* strategy.

"The Origin of Strategy," by Bruce D. Henderson, draws on Darwin to illuminate the competitive process. One of the pioneers of the strategy field, Henderson argues that no two firms can coexist if they make their livings in identical ways. He frames the problem of strategy as a continued struggle to distinguish a company from its rivals.

The next article, "How Competitive Forces Shape Strategy," introduces the tools of economic analysis to strategy formulation. Andrews *et al.* told managers to "examine the economic environment of the company, to determine the essential characteristics of the industry, to note its developments and trends, and to estimate future opportunity and risks for firms of varying resources and competences." Despite this recognition that industry conditions played an important role in a firm's success, managers lacked a systematic way of assessing their competitive environments.

In economics, the field of industrial organization had been studying the structural determinants of industry profitability for decades, but the implications in that work for managers had not been developed. In the past ten years, those floodgates have been opened. Research on industry and competitor analysis has shown how a system of forces, inside and outside an industry, collectively influence the nature and degree of competition within an industry and, ultimately, its profit potential. These insights have led to fundamental advancements in our understanding of competitive strategy.

Present research continues to affirm the important role industry conditions play in the performance of individual firms. Seeking to explain performance differences across firms, recent studies have repeatedly shown that average industry profitability is, by far, the most significant predictor of firm performance.[1] It is far more important than market share and much more important than the extent of a firm's diversification (see Exhibit II). In short, it is now

Exhibit II. **Relative Contributions to Firm Performance**

Effect	Percentage
Industry structure	19.48
Diversification	2.65
Market share	−.18

Source: Birger Wernerfelt and Cynthia A. Montgomery, "Tobin's q and the Importance of Focus in Firm Performance," *American Economic Review* (March 1988), p. 249. Reprinted with permission.

uncontestable that industry analysis should play a vital role in strategy formation.

Out of the work on industry analysis has come a body of research on positioning a firm within its industry. Any company's performance is partly a result of the structure of its industry. We regularly observe that some companies outperform others in the same field year in and year out. Positioning a company in its industry is based on the search for competitive advantage. Competitive advantage can arise either from lower cost or from the ability to differentiate the company in the eyes of its customers and command a premium price. These advantages, in turn, arise out of the discrete activities a firm performs in creating, producing, marketing, and delivering its product. These activities collectively are called the value chain. Choices about the pursuit of competitive advantage must also involve concomitant choices about competitive scope, or the breadth of the company's strategic target.[2]

Earlier concepts of competitive positioning were based exclusively on cost and the role of market share as the sole determinants of cost position, but more recent research has shown this view to be oversimplified. We now know that several firms can succeed within the same industry by pursuing various strategies, each seeking a different form of competitive advantage for a different subset of customers.

The next article, "Sustainable Advantage" by Pankaj Ghemawat, highlights some of these issues. Based on his review of 100 successful firms, Ghemawat characterizes the competitive conditions and specific firm advantages that have endured.

The final two articles in Part I, "Time—The Next Source of Competitive Advantage" by George Stalk, Jr., and "Getting Back to Strategy" by Kenichi Ohmae, focus on two positioning issues that are important in virtually every company. Stalk addresses the importance of time as a strategic weapon. Although faster is not always better, Stalk makes a persuasive case that eliminating unnecessary cycle time pays competitive dividends. In "Getting Back to Strategy," Ohmae reminds us that preoccupation with competitors may obscure the real source of superior performance—creating value for customers.

Linking Competitive Strategy and Functional Strategy

While the articles in the first section focus on the firm and its external competitive environment, the articles in Part II are more inwardly directed. Their focus is on what has been termed *internal consistency*—the extent to which a firm's plans and policies reinforce each other and can be mutually achieved.

The difference between identifying desirable ends and reaching those ends rests in the implementation of a firm's strategy. It has long been recognized that major operating policies at the functional level should be an explicit part of a firm's strategy. Further, the policies in the various functional areas should be coordinated and work in concert to achieve the overall goals of the strategy.

Despite the importance of tightly coordinated plans and functions, dramatic failures in internal consistency continue to plague firms. It is not uncommon to see grand strategic plans that fail to describe how those ends will be reached. Worse, functional areas often work at odds with one another, each guided by its own sense of priorities and not influenced by the firm's strategic goals.

The articles in this section provide important examples of how to forge the linkage between competitive strategy and functional policies. They provide concrete examples of functional policies that support a firm's strategy. In elucidating a more strategic role for areas such as manufacturing, finance, and information systems, these articles expand the number of options firms possess for creating competitive advantage. In "Information Technology Changes the Way You Compete," F. Warren McFarlan describes some of the important links between information technology and strategy. "Competing through Manufacturing" by Steven C. Wheelwright and

Robert H. Hayes and "Financial Goals and Strategic Consequences" by Gordon Donaldson do the same for manufacturing and finance.

We selected these three articles not because they cover every important function but because they illustrate particularly well the needed linkages between strategy and functional policies. The same necessary relationship applies to marketing, research and development, control, and other important disciplines.

Evolving Nature of International Competition

Increasingly, both business units and corporations must compete globally. Global strategies involve not only selling worldwide but also producing and even conducting research in more than one location. Many strategic issues are the same regardless of whether the company is competing in one nation or many. It is still essential for a company to understand the structure of its industry and position itself to gain a sustainable competitive advantage.

Yet two additional questions must be addressed in global strategy. The first involves location. In a global strategy, the firm can choose to locate the various activities in its value chain anywhere. It must choose how to configure these activities worldwide to best reinforce its competitive advantage.

The second distinctive question in global strategy addresses coordination. As the global firm spreads activities around the world, it must decide how these activities should be coordinated or, conversely, allowed to operate autonomously to reinforce competitive advantage. The dual issues of configuration and coordination give rise to a host of alternative forms of global strategy whose appropriateness depends on industry structure and the firm's own competitive position.

When studying international markets, classical economists have emphasized macroeconomic variables, including interest rates, currency values, natural resources, and labor pools—all of which are quite beyond the ability of an individual firm or industry to control. The adequacy of this view has been decisively challenged. "The Competitive Advantage of Nations" argues that national prosperity can be created and is not merely a result of inherited endowments. In fact, for competing in sophisticated industries, the factor conditions that matter the most are those a nation develops such as specialized human resources or specific scientific know-how. These factors, together with demanding local buyers, a sophisticated supplier network, and intense domestic rivalry, are the conditions that spawn successful global competitors.

This new research, like some of the business strategy work discussed earlier, highlights the fact that sustainable competitive positions (1) reflect certain economic regularities, (2) are often the product of advantages that are created, not inherited, and (3) are built around unusual sets of capabilities that are difficult for competitors to imitate. The new research adds an interesting twist by showing that the locus of some of those resources is not necessarily within the firm. In fact, a group of competitors that share an intense rivalry may also share a sophisticated competitive context that becomes part of each firm's competitive repertoire in dealing with the global marketplace.

From the perspective of business strategy or public policy, the bottom line remains the same. Firms that create sustainable competitive positions in industries that are economically viable will prevail. The skills and resources for reaching those ends may be housed within the firm, may be outsourced, or may be part of a more broadly defined competitive context.

The other articles in this section address some of the new learning about how to manage the multinational firm. A multinational with subsidiaries in many countries is not necessarily a global firm. What is important is the firm's ability to integrate and coordinate its worldwide activities in individual business areas. This proves to be a daunting organizational challenge, for reasons of language, culture, and organizational incentives. Christopher A. Bartlett and Sumantra Ghoshal raise some of the most important organizational issues facing any multinational and describe how multinationals can truly leverage their global positions. Theodore Levitt's "The Globalization of Markets" illustrates how important it is to adopt a global perspective. Levitt argues that for many products the potential markets are indeed worldwide. The article, which has been controversial, has challenged companies and scholars alike to refine their understanding of how products developed in one nation can be sold elsewhere. In "Managing in a Borderless World," Ohmae talks about how global firms can get preferred access to important country markets.

These articles and other work on global strategy make clear that the euphoria about the ability of the global firm to transcend countries was unwarranted. Although the world is increasingly borderless from the point of view of transporting and marketing goods, there are strong national differences that are crucial not only to gaining competitive advantage but also to penetrating foreign markets. Every multinational needs a clear home base for each of its business activities. In turn, these bases must serve as the foundation for a global strategy.

Corporate Strategy and Firm Scope

Corporate strategy, or strategy for multibusiness firms, has captured a good deal of management attention since the 1970s. Regrettably, strategy choices in this area have been based on far less understanding than those in business-level strategy. Studies have repeatedly shown the disastrous consequences of most corporate strategies not only in the United States but elsewhere. Much of the diversification has been unsuccessful. Indeed, the failed diversification of the past has created a whole new industry that has profited greatly from unwinding it.

"From Competitive Advantage to Corporate Strategy" identifies some of the central issues in corporate strategy. At the heart of corporate strategy is the ability of a diversified corporation to enhance the competitive advantage of its business units. Otherwise, little economic value is created. Although much of the writing on corporate strategy has been decidedly financial in its orientation, what is becoming apparent is that corporate strategy must be inextricably linked to strategy at the business level. "From Competitive Advantage to Corporate Strategy" develops the broad concepts by which the diversified firm adds value to its business units. The most robust of these concepts require the ability to transfer proprietary skills or share important activities across business units.

The skills and activities that form the underpinning of successful diversification are an increasing subject of study. Alfred Chandler's historical essay, "The Enduring Logic of Industrial Success," illustrates the process at work in the twentieth century. C. K. Prahalad and Gary Hamel's article, "The Core Competence of the Corporation," highlights the importance of competences that transcend businesses.

We have made a beginning; yet important questions remain un-answered. So far, the argument is dangerously close to being cir-cular—a core competence is something that has made a company successful. We need to understand what makes competences, or "resources" as some prefer to call them, truly valuable in compet-itive terms. At both the corporate and business level, this is likely to be a function of the ease with which the resources can be imitated by competitors, the ability of the firm to capture the profits gen-erated by the resources, and the market conditions in which the resources are applied. Progress on these very complex issues will not come easily, but the rewards should be substantial.

Rather than diversify, firms are increasingly turning to strategic alliances. Some firms are using alliances to acquire new resources; others are electing to reduce their scope by specializing in a limited number of activities in the value chain and outsourcing the rest. At issue in the different approaches is the ease with which certain capabilities can be exchanged across, versus within, company boundaries. Also of concern is a firm's ability to capture the profits from the capabilities it owns.

We have selected two articles, "Beyond Products: Services-Based Strategy," by James Brian Quinn, Thomas L. Doorley, and Penny C. Paquette and "The Strategic Benefits of Logistics Alliances" by Donald J. Bowersox, that raise these issues. These articles were chosen because they recognize the complex trade-offs involved in forming alliances with other firms. Alliances can obtain benefits, but they carry inevitable costs in terms of coordination and com-plexity. While much of present research celebrates alliances, we believe the role of alliances to be more subtle. They are the means to achieve carefully focused strategic objectives, not ends in them-selves.

As many of the articles in this collection suggest, some of the toughest strategic issues managers face are within their own firms and involve transforming their own organizations rather than con-quering external adversaries. Organizational capabilities must be carefully nurtured, and systems and processes must be put in place to guide their deployment and enhancement. As we have seen, these are very difficult challenges. On the other hand, precisely because no templates exist and because the needs are critical, gains in these areas, deeply woven into the texture of firms, should be difficult for competitors to imitate and thus may become the basis for a powerful competitive advantage.

The Process of Making Strategy

Within firms, a number of systems have been developed to facilitate the process of strategy formation. Unfortunately, these systems are not always true to the ideals of their mission. In particular, many strategic planning systems focus on operating and financial details, not competitive positioning, and many lose sight of the critical competitive issues that planning should address. Companies cannot afford to interpret these difficulties as a signal that strategic analysis cannot be institutionalized. As the articles in this section show, planning systems can be quite effective when guided by a deep understanding of the elements of strategy.

"Many Best Ways to Make Strategy" by Michael Goold and Andrew Campbell and "Scenarios: Uncharted Waters Ahead" by Pierre Wack illustrate some of the processes for strategic planning that do work. Goold and Campbell show how to tailor planning processes to organizations. Wack describes the Royal Dutch/Shell scenario planning technique for unfreezing managers' views about the future.

The marriage between strategic planning and financial planning has become a double-edged sword. As Alfred Rappaport discusses, many financial planning models depend upon accounting measures that do not provide adequate estimates of the true economic value of investments. There is also the issue of the relative weight such systems place on financial projections, often in the absence of rigorous strategic analysis. We are now far from being able to estimate precisely the value of many strategic investments, particularly in intangible resources, that may increase in value through extended usage. Treating these assets in the same manner as tangible physical investments, or ignoring their value altogether, can result in very shortsighted investment decisions.

At the root of this dilemma is the fact that many strategic planning systems do not facilitate rigorous strategic analysis, including industry and competitor evaluation, and careful crafting of goals and functional plans. Until these elements are given the attention they require, such systems will surely fail.

"Crafting Strategy" by Henry Mintzberg completes this part of the book by highlighting the basic purposes of the strategy-making process. Mintzberg's call to reduce complexity is a fitting lesson for many companies.

Corporate Governance

Historically, management texts have talked about the chief executive officer as the firm's chief strategist—the person ultimately responsible for determining organizational objectives and purpose and establishing the means to reach those ends. Embedded in this perspective is an orderly sense of continuity that intimately intertwines management and corporate governance.

Recent takeover activity raises serious doubts about this view of the world. Essentially at issue is the question of who has the right, or how one earns the right, to determine firm strategy. Chester Barnard long ago raised the distinction between "doing the right things" and "doing things right."[3] Serious errors of judgment or execution on either dimension can lead not only to the replacement of the CEO, but also the movement of decision-making responsibility into completely new hands, often those of a new set of owners. Such transitions may occur not only in the face of ineptness, but also when a firm has built a set of resources that another firm finds particularly valuable for its own purposes.

It is evident that takeover activity plays an important disciplining role, which Michael C. Jensen's "Eclipse of the Public Corporation" stresses. The power of the mechanism itself is consistent with the depth of responsibility corporate leadership bears. Were there no such mechanisms, or only weaker mechanisms, the vital checks and balances on high-level management and directors of firms would be diminished.

At the same time, it is not clear that the impact of these abrupt changes in corporate leadership and governance is universally positive. While early research has shown that takeovers have had a positive impact on the competitiveness of individual businesses, we cannot now assess the long-run implications of revolving door strategists.[4] In particular, it is difficult to predict how this activity might influence long-term, firm-specific investments in tangible and intangible resources.

Andrews' article, "Directors' Responsibility for Corporate Strategy," suggests a means by which chief executives can avoid some of the pitfalls that have led to takeovers in the first place. He shows how a board of directors, which truly represents firms' owners, can play a far more constructive role in developing strategy than is often the case.

It is prudent, then, to underscore the extent of responsibility that one bears in setting and carrying out corporate strategies. The checks and balances provided by supplier markets, product markets, and capital markets will continue to be an ever-present reminder of the seriousness of the task itself.

Notes

1. Richard Schmalensee, "Do Markets Differ Much?," *American Economic Review* (June 1985), pp. 341–351.

2. Michael E. Porter, *Competitive Strategy: Techniques for Analyzing Industries and Competitors* (New York: Free Press, 1980) and Michael E. Porter, *Competitive Advantage: Creating and Sustaining Superior Performance* (New York: Free Press, 1985).

3. Chester I. Barnard, *The Functions of the Executive* (Cambridge, MA: Harvard University Press, 1938).

4. Steven Kaplan, "The Effects of Management Buyouts on Operating Performance and Value," *Journal of Financial Economics*, vol. 24, no. 2 (October 1989), pp. 217–254.

Strategy

PART

I

Business Strategy

1
The Origin of Strategy

Bruce D. Henderson

Consider this lesson in strategy. In 1934, Professor G.F. Gause of Moscow University, known as "the father of mathematical biology," published the results of a set of experiments in which he put two very small animals (protozoans) of the same genus in a bottle with an adequate supply of food. If the animals were of different species, they could survive and persist together. If they were of the same species, they could not. This observation led to Gause's Principle of Competitive Exclusion: No two species can coexist that make their living in the identical way.

Competition existed long before strategy. It began with life itself. The first one-cell organisms required certain resources to maintain life. When these resources were adequate, the number grew from one generation to the next. As life evolved, these organisms became a resource for more complex forms of life, and so on up the food chain. When any pair of species competed for some essential resource, sooner or later one displaced the other. In the absence of counterbalancing forces that could maintain a stable equilibrium by giving each species an advantage in its own territory, only one of any pair survived.

Over millions of years, a complex network of competitive interaction developed. Today more than a million distinct existing species have been cataloged, each with some unique advantage in competing for the resources it requires. (There are thought to be millions more as yet unclassified.) At any given time, thousands of species are becoming extinct and thousands more are emerging.

What explains this abundance? *Variety.* The richer the environment, the greater the number of potentially significant variables that can give each species a unique advantage. But also, the richer the environment, the greater the potential number of competitors—and the more severe the competition.

For millions of years, natural competition involved no strategy. By chance and the laws of probability, competitors found the combinations of resources that best matched their different characteristics. This was not strategy but Darwinian natural selection, based on adaptation and the survival of the fittest. The same pattern exists in all living systems, including business.

In both the competition of the ecosphere and the competition of trade and commerce, random chance is probably the major, all-pervasive factor. Chance determines the mutations and variations that survive and thrive from generation to generation. Those that leave relatively fewer offspring are displaced. Those that adapt best displace the rest. Physical and structural characteristics evolve and adapt to match the competitive environment. Behavior patterns evolve too and become embedded as instinctual reactions.

In fact, business and biological competition would follow the same pattern of gradual evolutionary change except for one thing. Business strategists can use their imagination and ability to reason logically to accelerate the effects of competition and the rate of change. In other words, imagination and logic make strategy possible. Without them, behavior and tactics are either intuitive or the result of conditioned reflexes. But imagination and logic are only two of the factors that determine shifts in competitive equilibrium. Strategy also requires the ability to understand the complex web of natural competition.

If every business could grow indefinitely, the total market would grow to an infinite size on a finite earth. It has never happened. Competitors perpetually crowd each other out. The fittest survive and prosper until they displace their competitors or outgrow their resources. What explains this evolutionary process? Why do business competitors achieve the equilibrium they do?

Remember Gause's Principle. Competitors that make their living in the same way cannot coexist—no more in business than in nature. Each must be different enough to have a unique advantage. The continued existence of a number of competitors is proof per se that their advantages over each other are mutually exclusive. They may look alike, but they are different species.

Consider Sears, K mart, Wal-Mart, and Radio Shack. These stores overlap in the merchandise they sell, in the customers they serve, and in the areas where they operate. But to survive, each of these retailers has had to differentiate itself in important ways, to dominate different segments of the market. Each sells to different customers or offers different values, services, or products.

What differentiates competitors in business may be purchase price, function, time utility (the difference between instant gratification and "someday, as soon as possible"), or place utility (when your heating and cooling system quits, the manufacturer's technical expert is not nearly as valuable as the local mechanic). Or it may be nothing but the customer's perception of the product and its supplier. Indeed, image is often the only basis of comparison between similar but different alternatives. That is why advertising can be valuable.

Since businesses can combine these factors in many different ways, there will always be many possibilities for competitive coexistence. But also, many possibilities for each competitor to enlarge the scope of its advantage by changing what differentiates it from its rivals. Can evolution be planned for in business? That is what strategy is for.

Strategy is a deliberate search for a plan of action that will develop a business's competitive advantage and compound it. For any company, the search is an iterative process that begins with a recognition of where you are and what you have now. Your most dangerous competitors are those that are most like you. The differences between you and your competitors are the basis of your advantage. If you are in business and are self-supporting, you already have some kind of competitive advantage, no matter how small or subtle. Otherwise, you would have gradually lost customers faster than you gained them. The objective is to enlarge the scope of your advantage, which can happen only at someone else's expense.

Chasing market share is almost as productive as chasing the pot of gold at the end of the rainbow. You can never get there. Even if you could, you would find nothing. If you are in business, you already have 100% of your own market. So do your competitors. Your real goal is to expand the size of your market. But you will always have 100% of your market, whether it grows or shrinks.

Your present market is what, where, and to whom you are selling what you now sell. Survival depends on keeping 100% of this market. To grow and prosper, however, you must expand the market in which you can maintain an advantage over any and all competitors that might be selling to your customers.

Unless a business has a unique advantage over its rivals, it has no reason to exist. Unfortunately, many businesses compete in important areas where they operate at a disadvantage—often at great cost, until, inevitably, they are crowded out. That happened to Texas Instruments and its pioneering personal computer. TI invented the semiconductor; its business was built on instrumentation. Why was it forced out of the personal computer business?

Many executives have been led on a wild goose chase after market share by their inability to define the potential market in which they would, or could, enjoy a competitive advantage. Remember the Edsel? And the Mustang? Xerox invented the copying machine; why couldn't IBM become a major competitor in this field? What did Kodak do to virtually dominate the large-scale business copier market in the United States? What did Coca-Cola do to virtually dominate the soft drink business in Japan?

But what is market share? Grape Nuts has 100% of the Grape Nuts market, a smaller percentage of the breakfast cereal market, an even smaller percentage of the packaged-foods market, a still smaller percentage of the packaged-goods shelf-space market, a tiny percentage of the U.S. food market, a minuscule percentage of the world food market, and a microscopic percentage of total consumer expenditures.

Market share is a meaningless number unless a company defines the market in terms of the boundaries separating it from its rivals. These boundaries are the points at which the company and a particular competitor are equivalent in a potential customer's eyes. The trick lies in moving the boundary of advantage into the potential competitor's market and keeping that competitor from doing the same. The competitor that truly has an advantage can give potential customers more for their money and still have a larger margin between its cost and its selling price. That extra can be converted into either growth or larger payouts to the business's owners.

So what is new? The marketing wars are forever. But market share is malarkey.

Strategic competition compresses time. Competitive shifts that might take generations to evolve instead occur in a few short years. Strategic competition is not new, of course. Its elements have been recognized and used ever since humans combined intelligence, imagination, accumulated resources, and coordinated behavior to wage war. But strategic competition in business is a relatively recent phenomenon. It may well have as profound an impact on business productivity as the industrial revolution had on individual productivity.

The basic elements of strategic competition are these: (1) ability to understand competitive behavior as a system in which competitors, customers, money, people, and resources continually interact; (2) ability to use this understanding to predict how a given strategic move will rebalance the competitive equilibrium; (3) resources that can be permanently committed to new uses even though the benefits will be deferred; (4) ability to predict risk and return with enough accuracy and confidence to justify that commitment; and (5) willingness to act.

This list may sound like nothing more than the basic requirements for making any ordinary investment. But strategy is not that simple. It is all-encompassing, calling on the commitment and dedication of the whole organization. Any competitor's failure to react and then deploy and commit its own resources against the strategic move of a rival can turn existing competitive relationships upside down. That is why strategic competition compresses time. Natural competition has none of these characteristics.

Natural competition is wildly expedient in its moment-to-moment interaction. But it is inherently conservative in the way it changes a species's characteristic behavior. By contrast, strategic commitment is deliberate, carefully considered, and tightly reasoned. But the consequences may well be radical change in a relatively short period of time. Natural competition is evolutionary. Strategic competition is revolutionary.

Natural competition works by a process of low-risk, incremental trial and error. Small changes are tried and tested. Those that are beneficial are gradually adopted and maintained. No need for foresight or commitment, what matters is adaptation to the way things are now. Natural competition can and does evolve exquisitely complex and effective forms eventually. Humans are just such an end result. But unmanaged change takes thousands of generations. Often it cannot keep up with a fast-changing environment and with the adaptation of competitors.

By committing resources, strategy seeks to make sweeping changes in competitive relationships. Only two fundamental inhibitions moderate its revolutionary character. One is failure, which can be as far-reaching in its consequences as success. The other is the inherent advantage that an alert defender has over an attacker.

Success usually depends on the culture, perceptions, attitudes, and characteristic behavior of competitors and on their mutual awareness of each other.

This is why, in geopolitics and military affairs as well as in business, long periods of equilibrium are punctuated by sharp shifts in competitive relationships. It is the age-old pattern of war and peace and then war again. Natural competition continues during periods of peace. In business, however, peace is becoming increasingly rare. When an aggressive competitor launches a successful strategy, all the other businesses with which it competes must respond with equal foresight and dedication of resources.

In 1975, the British War Office opened its classified files on World War II. Serious readers of these descriptions of "war by other means" may feel inclined to revise their thinking about what happened in that war and about strategy generally, particularly the differences between actual strategies and apparent strategies.

The evidence is clear that the outcome of individual battles and campaigns often depended on highly subjective evaluations of the combatants' intentions, capabilities, and behavior. But until the records were unsealed, only people who were directly involved appreciated this. Historians and other observers ascribed victories and defeats to grand military plans or chance.

Also in 1975, Edward O. Wilson published *Sociobiology*, a landmark study in which he tried to synthesize all that is known about population biology, zoology, genetics, and animal behavior. What emerged was a framework for understanding the success of species in terms of social behavior—that is, competition for resources. This synthesis is the closest approach to a general theory of competition that I know of. It provides abundant parallels for business behavior as well as for the economic competition that characterizes our own species.

Human beings may be at the top of the ecological chain, but we are still members of the ecological community. That is why Darwin is probably a better guide to business competition than economists are.

Classical economic theories of business competition are so simplistic and sterile that they have been less contributions to understanding than obstacles. These theories postulate rational, self-interested behavior by individuals who interact through market exchanges in a fixed and static legal system of property and contracts. Their frame of reference is "perfect competition," a theoretical abstraction that never has existed and never could exist.

In contrast, Charles Darwin's *On the Origin of Species,* published in 1859, outlines a more fruitful perspective and point of departure for developing business strategy: "Some make the deep-seated error of considering the physical conditions of a country as the most important for its inhabitants; whereas it cannot, I think, be disputed that the nature of the other inhabitants with which each has to compete is generally a far more important element of success."

2
How Competitive Forces
Shape Strategy

Michael E. Porter

The essence of strategy formulation is coping with competition. Yet it is easy to view competition too narrowly and too pessimistically. While one sometimes hears executives complaining to the contrary, intense competition in an industry is neither coincidence nor bad luck.

Moreover, in the fight for market share, competition is not manifested only in the other players. Rather, competition in an industry is rooted in its underlying economics, and competitive forces exist that go well beyond the established combatants in a particular industry. Customers, suppliers, potential entrants, and substitute products are all competitors that may be more or less prominent or active depending on the industry.

The state of competition in an industry depends on five basic forces, which are diagrammed in Exhibit I. The collective strength of these forces determines the ultimate profit potential of an industry. It ranges from *intense* in industries like tires, metal cans, and steel, where no company earns spectacular returns on investment, to *mild* in industries like oil field services and equipment, soft drinks, and toiletries, where there is room for quite high returns.

In the economists' "perfectly competitive" industry, jockeying for position is unbridled and entry to the industry very easy. This kind of industry structure, of course, offers the worst prospect for long-run profitability. The weaker the forces collectively, however, the greater the opportunity for superior performance.

Whatever their collective strength, the corporate strategist's goal

Exhibit I.   Forces Governing Competition in an Industry

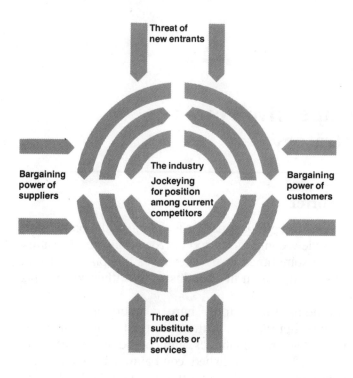

is to find a position in the industry where his or her company can best defend itself against these forces or can influence them in its favor. The collective strength of the forces may be painfully apparent to all the antagonists; but to cope with them, the strategist must delve below the surface and analyze the sources of each. For example, what makes the industry vulnerable to entry? What determines the bargaining power of suppliers?

Knowledge of these underlying sources of competitive pressure provides the groundwork for a strategic agenda of action. They highlight the critical strengths and weaknesses of the company, animate the positioning of the company in its industry, clarify the areas where strategic changes may yield the greatest payoff, and highlight the places where industry trends promise to hold the greatest significance as either opportunities or threats. Understanding these sources also proves to be of help in considering areas for diversification.

Contending Forces

The strongest competitive force or forces determine the profitability of an industry and so are of greatest importance in strategy formulation. For example, even a company with a strong position in an industry unthreatened by potential entrants will earn low returns if it faces a superior or a lower-cost substitute product—as the leading manufacturers of vacuum tubes and coffee percolators have learned to their sorrow. In such a situation, coping with the substitute product becomes the number one strategic priority.

Different forces take on prominence, of course, in shaping competition in each industry. In the ocean-going tanker industry the key force is probably the buyers (the major oil companies), while in tires it is powerful OEM buyers coupled with tough competitors. In the steel industry the key forces are foreign competitors and substitute materials.

Every industry has an underlying structure, or a set of fundamental economic and technical characteristics, that gives rise to these competitive forces. The strategist, wanting to position his company to cope best with its industry environment or to influence that environment in the company's favor, must learn what makes the environment tick.

This view of competition pertains equally to industries dealing in services and to those selling products. To avoid monotony in this article, I refer to both products and services as "products." The same general principles apply to all types of business.

A few characteristics are critical to the strength of each competitive force. I shall discuss them in this section.

THREAT OF ENTRY

New entrants to an industry bring new capacity, the desire to gain market share, and often substantial resources. Companies diversifying through acquisition into the industry from other markets often leverage their resources to cause a shake-up, as Philip Morris did with Miller beer.

The seriousness of the threat of entry depends on the barriers present and on the reaction from existing competitors that the entrant can expect. If barriers to entry are high and a newcomer can expect sharp retaliation from the entrenched competitors, obviously he will not pose a serious threat of entering.

There are six major sources of barriers to entry:

1. *Economies of scale*—These economies deter entry by forcing the aspirant either to come in on a large scale or to accept a cost disadvantage. Scale economies in production, research, marketing, and service are probably the key barriers to entry in the mainframe computer industry, as Xerox and GE sadly discovered. Economies of scale can also act as hurdles in distribution, utilization of the sales force, financing, and nearly any other part of a business.

2. *Product differentiation*—Brand identification creates a barrier by forcing entrants to spend heavily to overcome customer loyalty. Advertising, customer service, being first in the industry, and product differences are among the factors fostering brand identification. It is perhaps the most important entry barrier in soft drinks, over-the-counter drugs, cosmetics, investment banking, and public accounting. To create high fences around their businesses, brewers couple brand identification with economies of scale in production, distribution, and marketing.

3. *Capital requirements*—The need to invest large financial resources in order to compete creates a barrier to entry, particularly if the capital is required for unrecoverable expenditures in up-front advertising or R&D. Capital is necessary not only for fixed facilities but also for customer credit, inventories, and absorbing start-up losses. While major corporations have the financial resources to invade almost any industry, the huge capital requirements in certain fields, such as computer manufacturing and mineral extraction, limit the pool of likely entrants.

4. *Cost disadvantages independent of size*—Entrenched companies may have cost advantages not available to potential rivals, no matter what their size and attainable economies of scale. These advantages can stem from the effects of the learning curve (and of its first cousin, the experience curve), proprietary technology, access to the best raw materials sources, assets purchased at preinflation prices, government subsidies, or favorable locations. Sometimes cost advantages are legally enforceable, as they are through patents.

5. *Access to distribution channels*—The new boy on the block must, of course, secure distribution of his product or service. A new food

product, for example, must displace others from the supermarket shelf via price breaks, promotions, intense selling efforts, or some other means. The more limited the wholesale or retail channels are and the more that existing competitors have these tied up, obviously the tougher that entry into the industry will be. Sometimes this barrier is so high that, to surmount it, a new contestant must create its own distribution channels, as Timex did in the watch industry in the 1950s.

6. *Government policy*—The government can limit or even foreclose entry to industries with such controls as license requirements and limits on access to raw materials. Regulated industries like trucking, liquor retailing, and freight forwarding are noticeable examples; more subtle government restrictions operate in fields like ski-area development and coal mining. The government also can play a major indirect role by affecting entry barriers through controls such as air and water pollution standards and safety regulations.

The potential rival's expectations about the reaction of existing competitors also will influence its decision on whether to enter. The company is likely to have second thoughts if incumbents have previously lashed out at new entrants or if:

The incumbents possess substantial resources to fight back, including excess cash and unused borrowing power, productive capacity, or clout with distribution channels and customers.

The incumbents seem likely to cut prices because of a desire to keep market shares or because of industrywide excess capacity.

Industry growth is slow, affecting its ability to absorb the new arrival and probably causing the financial performance of all the parties involved to decline.

CHANGING CONDITIONS. From a strategic standpoint there are two important additional points to note about the threat of entry.

First, it changes, of course, as these conditions change. The expiration of Polaroid's basic patents on instant photography, for instance, greatly reduced its absolute cost entry barrier built by proprietary technology. It is not surprising that Kodak plunged into the market. Product differentiation in printing has all but disappeared. Conversely, in the auto industry economies of scale increased enormously with post-World War II automation and vertical integration—virtually stopping successful new entry.

Second, strategic decisions involving a large segment of an industry can have a major impact on the conditions determining the threat of entry. For example, the actions of many U.S. wine producers in the 1960s to step up product introductions, raise advertising levels, and expand distribution nationally surely strengthened the entry roadblocks by raising economies of scale and making access to distribution channels more difficult. Similarly, decisions by members of the recreational vehicle industry to vertically integrate in order to lower costs have greatly increased the economies of scale and raised the capital cost barriers.

POWERFUL SUPPLIERS AND BUYERS

Suppliers can exert bargaining power on participants in an industry by raising prices or reducing the quality of purchased goods and services. Powerful suppliers can thereby squeeze profitability out of an industry unable to recover cost increases in its own prices. By raising their prices, soft drink concentrate producers have contributed to the erosion of profitability of bottling companies because the bottlers, facing intense competition from powdered mixes, fruit drinks, and other beverages, have limited freedom to raise *their* prices accordingly. Customers likewise can force down prices, demand higher quality or more service, and play competitors off against each other—all at the expense of industry profits.

The power of each important supplier or buyer group depends on a number of characteristics of its market situation and on the relative importance of its sales or purchases to the industry compared with its overall business.

A *supplier* group is powerful if:

It is dominated by a few companies and is more concentrated than the industry it sells to.

Its product is unique or at least differentiated, or if it has built up switching costs. Switching costs are fixed costs buyers face in changing suppliers. These arise because, among other things, a buyer's product specifications tie it to particular suppliers, it has invested heavily in specialized ancillary equipment or in learning how to operate a supplier's equipment (as in computer software), or its production lines are connected to the supplier's manufacturing facilities (as in some manufacture of beverage containers).

It is not obliged to contend with other products for sale to the industry. For instance, the competition between the steel companies and the aluminum companies to sell to the can industry checks the power of each supplier.

It poses a credible threat of integrating forward into the industry's business. This provides a check against the industry's ability to improve the terms on which it purchases.

The industry is not an important customer of the supplier group. If the industry is an important customer, suppliers' fortunes will be closely tied to the industry, and they will want to protect the industry through reasonable pricing and assistance in activities like R&D and lobbying.

A *buyer* group is powerful if:

It is concentrated or purchases in large volumes. Large-volume buyers are particularly potent forces if heavy fixed costs characterize the industry—as they do in metal containers, corn refining, and bulk chemicals, for example—which raise the stakes to keep capacity filled.

The products it purchases from the industry are standard or undifferentiated. The buyers, sure that they can always find alternative suppliers, may play one company against another, as they do in aluminum extrusion.

The products it purchases from the industry form a component of its product and represent a significant fraction of its cost. The buyers are likely to shop for a favorable price and purchase selectively. Where the product sold by the industry in question is a small fraction of buyers' costs, buyers are usually much less price sensitive.

It earns low profits, which create great incentive to lower its purchasing costs. Highly profitable buyers, however, are generally less price sensitive (that is, of course, if the item does not represent a large fraction of their costs).

The industry's product is unimportant to the quality of the buyers' products or services. Where the quality of the buyers' products is very much affected by the industry's product, buyers are generally less price sensitive. Industries in which this situation obtains include oil field equipment, where a malfunction can lead to large losses, and enclosures for electronic medical and test instruments where the quality of the enclosure can influence the user's impression about the quality of the equipment inside.

The industry's product does not save the buyer money. Where the industry's product or service can pay for itself many times over, the buyer is rarely price sensitive; rather, he is interested in quality. This is true in services like investment banking and public accounting, where errors in judgment can be costly and embarrassing, and in businesses like the logging of oil wells, where an accurate survey can save thousands of dollars in drilling costs.

The buyers pose a credible threat of integrating backward to make the industry's product. The Big Three auto producers and major buyers of cars have often used the threat of self-manufacture as a bargaining lever. But sometimes an industry engenders a threat to buyers that its members may integrate forward.

Most of these sources of buyer power can be attributed to consumers as a group as well as to industrial and commercial buyers; only a modification of the frame of reference is necessary. Consumers tend to be more price sensitive if they are purchasing products that are undifferentiated, expensive relative to their incomes, and of a sort where quality is not particularly important.

The buying power of retailers is determined by the same rules, with one important addition. Retailers can gain significant bargaining power over manufacturers when they can influence consumers' purchasing decisions, as they do in audio components, jewelry, appliances, sporting goods, and other goods.

STRATEGIC ACTION.   A company's choice of suppliers to buy from or buyer groups to sell to should be viewed as a crucial strategic decision. A company can improve its strategic posture by finding suppliers or buyers who possess the least power to influence it adversely.

Most common is the situation of a company being able to choose whom it will sell to—in other words, buyer selection. Rarely do all the buyer groups a company sells to enjoy equal power. Even if a company sells to a single industry, segments usually exist within that industry that exercise less power (and that are therefore less price sensitive) than others. For example, the replacement market for most products is less price sensitive than the overall market.

As a rule, a company can sell to powerful buyers and still come away with above-average profitability only if it is a low-cost producer in its industry or if its product enjoys some unusual, if not unique, features. In supplying large customers with electric motors,

Emerson Electric earns high returns because its low-cost position permits the company to meet or undercut competitors' prices.

If the company lacks a low-cost position or a unique product, selling to everyone is self-defeating because the more sales it achieves, the more vulnerable it becomes. The company may have to muster the courage to turn away business and sell only to less potent customers.

Buyer selection has been a key to the success of National Can and Crown Cork & Seal. They focus on the segments of the can industry where they can create product differentiation, minimize the threat of backward integration, and otherwise mitigate the awesome power of their customers. Of course, some industries do not enjoy the luxury of selecting "good" buyers.

As the factors creating supplier and buyer power change with time or as a result of a company's strategic decisions, naturally the power of these groups rises or declines. In the ready-to-wear clothing industry, as the buyers (department stores and clothing stores) have become more concentrated and control has passed to large chains, the industry has come under increasing pressure and suffered falling margins. The industry has been unable to differentiate its product or engender switching costs that lock in its buyers enough to neutralize these trends.

SUBSTITUTE PRODUCTS

By placing a ceiling on prices it can charge, substitute products or services limit the potential of an industry. Unless it can upgrade the quality of the product or differentiate it somehow (as via marketing), the industry will suffer in earnings and possibly in growth.

Manifestly, the more attractive the price-performance trade-off offered by substitute products, the firmer the lid placed on the industry's profit potential. Sugar producers confronted with the large-scale commercialization of high-fructose corn syrup, a sugar substitute, are learning this lesson today.

Substitutes not only limit profits in normal times; they also reduce the bonanza an industry can reap in boom times. In 1978, the producers of fiberglass insulation enjoyed unprecedented demand as a result of high energy costs and severe winter weather. But the industry's ability to raise prices was tempered by the plethora of insulation substitutes, including cellulose, rock wool, and styrofoam. These substitutes are bound to become an even stronger force once the current round of plant additions by fiberglass insulation producers has boosted capacity enough to meet demand (and then some).

Substitute products that deserve the most attention strategically are those that (a) are subject to trends improving their price-performance trade-off with the industry's product, or (b) are produced by industries earning high profits. Substitutes often come rapidly into play if some development increases competition in their industries and causes price reduction or performance improvement.

JOCKEYING FOR POSITION

Rivalry among existing competitors takes the familiar form of jockeying for position—using tactics like price competition, product introduction, and advertising slugfests. Intense rivalry is related to the presence of a number of factors:

Competitors are numerous or are roughly equal in size and power. In many U.S. industries in recent years foreign contenders, of course, have become part of the competitive picture.

Industry growth is slow, precipitating fights for market share that involve expansion-minded members.

The product or service lacks differentiation or switching costs, which lock in buyers and protect one combatant from raids on its customers by another.

Fixed costs are high or the product is perishable, creating strong temptation to cut prices. Many basic materials businesses, like paper and aluminum, suffer from this problem when demand slackens.

Capacity is normally augmented in large increments. Such additions, as in the chlorine and vinyl chloride businesses, disrupt the industry's supply-demand balance and often lead to periods of overcapacity and price cutting.

Exit barriers are high. Exit barriers, like very specialized assets or management's loyalty to a particular business, keep companies competing even though they may be earning low or even negative returns on investment. Excess capacity remains functioning, and the profitability of the healthy competitors suffers as the sick ones hang on.[1] If the entire industry suffers from overcapacity, it may seek government help—particularly if foreign competition is present.

The rivals are diverse in strategies, origins, and "personalities." They have different ideas about how to compete and continually run head-on into each other in the process.

As an industry matures, its growth rate changes, resulting in declining profits and (often) a shakeout. In the booming recreational vehicle industry of the early 1970s, nearly every producer did well; but slow growth since then has eliminated the high returns, except for the strongest members, not to mention many of the weaker companies. The same profit story has been played out in industry after industry—snowmobiles, aerosol packaging, and sports equipment are just a few examples.

An acquisition can introduce a very different personality to an industry, as has been the case with Black & Decker's takeover of McCullough, the producer of chain saws. Technological innovation can boost the level of fixed costs in the production process, as it did in the shift from batch to continuous-line photo finishing in the 1960s.

While a company must live with many of these factors—because they are built into industry economics—it may have some latitude for improving matters through strategic shifts. For example, it may try to raise buyers' switching costs or increase product differentiation. A focus on selling efforts in the fastest-growing segments of the industry or on market areas with the lowest fixed costs can reduce the impact of industry rivalry. If it is feasible, a company can try to avoid confrontation with competitors having high exit barriers and can thus sidestep involvement in bitter price cutting.

Formulation of Strategy

Once having assessed the forces affecting competition in an industry and their underlying causes, the corporate strategist can identify the company's strengths and weaknesses. The crucial strengths and weaknesses from a strategic standpoint are the company's posture vis-à-vis the underlying causes of each force. Where does it stand against substitutes? Against the sources of entry barriers?

Then the strategist can devise a plan of action that may include (1) positioning the company so that its capabilities provide the best defense against the competitive force; and/or (2) influencing the balance of the forces through strategic moves, thereby improving the company's position; and/or (3) anticipating shifts in the factors underlying the forces and responding to them, with the hope of exploiting change by choosing a strategy appropriate for the new competitive balance before opponents recognize it. I shall consider each strategic approach in turn.

POSITIONING THE COMPANY

The first approach takes the structure of the industry as given and matches the company's strengths and weaknesses to it. Strategy can be viewed as building defenses against the competitive forces or as finding positions in the industry where the forces are weakest.

Knowledge of the company's capabilities and of the causes of the competitive forces will highlight the areas where the company should confront competition and where avoid it. If the company is a low-cost producer, it may choose to confront powerful buyers while it takes care to sell them only products not vulnerable to competition from substitutes.

The success of Dr Pepper in the soft drink industry illustrates the coupling of realistic knowledge of corporate strengths with sound industry analysis to yield a superior strategy. Coca-Cola and Pepsi-Cola dominate Dr Pepper's industry, where many small concentrate producers compete for a piece of the action. Dr Pepper chose a strategy of avoiding the largest-selling drink segment, maintaining a narrow flavor line, forgoing the development of a captive bottler network, and marketing heavily. The company positioned itself so as to be least vulnerable to its competitive forces while it exploited its small size.

In the $11.5 billion soft drink industry, barriers to entry in the form of brand identification, large-scale marketing, and access to a bottler network are enormous. Rather than accept the formidable costs and scale economies in having its own bottler network—that is, following the lead of the Big Two and of Seven-Up—Dr Pepper took advantage of the different flavor of its drink to "piggyback" on Coke and Pepsi bottlers who wanted a full line to sell to customers. Dr Pepper coped with the power of these buyers through extraordinary service and other efforts to distinguish its treatment of them from that of Coke and Pepsi.

Many small companies in the soft drink business offer cola

drinks that thrust them into head-to-head competition against the majors. Dr Pepper, however, maximized product differentiation by maintaining a narrow line of beverages built around an unusual flavor.

Finally, Dr Pepper met Coke and Pepsi with an advertising on-slaught emphasizing the alleged uniqueness of its single flavor. This campaign built strong brand identification and great customer loyalty. Helping its efforts was the fact that Dr Pepper's formula involved lower raw materials cost, which gave the company an absolute cost advantage over its major competitors.

There are no economies of scale in soft drink concentrate production, so Dr Pepper could prosper despite its small share of the business (6%). Thus Dr Pepper confronted competition in marketing but avoided it in product line and in distribution. This artful positioning combined with good implementation has led to an enviable record in earnings and in the stock market.

INFLUENCING THE BALANCE

When dealing with the forces that drive industry competition, a company can devise a strategy that takes the offensive. This posture is designed to do more than merely cope with the forces themselves; it is meant to alter their causes.

Innovations in marketing can raise brand identification or otherwise differentiate the product. Capital investments in large-scale facilities or vertical integration affect entry barriers. The balance of forces is partly a result of external factors and partly in the company's control.

EXPLOITING INDUSTRY CHANGE

Industry evolution is important strategically because evolution, of course, brings with it changes in the sources of competition I have identified. In the familiar product life-cycle pattern, for example, growth rates change, product differentiation is said to decline as the business becomes more mature, and the companies tend to integrate vertically.

These trends are not so important in themselves; what is critical is whether they affect the sources of competition. Consider vertical integration. In the maturing minicomputer industry, extensive vertical integration, both in manufacturing and in software development, is taking place. This very significant trend is greatly raising economies of scale as well as the amount of capital necessary to compete in the industry. This in turn is raising barriers to entry and may drive some smaller competitors out of the industry once growth levels off.

Obviously, the trends carrying the highest priority from a strategic standpoint are those that affect the most important sources of competition in the industry and thóse that elevate new causes to the forefront. In contract aerosol packaging, for example, the trend toward less product differentiation is now dominant. It has increased buyers' power, lowered the barriers to entry, and intensified competition.

The framework for analyzing competition that I have described can also be used to predict the eventual profitability of an industry. In long-range planning the task is to examine each competitive force, forecast the magnitude of each underlying cause, and then construct a composite picture of the likely profit potential of the industry.

The outcome of such an exercise may differ a great deal from the existing industry structure. Today, for example, the solar heating business is populated by dozens and perhaps hundreds of companies, none with a major market position. Entry is easy, and competitors are battling to establish solar heating as a superior substitute for conventional methods.

The potential of this industry will depend largely on the shape of future barriers to entry, the improvement of the industry's position relative to substitutes, the ultimate intensity of competition, and the power captured by buyers and suppliers. These characteristics will in turn be influenced by such factors as the establishment of brand identities, significant economies of scale or experience curves in equipment manufacture wrought by technological change, the ultimate capital costs to compete, and the extent of overhead in production facilities.

The framework for analyzing industry competition has direct benefits in setting diversification strategy. It provides a road map for answering the extremely difficult question inherent in diversification decisions: "What is the potential of this business?" Combining the framework with judgment in its application, a company may be able to spot an industry with a good future before this good future is reflected in the prices of acquisition candidates.

Multifaceted Rivalry

Corporate managers have directed a great deal of attention to defining their businesses as a crucial step in strategy formulation. Theodore Levitt, in his classic 1960 article in the *Harvard Business Review,* argued strongly for avoiding the myopia of narrow, product-oriented industry definition.[2] Numerous other authorities have also stressed the need to look beyond product to function in defining a business, beyond national boundaries to potential international competition, and beyond the ranks of one's competitors today to those that may become competitors tomorrow. As a result of these urgings, the proper definition of a company's industry or industries has become an endlessly debated subject.

One motive behind this debate is the desire to exploit new markets. Another, perhaps more important motive is the fear of overlooking latent sources of competition that someday may threaten the industry. Many managers concentrate so single-mindedly on their direct antagonists in the fight for market share that they fail to realize that they are also competing with their customers and their suppliers for bargaining power. Meanwhile, they also neglect to keep a wary eye out for new entrants to the contest or fail to recognize the subtle threat of substitute products.

The key to growth—even survival—is to stake out a position that is less vulnerable to attack from head-to-head opponents, whether established or new, and less vulnerable to erosion from the direction of buyers, suppliers, and substitute goods. Establishing such a position can take many forms—solidifying relationships with favorable customers, differentiating the product either substantively or psychologically through marketing, integrating forward or backward, establishing technological leadership.

Notes

1. For a more complete discussion of exit barriers and their implications for strategy, see my article, "Please Note Location of Nearest Exit," *California Management Review* (Winter 1976), p. 21.
2. Theodore Levitt, "Marketing Myopia," reprinted as a *Harvard Business Review* Classic (September–October 1975), p. 26.

3
Sustainable Advantage

Pankaj Ghemawat

"If a man . . . make a better mouse-trap than his neighbour, tho' he build his house in the woods, the world will make a beaten path to his door." Attributed to one of Emerson's lectures in the nineteenth century, these words seem to have anticipated the exhortations of the twentieth: Manage for uniqueness, develop a distinctive competence, create competitive advantage.

But that's not all Emerson had to say about investment in better mousetraps; he also remarked, "Invention breeds invention." What will restrain rivals from imitating or even improving on an invention? That question preoccupies the real mousetrap industry as it staggers from imported copies of its innovative glueboards and repeating traps.

That question is also central to competitive strategy. Strategists insist that for outstanding performance, a company has to beat out the competition. The trouble is that the competition has heard the same message. Deadlocks ensue. Look at the cross-industry findings about three competitive hot spots.

1. Product innovation. Competitors secure detailed information on 70% of all new products within a year of their development. Patenting usually fails to deter imitation. On average, imitation costs a third less than innovation and is a third quicker.[1]

2. Production. New processes are even harder to protect than new products. Incremental improvements to old processes are vulnerable too—if consultants are to be believed, 60% to 90% of all "learning" ultimately diffuses to competitors. Production often blurs competitive advantage: Recent studies show that unionized workers pocket two-thirds of the potential profits in U.S. manufacturing.[2]

3. Marketing. Nonprice instruments are usually ascribed more potency than price changes, partly because they are harder to match. Rivals often react to a particular move, however, by adjusting their entire marketing mix. Such reactions tend to be intense; limited data on advertising suggest that the moves and countermoves frequently cancel out.[3]

In principle, threats like these have always been part of doing business. In practice, they have multiplied with the intensification of domestic and international competition. How should a business cope with such competitive pressure? For guidance, we can turn from cross-industry findings to cases.

Keeping the Edge

This study of sustainable success grew out of a sample of 100 businesses that far outperformed their industries in the recent past. Not all of them promise to be as successful in the coming decade. The vulnerable ones have a lesson to impart.

Analog Devices, which focuses on specialized applications for analog semiconductors, has invested countercyclically to cash in on business upturns. The results: 80% faster growth and 50% higher profitability than the rest of the semiconductor industry. But existing competitors seem set to copy Analog's investment policy, and new ones—notably the Japanese—are invading its profitable niches.

Nike's leadership in athletic shoes was built on cheap Far Eastern labor and massive investments in product development and marketing. Over the past five years, Nike averaged thrice the profitability and four times the growth of the rest of the U.S. shoe industry. But competitors are busy cloning its strategy. Reebok International, for one, sources 95% of its shoes from South Korea, spends heavily on product styling, and has won endorsements from rock stars as well as athletes. Reebok's sales and profits expanded fivefold in 1985, while Nike's actually declined.

Piedmont Aviation's hubs at Baltimore, Charlotte, and Dayton tie together dozens of small and mid-sized cities. Since the major airlines had neglected these routes, Piedmont grew three times as fast as the rest of the industry and was six times as profitable. But others are now muscling in: People Express has started to encroach, and American Airlines' planned hub at Raleigh will hurt Piedmont's operations out of Baltimore and Charlotte.

Analog Devices, Nike, and Piedmont are very different from one another, yet they face the same threat: copying by competitors. Their competitive advantages are insecure, or contestable, because each can be duplicated. These examples also show that some success stories do revolve around contestable advantages: All of a company's competitors may be stupid some of the time. But can you count on your competitors being stupid *all* of the time? The historical record suggests otherwise. That is why sustainable advantages—advantages anchored in industry economics— command attention.

The literature on strategy is crammed with accounts of why a sustainable competitive advantage is A Good Thing To Have. But all those accounts beg two key questions: Which advantages tend to be sustainable, and why?

Sustainable advantages fall into three categories: size in the targeted market, superior access to resources or customers, and restrictions on competitors' options. Note that these advantages are nonexclusive. They can, and often do, interact. The more of them, the better.

BENEFITS OF SIZE

Size advantages exist because markets are finite. If a business can commit to being large, competitors may resign themselves to remaining smaller. What holds them back is the fear that if they matched the leader's size, supply might exceed demand by enough to make the market unprofitable for everyone.

Commitment to being large means making durable, irreversible investments. To exploit commitment opportunities, a business must be able to preempt its competitors. Caveat preemptor: First-movers have to be especially wary of environmental changes that can erode the value of their early investments.

Size is an advantage only if, net net, there are compelling economies to being large. Such economies have three possible bases: scale, experience, and scope.

Scale economies usually summon up a vision of a global factory running flat out. But it is important to remember that scale can work on a national, regional, or even local level, and that its effects need not be confined to manufacturing.

Wal-Mart, the discount merchandiser, illustrates the power of local and regional scale economies. Historically, it focused on small Sunbelt towns that its competitors had neglected. Most of these towns could not support two discounters, so once Wal-Mart made a long-lived, largely unrecoverable investment to service such a town, it gained a local monopoly. The company reinforced this advantage by wrapping its stores in concentric rings around regional distribution centers. By the time competitors realized that this policy cut distribution costs in half, Wal-Mart had preempted enough store sites to render competing regional warehouses unviable. Now you know why Sam Walton is one of the richest men in America.

The Wal-Mart story also shows the limits to scale economies. K mart and other discounters are beginning to enter some of Wal-Mart's larger locations. The problem, ironically, is market growth: Because of the boom in the Sunbelt, some of these towns can now accommodate two discounters. And even the warehousing advantages look insecure in the regions into which Wal-Mart is expanding; it probably won't be able to blanket these areas with stores before competitors move in.

Experience effects are based on size over time, rather than size at a particular point in time. If you think about it, experience is a kind of irreversible, market-specific investment. While it is usually cited in the context of the experience curve—the inverse relation between cumulative production and average cost—its ambit is actually much broader. For example, experience has been shown to increase the operating reliability of processing plants, the success rate of product introductions, and the marketability of high-tech products.

Experience effects—especially experience curves—have come under heavy fire recently because they were oversold in the 1970s. Yet some companies *have* parlayed them into competitive success. Take Lincoln Electric's experience in the electric welding industry. Ever since John Lincoln developed the portable arc welder in 1895, Lincoln Electric has outraced its competition down the experience curve. In its ninth decade it still commands a 7% to 15% cost advantage over its four largest rivals.

Lincoln is an object lesson about when and how to exploit experience effects. As the product pioneer it had a first-mover advantage; and that lead has proved durable because of the incrementalism of technological change. Lincoln has also kept its experience proprietary by integrating backward, customizing its production machinery, and holding annual worker turnover under 3%. Finally, it has continued to invest in experience by sharing cost reductions with customers. Competitors complain publicly that they have trouble matching Lincoln's prices, let alone undercutting them.

Scope economies are derived from activities in interrelated markets. If they are strong, a sustainable advantage in one market can be used to build sustainability in another. The term "scope economies" isn't just a newfangled name for synergy; it actually defines the conditions under which synergy works. To achieve economies of scope, a company must be able to share resources across markets, while making sure that the cost of those resources remains largely fixed. Only then can economies be effected by spreading assets over a greater number of markets.

Cincinnati Milacron, the largest U.S. machine tool manufacturer, shows how companies can capitalize on scope economies. For the past two decades it has led the U.S. machine tool industry in both R&D and the size of its sales and service networks—activities that account for a third of the value added by the industry. In the 1980s, it has pushed hard into robotics, with good reason. Its cumulative R&D experience gives the company such a big lead in the machine tool segment that no domestic challenger can rationally commit to matching its R&D, sales force, or service expenditures. Furthermore, the technologies and customers for its computerized, numerically controlled machine tools overlap with those for robotics. And the company's R&D, sales, and service activities are all very volume sensitive, which slashes the incremental costs of moving into robotics. These factors make it a formidable contender in the industry.

A company pursuing a sustainable scope advantage cannot afford to run its businesses as isolated units. Activities have to be coordinated and allowances must be made for contributions from one business to the success of another. This makes scope economies especially hard to implement.

ACCESS ADVANTAGES

Preferred access to resources or customers can award a business a sustainable advantage that is independent of size. The advantage persists because competitors are held back by an investment asymmetry: They would suffer a penalty if they tried to imitate the leader.

Access will lead to a sustainable advantage if two conditions are met: It must be secured under better terms than competitors will be able to get later, and the advantage has to be enforceable over the long run. Enforceability can come from ownership, binding contracts, or self-enforcing mechanisms such as switching costs. Without enforceability, the terms of access shift in line with overall market conditions, wiping out any competitive differences.

Enforceability can be a two-edged sword, however. The risk of pursuing sustainable access advantages is that they may saddle a business with worse terms than those available to its rivals.

KNOW-HOW.   Superior access to information may reflect the benefits of scale or experience. Boeing, for instance, has acquired superior know-how about commercial jet aircraft through billions of dollars of cumulative investments in R&D. More often, though, sustainability hinges on hidden know-how—what your rivals don't see. For example, IBM's size and the complexity of its operating environment make it hard for competitors to figure out exactly what makes it tick. If the cost of surmounting that kind of informational barrier exceeds the payoffs, rivals may not even attempt imitation.

Consider Du Pont's preemption of all the capacity expansion in the U.S. titanium dioxide industry in the 1970s. Thanks to a production process based on low-cost feedstock, Du Pont enjoyed a 20% cost advantage over competitors' processes. Mastering the cheaper feedstock technology was a black art—it could be accomplished only by investing $50 million to $100 million and several years of testing time in an efficiently scaled plant. The cost and risk of this alternative kept Du Pont's competitors from trying to imitate its demonstrably superior technology.

An obvious but important point: Know-how must be kept secret if it is to yield an advantage. Many high-tech and service companies have been devastated by the defection of key personnel in whom their know-how is vested. The Boston Consulting Group, for instance, has suffered more than a dozen spinoffs, eroding its competitive advantage in management consulting and its client base. Other sources of leaks include suppliers, customers, reverse engineering, and even patent documents.

INPUTS.   Tying up inputs will lead to a sustainable advantage only if the commodity's supply is bounded and the company has the right to use it on favorable terms. Boundedness here is interpreted broadly: It may imply either a strictly limited supply of the input or a supply that is elastic but of varying quality. In both cases, the supply of the preferred input is limited; as a result, tying it up can be very profitable.

This description covers a wide range of phenomena. Courtaulds' 10% to 15% cost advantage over its competitors in the viscose industry can be traced to its backward integration into dissolving pulp, which accounts for a third of the finished product's cost. Courtaulds gets its pulp from a well-located subsidiary for half what its competitors pay. James River Corporation has averaged a 24% ROE by buying obsolete commodity paper machines at fire-sale prices and converting them to specialty products, a stratagem that has held its assets-to-sales ratio to two-thirds the industry average. In diamonds, the Central Selling Organization (controlled by De Beers) has built up its marketing muscle by tying up contracts to market 80% of the Western hemisphere's supply.

Companies can also secure preferred access through their reputations or established relationships. In the record industry, for example, CBS has attracted promising artists because of its reputation for being able to take them to the top—at least partially a self-fulfilling prophecy.

Access advantages are vulnerable to shifts in input availability or prices. Courtaulds' cost advantage in dissolving pulp will wither as infrastructure development opens up more tropical and sub-tropical forests. And James River's competitors, particularly Hammermill, have begun to bid up the prices of the second-hand paper machines that it traditionally bought for a song. This constrains James River's growth, even though its cheap asset base will prop up profitability for years to come.

MARKETS.   In many ways, preferred access to markets is the mirror image of preferred access to inputs. But access to markets relies less on vertical integration or contracts and more on self-enforcing mechanisms such as reputation, relationships, switching costs, and product complementarities.

That is not to say that vertical integration and contracts are entirely missing from the picture. Tele-Communications' strategy in cable television systems shows otherwise. While competitors outbid each other in their scramble to secure big franchises, Tele-Communications concentrated on acquiring small, contiguous systems in areas that were poorly served because they were hard to get to or far from large population centers. Tele-Communications' current network faces no serious threats from substitutes or competitors, limits its exposure to the whims of any one regulatory authority, and allows the company to spread the costs of its microwave common-carrier network over several communities.

Still, self-enforcing mechanisms for market access crop up far more frequently. Let us look at just two examples. Tandem, which pioneered expansible, fault-tolerant computers for processing transactions, has gained preferred access to demand for upgrades and replacements because changeovers from one system to another are very costly. And Borden's brand of processed lemon juice, ReaLemon, attained a 50% premium over identical competing brands because as the pioneer, it benefited from consumer risk-aversion: Lemon juice doesn't cost very much and you don't buy it very often, so why take a chance with an untried brand?

You have probably already figured out that market access advantages are very sensitive to customer preferences. Even slight, apparently innocuous shifts in preferences can weaken an entrenched brand, dispel accumulated switching costs, or undercut long-standing relationships.

EXERCISING OPTIONS

Sometimes the sustainability of an advantage cannot be pinned on either size or access. Instead, competitors' options may differ fundamentally from yours, hamstringing their ability to imitate your company's strategy. Rivals may be frozen into their current positions for several reasons.

PUBLIC POLICY. Government intervention always affects the workings of markets; that is its avowed purpose. Sometimes its actions percolate so far as to affect competitive positions within an industry. The examples are familiar: Patents (try to) protect innovators from imitators, antitrust laws prevent large businesses from being as aggressive as smaller competitors, some companies get handouts while others do not. The lesson, strategically, is that a company that is on the right side of public policy can exploit its position to build sustainability against companies that are not.

Heileman Brewing exemplifies both the leverage from this source of sustainability and its limits. The shakeout in the U.S. brewing industry during the 1970s endangered many small, regional brewers. Antitrust laws prevented the national brewers—Anheuser-Busch, Miller, and Schlitz—from acquiring them. Heileman, then one of the larger regional brewers, faced no such constraints. It grew throughout the decade by buying out numerous smaller brewers lock, stock, and barrel. These cheap assets fed right through to the bottom line: With an average ROE of 29% over the past five years, Heileman is still ahead of its competitors. But the bloom on this particular strategy is fading. By 1982, Heileman's market share had tripled, and the Justice Department blocked its proposed acquisitions of Schlitz and Pabst. Other takeovers by Heileman are improbable.

Remember that what the government gives, the government can take away. Treat an advantage based on public policy as sustainable only if you are sure you will continue to be on the right side. If not, try a different route.

DEFENSE.   A business can also sustain an advantage if its competitors are restricted by past investments. If imitation threatens the cash flow from those investments, disadvantaged competitors may rationally stay put and defend them, thereby giving the innovator an opportunity to take the lead.

Examples of defensiveness are legion. Bic used its 19-cent Crystal to wrest leadership from Gillette in the U.S. pen market in the 1950s, when Bic's aggression went unmatched because Gillette did not want to decimate the sales of its more expensive Paper Mate line. In plain-paper copying, a number of competitors successfully attacked Xerox in the 1970s. Recognizing that its multibillion-dollar rental base was becoming obsolete, Xerox milked it by dragging its feet on price cuts and product innovation—even though these lags caused its share of new placements to fall from nearly 100% in 1972 to 14% by 1976.

Time often erodes defensiveness, however, as it depreciates the value of past investments. In 1970, Gillette introduced a low-priced line of Write Bros. pens to arrest Bic's advance. And since 1977, Xerox has restored its share of new copier placements to the 40% to 50% range by matching competitors' prices and product features.

RESPONSE LAGS.   The final restriction on rivals' options comes from response lags. One business can be every bit as efficient as another in terms of potential size or access without being equally prepared to make a specific move. In that event, the nimbler of the two can count on a lag in its competitor's response, or a period of sustainability.

The longer the response lag the better, as existing advantages stretch out and opportunities to create new ones multiply. Lag times vary enormously, of course, but I can make some broad generalizations. Responses to most pricing moves come in weeks if not days, while responses to nonprice competition and to R&D usually take a few years. And it may take a decade or more to match a competitor's scope economies or superior organization.[4]

Kodak vividly illustrates how you can sustain a lead by exploiting competitors' response lags. In the late 1950s, Du Pont and Bell & Howell formed a joint venture to challenge Kodak's dominance of the color film market. They found product development exasperating, however, because each time they improved their film, Kodak seemed, as if by magic, to make its film even better. When the Du Pont—Bell & Howell film was finally ready, Kodak administered the coup de grace by introducing the vastly superior Kodachrome II slide film. The competing entry never reached the market.

Guidelines for Strategy

I have outlined a set of factors that affect the sustainability of competitive advantages. How should these factors—and the broad notion of sustainability—be integrated into strategy formulation? Here are several points to remember:

1. Managers cannot afford to ignore contestable advantages. For one thing, even moves that offer ephemeral advantages may be worth making, if only to avoid a competitive *disadvantage*. For another, some contestable advantages may survive uncontested: Disadvantaged competitors may be tied up trying to meet their profit targets, constrained by their corporate strategies, or just ineptly managed.

2. The distinction between contestable and sustainable advantages is a matter of degree. Sustainability is greatest when based on several kinds of advantages rather than one, when the advantage is large, and when few environmental threats to it exist.

3. Not all industries offer equal opportunities to sustain an advantage. First-mover advantages tend to be most potent in industries characterized by durable, irreversible, market-specific assets, either tangible or intangible. Industries that evolve gradually offer more room to sustain advantages than those that are regularly rocked by drastic changes in technology or demand. And sustainability is more accessible in industries with more than one dominant strategy because competitors may not have the same options you do.

4. To create a sustainable advantage, you must either be blessed with competitors that have a restricted menu of options or be able to preempt them. Propitious times to preempt occur when an industry is undergoing wrenching changes in technology, demand patterns, or input availability. Scan the environment actively. If you notice any changes, see whether they play to your particular strengths.

Ultimately, the search for sustainability involves a series of decisions about the degree to which you are willing to commit your business to a particular way of doing things. You have to pick the relative emphasis you are going to place on two things: commitment to competing a particular way and retaining the flexibility to compete effectively in other ways.

Notes

1. Edwin Mansfield, "How Rapidly Does New Industrial Technology Leak Out?" *Journal of Industrial Economics* (December 1985), p. 217; Richard C. Levin et al., "Survey Research on R&D Appropriability and Technological Opportunity, Part I," Yale University Working Paper (New Haven: July 1984); and Edwin Mansfield, Mark Schwartz, and Samuel Wagner, "Imitation Costs and Patents: An Empirical Study," *Economic Journal* (December 1981), p. 907.

2. Michael A. Salinger, "Tobin's q, Unionization, and the Concentration-Profits Relationship," *Rand Journal of Economics*, Summer 1984, p. 159; and Thomas Karier, "Unions and Monopoly Profits," *Review of Economics and Statistics* (February 1985), p. 34.

3. M.M. Metwally, "Advertising and Competitive Behavior of Selected Australian Firms," *Review of Economics and Statistics* (November 1975), p. 417; Jean-Jaques Lambin, *Advertising, Competition, and Market Conduct in Oligopoly Over Time* (Amster-

dam: North-Holland, 1976); and Jeffrey M. Netter, "Excessive Advertising: An Empirical Analysis," *Journal of Industrial Economics* (June 1982), p. 361.

4. See, for example, David J. Teece, "The Diffusion of an Administrative Innovation," *Management Science* (May 1980), p. 464.

4
Time—The Next Source of Competitive Advantage

George Stalk, Jr.

Like competition itself, competitive advantage is a constantly moving target. For any company in any industry, the key is not to get stuck with a single simple notion of its source of advantage. The best competitors, the most successful ones, know how to keep moving and always stay on the cutting edge.

Today, *time* is on the cutting edge. The ways leading companies manage time—in production, in new product development and introduction, in sales and distribution—represent the most powerful new sources of competitive advantage. Though certain Western companies are pursuing these advantages, Japanese experience and practice provide the most instructive examples—not because they are necessarily unique but because they best illustrate the evolutionary stages through which leading companies have advanced.

In the period immediately following World War II, Japanese companies used their low labor costs to gain entry to various industries. As wage rates rose and technology became more significant, the Japanese shifted first to scale-based strategies and then to focused factories to achieve advantage. The advent of just-in-time production brought with it a move to flexible factories, as leading Japanese companies sought both low cost and great variety in the market. Cutting-edge Japanese companies today are capitalizing on time as a critical source of competitive advantage: shortening the planning loop in the product development cycle and trimming process time in the factory—managing time the way most companies manage costs, quality, or inventory.

In fact, as a strategic weapon, time is the equivalent of money, productivity, quality, even innovation. Managing time has enabled top Japanese companies not only to reduce their costs but also to offer broad product lines, cover more market segments, and upgrade the technological sophistication of their products. These companies are time-based competitors.

From Low Wages to Variety Wars

Since 1945, Japanese competitors have shifted their strategic focus at least four times. These early adaptations were straightforward; the shift to time-based competitive advantage is not nearly so obvious. It does, however, represent a logical evolution from the earlier stages.

In the immediate aftermath of World War II, with their economy devastated and the world around them in a shambles, the Japanese concentrated on achieving competitive advantage through low labor costs. Since Japan's workers were still productive and the yen was devalued by 98.8% against the dollar, its labor costs were extraordinarily competitive with those of the West's developed economies.

Hungry for foreign exchange, the Japanese government encouraged companies to make the most of their one edge by targeting industries with high labor content: textiles, shipbuilding, and steel—businesses where the low labor rates more than offset low productivity rates. As a result, Japanese companies took market share from their Western competition.

But this situation did not last long. Rising wages, caused by high inflation, combined with fixed exchange rates to erode the advantage. In many industries, manufacturers could not improve their productivity fast enough to offset escalating labor costs. By the early 1960s, for instance, the textile companies—comprising Japan's largest industry—were hard-pressed. Having lost their competitive edge in world markets, they spiraled downward, first losing share, then volume, then profits, and finally position and prestige. While the problem was most severe for the textile business, the rest of Japanese industry suffered as well.

The only course was adaptation: In the early 1960s, the Japanese shifted their strategy, using capital investment to boost work-force productivity. They inaugurated the era of scale-based strategies, achieving high productivity and low costs by building the largest and most capital-intensive facilities that were technologically feasible. Japanese shipbuilders, for example, revolutionized the industry in their effort to raise labor productivity. Adapting fabrication techniques from mass production processes and using automatic and semiautomatic equipment, they constructed vessels in modules. The approach produced two advantages for the Japanese. It drove up their own productivity and simultaneously erected a high capital-investment barrier to others looking to compete in the business.

The search for ways to achieve even higher productivity and lower costs continued, however. And in the mid-1960s, it led top Japanese companies to a new source of competitive advantage—the focused factory. Focused competitors manufactured products either made nowhere else in the world or located in the high-volume segment of a market, often in the heart of their Western competitors' product lines. Focusing of production allowed the Japanese to remain smaller than established broad-line producers, while still achieving higher productivity and lower costs—giving them great competitive power.

Factory costs are very sensitive to the variety of goods a plant produces. Reduction of the product-line variety by half, for example, raises productivity by 30%, cuts costs 17%, and substantially lowers the break-even point. Cutting the product line in half again boosts productivity by 75%, slashes costs 30%, and diminishes the break-even point to below 50% (see Exhibit I).

In industries like bearings, where competition was fierce in the late 1960s, the Japanese fielded product lines with one-half to one-quarter the variety of their Western competitors. Targeting the high-volume segments of the bearing business—bearings for automobile applications was one—the Japanese used the low costs of their highly productive focused factories to undercut the prices of Western competitors.

SKF was one victim. With factories scattered throughout Europe, each geared to a broad product line for the local market, the Swedish company was a big target for the Japanese. SKF reacted by trying to avoid direct competition with the Japanese: It added higher margin products to serve specialized applications. But SKF did not simultaneously drop any low-margin products, thereby complicating its plant operations and adding to production costs. In effect, SKF provided a cost umbrella for the Japanese. As long as they operated beneath it, the Japanese could expand their product line and move into more varied applications.

Avoiding price competition by moving into higher-margin prod-

Exhibit I.

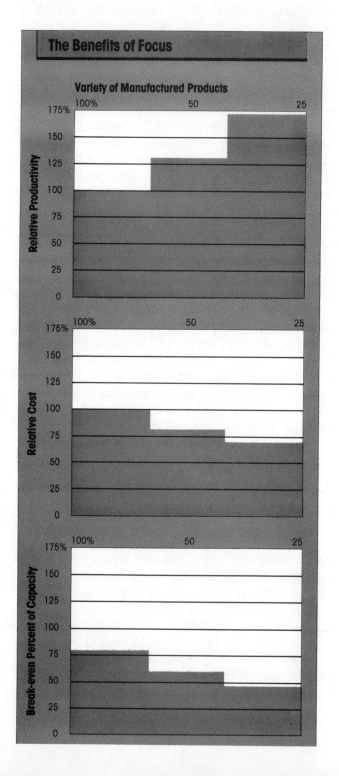

ucts is called margin retreat—a common response to stepped-up competition that eventually leads to corporate suicide. As a company retreats, its costs rise as do its prices, thus "subsidizing" an aggressive competitor's expansion into the vacated position. The retreating company's revenue base stops growing and may eventually shrink to the point where it can no longer support the fixed cost of the operation. Retrenchment, restructuring, and further shrinkage follow in a cycle that leads to inevitable extinction.

SKF avoided this fate by adopting the Japanese strategy. After a review of its factories, the company focused each on those products it was best suited to manufacture. If a product did not fit a particular factory, it was either placed in another, more suitable plant or dropped altogether. This strategy not only halted SKF's retreat but also beat back the Japanese advance.

At the same time, however, leading Japanese manufacturers began to move toward a new source of competitive advantage—the flexible factory. Two developments drove this move. First, as they expanded and penetrated more markets, their narrow product lines began to pinch, limiting their ability to grow. Second, with growth limited, the economics of the focus strategy presented them with an unattractive choice: either reduce variety further or accept the higher costs of broader product lines.

In manufacturing, costs fall into two categories: those that respond to volume or scale and those that are driven by variety. Scale-related costs decline as volume increases, usually falling 15% to 25% per unit each time volume doubles. Variety-related costs, on the other hand, reflect the costs of complexity in manufacturing: setup, materials handling, inventory, and many of the overhead costs of a factory. In most cases, as variety increases, costs increase, usually at a rate of 20% to 35% per unit each time variety doubles.

The sum of the scale- and variety-related costs represents the total cost of manufacturing. With effort, managers can determine the optimum cost point for their factories—the point where the combination of volume and variety yields the lowest total manufacturing cost for a particular plant. When markets are good, companies tend to edge toward increased variety in search of higher volumes, even though this will mean increased costs. When times are tough, companies pare their product lines, cutting variety to reduce costs.

In a flexible factory system, variety-driven costs start lower and increase more slowly as variety grows. Scale costs remain un-

Exhibit II.

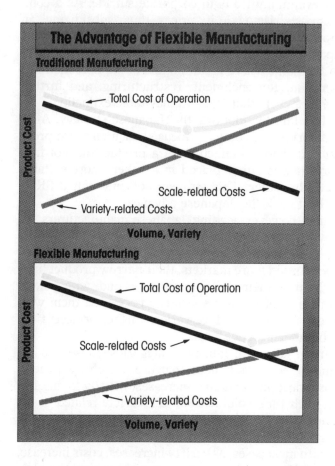

changed. Thus the optimum cost point for a flexible factory occurs at a higher volume and with greater variety than for a traditional factory. A gap emerges between the costs of the flexible and the traditional factory—a cost/variety gap that represents the competitive advantage of flexible production. Very simply, a flexible factory enjoys more variety with lower total costs than traditional factories, which are still forced to make the trade-off between scale and variety (see Exhibit II).

Yanmar Diesel illustrates how this process works. In 1973, with the Japanese economy in recession, Yanmar Diesel was mired in red ink. Worse, there was no promise that once the recession had passed, the existing strategy and program would guarantee real improvement in the company's condition.

As a Toyota supplier, Yanmar was familiar with the automaker's flexible manufacturing system. Moreover, Yanmar was impressed with the automaker's ability to weather the recession without losing money. Yanmar decided to install the Toyota procedure in its own two factories. The changeover took less than five years and produced dramatic results: Manufacturing costs declined 40% to 60%, depending on the product; factory break-even points dropped 80% to 50%; total manufacturing labor productivity improved by more than 100%.

But it was Yanmar's newfound capability in product variety that signaled the arrival of a unique strategic edge: During the restructuring Yanmar more than quadrupled its product line. With focused factories, Yanmar could have doubled productivity in such a short time only by reducing the breadth of the product line by 75%. The Toyota system made Yanmar's factories more flexible, reducing costs and producing a greater variety of products.

As its inventor, Taiichi Ohno, said, the Toyota production system was "born of the need to make many types of automobiles, in small quantities with the same manufacturing process." With its emphasis on just-in-time production, total quality control, employee decision making on the factory floor, and close supplier relations, the Toyota system gave the many Japanese manufacturers who adopted it in the mid-1970s a distinct competitive advantage.

A comparison of a U.S. company with a Japanese competitor in the manufacture of a particular automotive suspension component illustrates the nature and extent of the Japanese advantage. The U.S. company bases its strategy on scale and focus: It produces 10 million units per year—making it the world's largest producer— and offers only 11 types of finished parts. The Japanese company's strategy, on the other hand, is to exploit flexibility. It is both smaller and less focused: It manufactures only 3.5 million units per year but has 38 types of finished parts.

With one-third the scale and more than three times the product variety, the Japanese company also boasts total labor productivity that is half again that of its American competitor. Moreover, the unit cost of the Japanese manufacturer is less than half that of the U.S. company. But interestingly, the productivity of the Japanese direct laborers is not as high as that of the U.S. workers, a reflection of the difference in scale. The Japanese advantage comes from the

Exhibit III.

Flexible Manufacturing's Productivity Edge *(Automobile Suspension Component)*	U.S. Competitor	Japanese Competitor
Annual Volume	10M	3.5M
Employees		
Direct	107	50
Indirect	135	7
Total	242	57
Annual Units/Employee	43,100	61,400
Types of Finished Parts	11	38
Unit Cost for Comparable Part (index)	$100	$49

(1987 figures)

productivity of the overhead employees: with one-third the volume and three times the variety, the Japanese company has only one-eighteenth the overhead employees (see Exhibit III).

In the late 1970s, Japanese companies exploited flexible manufacturing to the point that a new competitive thrust emerged—the variety war. A classic example of a variety war was the battle that erupted between Honda and Yamaha for supremacy in the motorcycle market, a struggle popularly known in Japanese business circles as the H-Y War. Yamaha ignited the H-Y War in 1981 when it announced the opening of a new factory which would make it the world's largest motorcycle manufacturer, a prestigious position held by Honda. But Honda had been concentrating its corporate resources on the automobile business and away from its motorcycle operation. Now, faced with Yamaha's overt and public challenge, Honda chose to counterattack.

Honda launched its response with the war cry, "Yamaha wo tsubusu!" ("We will crush, squash, slaughter Yamaha!") In the no-holds-barred battle that ensued, Honda cut prices, flooded distribution channels, and boosted advertising expenditures. Most important—and most impressive to consumers—Honda also rapidly increased the rate of change in its product line, using variety to bury Yamaha. At the start of the war, Honda had 60 models of motorcycles. Over the next 18 months, Honda introduced or replaced 113 models, effectively turning over its entire product line twice. Yamaha also began the war with 60 models; it was able to manage only 37 changes in its product line during those 18 months.

Honda's new product introductions devastated Yamaha. First, Honda succeeded in making motorcycle design a matter of fashion, where newness and freshness were important attributes for consumers. Second, Honda raised the technological sophistication of its products, introducing four-valve engines, composites, direct drive, and other new features. Next to a Honda, Yamaha products looked old, unattractive, and out of date. Demand for Yamaha products dried up; in a desperate effort to move them, dealers were forced to price them below cost. But even that didn't work. At the most intense point in the H-Y War, Yamaha had more than 12 months of inventory in its dealers' showrooms. Finally Yamaha surrendered. In a public statement, Yamaha President Eguchi announced, "We want to end the H-Y War. It is our fault. Of course there will be competition in the future but it will be based on a mutual recognition of our respective positions."

Honda didn't go unscathed either. The company's sales and service network was severely disrupted, requiring additional investment before it returned to a stable footing. However, so decisive was its victory that Honda effectively had as much time as it wanted to recover. It had emphatically defended its title as the world's largest motorcycle producer and done so in a way that warned Suzuki and Kawasaki not to challenge that leadership. Variety had won the war.

Time-Based Competitive Advantage

The strength of variety as a competitive weapon raises an interesting question. How could Japanese companies accommodate such rapid rates of change? In Honda's case, there could be only three possible answers. The company did one of the following:

1. Began the development of more than 100 new models 10 to 15 years before the attack.

2. Authorized a sudden, massive spending surge to develop and manufacture products on a crash basis.
3. Used structurally different methods to develop, manufacture, and introduce new products.

In fact, what Honda and other variety-driven competitors pioneered was time-based competitiveness. They managed structural changes that enabled their operations to execute their processes much faster. As a consequence, time became their new source of competitive advantage.

While time is a basic business performance variable, management seldom monitors its consumption explicitly—almost never with the same precision accorded sales and costs. Yet time is a more critical competitive yardstick than traditional financial measurements.

Today's new-generation companies compete with flexible manufacturing and rapid-response systems, expanding variety and increasing innovation. A company that builds its strategy on this cycle is a more powerful competitor than one with a traditional strategy based on low wages, scale, or focus. These older, cost-based strategies require managers to do whatever is necessary to drive down costs: move production to or source from a low-wage country; build new facilities or consolidate old plants to gain economies of scale; or focus operations down to the most economic subset of activities. These tactics reduce costs but at the expense of responsiveness.

In contrast, strategies based on the cycle of flexible manufacturing, rapid response, expanding variety, and increasing innovation are time based. Factories are close to the customers they serve. Organization structures enable fast responses rather than low costs and control. Companies concentrate on reducing if not eliminating delays and using their response advantages to attract the most profitable customers.

Many—but certainly not all—of today's time-based competitors are Japanese. Some of them are Sony, Matsushita, Sharp, Toyota, Hitachi, NEC, Toshiba, Honda, and Hino; time-based Western companies include Benetton, The Limited, Federal Express, Domino's Pizza, Wilson Art, and McDonald's. For these leading competitors, time has become the overarching measurement of performance. By reducing the consumption of time in every aspect of the business, these companies also reduce costs, improve quality, and stay close to their customers.

Breaking the Planning Loop

Companies are systems; time connects all the parts. The most powerful competitors understand this axiom and are breaking the debilitating loop that strangles much of traditional manufacturing planning.

Traditional manufacturing requires long lead times to resolve conflicts between various jobs or activities that require the same resources. The long lead times, in turn, require sales forecasts to guide planning. But sales forecasts are inevitably wrong; by definition they are guesses, however informed. Naturally, as lead times lengthen, the accuracy of sales forecasts declines. With more forecasting errors, inventories balloon and the need for safety stocks at all levels increases. Errors in forecasting also mean more unscheduled jobs that have to be expedited, thereby crowding out scheduled jobs. The need for longer lead times grows even greater and the planning loop expands even more, driving up costs, increasing delays, and creating system inefficiencies.

Managers who find themselves trapped in the planning loop often respond by asking for better forecasts and longer lead times. In other words, they treat the symptoms and worsen the problem. The only way to break the planning loop is to reduce the consumption of time throughout the system; that will, in turn, cut the need for lead time, for estimates, for safety stocks, and all the rest. After all, if a company could ever drive its lead time all the way to zero, it would have to forecast only the next day's sales. While that idea of course is unrealistic, successful time-based competitors in Japan and in the West have kept their lead times from growing and some have even reduced them, thereby diminishing the planning loop's damaging effects.

Thirty years ago, Jay W. Forrester of MIT published a pioneering article in the *Harvard Business Review*, "Industrial Dynamics: A Major Breakthrough for Decision Makers" (July-August 1958), which established a model of time's impact on an organization's performance. Using "industrial dynamics"—a concept originally developed for shipboard fire control systems—Forrester tracked

Exhibit IV.

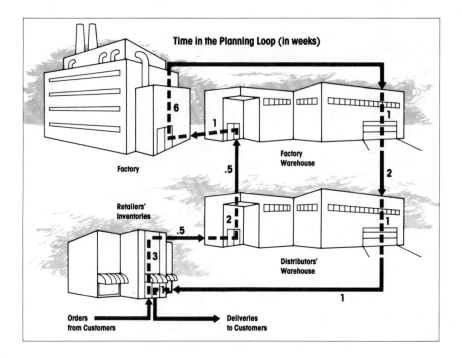

the effects of time delays and decision rates within a simple business system consisting of a factory, a factory warehouse, a distributor's inventory, and retailers' inventories. The numbers in Exhibit IV are the delays in the flow of information or product, measured in weeks. In this example, the orders accumulate at the retailer for three weeks, are in the mail for half a week, are delayed at the distributor for two weeks, go back into the mail for another half a week, and need eight weeks for processing at the factory and its warehouse. Then the finished product begins its journey back to the retailer. The cycle takes 19 weeks.

The system in this example is very stable—as long as retail demand is stable or as long as forecasts are accurate 19 weeks into the future. But if unexpected changes occur, the system must respond. Exhibit V, also taken from the Forrester article, shows what happens to this system when a simple change takes place: Demand goes up 10%, then flattens. Acting on new forecasts and seeking to cut delivery delays, the factory first responds by ramping up pro-

Exhibit V.

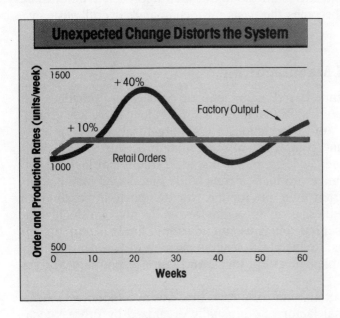

duction 40%. When management realizes—too late—that it has overshot the mark, it cuts production 30%. Too late again it learns that it has overcorrected. This ramping up and cutting back continue until finally the system stabilizes, more than a year after the initial 10% increase.

What distorts the system so badly is time: the lengthy delay between the event that creates the new demand and the time when the factory finally receives the information. The longer that delay, the more distorted is the view of the market. Those distortions reverberate throughout the system, producing disruption, waste, and inefficiency.

These distortions plague business today. To escape them, companies have a choice: They can produce to forecast or they can reduce the time delays in the flow of information and product through the system. The traditional solution is to produce to forecast. The new approach is to reduce time consumption.

Because time flows throughout the system, focusing on time-based competitive performance results in improvements across the board. Companies generally become time-based competitors by first correcting their manufacturing techniques, then fixing sales and distribution, and finally adjusting their approach to innovation. Ultimately, it becomes the basis for a company's overall strategy.

Time-Based Manufacturing

In general, time-based manufacturing policies and practices differ from those of traditional manufacturers along three key dimensions: length of production runs, organization of process components, and complexity of scheduling procedures.

When it comes to lot size, for instance, traditional factories attempt to maximize production runs while time-based manufacturers try to shorten their production runs as much as possible. In fact, many Japanese companies aim for run lengths of a single unit. The thinking behind this is as simple as it is fundamental to competitive success: Reduced run lengths mean more frequent production of the complete mix of products and faster response to customers' demands.

Factory layout also contributes to time-based competitive advantage. Traditional factories are usually organized by process technology centers. For example, metal goods manufacturers organize their factories into shearing, punching, and braking departments; electronic assemblers have stuffing, wave soldering, assembly, testing, and packing departments. Parts move from one process technology center to the next. Each step consumes valuable time: Parts sit, waiting to move; then move; then wait to be used in the next step. In a traditional manufacturing system, products usually receive value for only .05% to 2.5% of the time that they are in the factory. The rest of the time products sit waiting for something to happen.

Time-based factories, however, are organized by product. To minimize handling and moving of parts, the manufacturing functions for a component or a product are as close together as possible. Parts move from one activity to the next with little or no delay. Because the production process eliminates the need to pile and repile parts, they flow quickly and efficiently through the factory.

In traditional factories, scheduling is also a source of delay and waste. Most traditional factories use central scheduling that requires sophisticated materials resource planning and shop-floor control systems. Even though these systems are advanced, they still waste time: Work orders usually flow to the factory floor on a monthly or weekly basis. In the meantime, parts can sit idle.

In time-based factories, local scheduling enables employees to make more production control decisions on the factory floor, without the time-consuming loop back to management for approval. Moreover, the combination of the product-oriented layout of the factory and local scheduling makes the total production process run more smoothly. Once a part starts through the production run, many of the requirements between manufacturing steps are purely automatic and require no intermediate scheduling.

These differences between traditional and time-based factories add up. Flexible factories enjoy big advantages in both productivity and time: Labor productivity in time-based factories can be as much as 200% higher than in conventional plants; time-based factories can respond eight to ten times faster than traditional factories. Flexible production means significant improvements in labor and net-asset productivity. These, in turn, yield reductions of up to 20% in overall costs and increases in growth for much less investment.

Toyota offers a dramatic example of the kinds of improvements that leading time-based competitors are making. Dissatisfied with the response time of a supplier, Toyota went to work. It took the supplier 15 days to turn out a component after arrival of the raw materials at its factory. The first step was to cut lot sizes, reducing response time to 6 days. Next Toyota streamlined the factory layout, reducing the number of inventory holding points. The response time fell to 3 days. Finally Toyota eliminated all work-in-progress inventories at the supplier's plant. New response time: 1 day.

Toyota, of course, is not alone in improving manufacturing response times. Matsushita cut the time needed to make washing machines from 360 hours to just 2; Honda slashed its motorcycle fabricating time by 80%; in North America, companies making motor controllers and electrical components for unit air conditioners have improved their manufacturing response times by 90%.

Time-Based Sales and Distribution

A manufacturer's next challenge is to avoid dissipation of factory performance improvements in other parts of the organization. In Jay Forrester's example of the planning loop, the factory and its warehouse accounted for roughly one-half of the system's time. In actuality today, the factory accounts for one-third to one-half of the total time—often the most "visible" portion of time. But other parts of the system are just as important, if less apparent. For example, in the Forrester system, sales and distribution consume as much or more time than manufacturing.

What Forrester modeled, the Japanese experienced. By the late 1970s, leading Japanese companies were finding that inefficient sales and distribution operations undercut the benefits of their flexible manufacturing systems. Toyota, which at that time was divided into two separate companies, Toyota Motor Manufacturing and Toyota Motor Sales, again makes this point. Toyota Motor Manufacturing could manufacture a car in less than 2 days. But Toyota Motor Sales needed from 15 to 26 days to close the sale, transmit the order to the factory, get the order scheduled, and deliver the car to the customer. By the late 1970s, the cost-conscious, competition-minded engineers at Toyota Manufacturing were angry at their counterparts at Toyota Motor Sales, who were frittering away the advantage gained in the production process. The sales and distribution function was generating 20% to 30% of a car's cost to the customer—more than it cost Toyota to manufacture the car!

Finally, in 1982, Toyota moved decisively to remedy the problem. The company merged Toyota Motor Manufacturing and Toyota Motor Sales. The company announced that it wanted to become "more marketing driven." While Toyota assured the public that the reorganization only returned it to its configuration in the 1950s, within 18 months all the Toyota Motor Sales directors retired. Their jobs were left vacant or filled by executives from Toyota Motor Manufacturing.

The company wasted no time in implementing a plan to cut delays in sales and distribution, reduce costs, and improve customer service. The old system, Toyota found, had handled customer orders in batches. Orders and other crucial information would accumulate at one step of the sales and distribution process before dispatch to the next level, which wasted time and generated extra costs.

To speed the flow of information, Toyota had to reduce the size of the information batches. The solution came from a company-developed computer system that tied its salespeople directly to the factory scheduling operation. This link bypassed several levels of the sales and distribution function and enabled the modified system to operate with very small batches of orders.

Toyota expected this new approach to cut the sales and distribution cycle time in half—from four to six weeks to just two to three weeks across Japan. (For the Tokyo and Osaka regions, which account for roughly two-thirds of Japan's population, the goal was to reduce cycle time to just two days.) But by 1987, Toyota had reduced system responsiveness to eight days, including the time required to make the car. In the Forrester example, this achievement is equivalent to cutting the 19-week cycle to 6 weeks. The results were predictable: shorter sales forecasts, lower costs, happier customers.

Time-Based Innovation

A company that can bring out new products three times faster than its competitors enjoys a huge advantage. Today, in one industry after another, Japanese manufacturers are doing just that to their Western competition:

In projection television, Japanese producers can develop a new television in one-third the time required by U.S. manufacturers.

In custom plastic injection molds, Japanese companies can develop the molds in one-third the time of U.S. competitors and at one-third the cost.

In autos, Japanese companies can develop new products in half the time—and with half as many people—as the U.S. and German competition.

To accomplish their fast-paced innovations, leading Japanese manufacturers have introduced a series of organizational techniques that precisely parallel their approach to flexible manufacturing:

In manufacturing, the Japanese stress short production runs and small lot sizes. In innovation, they favor smaller increments of improvement in new products, but introduce them more often—versus the Western approach of more significant improvements made less often.

In the organization of product development work, the Japanese use factory cells that are cross-functional teams. Most Western new product development activity is carried out by functional centers.

In the scheduling of work, Japanese factories stress local responsibility, just as product development scheduling is decentralized. The Western approach to both requires plodding centralized scheduling, plotting, and tracking.

The effects of this time-based advantage are devastating; quite simply, American companies are losing leadership of technology and innovation—supposedly this country's source of long-term advantage.

Unless U.S. companies reduce their new product development and introduction cycles from 36-48 months to 12-18 months, Japanese manufacturers will easily out-innovate and outperform them. Taking the initiative in innovation will require even faster cycle times.

Residential air conditioners illustrate the Japanese ability to introduce more technological innovation in smaller increments—and how in just a few years these improvements add up to remarkably superior products. The Japanese introduce innovations in air conditioners four times faster than their American competitors; in technological sophistication the Japanese products are seven to ten years ahead of U.S. products.

Look at the changes in Mitsubishi Electric's three-horsepower heat pump between 1975 and 1985. From 1975 to 1979, the company did nothing to the product except change the sheet metal work, partly to improve efficiency but mostly to reduce materials costs. In 1979, the technological sophistication of the product was roughly equal to that of the U.S. competition. From this point on, the Japanese first established, and then widened the lead.

In 1980, Mitsubishi introduced its first major improvement: a new product that used integrated circuits to control the air-conditioning cycle. One year later, the company replaced the integrated circuits with microprocessors and added two important innovations to increase consumer demand. The first was "quick connect" freon lines. On the old product (and on the U.S. product), freon lines were made from copper tubing and cut to length, bent, soldered together, purged, and filled with freon—an operation requiring great skill to produce a reliable air conditioner. The Japanese substituted quick-connect freon lines—precharged hoses that simply clicked together. The second innovation was simplified wiring. On the old product (and still today on the U.S. product), the unit had six color-coded wires to connect. The advent of microprocessors made possible a two-wire connection with neutral polarity.

These two changes did not improve the energy-efficiency ratio of the product; nor were they intended to. Rather, the point was to fabricate a unit that would be simpler to install and more reliable, thereby broadening distribution and increasing demand. Because of these innovations, white-goods outlets could sell the new product, and local contractors could easily install it.

In 1982, Mitsubishi introduced a new version of the air conditioner featuring technological advances related to performance. A high-efficiency rotary compressor replaced the outdated reciprocating compressor. The condensing unit had louvered fins and inner fin tubes for better heat transfer. Because the balance of the system changed, all the electronics had to change. As a result, the energy-efficiency ratio improved markedly.

In 1983, Mitsubishi added sensors to the unit and more computing power, expanding the electronic control of the cycle and again improving the energy-efficiency ratio.

In 1984, Mitsubishi came out with another version of the product, this time with an inverter that made possible an even higher energy-efficiency ratio. The inverter, which requires additional electronics for the unit, allows unparalleled control over the speed of the electric motor, dramatically boosting the appliance's efficiency.

Using time-based innovation, Mitsubishi transformed its air conditioner. The changes came incrementally and steadily. Overall they gave Mitsubishi—and other Japanese companies on the same track—the position of technological leadership in the global residential air-conditioning industry.

In 1985, a U.S. air-conditioner manufacturer was just debating whether to use integrated circuits in its residential heat pump. In view of its four- to five-year product development cycle, it could not have introduced the innovation until 1989 or 1990—putting the American company ten years behind the Japanese. Faced with this situation, the U.S. air-conditioner company followed the example of many U.S. manufacturers that have lost the lead in technology and innovation: It decided to source its air conditioners and components from its Japanese competition.

Time-Based Strategy

The possibility of establishing a response time advantage opens new avenues for constructing winning competitive strategies. At most companies, strategic choices are limited to three options:

1. Seeking coexistence with competitors. This choice is seldom stable, since competitors refuse to cooperate and stay put.
2. Retreating in the face of competitors. Many companies choose this course; the business press fills its pages with accounts of companies retreating by consolidating plants, focusing their operations, outsourcing, divesting businesses, pulling out of markets, or moving upscale.
3. Attacking, either directly or indirectly. The direct attack involves the classic confrontation—cut price and add capacity, creating head-on competition. Indirect attack requires surprise. Competitors either do not understand the strategies being used against them or they do understand but cannot respond—sometimes because of the speed of the attack, sometimes because of their inability to mount a response.

Of the three options, only an attack creates the opportunity for real growth. Direct attack demands superior resources; it is always expensive and potentially disastrous. Indirect attack promises the most gain for the least cost. Time-based strategy offers a powerful new approach for successful indirect attacks against larger, established competitors.

Consider the remarkable example of Atlas Door, a ten-year-old U.S. company. It has grown at an average annual rate of 15% in an industry with an overall annual growth rate of less than 5%. In recent years, its pretax earnings were 20% of sales, about five times the industry average. Atlas is debt free. In its tenth year the company achieved the number one competitive position in its industry.

The company's product: industrial doors. It is a product with almost infinite variety, involving limitless choices of width and height and material. Because of the importance of variety, inventory is almost useless in meeting customer orders; most doors can be manufactured only after the order has been placed.

Historically, the industry had needed almost four months to respond to an order for a door that was out of stock or customized. Atlas's strategic advantage was time: It could respond in weeks to any order. It had structured its order-entry, engineering, manufacturing, and logistics systems to move information and products quickly and reliably.

First, Atlas built just-in-time factories. These are fairly simple in concept. They require extra tooling and machinery to reduce changeover times and a fabrication process organized by product and scheduled to start and complete all of the parts at the same time. But even the performance of the factory—critical to the company's overall responsiveness—still only accounted for 2 1/2 weeks of the completed product delivery cycle.

Second, Atlas compressed time at the front end of the system, where the order first entered and was processed. Traditionally, when customers, distributors, or salespeople called a door manufacturer with a request for price and delivery, they would have to wait more than one week for a response. If the desired door was not in stock, not in the schedule, or not engineered, the supplier's organization would waste even more time, pushing the search for an answer around the system.

Recognizing the opportunity to cut deeply into the time expenditure in this part of the system, Atlas first streamlined, then automated its entire order-entry, engineering, pricing, and scheduling processes. Today Atlas can price and schedule 95% of its incoming orders while the callers are still on the telephone. It can quickly engineer new special orders because it has preserved on computer the design and production data of all previous special orders—which drastically reduces the amount of re-engineering necessary.

Third, Atlas tightly controlled logistics so that it always shipped only fully complete orders to construction sites. Orders require many components. Gathering all of them at the factory and making sure that they are with the correct order can be a time-consuming task. It is even more time-consuming, however, to get the correct parts to the job site after they have missed the initial shipment. Atlas developed a system to track the parts in production and the purchased parts for each order, ensuring arrival of all necessary parts at the shipping dock in time—a just-in-time logistics operation.

When Atlas started operations, distributors were uninterested in its product. The established distributors already carried the door line of a larger competitor; they saw no reason to switch suppliers except, perhaps, for a major price concession. But as a start-up, Atlas was too small to compete on price alone. Instead, it positioned itself as the door supplier of last resort, the company people came to if the established supplier could not deliver or missed a key date.

Of course, with industry lead times of almost four months, some calls inevitably came to Atlas. And when it did get a call, Atlas commanded a higher price because of its faster delivery. Atlas not only got a higher price but its time-based processes also yielded lower costs: It thus enjoyed the best of both worlds.

In ten short years, the company replaced the leading door suppliers in 80% of the distributors in the country. With its strategic advantage the company could be selective, becoming the house supplier for only the strongest distributors.

In the wake of this indirect attack, the established competitors have not responded effectively. The conventional view is that Atlas is a "garage shop operator" that cannot sustain its growth: Competitors expect the company's performance to degrade to the industry average as it grows larger. But this response—or nonresponse—only reflects a fundamental lack of understanding of time as the source of competitive advantage. The extra delay in responding only adds to the insurmountable lead the indirect time-based attack has created. While the traditional companies track costs and size, the new competitor derives advantage from time, staying on the cutting edge, leaving its rivals behind.

5
Getting Back to Strategy

Kenichi Ohmae

"Competitiveness" is the word most commonly uttered these days in economic policy circles in Washington and most European capitals. The restoration of competitive vitality is a widely shared political slogan. Across the Atlantic, the sudden nearness of 1992 and the coming unification of the Common Market focus attention on European industries' ability to compete against global rivals. On both continents, senior managers, who started to wrestle with these issues long before politicians got hold of them, search actively for successful models to follow, for examples of how best to play the new competitive game. With few exceptions, the models they have found and the examples they are studying are Japanese.

To many Western managers, the Japanese competitive achievement provides hard evidence that a successful strategy's hallmark is the creation of sustainable competitive advantage by beating the competition. If it takes world-class manufacturing to win, runs the lesson, you have to beat competitors with your factories. If it takes rapid product development, you have to beat them with your labs. If it takes mastery of distribution channels, you have to beat them with your logistics systems. No matter what it takes, the goal of strategy is to beat the competition.

After a painful decade of losing ground to the Japanese, managers in the United States and Europe have learned this lesson very well indeed. As a guide to action, it is clear and compelling. As a metric of performance, it is unambiguous. It is also wrong.

Of course, winning the manufacturing or product development or logistics battle is no bad thing. But it is not really what strategy is—or should be—about. Because when the focus of attention is on ways to beat the competition, it is inevitable that strategy gets defined primarily in terms of the competition. For instance, if the competition has recently brought out an electronic kitchen gadget that slices, dices, and brews coffee, you had better get one just like it into your product line—and get it there soon. If the competition has cut production costs, you had better get out your scalpel. If they have just started to run national ads, you had better call your agency at once. When you go toe-to-toe with competitors, you cannot let them build up any kind of advantage. You must match their every move. Or so the argument goes.

Of course it is important to take the competition into account, but in making strategy that should not come first. It cannot come first. First comes painstaking attention to the needs of customers. First comes close analysis of a company's real degrees of freedom in responding to those needs. First comes the willingness to rethink, fundamentally, what products are and what they do, as well as how best to organize the business system that designs, builds, and markets them. Competitive realities are what you test possible strategies against; you define them in terms of customers. Tit-for-tat responses to what competitors do may be appropriate, but they are largely reactive. They come second, after your real strategy. Before you test yourself against competition, strategy takes shape in the determination to create value for customers.

It also takes shape in the determination to *avoid* competition whenever and wherever possible. As the great Sun Tzu observed 500 years before Christ, the smartest strategy in war is the one that allows you to achieve your objectives without having to fight. In just three years, for example, Nintendo's "family computer" sold 12 million units in Japan alone, during which time it had virtually no competition at all. In fact, it created a vast network of companies working to help it succeed. Ricoh supplied the critical Zylog chips; software houses produced special games to play on it like Dragon Quest I, II, and III. Everyone was making too much money to think of creating competition.

The visible clashing between companies in the marketplace— what managers frequently think of as strategy—is but a small fragment of the strategic whole. Like an iceberg, most of strategy is submerged, hidden out of sight. The visible part can foam and froth with head-to-head competition. But most of it is intentionally invisible—beneath the surface where value gets created, where competition gets avoided. Sometimes, of course, the foam and froth of direct competition cannot be avoided. The product is right, the company's direction is right, the perception of value is right, and managers have to buckle down and fight it out with competitors. But in my experience, managers too often and too willingly launch themselves into old-fashioned competitive battles. It's familiar ground. They know what to do, how to fight. They have a much harder time seeing when an effective customer-oriented strategy could avoid the battle altogether.

The Big Squeeze

During the late 1960s and early 1970s, most Japanese companies focused their attention on reducing costs through programs like quality circles, value engineering, and zero defects. As these companies went global, however, they began to concentrate instead on differentiating themselves from their competitors. This heavy investment in competitive differentiation has now gone too far; it has already passed the point of diminishing returns—too many models, too many gadgets, too many bells and whistles.

Today, as a result, devising effective customer-oriented strategies has a special urgency for these companies. A number of the largest and most successful face a common problem—the danger of being trapped between low-cost producers in the NIEs (newly industrialized economies) and high-end producers in Europe. While this threat concerns managers in all the major industrial economies, in Japan, where the danger is most immediate and pressing, it has quickly led companies to rethink their familiar strategic goals. As a consequence, they are rediscovering the primary importance of focusing on customers—in other words, the importance of getting back to what strategy is really about.

In Japan today, the handwriting is on the wall for many industries: The strategic positioning that has served them so well in the past is no longer tenable. On one side, there are German companies making top-of-the-line products like Mercedes or BMW in automobiles, commanding such high prices that even elevated cost levels do not greatly hurt profitability. On the other are low-price, high-volume producers like Korea's Hyundai, Samsung, and Lucky Goldstar. These companies can make products for less than half what it costs the Japanese. The Japanese are being caught in the middle: They are able neither to command the immense margins of the Germans nor to undercut the rock-bottom wages of the Koreans. The result is a painful squeeze.

If you are the leader of a Japanese company, what can you do? I see three possibilities. First, because Korean productivity is still quite low, you can challenge them directly on costs. Yes, their wages are often as little as one-seventh to one-tenth of yours. But if you aggressively take labor content out of your products, you can close or even reverse the cost gap. In practice, this means pushing hard—and at considerable expense—toward full automation, unmanned operations, and totally flexible manufacturing systems.

Examples prove that it can be done. NSK (Nikon Seiko), which makes bearings, has virtually removed its work force through an extensive use of computer-integrated manufacturing linked directly with the marketplace. Mazak Machinery has taken almost all the labor content out of key components in its products. Fujitsu Fanuc has so streamlined itself that it has publicly announced that it can break even with as little as 20% capacity utilization and can compete successfully with a currency as strong as 70 yen to the dollar.

This productivity-through-automation route is one way to go. In fact, for commodity products such as bearings it may be the only way. Once you start down this path, however, you have to follow it right to the end. No turning back. No stopping. Because Korean wages are so low that nothing less than a total commitment to eliminating labor content will suffice. And China, with wage rates just one-fifth of those in the newly industrialized economies, is not far behind Korea and Taiwan in such light industries as textiles, footwear, and watchbands. Although the currencies of the newly industrialized economies are now moving up relative to the dollar, the difference in wage rates is still great enough to require the fiercest kind of across-the-board determination to get rid of labor content.

A second way out of the squeeze is for you to move upmarket where the Germans are. In theory this might be appealing; in practice it has proven very hard for the Japanese to do. Their corporate cultures simply do not permit it. Just look, for example, at what happened with precision electronic products like compact disk players. As soon as the CD reached the market, customers went crazy with demand. Everybody wanted one. It was a perfect opportunity to move upscale with a "Mercedes" compact disk player. What did the Japanese do? Corporate culture and instinct took over, and they cut prices down to about one-fifth of what U.S. and European companies were going to ask for their CDs. Philips, of course, was trying to keep prices and margins up, but the Japanese were trying to drive them down. The Western companies wanted to make money; the Japanese instinct was to build share at any cost.

This is foolishness—or worse. Of course, it is perfectly clear why the Japanese respond this way. They are continuing to practice the approach that served them well in the past when they were playing the low-cost market entry game that the Koreans are playing now. It's the game they know how to play. But now there's a new game, and the Japanese companies have new positions. The actions that made sense for a low-cost player are way off course for a company trying to play at the high end of the market.

There is another reason for this kind of self-defeating behavior. Sony is really more worried about Matsushita than about Philips, and Matsushita is more worried about Sanyo. This furious internal competition fuels the Japanese impulse to slash prices whenever possible. That's also why it's so difficult for Japanese companies to follow the German route. To do it, they have to buck their own history. It means going their own way, and guarding against the instinct to backpedal, to do what their domestic competitors are doing.

Hard as it is, a number of companies *are* going their own way quite successfully. Some, like Seiko in its dogfight with Casio and Hong Kong-based watchmakers, had been badly burned in the low-price game and are now moving to restore profits at the high end of the market. Others, like Honda, Toyota, and Nissan in the automobile industry, are launching more expensive car lines and creating second dealer channels in the United States through which to compete directly for the upscale "German" segment. Still others, like Nakamichi in tape recorders, have always tried to operate at the high end and have never given in on price. Such companies are, however, very rare. Instinct runs deep. Japanese producers tend to compete on price even when they do not have to.

For most companies, following the Korean or German approach is neither an appealing nor a sustainable option. This is not only true in Japan but also in all the advanced industrial economies, if for different reasons. What sets Japanese companies apart is the consideration that they may have less room to maneuver than others, given their historical experience and present situation. For all these companies, there is a pressing need for a middle strategic course, a way to flourish without being forced to go head-to-head with competitors in either a low-cost or an upmarket game. Such a course exists—indeed, it leads managers back to the heart of what strategy is about: creating value for customers.

Five-Finger Exercise

Imagine for a moment that you are head of Yamaha, a company that makes pianos. What are your strategic choices? After strenuous and persistent efforts to become the leading producer of high-quality pianos, you have succeeded in capturing 40% of the global piano market. Unfortunately, just when you finally became the market leader, overall demand for pianos started to decline by 10% every year. As head of Yamaha, what do you do?

A piano is a piano. In most respects, the instrument has not changed much since Mozart. Around the world, in living rooms and dens and concert halls and rehearsal halls, there are some 40 million pianos. For the most part they simply sit. Market growth is stagnant, in polite terms. In business terms, the industry is already in decline; and Korean producers are now coming on-line with their usual low-cost offerings. Competing just to hold share is not an attractive prospect. Making better pianos will not help much; the market has only a limited ability to absorb additional volume. What do you do? What can you do?

According to some analysts, the right move would be to divest the business, labeling it a dog that no longer belongs in the corporate portfolio. But Yamaha reacted differently. Rather than selling the business, Yamaha thought long and hard about how to create value for customers. It took that kind of effort—the answers were far from obvious.

What Yamaha's managers did was look—they took a hard look at the customer and the product. What they saw was that most of these 40 million pianos sit around idle and neglected—and out of tune—most of the time. Not many people play them anymore. No one seems to have a lot of time anymore—and one thing learning to play the piano takes is lots of time. What sits in the homes of these busy people is a large piece of furniture that collects dust. Instead of music, it may even produce guilt. Certainly it is not a functioning musical instrument. No matter how good you are at strategy, you won't be able to sell that many new pianos—no matter how good they are—in such an environment. If you want to create value for customers, you're going to have to find ways to add value to the millions of pianos already out there.

So what do you do? What Yamaha did was to remember the old player piano—a pleasant idea with a not very pleasant sound. Yamaha worked hard to develop a sophisticated, advanced combination of digital and optical technology that can distinguish among 92 different degrees of strength and speed of key touch from pianissimo to fortissimo. Because the technology is digital, it can record and reproduce each keystroke with great accuracy, using the same kind of 3 1/2" disks that work on a personal computer. That means you can now record live performances by the pianists of your choice—or buy such recordings on a computerlike diskette—and then, in effect, invite the artists into your home to play the same compositions on your piano. Yamaha's strategy used technology to create new value for piano customers.

Think about it. For about $2,500 you can retrofit your idle, untuned, dust-collecting piece of oversized furniture so that great artists can play it for you in the privacy of your own home. You can invite your friends over and entertain them as well—and showcase the latest in home entertainment technology. If you are a flutist, you can invite someone over to accompany you on the piano and record her performance. Then, even when she is not there, you can practice the piece with full piano accompaniment.

Furthermore, if you have a personal computer at home in Cambridge and you know a good pianist living in California, you can have her record your favorite sonata and send it over the phone; you simply download it onto your computer, plug the diskette into your retrofitted piano, and enjoy her performance. Or you can join a club that will send you the concert that Horowitz played last night at Carnegie Hall to listen to at home on your own piano. There are all kinds of possibilities.

In terms of the piano market, this new technology creates the prospect of a $2,500 sale to retrofit each of 40 million pianos—not bad for a declining industry. In fact, the potential is even greater because there are also the software recordings to market.

Yamaha started marketing this technology last April, and sales in Japan have been explosive. This was a stagnant industry, remember, an industry which had suffered an annual 10% sales decline in each of the past five years. Now it's alive again—but in a different way. Yamaha did not pursue all the usual routes: It didn't buckle down to prune costs, proliferate models, slice overhead, and all the other usual approaches. It looked with fresh eyes for chances to create value for customers. And it found them.

It also found something else: It learned that the process of discovering value-creating opportunities is itself contagious. It spreads. For instance, now that customers have pianos that play the way Horowitz played last night at Carnegie Hall, they want their instrument tuned to professional standards. That means a tuner visits every six months and generates substantial additional revenue. (And it is substantial. Globally, the market for tuning is roughly $1.6 billion annually, a huge economic opportunity long ignored by piano manufacturers and distributors.) Yamaha can also give factory workers who might otherwise lose their jobs a chance to be tuners.

As the piano regains popularity, a growing number of people will again want to learn how to play the instrument themselves. And that means tutorials, piano schools, videocassettes, and a variety of other revenue-producing opportunities. Overall, the potential growth in the piano industry, hardware and software, is much bigger than anyone previously recognized. Creating value for the customer was the key that unlocked it.

But what about people's reluctance today to spend the time to learn piano the old-fashioned way? We are a society that prizes convenience, and as the many years of declining piano sales illustrate, learning to play a musical instrument is anything but convenient. Listening to music, as opposed to making music, is more popular than ever. Look at all the people going to school or to the office with earphones on; music is everywhere. It's not interest in music that's going down; it's the interest in spending years of disciplined effort to master an instrument. If you asked people if they would like to be able to play an instrument like the piano, they'd say yes. But most feel as if they've already missed the opportunity to learn. They're too old now; they don't have the time to take years of lessons.

With the new digital and sound-chip technologies, they don't have to. Nor do they have to be child prodigies. For $1,500 they can buy a Klavinova, a digital electronic piano, that allows them to do all kinds of wonderful things. They can program it to play and then croon along. They can program it to play the left hand part and join in with a single finger. They can listen to a tutorial cassette that directs which keys to push. They can store instructions in the computer's memory so that they don't have to play all the notes and chords simultaneously. Because the digital technology makes participation easy and accessible, "playing" the instrument becomes fun. Technology removes the learning barrier. No wonder this digital segment is now much bigger than the traditional analog segment of the market.

Most piano manufacturers, however, are sticking with traditional acoustic technologies and leaving their futures to fate. Faced with declining demand, they fight even harder against an ever more aggressive set of competitors for their share of a shrinking pie. Or they rely on government to block imports. Yamaha has not abandoned acoustic instruments; it is now the world leader in nearly all categories of acoustic and "techno" musical instruments. What it did, however, was to study its music-loving customers and to build a strategy based on delivering value linked to those customers' inherent interest in music. It left nothing to fate. It got back to strategy.

Cleaning Up

This is how you chart out a middle course between the Koreans and the Germans. This is how you revitalize an industry. More to the point, this is how you create a value-adding strategy: not by setting out to beat the competition but by setting out to understand how best to provide value for customers.

Kao is a Japanese toiletry company that spends 4% of its revenues on fundamental R&D, studying skin, hair, blood, circulation—things like that. (This 4% may, at first, sound low, but it excludes personnel cost. This matters because as many as 2,800 of the company's 6,700 or so employees are engaged in R&D.) Recently it developed a new product that duplicates the effect of a Japanese hot spring. A hot spring has a high mineral content under extreme pressure. Even the right chemicals thrown into a hot bath will not automatically give you the same effect. Babu, Kao's new bath additive, actually produces the same kind of improvement in circulation that a hot spring provides. It looks like a jumbo-sized Alka-Seltzer tablet. When you throw one Babu into a bath, it starts to fizz with carbon dioxide bubbles as minerals dissolve in the hot water.

Kao's strategy was to offer consumers something completely different from traditional bath gel. Because of its effects on overall health and good circulation, Babu competes on a different ground. In fact, it wiped out the old Japanese bath gel and additives industry in a single year. It's the only product of its kind that now sells in Japan. There is no competition because potential competitors cannot make anything like it. Kao is playing a different game.

For the new breed of Japanese companies, like Yamaha and Kao, strategy does not mean beating the competition. It means working hard to understand a customer's inherent needs and then rethinking what a category of product is all about. The goal is to develop the right product to serve those needs—not just a better version of competitors' products. In fact, Kao pays far less attention to other toiletry companies than it does to improving skin condition, circulation, or caring for hair. It now understands hair so well that its newest hair tonic product, called Success, falls somewhere between cosmetics and medicine. In that arena, there is no competition.

Brewing Wisdom

Getting back to strategy means getting back to a deep understanding of what a product is about. Some time back, for example, a Japanese home appliance company was trying to develop a coffee percolator. Should it be a General Electric-type percolator, executives wondered? Should it be the same drip-type that Philips makes? Larger? Smaller? I urged them to ask a different kind of question: Why do people drink coffee? What are they looking for when they do? If your objective is to serve the customer better, then shouldn't you understand why that customer drinks coffee in the first place? Then you know what kind of percolator to make.

The answer came back: good taste. I then asked the company's engineers what they were doing to help the consumer enjoy good taste in a cup of coffee. They said they were trying to design a good percolator. I asked them what influences the taste of a cup of coffee. No one knew. That became the next question we had to answer. It turns out that lots of things can affect taste—the beans, the temperature, the water. We did our homework and discovered all the things that affect taste. For the engineers, each factor represented a strategic degree of freedom in designing a percolator—that is, a factor about which something can be done. With beans, for instance, you can have different degrees of quality or freshness. You can grind them in various ways. You can produce different grain sizes. You can distribute the grains differently when pouring hot water over them.

Of all the factors, water quality, we learned, made the greatest difference. The percolator in design at the time, however, didn't take water quality into account at all. Everyone had simply assumed that customers would use tap water. We discovered next that the grain distribution and the time between grinding the beans and pouring in the water were crucial. As a result, we began to think about the product and its necessary features in a new way. It *had* to have a built-in dechlorinating function. It *had* to have a built-in grinder. All the customer should have to do is pour in water and beans; the machine should handle the rest. That's the way to assure great taste in a cup of coffee.

To start you have to ask the right questions and set the right kinds of strategic goals. If your only concern is that General Electric has just brought out a percolator that brews coffee in ten minutes, you will get your engineers to design one that brews it in seven minutes. And if you stick with that logic, market research will tell you that instant coffee is the way to go. If the General Electric machine consumes only a little electricity, you will focus on using even less.

Conventional marketing approaches won't solve the problem. You can get any results you want from the consumer averages. If you ask people whether they want their coffee in ten minutes or seven, they will say seven, of course. But it's still the wrong question. And you end up back where you started, trying to beat the competition at its own game. If your primary focus is on the competition, you will never step back and ask what the customer's inherent needs are or what the product really is about. Personally, I would much rather talk with three housewives for two hours each on their feelings about, say, washing machines than conduct a 1,000-person survey on the same topic. I get much better insight and perspective on what they are really looking for.

Taking Pictures

Back in the mid-1970s, single-lens reflex (SLR) cameras started to become popular, and lens-shutter cameras declined rapidly in popularity. To most people, the lens-shutter model looked cheap and nonprofessional and it took inferior quality pictures. These opinions were so strong that one camera company with which I was working had almost decided to pull out of the lens-shutter business entirely. Everyone knew that the trend was toward SLR and that only a better version of SLR could beat the competition.

I didn't know. So I asked a few simple questions: Why do people take pictures in the first place? What are they really looking for when they take pictures? The answer was simple. They were not looking for a good camera. They were looking for good pictures. Cameras—SLR or lens-shutter—and film were not the end products that consumers wanted. What they wanted were good pictures.

Why was it so hard to take good pictures with a lens-shutter camera? This time, no one knew. So we went to a film lab and collected a sample of some 18,000 pictures. Next we identified the 7% or so that were not very good; then we tried to analyze why each of these picture-taking failures had occurred. We found some obvious causes—even some categories of causes. Some failures were the result of poor distance adjustment. The company's design engineers addressed that problem in two different ways: They added a plastic lens designed to keep everything in focus beyond three feet (a kind of permanent focus), and they automated the focus process.

Another common problem with the bad pictures was not enough light. The company built a flash right into the camera. That way, the poor fellow who left his flash attachment on a closet shelf could still be equipped to take a good picture. Still another problem was the marriage of film and camera. Here the engineers added some grooves on the side of the film cartridges so that the camera could tell how sensitive the film is to light and could adjust. Double exposure was another common problem. The camera got a self-winder.

In all, we came up with some 200 ideas for improving the lens-shutter camera. The result—virtually a whole new approach to the product—helped revitalize the business. Today, in fact, the lens-shutter market is bigger than that for SLRs. And we got there because we did a very simple thing: We asked what the customer's inherent needs were and then rethought what a camera had to be in order to meet them. There was no point slugging it out with competitors. There was no reason to leave the business. We just got back to strategy—based on customers.

Making Dinner

There is no mystery to this process, no black box to which only a few gurus have access. The questions that have to be asked are straightforward, and the place to start is clear. Awhile ago, some people came to me with a set of excellent ideas for designing kitchen appliances for Japanese homes. They knew cooking, and their appliances were quite good. After some study, however, I told them not to go ahead.

What I did was to go and visit several hundred houses and apartments and take pictures of the kitchens. The answer became clear: There was no room. There were even things already stacked on top of the refrigerators. The counters were already full. There was no room for new appliances, no matter how appealing their attributes.

Thinking about these products, and understanding the customer's needs, however, did produce a different idea: Build this new equipment into something that is already in the kitchen. That way there is no new demand for space. What that led to, for example, was the notion of building a microwave oven into a regular oven. Everyone looked at the pictures of 200 kitchens and said, no space. The alternative was, rethink the product.

Aching Heads, Bad Logic

Looking closely at a customer's needs, thinking deeply about a product—these are no exotic pieces of strategic apparatus. They are, as they have always been, the basics of sound management. They have just been neglected or ignored. But why? Why have so many managers allowed themselves to drift so far away from what strategy is really about?

Think for a moment about aching heads. Is my headache the same as yours? My cold? My shoulder pain? My stomach discomfort? Of course not. Yet when a pharmaceutical company asked for help to improve its process for coming up with new products, what it wanted was help in getting into its development pipeline new remedies for standard problems like headache or stomach pain. It had assembled a list of therapeutic categories and was eager to match them up with appropriate R&D efforts.

No one had taken the time, however, to think about how people with various discomforts actually feel. So we asked 50 employees in the company to fill out a questionnaire—throughout a full year—about how they felt physically at all times of the day every day of the year. Then we pulled together a list of the symptoms described, sat down with the company's scientists, and asked them, item by item: Do you know why people feel this way? Do you have a drug for this kind of symptom? It turned out that there were no drugs for about 80% of the symptoms, these physical awarenesses of discomfort. For many of them, some combination of existing drugs worked just fine. For others, no one had ever thought to seek a particular remedy. The scientists were ignoring tons of profit.

Without understanding customers' needs—the specific types of discomfort they were feeling—the company found it all too easy to say, "Headache? Fine, here's a medicine, an aspirin, for headache. Case closed. Nothing more to do there. Now we just have to beat the competition in aspirin." It was easy not to take the next step and ask, "What does the headache feel like? Where does it come from? What is the underlying cause? How can we treat the cause, not just the symptom?" Many of these symptoms, for example, are psychological and culture-specific. Just look at television commercials. In the United States, the most common complaint is headache; in the United Kingdom, backache; in Japan, stomachache. In the United States, people say that they have a splitting headache; in Japan it is an ulcer. How can we truly understand what these people are feeling and why?

The reflex, of course, is to provide a headache pill for a headache—that is, to assume that the solution is simply the reverse of the diagnosis. That is bad medicine and worse logic. It is the kind of logic that reinforces the impulse to direct strategy toward beating the competition, toward cutting costs when making traditional musical instruments, or adding a different ingredient to the line of traditional soaps. It is the kind of logic that denies the need for a detailed understanding of intrinsic customer needs. It leads to fork-lift trucks that pile up boxes just fine but do not allow the operators to see directly in front of them. It leads to dishwashers that remove everything but the scorched eggs and rice that customers most want to get rid of. It leads to pianos standing idle and gathering dust.

Getting back to strategy means fighting that reflex, not giving in to it. It means resisting the easy answers in the search for better ways to deliver value to customers. It means asking the simple-sounding questions about what products are about. It means, in short, taking seriously the strategic part of management.

PART
II

Linking Competitive Strategy and Functional Strategy

1
Information Technology Changes the Way You Compete

F. Warren McFarlan

To solve customer service problems, a major distributor installs an on-line network to its key customers so that they can directly enter orders into its computer. The computer's main purpose is to cut order-entry costs and to provide more flexibility to customers in the time and process of order submission. The system yields a larger competitive advantage, adding value for customers and a substantial rise in their sales. The resulting sharp increase in the company's market share forces a primary competitor into a corporate reorganization and a massive systems development effort to contain the damage, but these corrective actions have gained only partial success.

A regional airline testifies before the U.S. Congress that it has been badly hurt by the reservation system of a national carrier. It claims that the larger airline, through access to the reservation levels on every one of the smaller line's flights, can pinpoint all mutually competitive routes where the regional is performing well and take competitive pricing and service action. Since the regional airline lacks access to the bigger carrier's data, it allegedly is at decided competitive disadvantage.

A large aerospace company has required major suppliers to acquire CAD (computer-aided design) equipment to link directly to its CAD installation. It claims this has dramatically reduced total cost and time of design changes, parts acquisition, and inventory, making it more competitive.

These examples are not unusual. With great speed, the sharp

reduction in the cost of information systems (IS) technology (i.e., computers, remote devices, and telecommunications[1]) has allowed computer systems to move from applications for back-office support to those offering significant competitive advantage. Particularly outstanding are systems that link customer and supplier. Though such links offer an opportunity for a competitive edge, they also bring a risk of strategic vulnerability. In the case of the aerospace manufacturer, operating procedures have shown much improvement, but this has been at the cost of vastly greater dependence, since it is now much harder for the manufacturer to change suppliers.

In many cases, the new technology has opened up a singular, one-time opportunity for a company to redeploy its assets and rethink its strategy. The technology has given the organization the potential for forging sharp new tools that can produce lasting gains in market share.

Of course, such opportunities vary widely from one company to another just as the intensity and the rules of competition vary widely from one industry to another. Similarly, a company's location, size, and basic product technology also shape potential IS technology applications. Computer advances have affected even the smallest companies. (Recently, for example, a $6 million manufacturer of electronic components profitably acquired CAD technology.) Further, in different situations, a company may appropriately attempt to be either a leader or an alert follower. The stakes can be so high, however, that this must be an explicit, well-planned decision.

Search for Opportunity

In assessing the ultimate impact of IS technology, companies must address the five questions that follow. If their answer to one or more of these questions is yes, information technology represents a strategic resource that requires attention at the highest level.

CAN IS TECHNOLOGY BUILD BARRIERS TO ENTRY?

In the example of the distributor, the company was able to open up a new electronic channel to its customers. Not only was the move highly successful but other companies could not replicate it. Customers did not want devices from different vendors on their premises.

A successful entry barrier offers not only a new service to appeal to customers but also features that keep the customers "hooked." The harder the service is to emulate, the higher the barrier for the competition. An example of such a defensible barrier is the development of a complex software package that adds value and is capable of evolution and refinement. A large financial services firm used this approach to launch a different and highly attractive financial product, depending on sophisticated software. Because of the complexity of the concept and its software, competitors lagged behind, giving the firm valuable time to establish market position. Further, the firm has been able to enhance its original product significantly, thus making itself a moving target.

The payoff from value-added features that increase both sales and market share is particularly noteworthy for industries in which there are great economies of scale and price is important to the customer. By moving first down the learning curve, a company can gain a cost advantage that enables it to put great pressure on its competitors.

Electronic tools for salespeople that increase the scope and speed of price quotes represent another kind of barrier. By permitting the sales force to prepare complex quotations on the customer's premises, portable microcomputers not only give better support but also make the sales force feel more confident (whether or not they have any reason to) and hence sell more aggressively. The sophisticated financial planning packages being used by sales forces of major insurance companies build similar barriers.

The flip side, of course, is the large capital investments these projects require and the uncertainty of their ultimate benefits. Further, in difficult economic times, investment in these electronic systems may create both serious cost rigidity and exit barriers against an orderly withdrawal from the industry. It is difficult, for example, for a large airline to scale its computing activity down sharply to deal with reduced operations or great cost pressures.

While a company may have difficulty in maintaining an individual advantage, it can parlay a series of innovations into a valuable image; it can be seen as a company that is at the leading edge. For example, Merrill Lynch has consistently improved the features of its cash management account. This image can help maintain market position, especially in periods when a line of products is not successfully competitive.

CAN IS TECHNOLOGY BUILD IN SWITCHING COSTS?

Are there ways to encourage customers to rely increasingly on the supplier's electronic support, building it into their operations so that increased operational dependence and normal human inertia make switching to a competitor unattractive? In the ideal case, the electronic support system is simple to use. It also contains, however, a series of increasingly complex and useful procedures that insinuate themselves into the customer's routines. Finally, the customer will have to spend too much time and money to change suppliers. Electronic home banking is a good example of this. When a customer has learned to use such a system and has coded all monthly creditors for the system, he or she will be much more reluctant to change banks than before.

A heavy machine manufacturer provides another example of electronic services and features that add value to and support a company's basic product line while increasing the switching cost. The company has attached electronic devices to its machinery installed on customer premises. In case of mechanical failure, the device signals a computer program at corporate headquarters and the program analyzes the data, diagnoses the problem, and either suggests changes in the machine's control settings or pinpoints the cause of the failure and identifies the defective parts. In the same vein, another manufacturer has supplemented such a service with immediate dispatching of spare parts.

CAN THE TECHNOLOGY CHANGE THE BASIS OF COMPETITION?

One revealing way to characterize competitive strategies is by means of Michael E. Porter's analysis.[2] He discusses three types, each with different ground rules. One is cost based, when a company can produce at a much lower cost than its competition. Companies selling commodities and high-technology products can use such strategies. A second type is based on product differentiation, when a company offers a different mix of product features such as service and quality. The third type is specialization in only one niche of a market, distinguishing itself by unusual cost or product features. Its strategies may be called focused.

In some industries dominated by cost-based competition, IS technology has permitted development of product features that are so different that they cause the basis of competition to change radically. For example, in the mid-1970s, a major distributor of magazines to newsstands and stores was in an industry segment dominated by cost-based competition. For years it had used electronic technology to drive costs down by developing cheaper methods of sorting and distributing magazines. While using less staff and lower inventory, it had achieved the position of low-cost producer.

In 1977, however, the distributor decided to build on the fact that its customers were small, unsophisticated, and unaware of their profit structures. By using its records of weekly shipments and returns from a newsstand, the distributor could identify what was selling on the newsstand. It developed programs that calculated profit per square foot for every magazine and compared these data with information from newsstands in economically and ethnically similar neighborhoods that often carried very different mixes of merchandise. The distributor could thus tell each newsstand every month how it could improve the product mix. Instead of just distributing magazines, the company has used technology to add a valuable inventory management feature that has permitted it to raise prices substantially and has changed the basis of competition from cost to product differentiation.

Other companies have used IS technology to change the basis of competition from product differentiation to low cost. For example, the suppliers to the aerospace manufacturer described earlier used to compete on the basis of quality, speedy handling of rush orders, and ability to meet customized requests as well as cost. The CAD-to-CAD link and the move to numerically controlled machine tools has negated the value of many of these elements of differentiation and made overall cost more important.

Dramatic cost reduction can significantly alter the old ground rules of competition. In a low-cost competitive environment, companies should look for a strategic opportunity from IS technology either through sharp cost reduction (for example, staff reduction or ability to grow without hiring staff, improved material use, increased machine efficiency through better scheduling or more cost-effective maintenance, and lower inventories) or by adding value to their products that will permit a change to competing on the basis of product differentiation. In the airline industry in the 1960s, American Airlines pioneered a new kind of reservation service, which brought a large increase in market share and competition. Today in the industry, airlines are fighting to get their on-line reservation systems into travel agencies and, through positioning of flight recommendations on a CRT screen, to influence the travel agent's purchase recommendation. In another example, relentless competition is taking place in the diversified financial services industry as insurance companies, banks, and brokerage houses merge, and companies jockey for position.

A large insurance carrier recently identified systems development as its biggest bottleneck in the introduction of new insurance products. It is, therefore, heavily investing in software packages and outside staff to complement its large (500-person) development organization. A cost-cutting activity in the 1960s and 1970s, the IS organization has become vital to the implementation of a product differentiation strategy in the 1980s. This company, which is cutting staff and financial expenditures overall, is increasing IS expenditures and staff as a strategic investment.

Just ahead are the risks and opportunities that will come with the timing and packaging of videotex and cable services as a new way of retailing, particularly to the upscale market. In many cases in a short time these changes could dramatically alter old processes and structures. No example is more striking than the situation confronting libraries. They have a 1,000-year-plus tradition of storing books made of parchment and wood pulp. Soaring materials costs, the advent of cheap microfiche and microfilm, expansion of computer data bases, and electronic links between libraries will make the research facility of the year 2000 unrecognizable from the large library of today. Those libraries that persist in spending 65% of their budget to keep aged wood pulp warm (and cool) will be irrelevant to the needs of their readers.

Though in the early stages it is difficult to distinguish the intriguing but ephemeral from an important structural innovation, if managers misread the issues in either direction the consequences can be devastating.

CAN IS CHANGE THE BALANCE OF POWER IN SUPPLIER RELATIONSHIPS?

The development of interorganizational systems can be a powerful asset; for example, just-in-time delivery systems can drastically reduce inventory levels in the automotive and other industries, thus permitting big cost savings. Similarly, electronic CAD links from one organization to another permit faster response, smaller inventory, and better service to the final consumer. In one case, a large retailer has linked its materials-ordering system electronically to its suppliers' order-entry system. If it wants 100 sofas for a particular region, its computer automatically checks the order-entry system of its primary sofa suppliers, and the one with the lowest cost gets the order.

Equally important, the retailer's computer continually monitors the suppliers' finished-goods inventories, factory scheduling, and commitments against the schedule to make sure enough inventory will be available to meet unexpected demand by the retailer. If inventories are inadequate, the retailer alerts the supplier. If suppliers are unwilling to go along with this system they may find their overall share of business dropping until they are replaced by others.

Such interorganizational systems can redistribute power between buyer and supplier. In the case of the aerospace manufacturer, the CAD-CAD systems increased dependence on an individual supplier, became hard to replace, and left the company vulnerable to major price increases. The retailer, on the other hand, was in a much stronger position to dictate the terms of its relationship to its suppliers.

CAN IS TECHNOLOGY GENERATE NEW PRODUCTS?

As described earlier, IS can lead to products that are of higher quality, that can be delivered faster, or that are cheaper. Similarly, at little extra cost, existing products can be tailored to customers' needs. Some companies may be able to combine one or more of these advantages. They should ask themselves if they can join an electronic support service with a product to increase the value in the consumer's eyes. Sometimes this can be done at little additional cost, as in the case of the on-line diagnostic system for machine failure described earlier.

Sometimes the data a company already has can be bundled or packaged to generate revenue. For example, Data Resources, Inc., the large econometrics subsidiary of McGraw-Hill, introduced a new product called VISILINK that for the first time permitted owners of personal computers to use DRI's econometrics data base and to extract desired information. This service significantly broadened DRI's appeal and allowed it to reach many small companies and individuals who either were unaware of DRI or who previously could not afford DRI's service. Similarly, the software developed to support a product may have commercial value.

The Challenge

Achieving advantages requires broad IS management and user dialogue plus imagination. The process is complicated by the fact that many IS products are strategic though the potential benefits are very subjective and not easily verified. Often a strict ROI focus by senior management may turn attention toward narrow, well-defined targets as opposed to broader strategic opportunities that are harder to analyze.

Visualizing their systems in terms of a strategic grid,[3] senior and IS management in a number of organizations have concluded that their company or business unit is located in either the support or the factory quadrant (see Exhibit I). They have set up staffing, organization, and planning activities accordingly. As a result of both the sharp change in IS technology performance and the evolution of competitive conditions, this categorization may be wrong. For the new conditions, for example, the competitor of the distributor described in the opening paragraph was complacent about its position in the support box. The company never realized what had happened until it was too late. Playing catch-up ball is difficult and expensive in this area.

A number of companies and industry groups are and will remain appropriately in the support and factory boxes. Technical changes, however, have been so sudden in the past several years that the role of a company's IS function needs reexamination to ensure its placement is still appropriate.

Exhibit I. Position of Information Systems in Various Types of Companies

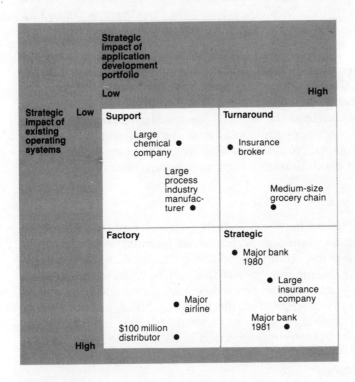

A New Point of View

Addressing the issues raised here requires management to change the way it operates.

1. The CEO must insist that the end products of IS planning clearly communicate the true competitive impact of the expenditures involved. Exhibit II shows how to accomplish this by identifying priorities for the allocation of financial and staff resources. In this connection, managers should realize that an embarrassingly large amount of development effort must be devoted to repair worn-out systems and to maintain them to meet changed business conditions.[4] Also, a vital but often unrecognized need exists for research and development to keep up with IS technology and to ensure that the company knows the full range of possibilities (for appropriate investments in the early phases).[5] Distinctly separate are the areas

where a company spends money to obtain pure competitive advantage (very exciting) or to regain or maintain competitive parity (not so exciting because the company is trying to recover from its short-sightedness). Finally, projects where the investment is defined for measurable ROI are also separate.

The aim underlying the ranking process in Exhibit II is to allocate resources to areas with the most growth potential. Each company should have a summary of the IS plan of about three pages that vividly communicates to the CEO the data derived from Exhibit II, why IS expenditures are allocated as they are, and what explicit types of competitive business benefits the company might expect from its IS expenditures. Today, many companies fall short of this goal.

2. Till now, it has been the industry norm for organizations and individuals to share data widely about information systems technology and plans, on the ground that no lasting competitive advantage would emerge from IS and that collaboration would allow all to reduce administrative headaches. But today, managers should take appropriate steps to ensure the confidentiality of strategic IS plans and thinking. Great care should be taken in choosing the attendees at industry meetings and in determining what they can talk about and what information they can share with vendors and competitors.

3. Executives should not permit the use of simplistic rules to calculate desirable IS expense levels. Judging an IS budget as a percentage of something, such as sales, has always been an easy way to compare the performance of different companies. In today's more volatile competitive arena, such comparisons are very dangerous. I have observed some companies that are spending 6% of their total sales in this area and that are clearly underinvesting. I have seen others making an outlay of 1% of their sales volume that are over-spending.

4. Interorganizational IS systems have hidden, second-order effects, that is, repercussions in other parts of the business. Managers should not ignore them. Interorganizational IS systems are not necessarily good in and of themselves just because they work and are technically sound. Both their development and operation pose opportunity for shifts in the balance of power between companies. Sourcing inflexibility, pricing, vulnerability, systems inefficiencies,

Exhibit II. Resource Allocation Priorities by Strategic Business Unit

Goal of IS expenditure	Growing, highly competitive industry	Relatively stable industry, known ground rules	Static or declining industry
Rehabilitate and maintain system	1	1	1
Experiment with new technology	2	3	3
Attain competitive advantage	2	2	3*
Maintain or regain competitive parity	2	3	4
Defined return on investment†	3	3	4

*Assuming the change is not so dramatic as to revolutionize the industry's overall performance.

†In an intensely cost-competitive environment, defined ROI is the same as gaining competitive advantage.

Note:
Numbers indicate relative attractiveness or importance of the investment, with 1 having the highest priority.

and excess expense are examples of these secondary effects. Assessing their implication requires careful examination.

5. Managers must not be too efficiency-oriented in IS resource allocation. They must encourage creativity in R&D during this period of technological discontinuity. The support or factory role (see Exhibit I) is correct for IS in some organizations; however, such a decision should result from careful, creative analysis.

Notes

1. See my article with James J. McKenney, "The Information Archipelago—Maps and Bridges," *Harvard Business Review* (September–October 1982), p. 109.

2. Michael E. Porter, "How Competitive Forces Shape Strategy," *Harvard Business Review* (March–April 1979), p. 137. Article is Chapter 2, Part I of this volume.

3. See my article with James J. McKenney and Philip Pyburn, "The Information Archipelago—Plotting a Course," *Harvard Business Review* (January–February 1983), p. 145.

4. See Martin D.J. Buss, "Penny-Wise Approach to Data Processing," *Harvard Business Review* (July–August 1981), p. 111.

5. See "The Information Archipelago—Plotting a Course."

2
Competing through Manufacturing

Steven C. Wheelwright and Robert H. Hayes

Manufacturing companies, particularly those in the United States, are today facing intensified competition. For many, it is a case of simple survival. What makes this challenge so difficult is that the "secret weapon" of their fiercest competitors is based not so much on better product design, marketing ingenuity, or financial strength as on something much harder to duplicate: superior over-all manufacturing capability. For a long time, however, many of these companies have systematically neglected their manufacturing organizations. Now, as the cost of that neglect grows ever clearer, they are not finding it easy to rebuild their lost excellence in production.

In most of these companies, the bulk of their labor force and assets are tied to the manufacturing function. The attitudes, expectations, and traditions that have developed over time in and around that function will be difficult to change. Companies cannot atone for years of neglect simply by throwing large chunks of investment dollars at the problem. Indeed, it normally takes several years of disciplined effort to transform manufacturing weakness into strength. In fact, it can take several years for a company to break the habit of "working around" the limitations of a manufacturing operation and to look on it as a source of competitive advantage.

In practice, of course, the challenge for managers is far more complex than is suggested by the simple dichotomy between "weakness" and "strength." There is no single end that every manufacturing function must serve—and serve well. There are, instead, several generic kinds of roles that the function can play in a company and—as Exhibit I suggests—these roles can be viewed as

Exhibit I.   Stages in Manufacturing's Strategic Role

Stage 1	**Minimize manufacturing's negative potential: "internally neutral"**	Outside experts are called in to make decisions about strategic manufacturing issues
		Internal, detailed management control systems are the primary means for monitoring manufacturing performance
		Manufacturing is kept flexible and reactive
Stage 2	**Achieve parity with competitors: "externally neutral"**	"Industry practice" is followed
		The planning horizon for manufacturing investment decisions is extended to incorporate a single-business cycle
		Capital investment is the primary means for catching up with competition or achieving a competitive edge
Stage 3	**Provide credible support to the business strategy: "internally supportive"**	Manufacturing investments are screened for consistency with the business strategy
		A manufacturing strategy is formulated and pursued
		Longer-term manufacturing developments and trends are addressed systematically
Stage 4	**Pursue a manufacturing-base competitive advantage: "externally supportive"**	Efforts are made to anticipate the potential of new manufacturing practices and technologies
		Manufacturing is involved "up front" in major marketing and engineering decisions (and vice versa)
		Long-range programs are pursued in order to acquire capabilities in advance of needs

stages of development along a continuum. At one extreme, production can offer little contribution to a company's market success; at the other, it provides a major source of competitive advantage.

Understanding the possibilities along this continuum can help managers identify both their company's current position and the transformations in attitude and approach that will be necessary if it is to advance to a higher stage of competitive effectiveness. Such understanding is also useful in judging how quickly a company may reasonably be expected to progress from stage to stage. It is useful, too, in pointing out the changes that must be made in other

Exhibit II. Major Types of Manufacturing Choices

Capacity	Amount, timing, type
Facilities	Size, location, specialization
Equipment and process technologies	Scale, flexibility, interconnectedness
Vertical integration	Direction, extent, balance
Vendors	Number, structure, relationship
New products	Hand-off, start-up, modification
Human resources	Selection and training, compensation, security
Quality	Definition, role, responsibility
Systems	Organization, schedules, control.

parts of the company in order to sustain each higher level of manufacturing's contribution.

Stages of Manufacturing Effectiveness

Before describing each of these generic roles (or stages) in detail and outlining the problems that can arise when trying to move from one to the next, we must say a few things about the kind of framework we are proposing. First, the stages are not mutually exclusive. Every manufacturing operation embodies a set of important choices about such factors as capacity, vertical integration, human resource policies, and the like. (See Exhibit II for a listing of these.) A given operation may be—and often is—composed of factors that are themselves at different levels of development. What determines the overall level of the operation is where the balance among these factors falls—that is, where in the developmental scheme the operation's center of gravity rests.

Second, it is difficult, if not impossible, for a company to skip a stage. A new business can, of course, attempt to begin operations at any level it chooses, but a manufacturing function that is already up and running has far less freedom of choice. Attitudes and established modes of doing things are well entrenched, and it takes a tremendous effort just to move things along from one level to the next. Hence, the organizational strain imposed by an effort to leapfrog a stage makes the probability of failure uncomfortably high. In addition, it is the mastery of activities at one stage that usually provides the underpinnings for a successful transition to the next.

It is possible, however, for a given operation to contain factors of the sort already mentioned that are well separated on the developmental continuum. But here, too, the forces of organizational gravity are remorselessly at work. Over time, the less advanced part of the operation will tend to draw the more advanced part back to its own level. The production group responsible for Apple's Macintosh computer has, for example, tried to push its capability in materials handling and test processes well ahead of the rest of its capabilities. The resulting strain has made it hard for the group to maintain a stable organization. By contrast, Hewlett-Packard's personal computer manufacturing group has tried to push ahead at a slower and steadier pace—but along a very broad front.

Third, although it is appealing in theory for companies to move as a single entity through these stages, the real work of development occurs at the business unit level. Certainly, it is nice to have backing from a central corporate office so that several business units can evolve together and help each other, but it is at the business unit, not corporate, level that the critical nuts-and-bolts coordination among factors and across functions takes place.

With these three points in mind, we now turn to a consideration of the stages themselves. We will give special attention to the shift from Stage 3 to Stage 4 because this transition is the most difficult of all and because reaching Stage 4 has the largest payoff in terms of competitive success. In fact, Stage 4 operations characterize all companies that have achieved the status of world-class manufacturers.

STAGE 1

This lowest stage represents an "internally neutral" orientation toward manufacturing: Top managers regard the function as neutral—incapable of influencing competitive success. Consequently, they seek only to minimize any negative impact it may have. They do not expect manufacturing (indeed, they tend to discourage it from trying) to make a positive contribution.

Stage 1 organizations typically view manufacturing capability as the direct result of a few structural decisions about capacity, facilities, technology, and vertical integration. Managers attach little or no strategic importance to such infrastructure issues as work force policies, planning and measurement systems, and incremental process improvements. When strategic issues involving manufacturing do arise, management usually calls in outside experts in the belief that their own production organization lacks the necessary expertise (a self-fulfilling prophecy).

When faced with the need to make a change in facilities, location, or process technology, their production managers run into top-level insistence to remain flexible and reactive so as not to get locked into the wrong decisions. Similarly, they are expected to source all manufacturing equipment from outside suppliers and to rely on these suppliers for most of their information about manufacturing technology and new technological developments.

On balance, Stage 1 organizations think of production as a low-tech operation that can be staffed with low-skilled workers and managers. They employ detailed measurements and controls of operating performance, oriented to near-term performance, to ensure that manufacturing does not get too far offtrack before corrective action can be taken. The aim is not to maximize the function's competitive value but to guard against competitively damaging problems.

Not surprisingly, the top managers of such companies try to minimize their involvement with, and thus their perceived dependence on, manufacturing. They concern themselves primarily with major investment decisions, as viewed through the prism of their capital budgeting process. As a result, they tend to regard their company's production facilities and processes as the embodiment of a series of once-and-for-all decisions. They are uneasy with the notion that manufacturing is a *learning* process that can create and expand its own capabilities—and may therefore not be totally controllable. Hence, they will agree to add capacity only when the need becomes obvious and, when they do, prefer to build large general-purpose facilities employing known—that is, "safe"—technologies purchased from outside vendors. Eager to keep the manufacturing function as simple as possible, they feel justified in thinking that "anybody ought to be able to manage manufacturing," an attitude reflected in their assignment of people to that department.

This Stage 1 view occurs both in companies whose managers see the manufacturing process as simple and straightforward and in those whose managers do not think it likely to have much impact on overall competitive position. Many consumer products and service companies fall into this category. So, too, do a number of sophisticated high-technology companies, which regard *product* technology as the key to competitive success and *process* technology as, at best, neutral.

Experience shows, however, that the competitive difficulties encountered by many U.S. consumer electronics and electrical equipment manufacturers have their roots in the attitude that manufacturing's role is simply to assemble and test products built from purchased components. Even in these high-tech companies, the manufacturing operation can appear clumsy and unprepared when confronted with such straightforward tasks as providing adequate production capacity, helping suppliers solve problems, and keeping equipment and systems up-to-date. With a self-limiting view of what manufacturing can do, managers find it difficult to upgrade their labor-intensive, low-technology processes when products involving a new generation of technology appear. Nor can their unfocused, general-purpose facilities compete effectively with the highly focused, specialized plants of world-class competitors.

STAGE 2

The second stage in our progression also represents a form of manufacturing "neutrality," but Stage 2 companies seek a competitive or "external" neutrality (parity with major competitors) on the manufacturing dimension rather than the internal ("don't upset the apple cart") neutrality of Stage 1. Typified by—but not restricted to—companies in traditional, manufacturing-intensive industries like steel, autos, and heavy equipment, Stage 2 organizations seek competitive neutrality by:

Following industry practice in matters regarding the work force (industrywide bargaining agreements with national unions, for example), equipment purchases, and the timing and scale of capacity additions.

Avoiding, where possible, the introduction of major, discontinuous changes in product or process. In fact, such changes tend to come—if at all—from competitors well outside the mainstream of an industry.

Treating capital investments in new equipment and facilities as the most effective means for gaining a temporary competitive advantage.

Viewing economies of scale related to the production rate as the most important source of manufacturing efficiency.

As noted, this approach to manufacturing is quite common in America's smokestack industries, most of which have an oligopolistic market structure and a well-defined set of competitors who share a vested interest in maintaining the status quo. It is also common in many companies engaged in electronic instrument assembly and pharmaceutical production, which consider manufacturing to be largely standardized and unsophisticated and which assume product development people can be entrusted with designing process changes whenever they are needed. Like those in Stage 1, Stage 2 companies—when they make an improvement in their process technology—rely on sources outside of manufacturing; unlike companies in Stage 1, however, they often turn to their own (largely product-oriented) R&D labs as well as to outside suppliers.

Top managers of Stage 2 companies regard resource allocation decisions as the most effective means of addressing the major strategic issues in manufacturing. Offensive investments to gain competitive advantage are usually linked to new products; manufacturing investments (other than those for additional capacity to match increases in the demand for existing products) are primarily defensive and cost-cutting in nature. They are usually undertaken only when manufacturing's shortcomings have become obvious.

STAGE 3

Stage 3 organizations expect manufacturing actively to support and strengthen the company's competitive position. As noted in Exhibit I, these organizations view manufacturing as "internally supportive" in that its contribution derives from and is dictated by overall business strategy. That contribution includes:

Screening decisions to be sure that they are consistent with the organization's competitive strategy.

Translating that strategy into terms meaningful to manufacturing personnel.

Seeking consistency within manufacturing through a carefully thought-out sequence of investments and systems changes over time.

Being on the lookout for longer-term developments and trends that may have a significant effect on manufacturing's ability to respond to the needs of other parts of the organization.

Formulating a manufacturing strategy, complete with plant charters and mission statements, to guide manufacturing activities over an extended period of time.

Companies often arrive at Stage 3 as a natural consequence of both their success in developing an effective business strategy, based on formal planning processes, and their wish to support that strategy in all functional areas. They want manufacturing to be creative and to take a long-term view in managing itself. When push comes to shove, however, the majority of them act as if such creativity is best expressed by making one or two bold moves—the introduction of robots, just-in-time, or CAD/CAM, for example—while they continue to run most of the function as a Stage 2 activity. The beer industry is a good case in point: After building a number of new, large-scale facilities in the 1970s and rationalizing existing operations, it began to drift back into a "business as usual" attitude toward the manufacturing function.

While Stage 2 companies at times also pursue advances in manufacturing practice, they tend to regard these in strictly defensive terms: as a means of keeping up with their industry. Stage 3 companies, however, view technological progress as a natural response to changes in business strategy and competitive position.

Another characteristic of Stage 3 organizations is that their manufacturing managers take a broad view of their role by seeking to understand their company's business strategy and the kind of competitive advantage it is pursuing. Some of these managers even follow career paths that lead to general management. Notwithstanding the potential for advancement or the greater equality of titles and pay across all functions in Stage 3 companies, manufacturing managers are expected only to support the company's business strategy, not to become actively involved in helping to formulate it.

STAGE 4

The fourth and most progressive stage of manufacturing development arises when competitive strategy rests to a significant degree on a company's manufacturing capability. By this we do not mean that manufacturing dictates strategy to the rest of the company but only that strategy derives from a coordinated effort among functional peers—manufacturing very much among them.

As noted in Exhibit I, the role of manufacturing in Stage 4 companies is "externally supportive," in that it is expected to make an important contribution to the competitive success of the organization. The leading companies in process-intensive industries, for example, usually give manufacturing a Stage 4 role, for here the evolution of product and process technologies is so intertwined that a company virtually must be in Stage 4 to gain a sustainable product advantage.

What then is special about Stage 4 companies?

They anticipate the potential of new manufacturing practices and technologies and seek to acquire expertise in them long before their implications are fully apparent.

They give sufficient credibility and influence to manufacturing for it to extract the full potential from production-based opportunities.

They place equal emphasis on structural (buildings and equipment) and infrastructural (management policies) activities as potential sources of continual improvement and competitive advantage.

They develop long-range business plans in which manufacturing capabilities are expected to play a meaningful role in securing the company's strategic objectives. By treating the manufacturing function as a strategic resource—that is, as a source of strength by itself as well as a means for enhancing the contribution of other functions—they encourage the interactive development of business, manufacturing, and other functional strategies.

Stage 4 organizations are generally of two types. The first includes those companies like Emerson Electric, Texas Instruments, Mars (candy), and Blue Bell, whose business strategies place primary emphasis on a manufacturing-based competitive advantage such as low cost. In fact, these companies sometimes regard their manufacturing functions as so important a source of competitive advantage that they relegate other functions to a secondary or derivative role—an action which can be just as dysfunctional as relegating manufacturing to a reactive role. The other type of Stage 4 company seeks a balance of excellence in all its functions and pursues "externally supportive" Stage 4 roles for each of its integrated functions. We describe in detail two such organizations in a later section of this article.

In both types of organization, manufacturing complements its traditional involvement in the capital budgeting process with a considerable amount of qualitative analysis to compensate for the blind spots and biases inherent in financial data. In addition, there are extensive formal and informal horizontal interactions between manufacturing and other functions that greatly facilitate such activities as product design, field service, and sales training. Manufacturing's direct participation in formulating overall business strategy further enhances this functional interaction. Finally, equally with the other functions, manufacturing is a valued source of general management talent for the entire organization.

Managing the Transition

Because the four stages just outlined fall along a continuum, they suggest the path that a company might follow as it seeks to enhance the contribution of its manufacturing function. They suggest, too, the speed with which a company might follow that path. The inertia of most large organizations—their entrenched attitudes and practices—favors a gradual, systematic, and cumulative movement from one developmental stage to the next, not an effort to skip a stage by throwing more resources at problems. Getting from here to there is not simply a question of applying endless resources. Indeed, managing the transition between stages represents a significant and often dramatic challenge for most organizations.

At the least, successfully negotiating such a transition requires leadership from within the manufacturing function. Managing change in an established operation is always difficult, but here that difficulty is compounded by the need to bring all manufacturing personnel to a new view of things long familiar. Consider, for example, the kinds of production choices mentioned in Exhibit II.

As a company or business unit moves along the continuum, dealing with vendors or making facilities choices requires many changes: Cost-minimization goals give way to a concern for enlisting vendors' critical capabilities, and planning for general-purpose facilities gives way to an appreciation of focused factories. Said another way, managing these transitions requires a special kind of leadership because the task at hand is to change how people think, not merely how they can be instructed to act.

Exhibit III. Alternative Views of Work Force Management

Stages 1, 2, and 3 traditional, static	Stage 4 broad potential, dynamic
Command and control	Learning
Management of effort	Management of attention
Coordinating information	Problem-solving information
Direct (supervisory) control	Indirect (systems and values) control
Process stability/ worker independence	Process evolution/worker dependence

Nowhere is this deep shift in viewpoint more important than in attitudes toward a company's human resources. As Exhibit III (courtesy of our colleague, Earl Sasser) suggests, Stages 1, 2, and 3 adhere fairly closely to the traditional "command-and-control" style of human resource management. Now, to be sure, moving from Stage 1 to Stage 2 and then on to Stage 3 requires an ever more polished execution of that style, with enhanced management development efforts and more thoughtful analysis of underlying commands. But there is no radical shift within these stages in the way managers think of the work force's contribution to overall competitive performance. In Stage 4, however, the dominant approach to the work force must be in terms of teamwork and problem solving, not command-and-control. In the earlier stages the key leadership task is the management of controlled effort, but getting to Stage 4—and prospering there—demands instead the management of creative experimentation and organizational learning.

WHY MOVE AT ALL?

Most young companies assign either Stage 1 or Stage 2 roles to manufacturing, to some extent because these roles require little attention and specific knowledge on the part of senior managers.

In the United States, companies tend to start out with a unique product or with the identification of an unexploited niche in a market. As a result, they place primary emphasis on marketing, product design, or other nonmanufacturing functions. Top management does not see the need to become smart about—or give close attention to—the work of production.

Companies are likely to remain at their initial stage until external pressures force a move. As long as no direct competitor successfully develops Stage 3 or Stage 4 manufacturing capabilities, they will find Stages 1 and 2 comfortable, secure, and apparently effective. The post-World War II experience of many U.S. industries convinced a generation of managers that a policy of stability can remain satisfactory for decades, a view reinforced by the stable economic growth associated with the 1960s. What they first saw as common practice they came to see as *good* practice.

In general, the transition from Stage 1 to Stage 2 comes when problems arise in the manufacturing function that can be solved by the "safe" application of an already proven practice. It can also occur if managers decide that the leading companies in their industry owe at least part of their success to their manufacturing process. The transition to Stage 3, however, usually begins when managers come to doubt the effectiveness of their traditional approaches or to wonder about the implications of new manufacturing technologies. A direct threat from a major competitor that has moved to a higher stage or a recognition of the competitive advantages of moving to Stage 3 (or the potential perils of not doing so) may also trigger action.

During the early 1980s, all these factors came together to encourage literally hundreds of companies to shift toward Stage 3. In many industries, long dominated by a few large companies following stable competitive ground rules, the sudden appearance of foreign competition and globalized markets jolted laggards into action. With no end to such competitive pressures in sight, many more companies are likely to attempt transitions to Stage 3 over the next several years.

Unfortunately many, if not most, of these companies are unlikely to achieve a full, lasting move to Stage 3 before they revert to Stage 2. The reasons for such a retreat are subtle, yet powerful. Moving from Stage 2 to Stage 3 often occurs in a crisis atmosphere when— as with U.S. producers of steel, autos, and machine tools—managers and workers alike see their real objective as regaining competitive parity with their attackers. The changes that are required to adapt fully to Stage 3 require such sustained effort and broad-based support, however, that these companies may not be able to cement them in place before improved business conditions relieve some of the competitive pressure. The natural tendency, of course, is to return to a "business as usual" Stage 2 mentality as soon as the crisis appears to have passed.

The great irony here is that too quick success often spells doom for permanent change. If, as often happens, the managers responsible for building manufacturing to Stage 3 levels are quickly promoted into other responsibilities and other, lesser managers are left to be the caretakers of recent changes, the necessary follow-up activities may not occur.

THE BIG JUMP TO STAGE 4

However difficult it is to get from Stage 2 to Stage 3, our experience suggests that the shift from Stage 3 to Stage 4 demands an effort substantially greater both in kind and in degree. Earlier transitions, which take place largely within the manufacturing function, are a form of "manufacturing fixing itself." Moving to Stage 4, however, involves changing the way that the *rest* of the organization thinks about manufacturing and interacts with it. Because coordination among functions is crucial, manufacturing must first have its own house in order. Entering Stage 4 is not something an organization simply chooses to do. It must first pay its dues by having done all the appropriate groundwork.

The differences between Stages 3 and 4 should not be underestimated. In Stage 3, manufacturing considerations feed into business strategy, but the function itself is still seen as reactive (in that its role is a derived one), not as a source of potential competitive advantage. Stage 4 implies a deep shift in manufacturing's role, in its self-image, and in the view of it held by managers in other functions. It is, at last, regarded as an equal partner and is therefore expected to play a major role in strengthening a company's market position. Equally important, it helps the rest of the organization see the world in a new way. Stage 3 companies will, for example, treat automation as essentially a cost-cutting and labor-saving activity. A Stage 4 manufacturing operation will bring automation into focus as a means of boosting process precision and product quality.

There is an expectation in Stage 4 that all levels of management will possess a high degree of technical competence and will be aware of how their actions may affect manufacturing activities. Further, they are expected to have a general understanding of the way products, markets, and processes interact and to manage actively these interactions across functions. Traditional approaches to improving performance—providing flexibility through excess capacity, for example, or raising delivery dependability through holding finished-goods inventory, or reducing costs through improvements in labor productivity—no longer are considered as the only way to proceed. Tighter integration of product design and process capabilities can also lead to increased flexibility, as well as to faster deliveries (through shorter production cycle times) and to lower costs (through improved product quality and reliability).

Most American top managers, in our experience, regard the transition from Stage 1 to Stage 2, and then on to Stage 3, as a desirable course to pursue. Yet few view achieving Stage 4 capabilities as an obvious goal or strengthen their companies' manufacturing functions with the clear intent of moving there.

In fact, most companies that reach Stage 3 do not perceive a move to Stage 4 as either essential or natural. Their managers, believing that Stage 3 provides 90% of the benefits attainable, resist spending the extra effort to advance further. Many prefer to play it safe by remaining in Stage 3 for a sustained period before deciding how and whether to move on. A sizable number doubt the value of Stage 4—some because they think it extremely risky in organizational terms; others because they feel threatened by the kind of initiatives manufacturing might take when unleashed. One company, in fact, ruled out a move to Stage 4 as being potentially destabilizing to its R&D group, which historically had played the key role in establishing the company's competitive advantage.

Although the benefits of operating in Stage 4 will vary from company to company and will often be invisible to managers until they are just on the edge of Stage 4 operations, four variables can serve as a sort of litmus test for a company's real attitude toward the competitive role its manufacturing organization can—and should—play and thus indicate its placement in Stage 3 or Stage 4.

THE AMOUNT OF ONGOING IN-HOUSE INNOVATION. Stage 4 organizations continually invest in process improvements, not only because they benefit existing products but also because they will benefit future products. This is not to say these companies are uninterested in big-step improvements, but that they place great importance on the cumulative value of continual enhancements in process technology.

THE EXTENT TO WHICH A COMPANY DEVELOPS ITS OWN MANU-FACTURING EQUIPMENT. The typical Stage 3 operation continues to rely on outside suppliers for equipment development. A Stage 4 company wants to know more than its suppliers about everything that is critical to its business. It may continue to buy much of its equipment, but it will also produce enough internally to ensure that it is close to the state-of-the-art in equipment technology.

Our experience with Stage 4 German and Japanese manufacturers is that they follow this practice much more than most of their American counterparts. Yet even in Germany, where leading companies develop their own equipment, suppliers such as those making machine tools remain strong and innovative. Reducing their market does not cripple their competitive viability. Instead, the increased competition and the greater technical sophistication among equipment users have made the interactions between manufacturers and suppliers more innovative for both.

THE ATTENTION PAID TO MANUFACTURING INFRASTRUCTURE. Stage 4 managers take care to integrate measurement systems, manufacturing planning and control procedures, and work force policies in their structural decisions on capacity, vertical integration, and the like. They do not necessarily give infrastructure and structural elements equal weight, but they look on both as important, and complementary, sources of competitive strength.

THE LINK BETWEEN PRODUCT DESIGN AND MANUFACTURING PRO-CESS DESIGN. Stage 3 companies focus on improving the hand-offs from product design to manufacturing; in Stage 4 the emphasis is on the parallel and interactive development of both products and processes.

If managers choose not to attempt the transition to Stage 4, that choice should be made intentionally, not by default or through a failure to understand the kind of benefits that new stage could offer. Rather, it should reflect a reasoned judgment that the risks were too great or the rewards insufficient.

Getting There from Here

Two examples of organizations that, in the early 1980s, chose to attempt the transition to Stage 4 are General Electric's dishwasher operation (at the business unit level) and IBM (at the corporate level). Taking a closer look at these two experiences may help bring into focus the benefits of, and the obstacles to, a successfully managed transition.

GENERAL ELECTRIC DISHWASHER

Dishwashers are one of several major consumer appliances that GE has produced for decades. In the late 1970s, GE's dishwasher strategic business unit (SBU) did a careful self-analysis and concluded that it had dated and aging resources: a 20-year-old product design, a 10- to 20-year-old manufacturing process, and an aging work force (average seniority of 15 to 16 years) represented by a strong, traditional union. Its manufacturing operations were primarily located, together with five other major appliance plants, at GE's Appliance Park in Louisville, Kentucky. A single labor relations group dealt with all of the site's 14,000 hourly workers, whose relations with management were neutral at best.

Nevertheless, it was a very successful business, holding the leading position in the U.S. dishwasher market and turning out about one-third of the units sold. In late 1977, as part of its normal planning for product redesign, the SBU proposed to corporate management that it invest $18 million in the incremental improvement of the product and its manufacturing process. With dishwasher manufacturing more or less at Stage 2 (it was essentially following "GE Appliance Park manufacturing practice"), those involved saw the request as a proposed foray into Stage 3, and expected the unit to return to Stage 2 once the improvements in products and processes began to age.

GE's senior managers normally would have approved such an investment and allowed the SBU to carry on with its traditional approach. In this case, however, they asked a number of tough questions about the long-term prospects for the business and encouraged SBU managers to think about pursuing a more innovative and aggressive course. The idea of making a fundamental change in the SBU's strategy gained rapid support from some key middle managers, who saw major opportunities if GE could break out of its traditional thinking. They began laying the groundwork for a solid move to Stage 3.

Over the next several months, as this reformulated proposal to upgrade product design and manufacturing processes began to take shape, the nature of the dishwasher business suggested possible benefits from moving on through Stage 3 to Stage 4:

> GE product designers had developed a top-of-the-line product with a plastic tub and plastic door liner. Although currently more expensive than the standard steel model, it offered significantly improved operating performance and used proprietary GE materials.

> More disciplined product design could increase component standardization because little of the product was visible after installation.

> Since only 55% of U.S. households owned dishwashers, there was considerable growth potential in the primary market as well as a sizable replacement market.

In combination with GE's strong competitive position, these factors led management to conclude that if the "right" product were introduced at the "right" price and with the "right" quality, GE could greatly expand both industry demand and its own market share, particularly in the private label business.

Accordingly, SBU managers decided not just to fix current problems but to do it right. They jettisoned their modest proposal for incremental product and process improvement and developed much bolder proposals requiring an investment of more than $38 million.

This revised plan rested on a major commitment to improve the factory's working environment through better communication with the work force as well as to encourage its involvement in redesigning the manufacturing process. Laying the groundwork for this new relationship took almost two years, but the time was well spent. Once established, this relationship markedly enhanced the contribution manufacturing could make to the overall business of the SBU.

The new plan also called for a complete redesign of the product around a central core consisting of a single-piece plastic tub and a single-piece plastic door. To ensure that the product would meet quality standards, management established stringent specifications for GE and for its vendors and demanded that both internal and external suppliers reduce their incidence of defects to one-twentieth of the levels formerly allowed. To meet the new specifications and the new cost targets, managers now had to carry out process and product development in tandem, not separate them as they had done in the past.

The revised proposal addressed, as well, the design of the production process. Automation was essential—not just to reduce costs but also to improve quality. Thus, modifications in product design had to reflect the capabilities and constraints of the new process. In addition, that process had to accommodate more worker control and shorter manufacturing cycle times, along with other nontraditional approaches to improve flexibility, quality, delivery dependability, and the integration of product testing with manufacturing.

By late 1980, there was general agreement on the major building blocks of this new strategy. Each of the functions—product design, marketing, and manufacturing—was to move aggressively toward defining its contribution in Stage 4 terms. To manufacturing management also fell the task of helping to develop performance measures that, if tracked over subsequent years, would indicate how well the function was carrying out its responsibilities.

As Exhibit IV shows, by the end of 1983, there was pronounced improvement in such important areas as service call rates, unit costs, materials handling, inventory turns, reject rates, and productivity—with a promise of still further improvements in 1984. Nor was this all. Other benefits included a 70% reduction in the number of parts, the elimination of 20 pounds of weight in the finished product (and thus reduced freight costs), and much more positive worker attitudes. Perhaps most important of all was the large jump in market share that GE won in the 12 months following the new product's introduction. Indeed, during the summer of 1983, *Consumer Reports* rated it as offering the best value among U.S. dishwashers. Although these results were impressive, SBU managers also gained a much better understanding of the effort needed to secure fully a Stage 4 position for manufacturing. Their experience underlined the need to treat product and process design in a

Exhibit IV. *General Electric Dishwasher SBU Redesign*

Performance measure	1980-1981	1983	1984 Goal
Service call rate (index)*	100	70	55
Unit cost (index)	100	90	88
Number of times tub or door is handled	27 + 27	1 + 3	1 + 3
Inventory turns	13	25	28
Reject rates (mechanical/electrical test)	10 %	3 %	2.5 %
Output per employee (index)	100	133	142

*Lower is better.

more iterative and interactive fashion and the importance of involving the work force in solving problems.

Of late, a rebounding economy with increased consumer demand has turned up pressure on the SBU to revert to its traditional view that output is paramount, no matter the compromises. Hence, even though the SBU's manufacturing function is now in Stage 4, it must doggedly fight to stay there and to help the rest of the organization complete the transition rather than allow itself to drift back toward Stage 3.

IBM CORPORATION

In the early 1980s, IBM viewed its worldwide activities as comprising 13 major businesses including, for example, typewriters and large computer systems. Like its competitors in each of these product markets, IBM faced rapidly changing environments and so had to be especially careful in designing and coordinating strategies. Hence, in each, the manufacturing organization was expected to play a role equal to that of the other major functions in developing and executing overall business strategy. Unlike its competitors, most of whom still assigned Stage 2 or Stage 3 roles to manufacturing, IBM recognized that production—responsible for 49% of IBM's assets, 110,000 of its employees, and 40% of its final product costs—had much to contribute to the competitive advantage of each business.

IBM's worldwide strategy for moving the manufacturing operations of each business into Stage 4 required those businesses to address seven areas of concern in a manner consistent with a Stage 4 approach to production. These areas were:

LOW COST.   IBM firmly believed that to be successful it must be the low-cost producer in each of its businesses, success being defined as having the best product quality, growing as fast or faster than the market, and being profitable. Reaching this low-cost position required stabilizing the manufacturing environment (reducing uncertainty wherever possible) and linking manufacturing more effectively to marketing and distribution. To this end, marketing had "ownership" of finished-goods inventory, and factory production rates were to be smoothed out by the adoption of a 90-day shipping horizon. In addition, IBM decided to design products around certain standard modules and, although it produced different configurations of these standard modules to customer order, it would not manufacture customized modules.

INVENTORIES.   IBM's goal was to reduce inventories significantly, first by measuring stock carefully and frequently and then by reducing "order churn" (the fluctuation in mix and volume that occurs before an order actually gets into the final production schedule). Lower in-process inventories, derived in part from the adoption of a just-in-time philosophy and from the standardization of components, helped IBM cut its inventory costs by hundreds of millions of dollars within 18 months while supporting ever-increasing sales.

QUALITY.   IBM estimated that 30% of its products' manufacturing cost—the *total* cost of quality prevention, detection, and appraisal—arose directly from not doing it right the first time. Significant improvements in the quality and manufacturability of design, the pursuit of zero defects, and the systematic stress testing of products during design and manufacturing all contributed to the lowering of these costs.

AUTOMATION.   Automation in a Stage 4 orientation is of value in that it leads to higher product quality, encourages interaction between product design and process design, and cuts overhead. This, in turn, means managing the evolution of the manufacturing process according to a long-term plan, just as with product evolution.

ORGANIZATION.   To provide the product design and marketing functions with a better linkage with manufacturing, IBM defined an additional level of line manufacturing management, a "production management center," which was responsible for all plants manufacturing a product line. For example, the three large system plants (located in France, Japan, and the United States) were all under a single production management center that served as the primary linkage with marketing for that product line, as well as with R&D's efforts to design new products. Such centers were intended not only to create effective functional interfaces but also to be responsible for planning manufacturing processes, defining plant charters, measuring plant performance, and ensuring that the processes and systems employed by different facilities were uniformly excellent.

MANUFACTURING SYSTEMS.   The purpose here was to develop integrated systems that provided information, linked directly to strategic business variables, for both general and functional managers. Such systems had to be compatible with each other yet flexible enough for each business to be able to select the modules it needed. As part of this systems effort, IBM rethought its entire manufacturing measurement system with the intent of reducing its historical focus on direct labor and giving more emphasis to materials, overhead, energy, and indirect labor. IBM believed that its manufacturing systems, like its product lines, should be made up of standard modules based on a common architecture. Each business could then assemble its own customized configuration yet still communicate effectively with other IBM businesses.

AFFORDABILITY.   By making external competitiveness, not internal rules of thumb, the basis for evaluating manufacturing performance, IBM no longer evaluated manufacturing against its own history but rather against its competitors. As part of this concern with affordability, IBM also sought to reduce its overhead, which exceeded 25% of total manufacturing costs.

Out of these seven areas of concern emerged a set of three management principles fully in harmony with the move to a Stage 4 appreciation of the competitive contribution that manufacturing can make. The first—emphasizing activities that facilitate, encourage, and reward effective interaction between manufacturing and both marketing and engineering—requires people able to regard each other as equals and to make significant contributions to areas other than their own. Information, influence, and support should—and must—flow in both directions.

The second principle recognizes that product and process technologies must interact. Process evolution (including automation) and product evolution must proceed in tandem. Indeed, IBM uses the terms "process windows" and "product windows" to describe these parallel paths and the opportunities they offer to exploit state-of-the-art processes in meeting customer needs and competitive realities.

The third principle is a focus of attention and resources on only those factors—manufacturing, quality, and overhead reduction, for example—that are essential to the long-term success of the business.

Getting Things Moving in Your Company

Our experience suggests that building manufacturing excellence requires that managers do more than simply understand the nature of the current role that manufacturing plays in their organizations and develop a plan for enhancing its competitive contribution. They must also communicate their vision to their organizations and prepare the ground for the changes that have to be made.

In virtually all the Stage 4 companies we have seen, at least one senior manager has been a key catalyst for the transition. Such leaders spring from all functional backgrounds and are concerned not to elevate manufacturing at the expense of other functions but to see their companies "firing on all cylinders." Seeking ways to integrate all functions into an effective whole, they must be strong enough, persuasive enough, and tough enough to push beyond conventional management thinking and to force their organizations to grapple with the deeper challenges prevailing in the increasingly competitive world of industry.

Today, there is considerable pessimism in some quarters about the long-term prospects for U.S. manufacturing. We are neither pessimistic nor optimistic; the answer "lies not in our stars but in ourselves." We have seen many organizations focus their efforts on achieving Stage 4 and make incredible improvements in short periods of time. Unfortunately, we have also seen many of them subsequently lose that commitment. After making tremendous strides, they begin to get comfortable and fall behind again.

Manufacturing can contribute significantly to the competitive success of any business. But it takes managers with determination, vision, and the ability to sustain focused effort over a long period of time and often in the face of stiff organizational resistance. The industrial race is no longer decided (if it ever was) by a fast and furious last-minute cavalry charge. It is a long, patient, persistent process of working together to clear the land, cultivate the fields, and continually extend the frontiers of an organization's capabilities.

3
Financial Goals and Strategic Consequences

Gordon Donaldson

One of the primary responsibilities of the CEO of any major corporation is to articulate the company's financial goals as a tangible focus for its business mission and strategy. In theory, these goals are imposed by shareholders through stock market responses to company performance. In practice, they are deeply rooted in the CEO's values and political philosophy, and they draw persuasive power from the depth of that conviction.

Despite this power, and because a company's financial goals are so visible and tangible, they often become the focal point for tension and dispute at the higher levels of the organization. Consider the way that two numbers—return on investment and rate of sales growth—came to symbolize opposing views of the corporate strategy and environment in Company A. Company A has been a leader in its field for several decades and remains highly regarded by the financial and investment community as profitable, reliable, and conservative. During the 1960s and early 1970s, its CEO knew exactly what the corporate and financial goals should be, and held onto them with unswerving commitment. He saw Company A as an unchallenged leader in technology and product innovation. His was a simple standard of excellence: return on investment. "I don't care about sales growth," he would say. "Give me technological leadership and the promise of a superior ROI, and growth will take care of itself."

For much of his tenure, he was apparently right. The company's profits more than satisfied required funds for investment, and Company A accumulated substantial financial reserves. The CEO's leadership was strongly supported by the board and applauded by the financial community.

One level down, the manager destined to be the CEO's successor had a different vision of the business. As he rose through the ranks of line management, he saw a number of the company's principal product lines gradually mature and their markets develop the traits of a commodity; high sales volume, low costs, and declining profit margins now characterized a sustainable competitive position. Success depended more critically on market share.

For this manager, the corporate growth rate was equal to, if not more important than, ROI as the focus of corporate strategy. Without a growth rate that matched or exceeded that of the industry, Company A's market share would not only decline but so would its potential to maximize ROI. In contrast to his boss, he would say, "Give me a superior growth rate and ROI will take care of itself." The opposing views produced a persistent tension at the top of Company A, a tension that was resolved only when the new CEO took over.

In fact, both executives may have been right—for their time. In a new-product market, companies with a proprietary entry-level position can demand superior returns as a condition of investment. As competition erodes that position, however, companies can succeed only if they continue to fund the investment necessary to maintain a healthy share of market even when that is accompanied by a declining ROI.

My study of organizations like Company A has revealed certain characteristics of the corporate financial goals system that have often been overlooked and that contribute to misunderstanding of the goal-setting process. For example:

Contrary to popular belief, companies do not put maximum profit before all else. In practice, no absolute or eternal financial priorities exist; they change as the economic and competitive environments change.

Mature companies assign priorities to multiple financial goals based on the relative power of the economic constituencies represented by these individual goals—whether capital or product markets or the market for human resources.

Companies do not have an inalienable right to "dream the impossible dream" and set any goal. From the moment a company decides to enter a particular segment of the product or capital market, its competition imposes limits and sets conditions on the goals it can realistically attain.

Managing a company's financial goals system is an unending process in which competing and conflicting priorities must be balanced. At any point, the system is potentially unstable because of the changing corporate environment and shifts in power and influence among constituencies.

A company's internal capital market must continuously try to reconcile the demand for and supply of funds. It imposes an impersonal and objective discipline on the conflicting goals that affect the flow of funds and requires that those driving demand balance with those driving supply. An executive cannot change any goal without considering the impact on all others.

Most managers find it difficult to understand and accept the entire goals system. Although financial goals appear objective and precise, they are in fact relative, changeable, and unstable. Moreover, subordinate managers normally see them from the limited perspective of their immediate responsibilities. Even top executives, tending to be more disposed to one constituency as against another, have difficulty accepting this system as a legitimate political compromise among these competing and conflicting priorities. Managers widely regard their company's financial goals system at best as capricious and at worst as inconsistent and even hostile. Though they may dutifully salute when the system is run up the flagpole, they harbor dark thoughts about whether it truly represents their self-interest.

I hope this article will contribute to a better understanding among all members of the management team of the nature and operation of a financial goals system. Although the members will no doubt continue to differ in their views of the correct priorities, they should understand how the system works, that objective boundaries on management choice exist, that goals are interdependent, and that a change in one goal always necessitates a trade-off with another.

How the System Works

A company's planning process sets a number of corporate goals in response to different priorities. Headquarters tries to include something for everyone as it exhorts the company to: grow aggressively in promising market segments; stay number one in product quality, markets, and technology; attract and hold superior management and technical personnel; diversify; provide a stable revenue stream, a superior return on investment, steady dividends, a superior price-earnings ratio; and maintain a conservative debt policy. Headquarters views these goals both as supportive of the company's broadest mission and responsive to the needs of investors, managers, employees, customers, and host communities.

Why do top managers expect so much? Aren't they aware that no one company can accomplish all this without compromise? Obviously they know. But many sincerely believe that all members of the extended corporate family share the same interests, that they agree that what's good for one is good for all, and that they will understand if their particular interests sometimes have to take a back seat.

In a world of scarce resources and finite horizons, however, such altruism does not always exist. Certainly in the short run, someone's self-interest must bow to the greater good. But for many of the parties involved, the short run—or a series of short runs—is the only long run. Everyone learns that economics does not ensure the equitable distribution of the corporation's ultimate benefits.

The company has to make trade-offs. Take its relations with the capital markets. Only a few companies, and then for only brief periods, so capture the attention and enthusiasm of the equity markets that they receive the equivalent of a blank check for new investment. For the majority, the public capital market window appears to open and close at random, without regard for their individual needs. The feeling of that window coming down on their fingers has instilled a spirit of self-sufficiency in many managers. To fuel growth, they rely primarily on internally generated funds coupled with conservative debt limits linked to the equity base. Reliable funds, even in large, mature, and successful corporations, are finite.

THE SELF-SUSTAINING MODEL

All corporate goals that affect the flow of funds within a company are the result of both explicit and implicit trade-offs among competing interests. A company can express these goals—and the trade-offs—quantitatively. The graph in Exhibit I reduces the goals system in a typical company to four key variables: the targets for

Exhibit I. A Balanced Financial Goals System

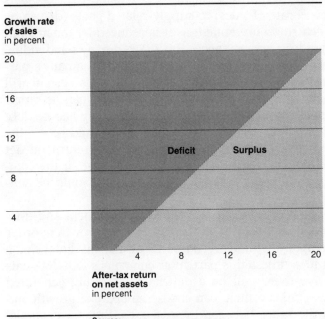

Source:
Gordon Donaldson, *Managing Corporate Wealth: The Operation of a Comprehensive Financial Goals System* (New York: Praeger Publishers, 1984), p. 69. Adapted with permission.

sales growth and return on net assets (RONA) and the ratios for dividend payout and debt-equity. Although other goals can be included to enhance the graph's sophistication, I begin with a simple model to show the primary goals and the basic technique. (For an explanation of the formula on which this graph is based, please see the Appendix.)

The diagonal line in Exhibit I defines the acceptable pairs of growth and RONA targets for self-sustaining growth in a company with a debt/equity target of .50 and a dividend payout target of .30. (The after-tax interest rate is assumed to be 6%.) These numbers define both the slope and position of the line as well as the division between the deficit and surplus sectors. The example makes normal planning assumptions: a stable ratio of sales to assets and assets to net assets, a replacement cost of the existing asset base no larger than the amount of the depreciation charges, and a moderate rate of inflation.

The graph shows the relationship of demand-related goals (driven by growth rate of sales) to supply-related goals (driven by the corporate return on investment as it is reduced by the amount paid to stockholders and enhanced by the company's individual debt level). The graph demonstrates that, given a company's particular dividend and debt policies, its financial goals system will be self-sustaining only if its growth and ROI targets can be represented by a single point on the diagonal. If a company had no debt and paid no dividends, the slope of the diagonal would be 45, the diagonal would divide the graph in half, and the return on net assets would equal the return on equity. In that case, if the company's rate of sales growth was equal to RONA, it would be self-funding.

In Exhibit I, however, RONA is affected by both debt and dividends, and it must be greater than the rate of sales growth in order to fund the company without recourse to capital markets. For a growth rate of 10%, unless this particular company's RONA equals or exceeds 11.5%, there will be a deficit of internally generated funds. Of course, management can choose any pair of growth and ROI targets in the space between the two axes. But, for example, if this company were to target a sales growth rate of 16%, and a RONA of 12%, it would imply a significant funds deficit—an unsustainable strategic position in the long run, if not in the short run.

A company's debt and dividend policies define the slope of the line of corporate self-sufficiency and its points of intersection with the axes. A more aggressive debt/equity goal combined with a lower dividend payment would expand the area of surplus, shrink the area of deficit, and raise the growth potential of any given RONA.

Top managers can use this kind of graph to communicate the meaning and discipline of an integrated set of financial goals to subordinates and to track performance against goals. The graph shows the impact of the trade-offs constantly necessitated by competing goals and objectives.

Unbalanced Goals

To help guide its senior managers, Company B developed a statement of corporate mission and goals that contained 24 items.

Some had a direct bearing on the nature, magnitude, and rate of new investment: The CEO targeted certain product lines for rapid development, the achievement of a specific share of market and rank in the industry, rates of growth in volume of operations, a balanced portfolio of business activities, and overseas expansion. Others focused on the sources of new investment funds: the target return on investment, the rate of profit growth, the proportion of retained earnings, dampened cyclicality of earnings, maximum debt levels, and minimum bond ratings.

The CEO expressed some goals in qualitative terms but quantified others, which I have depicted in Exhibit II. The 18% growth rate and 14% RONA target chosen by the company are at the intersection of the grid dividing the graph into four performance zones. The line of self-sustaining growth dividing the deficit and surplus sectors is defined by a target debt-equity ratio of .33 and a target earnings-retention ratio of .67.

WHY AN IMBALANCE?

The graph makes clear that an imbalance in the company's goals system resulted in a substantial funds-flow deficit. Why? Was this imbalance deliberate or inadvertent? Such a deliberate cash flow funding strategy can be supported by liquid reserves, underutilized invested capital, or an acquisition. Management cannot, however, sustain such strategies indefinitely. In this case, the imbalance resulted when management developed each goal in response to pressures of the moment. Moreover, the performance criteria of each lay outside this particular goals system.

To ensure better than average sales growth, for example, management set its target growth rate as an arbitrary multiple of real growth in GNP. At the same time, the company's goal—to be number one in each product market segment—implied that the company would meet or exceed the growth rate in each product industry. Nothing in the planning process guaranteed that these two growth concepts would naturally or necessarily converge.

The supply side of the funds-flow equation held unresolved inconsistencies as well. The company tied its earnings growth to sales and, hence, GNP. On the other hand, the ROI target was more arbitrary, chosen to be in advance of current performance and linked to past achievement. The company had not tested whether the two goals were consistent, yet they were obviously linked.

Exhibit II.   Company B's Performance Against Goals 1970–1978

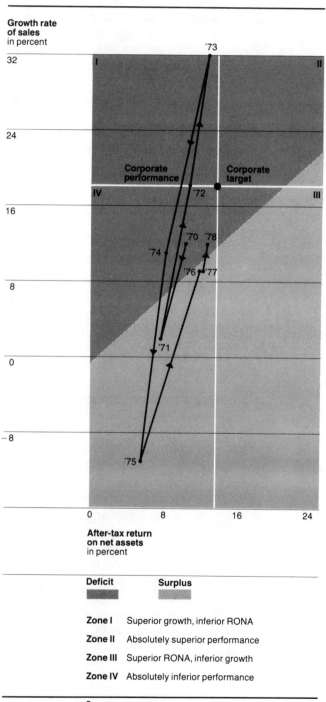

Zone I   Superior growth, inferior RONA

Zone II   Absolutely superior performance

Zone III Superior RONA, inferior growth

Zone IV   Absolutely inferior performance

Source:
Donaldson, *Managing Corporate Wealth*,
p. 138. Adapted with permission.

By themselves, the goals made perfect sense. Each had a sound organizational and economic rationale. Each would legitimately contribute to the health of the business. Each represented a piece of corporate reality. But management failed to recognize the consequences of their interaction for the flow of funds. They could not all be attained. Management had failed to choose among them, to make trade-offs. And the imbalance shown in Exhibit II was the result of management's oversight.

Of course, any company's year-to-year performance will often miss its target, at times by a wide margin. In the short term, management may have to make deliberate trade-offs between growth rate and RONA. Accelerated growth often entails accelerated, up-front investment, increased costs, and a possible shaving of profit margins to gain market share. Economic and competitive vicissitudes also produce unexpected swings in performance. Nevertheless, a corporate target's central function is to direct all managerial decisions and actions toward Zone II—where both primary goals are exceeded.

Judged by past performance, Company B's financial goals, if achieved, would set new highs. From 1970 to 1978, however, the company never penetrated Zone II, although it appeared within striking distance in 1978. The diagram shows how sales performance failed to dampen cyclicality, how the recession of 1974 and 1975 damaged both growth and ROI, and how Company B operated at an unsustainable deficit and was, in a sense, bailed out of the problem by the recession and its enforced retrenchment. The years 1976 and 1977 were important because, with a RONA of 12% and a sales rate of 9%, the company stood very close to what its target should have been for a balanced goals system (assuming the company's RONA was at or near the maximum potential of its collective industrial environment). If the existing goals system was going to survive, however, the next few years would have to show a radical change from the past.

Unbalanced goals and unbalanced performance strain a system's credibility—and viability. In time the relationship of target growth to target ROI proves unbalanced and one emerges as dominant. If Company B is committed to its 18% sales growth rate, but unable to generate the 22% RONA necessary to fund that growth on a sustained basis, then management's initial response may be to try to decrease the potential funds deficit by raising debt or lowering the dividend payout.

IS THERE A WAY OUT?

In this case, the gap is too great. We can measure the magnitude of the required shift. It is beyond reason. Company B would have to raise debt levels from the target of 33% to 134% of equity. Alternatively, the earnings-retention ratio would have to rise to 1.05 from a target of .67—an obvious impossibility. While a combination of the two targets is theoretically possible, it would be impractical or only partially successful in balancing the flow of funds. To sustain these goals, the one remaining option is to turn to the external capital market.

Ultimately, the drive for growth and needed expansion of investment will collide with the risk-return preferences of the capital markets and the availability of further investment on the part of lenders and shareholders. My research suggests that—having pushed the limits of internally generated funds and conservative debt and dividend payout policies—most companies have preferred to scale back growth rather than go to the public equity market for the further funding of established product market positions. Over the period I studied them, the 12 companies in my research sample made only two issues of common stock for cash.

Whether any company could sustain such a high degree of financial self-sufficiency over the next decade remains to be seen. Inevitably, the accelerated inflation of the late 1970s and its potential resurgence in the 1980s will require the aggregate U.S. corporate asset base to be funded again in the domestic capital markets. To the extent that companies will have to go to the equity market again to fund the established asset base, they will find it more difficult to use equity concurrently as an attractive vehicle for expansion and for acquisitions to support their diversification.

What Drives the System

By recognizing that all financial goals are interdependent, a company soon learns that a change in one demands a compensating adjustment somewhere else in the funds-flow equation. Where that change originates and what goals drive or dominate the financial goals system are the next important questions to answer. Academics and CEOs have nurtured the belief that shareholder wealth and return on investment are a company's ultimate priorities at all times. But that belief is not supported by my observations. I do not want to suggest that ROI is not critical; only that it and related goals that represent some version of the stockholder interest do not at all times drive the flow of funds. In fact, a preoccupation with one constituency or one goal distorts the reality of the diverse communities to be accommodated.

As a rule, market priorities are crucial to any corporate strategy and will tend to dominate the financial goals system and any change contemplated. Exhibit III characterizes a typical life cycle of the changes in corporate priorities.

Consider a single product market company operating in a highly mature and competitive industry (Zone IV). Both sales growth and ROI performance are below historic levels. The company may or may not be able to fund its own growth (position 5 versus position 1).

Some of America's basic smokestack industries have been in such a situation recently. In these cases, the near-term priorities of the product market have driven the financial goals system. At a minimum, the company feels impelled to grow at least as fast as its industry in order to preserve if not increase market share. It will also reinvest in existing facilities to maintain or improve efficiency and cost effectiveness. The rationale is basic: In any game, you're in until you're out, especially if you think it's the only game in town. According to the best American competitive traditions, when you're number two—or five or ten—you try harder.

THE STRATEGIC CYCLE

At some point, however, other organizational variables—such as the need to attract and hold superior management—render such conditions intolerable. The company may move to escape the relentless investment imperative of its traditional industry base. The degree, direction, and method of this diversification vary from company to company, whether internally or by acquisition.

Expressed in the terms of Exhibit III, the company is moving from Zone IV to Zone I. Ideally, it is searching for both higher growth and ROI. Both can be most easily accomplished by moving performance along the diagonal. Frequently, however, growth and investment precede ROI and may even require its near-term sac-

Exhibit III.   The Life Cycle of Corporate Financial Priorities

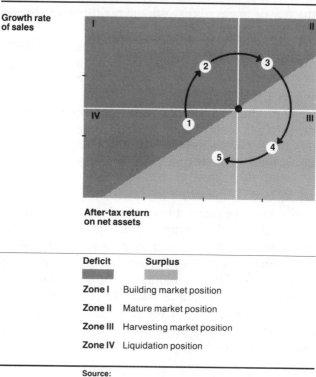

Deficit	Surplus

Zone I   Building market position

Zone II   Mature market position

Zone III   Harvesting market position

Zone IV   Liquidation position

Source:
Donaldson, *Managing Corporate Wealth*,
p. 148. Adapted with permission.

rifice. The company must penetrate new and unfamiliar product markets to establish a profitable and stable market share.

In the case of Company A, mentioned at the outset, a change in priorities grew out of the competitive evolution in its product markets. By insisting on the absolute priority of ROI, the first CEO had driven Company A into Zone III (position 4), where it had a highly liquid balance sheet. Recognizing the maturity of the product market, his successor sought to take the most direct route to Zone I (position 2) in order to avoid the unacceptable alternative of position 5. In fact, Company A's large liquid reserves allowed it to operate for some time in the deficit cycle from position 1 to position 3.

Companies without liquid reserves or financial slack cannot operate in Zone I with superior growth rates but inferior returns for long. At some point, they will feel great pressure to shrink the deficit by either increasing the debt-equity ratio or lowering dividend payment. But the dormant concerns of the capital market constituency will be roused by such actions. Lenders will see their limits of creditworthiness stretched, or shareholders will feel that their norms of the rate of reinvestment of earnings have been exceeded. Capital markets will press for more attention to their priorities. If the company diversifies by acquisition and resorts to equity securities as the medium of exchange, it will be most sensitive to capital market priorities. Capital becomes critical. Thus by initially responding to product market forces and priorities of growth and diversification, the company becomes more dependent on the external capital market, and must then reemphasize ROI and shareholder benefit as the price of that dependency.

If the strategy succeeds, the company eventually will reach position 3 or 4 in Zone II or III. After regaining self-sufficiency, the company can move again to a more conservative debt policy or increased dividend payout. It will then become less dependent on the external capital market and the priority of its goals.

Few companies can follow this path without a number of unexpected twists and turns. Nonetheless, this model helps point out how strategies evolve and how the priority of financial goals shifts in response to a changing corporate environment.

To Diversify—Or Not?

Financial self-sufficiency is a natural and appropriate prerequisite for a high degree of managerial independence. Whatever the merits from society's perspective, the American industrial corporation has been able to create its own private capital market. When all goes well, it assures a minimum of external financial discipline. Of course, freedom from external discipline is a matter of degree, but corporate financial management has as its implicit, if not explicit, objective decreased dependence on capital market uncertainty and interference.

Another element in the achievement of corporate and managerial independence is diversification. A number of corporate critics have questioned whether the recent spate of corporate diversification by acquisition or merger is appropriate. Such concern is not new. Most mature companies pursue diversification at some stage in their histories and inevitably suffer conflicts between the interests of stockholders and those of the organization and its professional managers. Though they often couch their motives for merger in terms of stockholder interest, managers pursue diversification because such a strategy:

> Lays the foundation for an internal capital market that affords the company a high degree of financial self-sufficiency over a long period of time.

> Stabilizes corporate income and ensures more efficient use of human and financial resources.

> Allows the organization to survive the inevitable demise of particular product markets.

Such objectives are rational and justifiable. Society should value them. Diversification, however, can impose some cost on the community of professional investors by: reducing the number and variety of investment vehicles accessible to the individual portfolio, reducing the information available on individual corporate units, and at times placing resources in the hands of managers with inferior objectives or ability. A professional investor doesn't need the diversification benefits that reduce risk through merger or acquisition, benefits valued by the undiversified management of the acquiring or acquired company.

Nor is the investment community the only potential loser. Widening of the company's earnings base with multiple sources reduces the power of any one consumer, competitor, or employee to discipline the management decision process.

A WINNING MOVE

A national commodity food producer and marketer embarked on an ambitious diversification strategy shortly after World War II. Its technology was simple and mature, the market highly competitive, profit margins narrow, and growth modest. New postwar management decided to undertake a radical change. While rationalizing the production and distribution facilities of existing products, the company began aggressively to acquire food and related products for national or regional distribution.

Over ten years, the company became highly diversified; the original product came to represent only a modest share of its sales. Though management admitted it had made some mistakes, it regarded the strategy as a success. During the initial period of rapid diversification and growth, the company's price-earnings ratio was superior but declined to average levels after the program was completed.

Not all diversification strategies are this successful; everybody won, from the organization and its managers to the original shareholders (if they hung on long enough and sold out soon enough). The shareholders won, not because the company had reduced their risk by diversification but by its shrewd selection and good management. Instead of getting out of the original one-industry company and diversifying on their own, they stuck with management and took a chance that it would do a better job in the long run.

There was one loser: the members of the original product market constituency who lost bargaining power and influence. Previously they had held the power to dominate corporate priorities since their cooperation was essential to organizational survival. In the diversified company, that power was gone. Management could now, if it chose, abandon the original product market without seriously threatening the organization.

Sometimes, diversified companies carry the goal of financial self-sufficiency—essential to the organization as a whole—indiscriminately down to the divisional or individual product market level. One company went so far as to tell its product market managers that their failure to earn a return capable of supporting their individual growth was "proof of second-class citizenship."

In fact, individual product market positions may appropriately function, at any given time, in surplus or deficit mode. To require the self-sufficiency of all product market positions is to deny not only reality but also one of diversification's primary objectives—to make an orderly transition from an income stream that has dried up to one that is still abundant. The phase-out of a mature product position should ideally coincide with the phase-in of an entry-level position in a high-growth industry, which will operate at a deficit. In practice, of course, the financial goals system is designed to motivate as well as discipline. Like a parent, management often becomes impatient for its infant product positions to grow up and become self-sufficient, thus assisting in the support of the younger siblings.

What Is Financial Reality?

Heated debate has raged over which financial goals govern corporate management, whether they are imposed from without (by myopic investors) or developed from within (by career managers), and whether they serve the best interests of the company and society. I have found that the issue cuts deeper than the familiar question of whether short-term financial priorities distort the resource allocation process.

A company's goals do not exist in a vacuum. Inevitably, they confront the reality of the existing corporate environment and established strategy. A serious inconsistency with that reality threatens the discipline of the system. In such cases, either management persistently rationalizes and ignores discrepancies between goals and performance or, worse, warps actions and reported results to meet expectations.

In the near term, financial goals are largely set for—and not by—management. They may result from past strategic decisions that placed the company in a certain product market, involved it in a long-term lending arrangement with a particular institution, made certain contractual commitments, or designed a particular organizational structure to effect the strategy. These things together determine an environment that imposes a set of specific and objective financial conditions of successful performance. These realities dominate the design of the goals system in the short term. Following naturally from the implementation of the existing competitive strategy, they remain in place as long as the strategy continues. Existing market forces outline required rates of growth and return as well as debt and dividend constraints. Competitive environments narrow the limits of choice.

Much confusion often results, however, from the indiscriminate mingling of short- and long-term goals. Implementation of the existing strategy in existing product markets determines short-term goals, while new strategic directions implicitly or explicitly map out new long-term priorities. The difference in time frame depends on the time necessary to implement strategic redirection in product or capital markets, organizational structure or staff. For companies whose current competitive environment satisfies long-term expectations, this issue represents a distinction without a difference. For managements or investors dissatisfied with near-term performance, however, it is important to keep the two horizons and their related goals systems separate.

Whether qualitative or quantitative, long-term goals relate the company's performance to the business universe in which it competes for capital, human resources, and market opportunities. Short-term goals relate performance in the current industry setting to primary competitors. In defining long-term goals, managers are free—and indeed have the responsibility—to ignore the current environment and to set goals that meet or exceed the best performance in the country for companies in their risk class. Company B, referred to in Exhibit II, wanted to grow faster than GNP, thus outperforming the average industrial company in growth rate. Other companies have done the same by trying to match the top quartile of the *Fortune* "500" or double in size every five years (an obviously above-average performance).

Such goals transcend existing competitive conditions. To mix the two planning horizons in one planning document, as Company B did, is to create confusion among management rank and file. Because Company B's long-term goal related to aggregate corporate performance, it was either a vague gleam in the CEO's eye or an indirect way to alert management to an impending change in the locus of product market operations. Unless the company makes the goal more precise by specifying plans and a timetable for strategic redirection, the goal will have little impact on the organization's behavior. The long-term goal may be a cause for concern by those responsible for current performance, but the immediacy of short-term goals will drive the long-term goals out every time.

A significant conflict of goals often occurs when companies quantify their ROI targets. In the broad sense, every company should try to find the highest sustainable ROI while maintaining a strong position in the market and a top-quality management team. Expressed in operational terms, that means equaling or exceeding company or industry performance.

But management usually chooses an ROI target that is: (1) purely arbitrary, chosen because it exceeds the company's past performance and tests the corporate "reach"; (2) more specific to fit the self-sustaining growth equation, fund anticipated growth, and free the organization from excessive dependence on public capital markets; or (3) based on a capital market measure of the company's cost of capital, debt, and equity, and adjusted for its risk class or "beta."

The last two ROI goals underline the contrast between short- and long-term goals and point up the confusion that can surface in the corporate financial goals system when management doesn't clearly identify the time horizon for achievement. A company bases the ROI required for self-sustaining growth on the dictates of the current business environment and competitive strategy. Management can properly describe it as a short-term goal related to existing strategy and the need for a balanced flow of funds.

On the other hand, the corporate cost of capital tests individual against aggregate corporate performance. As judged by the capital markets in which the company competes for funds, the measure tests the need for—or the wisdom of—strategic redirection of resources, addresses long-term issues, and is properly described as a long-term goal. Many companies commonly and, I believe, mistakenly use this measure in the capital-budgeting process as a short-term target or hurdle rate in the evaluation of ongoing investment projects. In such implementation of existing strategy, a self-sustaining ROI target or other short-term standard would be more appropriate. The market cost of capital implies a realistic and feasible strategic alternative that frequently doesn't exist. Only when the company is actively considering a strategic redirection of investment—and most do only infrequently—is the market rate for the cost of capital, debt, and equity the appropriate standard.

My hope is that managers will recognize the complexity inherent in any well-designed financial goals system and the care needed in selecting and applying individual goals. Unless managers make certain that all primary goals are consistent with each other, their company's economic and competitive environment, and its operative business strategy, the goals will not serve as an effective discipline.

Appendix

The Self-Sustaining Growth Equation

The idea that a company's financial goals system can reach equilibrium if the goals that drive the aggregate supply of funds are in balance with the goals that drive the demand for them can be represented by the self-sustaining growth equation shown below. Included in the mathematical formula are all the principal elements of the internal financial system of a company as it relates to its established product markets.

My research has found that the equation illustrates a fundamental assumption of management: that a company should expect to fund the long-term growth in its established product markets from retained earnings supplemented by a conservative amount of debt. In fact, five of the companies studied used some form of this equation in their financial planning:

$$g(S) = r[RONA + d(RONA - i)]$$

Where:

$g(S)$ = growth rate of sales

r = earnings-retention rate

d = debt-equity ratio

i = after-tax interest rate on debt

$RONA$ = return on net assets (return on investment)

PART

III

Evolving Nature of
International Competition

1
The Competitive Advantage of Nations

Michael E. Porter

National prosperity is created, not inherited. It does not grow out of a country's natural endowments, its labor pool, its interest rates, or its currency's value, as classical economics insists.

A nation's competitiveness depends on the capacity of its industry to innovate and upgrade. Companies gain advantage against the world's best competitors because of pressure and challenge. They benefit from having strong domestic rivals, aggressive home-based suppliers, and demanding local customers.

In a world of increasingly global competition, nations have become more, not less, important. As the basis of competition has shifted more and more to the creation and assimilation of knowledge, the role of the nation has grown. Competitive advantage is created and sustained through a highly localized process. Differences in national values, culture, economic structures, institutions, and histories all contribute to competitive success. There are striking differences in the patterns of competitiveness in every country; no nation can or will be competitive in every or even most industries. Ultimately, nations succeed in particular industries because their home environment is the most forward-looking, dynamic, and challenging.

These conclusions, the product of a four-year study of the patterns of competitive success in ten leading trading nations, contradict the conventional wisdom that guides the thinking of many companies and national governments—and that is pervasive today in the United States. According to prevailing thinking, labor costs,

Author's note: Michael J. Enright, who served as project coordinator for this study, has contributed valuable suggestions.

interest rates, exchange rates, and economies of scale are the most potent determinants of competitiveness. In companies, the words of the day are merger, alliance, strategic partnerships, collaboration, and supranational globalization. Managers are pressing for more government support for particular industries. Among governments, there is a growing tendency to experiment with various policies intended to promote national competitiveness—from efforts to manage exchange rates to new measures to manage trade to policies to relax antitrust—which usually end up only undermining it. (See the Appendix.)

These approaches, now much in favor in both companies and governments, are flawed. They fundamentally misperceive the true sources of competitive advantage. Pursuing them, with all their short-term appeal, will virtually guarantee that the United States—or any other advanced nation—never achieves real and sustainable competitive advantage.

We need a new perspective and new tools—an approach to competitiveness that grows directly out of an analysis of internationally successful industries, without regard for traditional ideology or current intellectual fashion. We need to know, very simply, what works and why. Then we need to apply it.

How Companies Succeed in International Markets

Around the world, companies that have achieved international leadership employ strategies that differ from each other in every respect. But while every successful company will employ its own particular strategy, the underlying mode of operation—the character and trajectory of all successful companies—is fundamentally the same.

Companies achieve competitive advantage through acts of innovation. They approach innovation in its broadest sense, including both new technologies and new ways of doing things. They perceive a new basis for competing or find better means for competing in old ways. Innovation can be manifested in a new product design, a new production process, a new marketing approach, or a new way of conducting training. Much innovation is mundane and incremental, depending more on a cumulation of small insights and advances than on a single, major technological breakthrough. It often involves ideas that are not even "new"—ideas that have been around, but never vigorously pursued. It always involves investments in skill and knowledge, as well as in physical assets and brand reputations.

Some innovations create competitive advantage by perceiving an entirely new market opportunity or by serving a market segment that others have ignored. When competitors are slow to respond, such innovation yields competitive advantage. For instance, in industries such as autos and home electronics, Japanese companies gained their initial advantage by emphasizing smaller, more compact, lower-capacity models that foreign competitors disdained as less profitable, less important, and less attractive.

In international markets, innovations that yield competitive advantage anticipate both domestic and foreign needs. For example, as international concern for product safety has grown, Swedish companies like Volvo, Atlas Copco, and AGA have succeeded by anticipating the market opportunity in this area. On the other hand, innovations that respond to concerns or circumstances that are peculiar to the home market can actually retard international competitive success. The lure of the huge U.S. defense market, for instance, has diverted the attention of U.S. materials and machine-tool companies from attractive, global commercial markets.

Information plays a large role in the process of innovation and improvement—information that either is not available to competitors or that they do not seek. Sometimes it comes from simple investment in research and development or market research; more often, it comes from effort and from openness and from looking in the right place unencumbered by blinding assumptions or conventional wisdom.

This is why innovators are often outsiders from a different industry or a different country. Innovation may come from a new company, whose founder has a nontraditional background or was simply not appreciated in an older, established company. Or the capacity for innovation may come into an existing company through senior managers who are new to the particular industry and thus more able to perceive opportunities and more likely to pursue them. Or innovation may occur as a company diversifies, bringing new resources, skills, or perspectives to another industry. Or innovations may come from another nation with different circumstances or different ways of competing.

With few exceptions, innovation is the result of unusual effort. The company that successfully implements a new or better way of competing pursues its approach with dogged determination, often in the face of harsh criticism and tough obstacles. In fact, to succeed, innovation usually requires pressure, necessity, and even adversity: The fear of loss often proves more powerful than the hope of gain.

Once a company achieves competitive advantage through an innovation, it can sustain it only through relentless improvement. Almost any advantage can be imitated. Korean companies have already matched the ability of their Japanese rivals to mass-produce standard color televisions and VCRs; Brazilian companies have assembled technology and designs comparable to Italian competitors in casual leather footwear.

Competitors will eventually and inevitably overtake any company that stops improving and innovating. Sometimes early-mover advantages such as customer relationships, scale economies in existing technologies, or the loyalty of distribution channels are enough to permit a stagnant company to retain its entrenched position for years or even decades. But sooner or later, more dynamic rivals will find a way to innovate around these advantages or create a better or cheaper way of doing things. Italian appliance producers, which competed successfully on the basis of cost in selling midsize and compact appliances through large retail chains, rested too long on this initial advantage. By developing more differentiated products and creating strong brand franchises, German competitors have begun to gain ground.

Ultimately, the only way to sustain a competitive advantage is to *upgrade it*—to move to more sophisticated types. This is precisely what Japanese automakers have done. They initially penetrated foreign markets with small, inexpensive compact cars of adequate quality and competed on the basis of lower labor costs. Even while their labor-cost advantage persisted, however, the Japanese companies were upgrading. They invested aggressively to build large modern plants to reap economies of scale. Then they became innovators in process technology, pioneering just-in-time production and a host of other quality and productivity practices. These process improvements led to better product quality, better repair records, and better customer-satisfaction ratings than foreign competitors had. Most recently, Japanese automakers have advanced to the vanguard of product technology and are introducing new, premium brand names to compete with the world's most prestigious passenger cars.

The example of the Japanese automakers also illustrates two additional prerequisites for sustaining competitive advantage. First, a company must adopt a global approach to strategy. It must sell its product worldwide, under its own brand name, through international marketing channels that it controls. A truly global approach may even require the company to locate production or R&D facilities in other nations to take advantage of lower wage rates, to gain or improve market access, or to take advantage of foreign technology. Second, creating more sustainable advantages often means that a company must make its existing advantage obsolete—even while it is still an advantage. Japanese auto companies recognized this; either they would make their advantage obsolete, or a competitor would do it for them.

As this example suggests, innovation and change are inextricably tied together. But change is an unnatural act, particularly in successful companies; powerful forces are at work to avoid and defeat it. Past approaches become institutionalized in standard operating procedures and management controls. Training emphasizes the one correct way to do anything; the construction of specialized, dedicated facilities solidifies past practice into expensive brick and mortar; the existing strategy takes on an aura of invincibility and becomes rooted in the company culture.

Successful companies tend to develop a bias for predictability and stability; they work on defending what they have. Change is tempered by the fear that there is much to lose. The organization at all levels filters out information that would suggest new approaches, modifications, or departures from the norm. The internal environment operates like an immune system to isolate or expel "hostile" individuals who challenge current directions or established thinking. Innovation ceases; the company becomes stagnant; it is only a matter of time before aggressive competitors overtake it.

The Diamond of National Advantage

Why are certain companies based in certain nations capable of consistent innovation? Why do they ruthlessly pursue improvements, seeking an ever-more sophisticated source of competitive advantage? Why are they able to overcome the substantial barriers to change and innovation that so often accompany success?

The answer lies in four broad attributes of a nation, attributes that individually and as a system constitute the diamond of national advantage, the playing field that each nation establishes and operates for its industries. These attributes are:

1. *Factor Conditions.* The nation's position in factors of production, such as skilled labor or infrastructure, necessary to compete in a given industry.
2. *Demand Conditions.* The nature of home-market demand for the industry's product or service.
3. *Related and Supporting Industries.* The presence or absence in the nation of supplier industries and other related industries that are internationally competitive.
4. *Firm Strategy, Structure, and Rivalry.* The conditions in the nation governing how companies are created, organized, and managed, as well as the nature of domestic rivalry.

These determinants create the national environment in which companies are born and learn how to compete (see Exhibit I). Each point on the diamond—and the diamond as a system—affects essential ingredients for achieving international competitive success: the availability of resources and skills necessary for competitive advantage in an industry; the information that shapes the opportunities that companies perceive and the directions in which they deploy their resources and skills; the goals of the owners, managers, and individuals in companies; and most important, the pressures on companies to invest and innovate.

When a national environment permits and supports the most rapid accumulation of specialized assets and skills—sometimes simply because of greater effort and commitment—companies gain a competitive advantage. When a national environment affords better ongoing information and insight into product and process needs, companies gain a competitive advantage. Finally, when the national environment pressures companies to innovate and invest, companies both gain a competitive advantage and upgrade those advantages over time.

FACTOR CONDITIONS

According to standard economic theory, factors of production—labor, land, natural resources, capital, infrastructure—will deter-

Exhibit I.

Determinants of National Competitive Advantage

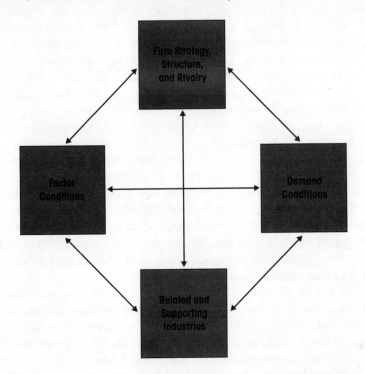

mine the flow of trade. A nation will export those goods that make most use of the factors with which it is relatively well endowed. This doctrine, whose origins date back to Adam Smith and David Ricardo and that is embedded in classical economics, is at best incomplete and at worst incorrect.

In the sophisticated industries that form the backbone of any advanced economy, a nation does not inherit but instead creates the most important factors of production—such as skilled human resources or a scientific base. Moreover, the stock of factors that a nation enjoys at a particular time is less important than the rate and efficiency with which it creates, upgrades, and deploys them in particular industries.

The most important factors of production are those that involve sustained and heavy investment and are specialized. Basic factors, such as a pool of labor or a local raw-material source, do not constitute an advantage in knowledge-intensive industries. Companies can access them easily through a global strategy or circumvent them through technology. Contrary to conventional wisdom, simply having a general work force that is high school or even college educated represents no competitive advantage in modern international competition. To support competitive advantage, a factor must be highly specialized to an industry's particular needs— a scientific institute specialized in optics, a pool of venture capital to fund software companies. These factors are more scarce, more difficult for foreign competitors to imitate—and they require sustained investment to create.

Nations succeed in industries where they are particularly good at factor creation. Competitive advantage results from the presence of world-class institutions that first create specialized factors and then continually work to upgrade them. Denmark has two hospitals that concentrate in studying and treating diabetes—and a world-leading export position in insulin. Holland has premier research institutes in the cultivation, packaging, and shipping of flowers, where it is the world's export leader.

What is not so obvious, however, is that selective disadvantages in the more basic factors can prod a company to innovate and upgrade—a disadvantage in a static model of competition can become an advantage in a dynamic one. When there is an ample supply of cheap raw materials or abundant labor, companies can simply rest on these advantages and often deploy them inefficiently. But when companies face a selective disadvantage, like high land costs, labor shortages, or the lack of local raw materials, they *must* innovate and upgrade to compete.

Implicit in the oft-repeated Japanese statement, "We are an island nation with no natural resources," is the understanding that these deficiencies have only served to spur Japan's competitive innovation. Just-in-time production, for example, economized on prohibitively expensive space. Italian steel producers in the Brescia area faced a similar set of disadvantages: high capital costs, high energy costs, and no local raw materials. Located in Northern Lombardy, these privately owned companies faced staggering logistics costs because of their distance from southern ports and the inefficiencies of the state-owned Italian transportation system. The result: They pioneered technologically advanced minimills that require only modest capital investment, use less energy, employ scrap metal as the feedstock, are efficient at small scale, and permit producers to locate close to sources of scrap and end-use customers. In other words, they converted factor disadvantages into competitive advantage.

Disadvantages can become advantages only under certain conditions. First, they must send companies proper signals about circumstances that will spread to other nations, thereby equipping them to innovate in advance of foreign rivals. Switzerland, the nation that experienced the first labor shortages after World War II, is a case in point. Swiss companies responded to the disadvantage by upgrading labor productivity and seeking higher value, more sustainable market segments. Companies in most other parts of the world, where there were still ample workers, focused their attention on other issues, which resulted in slower upgrading.

The second condition for transforming disadvantages into advantages is favorable circumstances elsewhere in the diamond—a consideration that applies to almost all determinants. To innovate, companies must have access to people with appropriate skills and have home-demand conditions that send the right signals. They must also have active domestic rivals who create pressure to innovate. Another precondition is company goals that lead to sustained commitment to the industry. Without such a commitment and the presence of active rivalry, a company may take an easy way around a disadvantage rather than using it as a spur to innovation.

For example, U.S. consumer-electronics companies, faced with high relative labor costs, chose to leave the product and production process largely unchanged and move labor-intensive activities to Taiwan and other Asian countries. Instead of upgrading their sources of advantage, they settled for labor-cost parity. On the other hand, Japanese rivals, confronted with intense domestic competition and a mature home market, chose to eliminate labor through automation. This led to lower assembly costs, to products with fewer components and to improved quality and reliability. Soon Japanese companies were building assembly plants in the United States—the place U.S. companies had fled.

DEMAND CONDITIONS

It might seem that the globalization of competition would diminish the importance of home demand. In practice, however, this is simply not the case. In fact, the composition and character of the home market usually has a disproportionate effect on how companies perceive, interpret, and respond to buyer needs. Nations gain competitive advantage in industries where the home demand gives their companies a clearer or earlier picture of emerging buyer needs, and where demanding buyers pressure companies to innovate faster and achieve more sophisticated competitive advantages than their foreign rivals. The size of home demand proves far less significant than the character of home demand.

Home-demand conditions help build competitive advantage when a particular industry segment is larger or more visible in the domestic market than in foreign markets. The larger market segments in a nation receive the most attention from the nation's companies; companies accord smaller or less desirable segments a lower priority. A good example is hydraulic excavators, which represent the most widely used type of construction equipment in the Japanese domestic market—but which comprise a far smaller proportion of the market in other advanced nations. This segment is one of the few where there are vigorous Japanese international competitors and where Caterpillar does not hold a substantial share of the world market.

More important than the mix of segments per se is the nature of domestic buyers. A nation's companies gain competitive advantage if domestic buyers are the world's most sophisticated and demanding buyers for the product or service. Sophisticated, demanding buyers provide a window into advanced customer needs; they pressure companies to meet high standards; they prod them to improve, to innovate, and to upgrade into more advanced segments. As with factor conditions, demand conditions provide advantages by forcing companies to respond to tough challenges.

Especially stringent needs arise because of local values and circumstances. For example, Japanese consumers, who live in small, tightly packed homes, must contend with hot, humid summers and high-cost electrical energy—a daunting combination of circumstances. In response, Japanese companies have pioneered compact, quiet air-conditioning units powered by energy-saving rotary compressors. In industry after industry, the tightly constrained requirements of the Japanese market have forced companies to innovate, yielding products that are *kei-haku-tansho*—light, thin, short, small—and that are internationally accepted.

Local buyers can help a nation's companies gain advantage if their needs anticipate or even shape those of other nations—if their needs provide ongoing "early-warning indicators" of global market trends. Sometimes anticipatory needs emerge because a nation's political values foreshadow needs that will grow elsewhere. Sweden's long-standing concern for handicapped people has spawned an increasingly competitive industry focused on special needs. Denmark's environmentalism has led to success for companies in water-pollution control equipment and windmills.

More generally, a nation's companies can anticipate global trends if the nation's values are spreading—that is, if the country is exporting its values and tastes as well as its products. The international success of U.S. companies in fast food and credit cards, for example, reflects not only the American desire for convenience but also the spread of these tastes to the rest of the world. Nations export their values and tastes through media, through training foreigners, through political influence, and through the foreign activities of their citizens and companies.

RELATED AND SUPPORTING INDUSTRIES

The third broad determinant of national advantage is the presence in the nation of related and supporting industries that are internationally competitive. Internationally competitive home-based suppliers create advantages in downstream industries in several ways. First, they deliver the most cost-effective inputs in an efficient, early, rapid, and sometimes preferential way. Italian gold and silver jewelry companies lead the world in that industry in part because other Italian companies supply two-thirds of the world's jewelry-making and precious-metal recycling machinery.

Far more significant than mere access to components and machinery, however, is the advantage that home-based related and supporting industries provide in innovation and upgrading—an advantage based on close working relationships. Suppliers and end-users located near each other can take advantage of short lines of communication, quick and constant flow of information, and an ongoing exchange of ideas and innovations. Companies have the opportunity to influence their suppliers' technical efforts and can serve as test sites for R&D work, accelerating the pace of innovation.

Exhibit II offers a graphic example of how a group of close-by,

Exhibit II.

The Italian Footwear Cluster

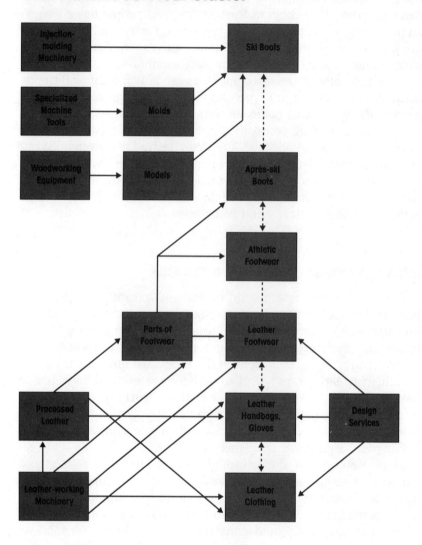

supporting industries creates competitive advantage in a range of interconnected industries that are all internationally competitive. Shoe producers, for instance, interact regularly with leather manufacturers on new styles and manufacturing techniques and learn about new textures and colors of leather when they are still on the drawing boards. Leather manufacturers gain early insights into fashion trends, helping them to plan new products. The interaction is mutually advantageous and self-reinforcing, but it does not happen automatically: It is helped by proximity, but occurs only because companies and suppliers work at it.

The nation's companies benefit most when the suppliers are, themselves, global competitors. It is ultimately self-defeating for a company or country to create "captive" suppliers that are totally dependent on the domestic industry and prevented from serving foreign competitors. By the same token, a nation need not be competitive in all supplier industries for its companies to gain competitive advantage. Companies can readily source from abroad materials, components, or technologies without a major effect on innovation or performance of the industry's products. The same is true of other generalized technologies—like electronics or software—where the industry represents a narrow application area.

Home-based competitiveness in related industries provides similar benefits: Information flow and technical interchange speed the rate of innovation and upgrading. A home-based related industry also increases the likelihood that companies will embrace new skills, and it also provides a source of entrants who will bring a novel approach to competing. The Swiss success in pharmaceuticals emerged out of previous international success in the dye industry, for example; Japanese dominance in electronic musical keyboards grows out of success in acoustic instruments combined with a strong position in consumer electronics.

FIRM STRATEGY, STRUCTURE, AND RIVALRY

National circumstances and context create strong tendencies in how companies are created, organized, and managed, as well as what the nature of domestic rivalry will be. In Italy, for example, successful international competitors are often small or medium-sized companies that are privately owned and operated like extended families; in Germany, in contrast, companies tend to be strictly hierarchical in organization and management practices, and top managers usually have technical backgrounds.

No one managerial system is universally appropriate—notwithstanding the current fascination with Japanese management. Competitiveness in a specific industry results from convergence of the management practices and organizational modes favored in the country and the sources of competitive advantage in the industry. In industries where Italian companies are world leaders—such as lighting, furniture, footwear, woolen fabrics, and packaging machines—a company strategy that emphasizes focus, customized products, niche marketing, rapid change, and breathtaking flexibility fits both the dynamics of the industry and the character of the Italian management system. The German management system, in contrast, works well in technical or engineering-oriented industries—optics, chemicals, complicated machinery—where complex products demand precision manufacturing, a careful development process, after-sale service, and thus a highly disciplined management structure. German success is much rarer in consumer goods and services where image marketing and rapid new-feature and model turnover are important to competition.

Countries also differ markedly in the goals that companies and individuals seek to achieve. Company goals reflect the characteristics of national capital markets and the compensation practices for managers. For example, in Germany and Switzerland, where banks comprise a substantial part of the nation's shareholders, most shares are held for long-term appreciation and are rarely traded. Companies do well in mature industries, where ongoing investment in R&D and new facilities is essential but returns may be only moderate. The United States is at the opposite extreme, with a large pool of risk capital but widespread trading of public companies and a strong emphasis by investors on quarterly and annual share-price appreciation. Management compensation is heavily based on annual bonuses tied to individual results. America does well in relatively new industries, like software and biotechnology, or ones where equity funding of new companies feeds active domestic rivalry, like specialty electronics and services. Strong pressures leading to underinvestment, however, plague more mature industries.

Individual motivation to work and expand skills is also important to competitive advantage. Outstanding talent is a scarce resource in any nation. A nation's success largely depends on the types of education its talented people choose, where they choose to work, and their commitment and effort. The goals a nation's institutions and values set for individuals and companies, and the prestige it attaches to certain industries, guide the flow of capital and human resources—which, in turn, directly affects the competitive performance of certain industries. Nations tend to be competitive in activities that people admire or depend on—the activities from which the nation's heroes emerge. In Switzerland, it is banking and pharmaceuticals. In Israel, the highest callings have been agriculture and defense-related fields. Sometimes it is hard to distinguish between cause and effect. Attaining international success can make an industry prestigious, reinforcing its advantage.

The presence of strong local rivals is a final, and powerful, stimulus to the creation and persistence of competitive advantage. This is true of small countries, like Switzerland, where the rivalry among its pharmaceutical companies, Hoffmann-La Roche, Ciba-Geigy, and Sandoz, contributes to a leading worldwide position. It is true in the United States in the computer and software industries. Nowhere is the role of fierce rivalry more apparent than in Japan, where there are 112 companies competing in machine tools, 34 in semiconductors, 25 in audio equipment, 15 in cameras—in fact, there are usually double figures in the industries in which Japan boasts global dominance (see Exhibit III). Among all the points on the diamond, domestic rivalry is arguably the most important because of the powerfully stimulating effect it has on all the others.

Conventional wisdom argues that domestic competition is wasteful: It leads to duplication of effort and prevents companies from achieving economies of scale. The "right solution" is to embrace one or two national champions, companies with the scale and strength to tackle foreign competitors, and to guarantee them the necessary resources, with the government's blessing. In fact, however, most national champions are uncompetitive, although heavily subsidized and protected by their government. In many of the prominent industries in which there is only one national rival, such as aerospace and telecommunications, government has played a large role in distorting competition.

Static efficiency is much less important than dynamic improvement, which domestic rivalry uniquely spurs. Domestic rivalry, like any rivalry, creates pressure on companies to innovate and improve. Local rivals push each other to lower costs, improve quality and service, and create new products and processes. But

Exhibit III.

Estimated Number of Japanese Rivals in Selected Industries

Air conditioners	13
Audio Equipment	25
Automobiles	9
Cameras	15
Car Audio	12
Carbon Fibers	7
Construction Equipment *	15
Copiers	14
Facsimile Machines	10
Large-scale Computers	6
Lift Trucks	8
Machine Tools	112
Microwave Equipment	5
Motorcycles	4
Musical Instruments	4
Personal Computers	16
Semiconductors	34
Sewing Machines	20
Shipbuilding†	33
Steel‡	5
Synthetic Fibers	8
Television Sets	15
Truck and Bus Tires	5
Trucks	11
Typewriters	14
Videocassette Recorders	10

Sources: Field interviews; *Nippon Kogyo Shinbun, Nippon Kogyo Nenkan,* 1987; Yano Research, *Market Share Jitan.* 1987; researchers' estimates.

*The number of companies varied by product area. The smallest number, 10, produced bulldozers. Fifteen companies produced shovel trucks, truck cranes, and asphalt-paving equipment. There were 20 companies in hydraulic excavators, a product area where Japan was particularly strong.
†Six companies had annual production exports in excess of 10,000 tons.
‡Integrated companies.

unlike rivalries with foreign competitors, which tend to be analytical and distant, local rivalries often go beyond pure economic or business competition and become intensely personal. Domestic rivals engage in active feuds; they compete not only for market share but also for people, for technical excellence, and perhaps most important, for "bragging rights." One domestic rival's success proves to others that advancement is possible and often attracts new rivals to the industry. Companies often attribute the success of foreign rivals to "unfair" advantages. With domestic rivals, there are no excuses.

Geographic concentration magnifies the power of domestic rivalry. This pattern is strikingly common around the world: Italian jewelry companies are located around two towns, Arezzo and Valenza Po; cutlery companies in Solingen, West Germany, and Seki, Japan; pharmaceutical companies in Basel, Switzerland; motorcycles and musical instruments in Hamamatsu, Japan. The more localized the rivalry, the more intense. And the more intense, the better.

Another benefit of domestic rivalry is the pressure it creates for constant upgrading of the sources of competitive advantage. The presence of domestic competitors automatically cancels the types of advantage that come from simply being in a particular nation—factor costs, access to or preference in the home market, or costs to foreign competitors who import into the market. Companies are forced to move beyond them, and as a result, gain more sustainable advantages. Moreover, competing domestic rivals will keep each other honest in obtaining government support. Companies are less likely to get hooked on the narcotic of government contracts or creeping industry protectionism. Instead, the industry will seek—and benefit from—more constructive forms of government support, such as assistance in opening foreign markets, as well as investments in focused educational institutions or other specialized factors.

Ironically, it is also vigorous domestic competition that ultimately pressures domestic companies to look at global markets and toughens them to succeed in them. Particularly when there are economies of scale, local competitors force each other to look outward to foreign markets to capture greater efficiency and higher profitability. And having been tested by fierce domestic competition, the stronger companies are well equipped to win abroad. If Digital

Equipment can hold its own against IBM, Data General, Prime, and Hewlett-Packard, going up against Siemens or Machines Bull does not seem so daunting a prospect.

The Diamond as a System

Each of these four attributes defines a point on the diamond of national advantage; the effect of one point often depends on the state of others. Sophisticated buyers will not translate into advanced products, for example, unless the quality of human resources permits companies to meet buyer needs. Selective disadvantages in factors of production will not motivate innovation unless rivalry is vigorous and company goals support sustained investment. At the broadest level, weaknesses in any one determinant will constrain an industry's potential for advancement and upgrading.

But the points of the diamond are also self-reinforcing: They constitute a system. Two elements, domestic rivalry and geographic concentration, have especially great power to transform the diamond into a system—domestic rivalry because it promotes improvement in all the other determinants and geographic concentration because it elevates and magnifies the interaction of the four separate influences.

The role of domestic rivalry illustrates how the diamond operates as a self-reinforcing system. Vigorous domestic rivalry stimulates the development of unique pools of specialized factors, particularly if the rivals are all located in one city or region: The University of California at Davis has become the world's leading center of wine-making research, working closely with the California wine industry. Active local rivals also upgrade domestic demand in an industry. In furniture and shoes, for example, Italian consumers have learned to expect more and better products because of the rapid pace of new-product development that is driven by intense domestic rivalry among hundreds of Italian companies. Domestic rivalry also promotes the formation of related and supporting industries. Japan's world-leading group of semiconductor producers, for instance, has spawned world-leading Japanese semiconductor-equipment manufacturers.

The effects can work in all directions: Sometimes world-class suppliers become new entrants in the industry they have been supplying. Or highly sophisticated buyers may themselves enter a supplier industry, particularly when they have relevant skills and view the new industry as strategic. In the case of the Japanese robotics industry, for example, Matsushita and Kawasaki originally designed robots for internal use before beginning to sell robots to others. Today they are strong competitors in the robotics industry. In Sweden, Sandvik moved from specialty steel into rock drills, and SKF moved from specialty steel into ball bearings.

Another effect of the diamond's systemic nature is that nations are rarely home to just one competitive industry; rather, the diamond creates an environment that promotes *clusters* of competitive industries. Competitive industries are not scattered helter-skelter throughout the economy but are usually linked together through vertical (buyer-seller) or horizontal (common customers, technology, channels) relationships. Nor are clusters usually scattered physically; they tend to be concentrated geographically. One competitive industry helps to create another in a mutually reinforcing process. Japan's strength in consumer electronics, for example, drove its success in semiconductors toward the memory chips and integrated circuits these products use. Japanese strength in laptop computers, which contrasts to limited success in other segments, reflects the base of strength in other compact, portable products and leading expertise in liquid-crystal display gained in the calculator and watch industries.

Once a cluster forms, the whole group of industries becomes mutually supporting. Benefits flow forward, backward, and horizontally. Aggressive rivalry in one industry spreads to others in the cluster, through spinoffs, through the exercise of bargaining power, and through diversification by established companies. Entry from other industries within the cluster spurs upgrading by stimulating diversity in R&D approaches and facilitating the introduction of new strategies and skills. Through the conduits of suppliers or customers who have contact with multiple competitors, information flows freely and innovations diffuse rapidly. Interconnections within the cluster, often unanticipated, lead to perceptions of new ways of competing and new opportunities. The cluster becomes a vehicle for maintaining diversity and overcoming the inward focus, inertia, inflexibility, and accommodation among rivals that slows or blocks competitive upgrading and new entry.

The Role of Government

In the continuing debate over the competitiveness of nations, no topic engenders more argument or creates less understanding than the role of the government. Many see government as an essential helper or supporter of industry, employing a host of policies to contribute directly to the competitive performance of strategic or target industries. Others accept the "free market" view that the operation of the economy should be left to the workings of the invisible hand.

Both views are incorrect. Either, followed to its logical outcome, would lead to the permanent erosion of a country's competitive capabilities. On one hand, advocates of government help for industry frequently propose policies that would actually hurt companies in the long run and only create the demand for more helping. On the other hand, advocates of a diminished government presence ignore the legitimate role that government plays in shaping the context and institutional structure surrounding companies and in creating an environment that stimulates companies to gain competitive advantage.

Government's proper role is as a catalyst and challenger; it is to encourage—or even push—companies to raise their aspirations and move to higher levels of competitive performance, even though this process may be inherently unpleasant and difficult. Government cannot create competitive industries; only companies can do that. Government plays a role that is inherently partial, that succeeds only when working in tandem with favorable underlying conditions in the diamond. Still, government's role of transmitting and amplifying the forces of the diamond is a powerful one. Government policies that succeed are those that create an environment in which companies can gain competitive advantage rather than those that involve government directly in the process, except in nations early in the development process. It is an indirect, rather than a direct, role.

Japan's government, at its best, understands this role better than anyone—including the point that nations pass through stages of competitive development and that government's appropriate role shifts as the economy progresses. By stimulating early demand for advanced products, confronting industries with the need to pioneer frontier technology through symbolic cooperative projects, establishing prizes that reward quality, and pursuing other policies that magnify the forces of the diamond, the Japanese government accelerates the pace of innovation. But like government officials anywhere, at their worst Japanese bureaucrats can make the same mistakes: attempting to manage industry structure, protecting the market too long, and yielding to political pressure to insulate inefficient retailers, farmers, distributors, and industrial companies from competition.

It is not hard to understand why so many governments make the same mistakes so often in pursuit of national competitiveness: Competitive time for companies and political time for governments are fundamentally at odds. It often takes more than a decade for an industry to create competitive advantage; the process entails the long upgrading of human skills, investing in products and processes, building clusters, and penetrating foreign markets. In the case of the Japanese auto industry, for instance, companies made their first faltering steps toward exporting in the 1950s—yet did not achieve strong international positions until the 1970s.

But in politics, a decade is an eternity. Consequently, most governments favor policies that offer easily perceived short-term benefits, such as subsidies, protection, and arranged mergers—the very policies that retard innovation. Most of the policies that would make a real difference either are too slow and require too much patience for politicians or, even worse, carry with them the sting of short-term pain. Deregulating a protected industry, for example, will lead to bankruptcies sooner and to stronger, more competitive companies only later.

Policies that convey static, short-term cost advantages but that unconsciously undermine innovation and dynamism represent the most common and most profound error in government industrial policy. In a desire to help, it is all too easy for governments to adopt policies such as joint projects to avoid "wasteful" R&D that undermine dynamism and competition. Yet even a 10% cost saving through economies of scale is easily nullified through rapid product and process improvement and the pursuit of volume in global markets—something that such policies undermine.

There are some simple, basic principles that governments should embrace to play the proper supportive role for national competitiveness: encourage change, promote domestic rivalry, stimulate innovation. Some of the specific policy approaches to guide nations seeking to gain competitive advantage include the following:

FOCUS ON SPECIALIZED FACTOR CREATION

Government has critical responsibilities for fundamentals like the primary and secondary education systems, basic national infrastructure, and research in areas of broad national concern such as health care. Yet these kinds of generalized efforts at factor creation rarely produce competitive advantage. Rather, the factors that translate into competitive advantage are advanced, specialized, and tied to specific industries or industry groups. Mechanisms such as specialized apprenticeship programs, research efforts in universities connected with an industry, trade association activities, and, most important, the private investments of companies ultimately create the factors that will yield competitive advantage.

AVOID INTERVENING IN FACTOR AND CURRENCY MARKETS

By intervening in factor and currency markets, governments hope to create lower factor costs or a favorable exchange rate that will help companies compete more effectively in international markets. Evidence from around the world indicates that these policies—such as the Reagan administration's dollar devaluation—are often counterproductive. They work against the upgrading of industry and the search for more sustainable competitive advantage.

The contrasting case of Japan is particularly instructive, although both Germany and Switzerland have had similar experiences. Over the past 20 years, the Japanese have been rocked by the sudden Nixon currency devaluation shock, two oil shocks, and, most recently, the yen shock—all of which forced Japanese companies to upgrade their competitive advantages. The point is not that government should pursue policies that intentionally drive up factor costs or the exchange rate. Rather, when market forces create rising factor costs or a higher exchange rate, government should resist the temptation to push them back down.

ENFORCE STRICT PRODUCT, SAFETY, AND ENVIRONMENTAL STANDARDS

Strict government regulations can promote competitive advantage by stimulating and upgrading domestic demand. Stringent standards for product performance, product safety, and environmental impact pressure companies to improve quality, upgrade technology, and provide features that respond to consumer and social demands. Easing standards, however tempting, is counterproductive.

When tough regulations anticipate standards that will spread internationally, they give a nation's companies a head start in developing products and services that will be valuable elsewhere. Sweden's strict standards for environmental protection have promoted competitive advantage in many industries. Atlas Copco, for example, produces quiet compressors that can be used in dense urban areas with minimal disruption to residents. Strict standards, however, must be combined with a rapid and streamlined regulatory process that does not absorb resources and cause delays.

SHARPLY LIMIT DIRECT COOPERATION AMONG INDUSTRY RIVALS

The most pervasive global policy fad in the competitiveness arena today is the call for more cooperative research and industry consortia. Operating on the belief that independent research by rivals is wasteful and duplicative, that collaborative efforts achieve economies of scale, and that individual companies are likely to underinvest in R&D because they cannot reap all the benefits, governments have embraced the idea of more direct cooperation. In the United States, antitrust laws have been modified to allow more cooperative R&D; in Europe, megaprojects such as ESPRIT, an information-technology project, bring together companies from several countries. Lurking behind much of this thinking is the fascination of Western governments with—and fundamental misunderstanding of—the countless cooperative research projects sponsored by the Ministry of International Trade and Industry (MITI), projects that appear to have contributed to Japan's competitive rise.

But a closer look at Japanese cooperative projects suggests a different story. Japanese companies participate in MITI projects to maintain good relations with MITI, to preserve their corporate images, and to hedge the risk that competitors will gain from the project—largely defensive reasons. Companies rarely contribute their best scientists and engineers to cooperative projects and usually spend much more on their own private research in the same field. Typically, the government makes only a modest financial contribution to the project.

The real value of Japanese cooperative research is to signal the importance of emerging technical areas and to stimulate proprietary company research. Cooperative projects prompt companies to explore new fields and boost internal R&D spending because companies know that their domestic rivals are investigating them.

Under certain limited conditions, cooperative research can prove beneficial. Projects should be in areas of basic product and process research, not in subjects closely connected to a company's proprietary sources of advantage. They should constitute only a modest portion of a company's overall research program in any given field. Cooperative research should be only indirect, channeled through independent organizations to which most industry participants have access. Organizational structures, like university labs and centers of excellence, reduce management problems and minimize the risk to rivalry. Finally, the most useful cooperative projects often involve fields that touch a number of industries and that require substantial R&D investments.

PROMOTE GOALS THAT LEAD TO SUSTAINED INVESTMENT

Government has a vital role in shaping the goals of investors, managers, and employees through policies in various areas. The manner in which capital markets are regulated, for example, shapes the incentives of investors and, in turn, the behavior of companies. Government should aim to encourage sustained investment in human skills, in innovation, and in physical assets. Perhaps the single most powerful tool for raising the rate of sustained investment in industry is a tax incentive for long-term (five years or more) capital gains restricted to new investment in corporate equity. Long-term capital gains incentives should also be applied to pension funds and other currently untaxed investors, who now have few reasons not to engage in rapid trading.

DEREGULATE COMPETITION

Regulation of competition through such policies as maintaining a state monopoly, controlling entry into an industry, or fixing prices

The Competitive Advantage of Nations 159

has two strong negative consequences: It stifles rivalry and innovation as companies become preoccupied with dealing with regulators and protecting what they already have; and it makes the industry a less dynamic and less desirable buyer or supplier. Deregulation and privatization on their own, however, will not succeed without vigorous domestic rivalry—and that requires, as a corollary, a strong and consistent antitrust policy.

ENFORCE STRONG DOMESTIC ANTITRUST POLICIES

A strong antitrust policy—especially for horizontal mergers, alliances, and collusive behavior—is fundamental to innovation. While it is fashionable today to call for mergers and alliances in the name of globalization and the creation of national champions, these often undermine the creation of competitive advantage. Real national competitiveness requires governments to disallow mergers, acquisitions, and alliances that involve industry leaders. Furthermore, the same standards for mergers and alliances should apply to both domestic and foreign companies. Finally, government policy should favor internal entry, both domestic and international, over acquisition. Companies should, however, be allowed to acquire small companies in related industries when the move promotes the transfer of skills that could ultimately create competitive advantage.

REJECT MANAGED TRADE

Managed trade represents a growing and dangerous tendency for dealing with the fallout of national competitiveness. Orderly marketing agreements, voluntary restraint agreements, or other devices that set quantitative targets to divide up markets are dangerous, ineffective, and often enormously costly to consumers. Rather than promoting innovation in a nation's industries, managed trade guarantees a market for inefficient companies.

Government trade policy should pursue open market access in every foreign nation. To be effective, trade policy should not be a passive instrument; it cannot respond only to complaints or work only for those industries that can muster enough political clout; it should not require a long history of injury or serve only distressed industries. Trade policy should seek to open markets wherever a nation has competitive advantage and should actively address emerging industries and incipient problems.

Where government finds a trade barrier in another nation, it should concentrate its remedies on dismantling barriers, not on regulating imports or exports. In the case of Japan, for example, pressure to accelerate the already rapid growth of manufactured imports is a more effective approach than a shift to managed trade. Compensatory tariffs that punish companies for unfair trade practices are better than market quotas. Other increasingly important tools to open markets are restrictions that prevent companies in offending nations from investing in acquisitions or production facilities in the host country—thereby blocking the unfair country's companies from using their advantage to establish a new beachhead that is immune from sanctions.

Any of these remedies, however, can backfire. It is virtually impossible to craft remedies to unfair trade practices that avoid both reducing incentives for domestic companies to innovate and export and harming domestic buyers. The aim of remedies should be adjustments that allow the remedy to disappear.

The Company Agenda

Ultimately, only companies themselves can achieve and sustain competitive advantage. To do so, they must act on the fundamentals described above. In particular, they must recognize the central role of innovation—and the uncomfortable truth that innovation grows out of pressure and challenge. It takes leadership to create a dynamic, challenging environment. And it takes leadership to recognize the all-too-easy escape routes that appear to offer a path to competitive advantage, but are actually short-cuts to failure. For example, it is tempting to rely on cooperative research and development projects to lower the cost and risk of research. But they can divert company attention and resources from proprietary research efforts and will all but eliminate the prospects for real innovation.

Competitive advantage arises from leadership that harnesses and amplifies the forces in the diamond to promote innovation and upgrading. Here are just a few of the kinds of company policies that will support that effort.

CREATE PRESSURES FOR INNOVATION

A company should seek out pressure and challenge, not avoid them. Part of strategy is to take advantage of the home nation to create the impetus for innovation. To do that, companies can sell to the most sophisticated and demanding buyers and channels; seek out those buyers with the most difficult needs; establish norms that exceed the toughest regulatory hurdles or product standards; source from the most advanced suppliers; treat employees as permanent in order to stimulate upgrading of skills and productivity.

SEEK OUT THE MOST CAPABLE COMPETITORS AS MOTIVATORS

To motivate organizational change, capable competitors and respected rivals can be a common enemy. The best managers always run a little scared; they respect and study competitors. To stay dynamic, companies must make meeting challenge a part of the organization's norms. For example, lobbying against strict product standards signals the organization that company leadership has diminished aspirations. Companies that value stability, obedient customers, dependent suppliers, and sleepy competitors are inviting inertia and, ultimately, failure.

ESTABLISH EARLY-WARNING SYSTEMS

Early-warning signals translate into early-mover advantages. Companies can take actions that help them see the signals of change and act on them, thereby getting a jump on the competition. For example, they can find and serve those buyers with the most anticipatory needs; investigate all emerging new buyers or channels; find places whose regulations foreshadow emerging regulations elsewhere; bring some outsiders into the management team; maintain ongoing relationships with research centers and sources of talented people.

IMPROVE THE NATIONAL DIAMOND

Companies have a vital stake in making their home environment a better platform for international success. Part of a company's responsibility is to play an active role in forming clusters and to work with its home-nation buyers, suppliers, and channels to help them upgrade and extend their own competitive advantages. To upgrade home demand, for example, Japanese musical instrument manufacturers, led by Yamaha, Kawai, and Suzuki, have established music schools. Similarly, companies can stimulate and support local suppliers of important specialized inputs—including encouraging them to compete globally. The health and strength of the national cluster will only enhance the company's own rate of innovation and upgrading.

In nearly every successful competitive industry, leading companies also take explicit steps to create specialized factors like human resources, scientific knowledge, or infrastructure. In industries like wool cloth, ceramic tiles, and lighting equipment, Italian industry associations invest in market information, process technology, and common infrastructure. Companies can also speed innovation by putting their headquarters and other key operations where there are concentrations of sophisticated buyers, important suppliers, or specialized factor-creating mechanisms, such as universities or laboratories.

WELCOME DOMESTIC RIVALRY

To compete globally, a company needs capable domestic rivals and vigorous domestic rivalry. Especially in the United States and Europe today, managers are wont to complain about excessive competition and to argue for mergers and acquisitions that will produce hoped-for economies of scale and critical mass. The complaint is only natural—but the argument is plain wrong. Vigorous domestic rivalry creates sustainable competitive advantage. Moreover, it is better to grow internationally than to dominate the domestic market. If a company wants an acquisition, a foreign one that can speed globalization and supplement home-based advantages or offset home-based disadvantages is usually far better than merging with leading domestic competitors.

GLOBALIZE TO TAP SELECTIVE ADVANTAGES IN OTHER NATIONS

In search of "global" strategies, many companies today abandon their home diamond. To be sure, adopting a global perspective is important to creating competitive advantage. But relying on foreign activities that supplant domestic capabilities is always a second-best solution. Innovating to offset local factor disadvantages is better than outsourcing; developing domestic suppliers and buyers is better than relying solely on foreign ones. Unless the critical underpinnings of competitiveness are present at home, companies will not sustain competitive advantage in the long run. The aim should be to upgrade home-base capabilities so that foreign activities are selective and supplemental only to overall competitive advantage.

The correct approach to globalization is to tap selectively into sources of advantage in other nations' diamonds. For example, identifying sophisticated buyers in other countries helps companies understand different needs and creates pressures that will stimulate a faster rate of innovation. No matter how favorable the home diamond, moreover, important research is going on in other nations. To take advantage of foreign research, companies must station high-quality people in overseas bases and mount a credible level of scientific effort. To get anything back from foreign research ventures, companies must also allow access to their own ideas—recognizing that competitive advantage comes from continuous improvement, not from protecting today's secrets.

USE ALLIANCES ONLY SELECTIVELY

Alliances with foreign companies have become another managerial fad and cure-all: They represent a tempting solution to the problem of a company wanting the advantages of foreign enterprises or hedging against risk, without giving up independence. In reality, however, while alliances can achieve selective benefits, they always exact significant costs: They involve coordinating two separate operations, reconciling goals with an independent entity, creating a competitor, and giving up profits. These costs ultimately make most alliances short-term transitional devices, rather than stable, long-term relationships.

Most important, alliances as a broad-based strategy will only ensure a company's mediocrity, not its international leadership. No company can rely on another outside, independent company for skills and assets that are central to its competitive advantage. Alliances are best used as a selective tool, employed on a temporary basis or involving noncore activities.

LOCATE THE HOME BASE TO SUPPORT COMPETITIVE ADVANTAGE

Among the most important decisions for multinational companies is the nation in which to locate the home base for each distinct business. A company can have different home bases for distinct businesses or segments. Ultimately, competitive advantage is created at home: It is where strategy is set, the core product and process technology is created, and a critical mass of production takes place. The circumstances in the home nation must support innovation; otherwise the company has no choice but to move its home base to a country that stimulates innovation and that provides the best environment for global competitiveness. There are no half-measures: The management team must move as well.

The Role of Leadership

Too many companies and top managers misperceive the nature of competition and the task before them by focusing on improving financial performance, soliciting government assistance, seeking stability, and reducing risk through alliances and mergers.

Today's competitive realities demand leadership. Leaders believe in change; they energize their organizations to innovate continuously; they recognize the importance of their home country as integral to their competitive success and work to upgrade it. Most important, leaders recognize the need for pressure and challenge. Because they are willing to encourage appropriate—and painful—

government policies and regulations, they often earn the title "statesmen," although few see themselves that way. They are prepared to sacrifice the easy life for difficulty and, ultimately, sustained competitive advantage. That must be the goal, for both nations and companies: not just surviving, but achieving international competitiveness.

And not just once, but continuously.

Appendix

WHAT IS NATIONAL COMPETITIVENESS?

National competitiveness has become one of the central preoccupations of government and industry in every nation. Yet for all the discussion, debate, and writing on the topic, there is still no persuasive theory to explain national competitiveness. What is more, there is not even an accepted definition of the term "competitiveness" as applied to a nation. While the notion of a competitive company is clear, the notion of a competitive nation is not.

Some see national competitiveness as a macroeconomic phenomenon, driven by variables such as exchange rates, interest rates, and government deficits. But Japan, Italy, and South Korea have all enjoyed rapidly rising living standards despite budget deficits; Germany and Switzerland despite appreciating currencies; and Italy and Korea despite high interest rates.

Others argue that competitiveness is a function of cheap and abundant labor. But Germany, Switzerland, and Sweden have all prospered even with high wages and labor shortages. Besides, shouldn't a nation seek higher wages for its workers as a goal of competitiveness?

Another view connects competitiveness with bountiful natural resources. But how, then, can one explain the success of Germany, Japan, Switzerland, Italy, and South Korea—countries with limited natural resources?

More recently, the argument has gained favor that competitiveness is driven by government policy: targeting, protection, import promotion, and subsidies have propelled Japanese and South Korean auto, steel, shipbuilding, and semiconductor industries into global preeminence. But a closer look reveals a spotty record. In Italy, government intervention has been ineffectual—but Italy has experienced a boom in world export share second only to Japan. In Germany, direct government intervention in exporting industries is rare. And even in Japan and South Korea, government's role in such important industries as facsimile machines, copiers, robotics, and advanced materials has been modest; some of the most frequently cited examples, such as sewing machines, steel and shipbuilding, are now quite dated.

A final popular explanation for national competitiveness is differences in management practices, including management-labor relations. The problem here, however, is that different industries require different approaches to management. The successful management practices governing small, private, and loosely organized Italian family companies in footwear, textiles, and jewelry, for example, would produce a management disaster if applied to German chemical or auto companies, Swiss pharmaceutical makers, or American aircraft producers. Nor is it possible to generalize about management-labor relations. Despite the commonly held view that powerful unions undermine competitive advantage, unions are strong in Germany and Sweden—and both countries boast internationally preeminent companies.

Clearly, none of these explanations is fully satisfactory; none is sufficient by itself to rationalize the competitive position of industries within a national border. Each contains some truth; but a broader, more complex set of forces seems to be at work.

The lack of a clear explanation signals an even more fundamental question. What is a "competitive" nation in the first place? Is a "competitive" nation one where every company or industry is competitive? No nation meets this test. Even Japan has large sectors of its economy that fall far behind the world's best competitors.

Is a "competitive" nation one whose exchange rate makes its goods price competitive in international markets? Both Germany and Japan have enjoyed remarkable gains in their standards of living—and experienced sustained periods of strong currency and rising prices. Is a "competitive" nation one with a large positive balance of trade? Switzerland has roughly balanced trade; Italy has a chronic trade deficit—both nations enjoy strongly rising national income. Is a "competitive" nation one with low labor costs? India and Mexico both have low wages and low labor costs—but neither seems an attractive industrial model.

The only meaningful concept of competitiveness at the national level is *productivity*. The principal goal of a nation is to produce a high and rising standard of living for its citizens. The ability to do so depends on the productivity with which a nation's labor and capital are employed. Productivity is the value of the output produced by a unit of labor or capital. Productivity depends on both the quality and features of products (which determine the prices that they can command) and the efficiency with which they are produced. Productivity is the prime determinant of a nation's long-run standard of living; it is the root cause of national per capita income. The productivity of human resources determines employee wages; the productivity with which capital is employed determines the return it earns for its holders.

A nation's standard of living depends on the capacity of its companies to achieve high levels of productivity—and to increase productivity over time. Sustained productivity growth requires that an economy continually *upgrade itself*. A nation's companies must relentlessly improve productivity in existing industries by raising product quality, adding desirable features, improving product technology, or boosting production efficiency. They must develop the necessary capabilities to compete in more and more sophisticated industry segments, where productivity is generally high. They must finally develop the capability to compete in entirely new, sophisticated industries.

International trade and foreign investment can both improve a nation's productivity as well as threaten it. They support rising national productivity by allowing a nation to specialize in those industries and segments of industries where its companies are more productive and to import where its companies are less productive. No nation can be competitive in everything. The ideal is to deploy the nation's limited pool of human and other resources into the most productive uses. Even those nations with the highest standards of living have many industries in which local companies are uncompetitive.

Yet international trade and foreign investment also can threaten productivity growth. They expose a nation's industries to the test of international standards of productivity. An industry will lose out if its productivity is not sufficiently higher than foreign rivals' to offset any advantages in local wage rates. If a nation loses the ability to compete in a range of high-productivity/high-wage industries, its standard of living is threatened.

Defining national competitiveness as achieving a trade surplus or balanced trade per se is inappropriate. The expansion of exports because of low wages and a weak currency, at the same time that the nation imports sophisticated goods that its companies cannot produce competitively, may bring trade into balance or surplus but lowers the nation's standard of living. Competitiveness also does not mean jobs. It's the *type* of jobs, not just the ability to employ citizens at low wages, that is decisive for economic prosperity.

Seeking to explain "competitiveness" at the national level, then, is to answer the wrong question. What we must understand instead is the determinants of productivity and the rate of productivity growth. To find answers, we must focus not on the economy as a whole but on *specific industries and industry segments*. We must understand how and why commercially viable skills and technology are created, which can only be fully understood at the level of particular industries. It is the outcome of the thousands of struggles for competitive advantage against foreign rivals in particular segments and industries, in which products and processes are created and improved, that underpins the process of upgrading national productivity.

When one looks closely at any national economy, there are striking differences among a nation's industries in competitive success. International advantage is often concentrated in particular industry segments. German exports of cars are heavily skewed toward high-performance cars, while Korean exports are all compacts and sub-compacts. In many industries and segments of industries, the competitors with true international competitive advantage are *based in only a few nations.*

Our search, then, is for the decisive characteristic of a nation that allows its companies to create and sustain competitive advantage in particular fields—the search is for the competitive advantage of nations. We are particularly concerned with the determinants of international success in technology- and skill-intensive segments and industries, which underpin high and rising productivity.

Classical theory explains the success of nations in particular industries based on so-called factors of production such as land, labor, and natural resources. Nations gain factor-based comparative advantage in industries that make intensive use of the factors they possess in abundance. Classical theory, however, has been overshadowed in advanced industries and economies by the globalization of competition and the power of technology.

A new theory must recognize that in modern international competition, companies compete with global strategies involving not only trade but also foreign investment. What a new theory must explain is why a nation provides a favorable *home base* for companies that compete internationally. The home base is the nation in which the essential competitive advantages of the enterprise are created and sustained. It is where a company's strategy is set, where the core product and process technology is created and maintained, and where the most productive jobs and most advanced skills are located. The presence of the home base in a nation has the greatest positive influence on other linked domestic industries and leads to other benefits in the nation's economy. While the ownership of the company is often concentrated at the home base, the nationality of shareholders is secondary.

A new theory must move beyond comparative advantage to the competitive advantage of a nation. It must reflect a rich conception of competition that includes segmented markets, differentiated products, technology differences, and economies of scale. A new theory must go beyond cost and explain why companies from some nations are better than others at creating advantages based on quality, features, and new product innovation. A new theory must begin from the premise that competition is dynamic and evolving; it must answer the questions: Why do some companies based in some nations innovate more than others? Why do some nations provide an environment that enables companies to improve and innovate faster than foreign rivals?

2
Tap Your Subsidiaries for Global Reach

Christopher A. Bartlett and Sumantra Ghoshal

In 1972, EMI developed the CAT scanner. This technological breakthrough seemed to be the innovation that the U.K.-based company had long sought in order to relieve its heavy dependence on the cyclical music and entertainment business and to strengthen itself in international markets. The medical community hailed the product, and within four years EMI had established a medical electronics business that was generating 20% of the company's worldwide earnings. The scanner enjoyed a dominant market position, a fine reputation, and a strong technological leadership situation.

Nevertheless, by mid-1979 EMI had started losing money in this business, and the company's deteriorating performance eventually forced it to accept a takeover bid from Thorn Electric. Thorn immediately divested the ailing medical electronics business. Ironically, the takeover was announced the same month that Godfrey Hounsfield, the EMI scientist who developed the CAT scanner, was awarded a Nobel Prize for the invention.

How could such a fairy-tale success story turn so quickly into a nightmare? There were many contributing causes, but at the center were a structure and management process that impeded the company's ability to capitalize on its technological assets and its worldwide market position.

The concentration of EMI's technical, financial, and managerial resources in the United Kingdom made it unresponsive to the varied and changing needs of international markets. As worldwide demand built up, delivery lead times for the scanner stretched out more than 12 months. Despite the protests of EMI's U.S. managers that these delays were opening opportunities for competitive entry, headquarters continued to fill orders on the basis of when they were received rather than on how strategically important they were. Corporate management would not allow local sourcing or duplicate manufacturing of the components that were the bottlenecks causing delays.

The centralization of decision making in London also impaired the company's ability to guide strategy to meet the needs of the market. For example, medical practitioners in the United States, the key market for CAT scanners, considered reduction of scan time to be an important objective, while EMI's central research laboratory, influenced by feedback from the domestic market, concentrated on improving image resolution. When General Electric eventually brought out a competitive product with a shorter scan time, customers deserted EMI.

In the final analysis, it was EMI's limited organizational capability that prevented it from capitalizing on its large resource base and its strong global competitive position. The company lacked:

The ability to sense changes in market needs and industry structure occurring away from home.

The resources to analyze data and develop strategic responses to competitive challenges that were emerging worldwide.

The managerial initiative, motivation, and capability in its overseas operations to respond imaginatively to diverse and fast-changing operating environments.

While the demise of its scanner business represents an extreme example, the problems EMI faced are common. With all the current attention being given to global strategy, companies risk underestimating the organizational challenge of managing their global operations. Indeed, the top management in almost every one of the MNCs we have studied has had an excellent idea of what it needed to do to become more globally competitive; it was less clear on how to organize to achieve its global strategic objectives.

United Nations Model and HQ Syndrome

Our study covered nine core companies in three industries and a dozen secondary companies from a more diverse industrial spectrum. They were selected from three areas of origin—the United

States, Europe, and Japan. Despite this diversity, most of these companies had developed their international operations around two common assumptions on how to organize. We dubbed these well-ingrained beliefs the "U.N. model assumption" and the "headquarters hierarchy syndrome."

Although there are wide differences in importance of operations in major markets like Germany, Japan, or the United States, compared with subsidiaries in Argentina, Malaysia, or Nigeria, for example, most multinationals treat their foreign subsidiaries in a remarkably uniform manner. One executive we talked to termed this approach "the U.N. model of multinational management." Thus it is common to see managers express subsidiary roles and responsibilities in the same general terms, apply their planning control systems uniformly systemwide, involve country managers to a like degree in planning, and evaluate them against standardized criteria. The uniform systems and procedures tend to paper over any differences in the informal treatment of subsidiaries.

When national units are operationally self-sufficient and strategically independent, uniform treatment may allow each to develop a plan for dealing with its local environment. As a company reaches for the benefits of global integration, however, there is little need for uniformity and symmetry among units. Yet the growing complexity of the corporate management task heightens the appeal of a simple system.

The second common assumption we observed, the headquarters hierarchy syndrome, grows out of and is reinforced by the U.N. model assumption. The symmetrical organization approach encourages management to envision two roles for the organization, one for headquarters and another for the national subsidiaries. As companies moved to build a consistent global strategy, we saw a strong tendency for headquarters managers to try to coordinate key decisions and control global resources and have the subsidiaries act as implementers and adapters of the global strategy in their localities.

As strategy implementation proceeded, we observed country managers struggling to retain their freedom, flexibility, and effectiveness, while their counterparts at the center worked to maintain their control and legitimacy as administrators of the global strategy. It's not surprising that relationships between the center and the periphery often became strained and even adversarial.

The combined effect of these two assumptions is to severely limit the organizational capability of a company's international operations in three important ways. First, the doctrine of symmetrical treatment results in an overcompensation for the needs of smaller or less crucial markets and a simultaneous underresponsiveness to the needs of strategically important countries. Moreover, by relegating the national subsidiaries to the role of local implementers and adapters of global directives, the head office risks grossly underutilizing the company's worldwide assets and organizational capabilities. And finally, ever-expanding control by headquarters deprives the country managers of outlets for their skills and creative energy. Naturally, they come to feel demotivated and even disenfranchised.

Dispersed Responsibility

The limitations of the symmetrical, hierarchical mode of operation have become increasingly clear to MNC executives, and in many of the companies we surveyed we found managers experimenting with alternative ways of managing their worldwide operations. And as we reviewed these various approaches, we saw a new pattern emerging that suggested a significantly different model of global organization based on some important new assumptions and beliefs. We saw companies experimenting with ways of selectively varying the roles and responsibilities of their national organizations to reflect explicitly the differences in external environments and internal capabilities. We also saw them modifying central administrative systems to legitimize the differences they encountered.

Such is the case with Procter & Gamble's European operations. More than a decade ago, P&G's European subsidiaries were free to adapt the parent company's technology, products, and marketing approaches to their local situation as they saw fit—while being held responsible, of course, for sales and earnings in their respective countries. Many of these subsidiaries had become large and powerful. By the mid-1970s, economic and competitive pressures were squeezing P&G's European profitability. The head office in Cincinnati decided that the loose organizational arrangement inhibited product development, curtailed the company's ability to capture Europewide scale economies, and afforded poor protection against competitors' attempts to pick off product lines country by country.

So the company launched what became known as the Pampers experiment—an approach firmly grounded in the classic U.N. and HQ assumptions. It created a position at European headquarters in Brussels to develop a Pampers strategy for the whole continent. By giving this manager responsibility for the Europewide product and marketing strategy, management hoped to be able to eliminate the diversity in brand strategy by coordinating activities across subsidiary boundaries. Within 12 months, the Pampers experiment had failed. It not only ignored local knowledge and underutilized subsidiary strengths but also demotivated the country managers to the point that they felt no responsibility for sales performance of the brand in their areas.

Obviously, a different approach was called for. Instead of assuming that the best solutions were to be found in headquarters, top management decided to find a way to exploit the expertise of the national units. For most products, P&G had one or two European subsidiaries that had been more creative, committed, and successful than the others. By extending the responsibilities and influence of these organizations, top management reasoned, the company could make the success infectious. All that was needed was a means for promoting intersubsidiary cooperation that could offset the problems caused by the company's dispersed and independent operations. For P&G the key was the creation of "Eurobrand" teams.

For each important brand the company formed a management team that carried the responsibility for development and coordination of marketing strategy for Europe. Each Eurobrand team was headed not by a manager from headquarters but by the general manager and the appropriate brand group from the "lead" subsidiary—a unit selected for its success and creativity with the brand. Supporting them were brand managers from other subsidiaries, functional managers from headquarters, and anyone else involved in strategy for the particular product. Team meetings became forums for the lead-country group to pass on ideas, propose action, and hammer out agreements.

The first Eurobrand team had charge of a new liquid detergent called Vizir. The brand group in the lead country, West Germany, had undertaken product and market testing, settled on the package design and advertising theme, and developed the marketing strategy. The Eurobrand team ratified all these elements, then launched Vizir in six new markets within a year. This was the first time the company had ever introduced a new product in that many markets in so brief a span. It was also the first time the company had got agreement in several subsidiaries on a single product formulation, a uniform advertising theme, a standard packaging line, and a sole manufacturing source. Thereafter, Eurobrand teams proliferated; P&G's way of organizing and directing subsidiary operations had changed fundamentally.

On reflection, company managers feel that there were two main reasons why Eurobrand teams succeeded where the Pampers experiment had failed. First, they captured the knowledge, the expertise, and most important, the commitment of managers closest to the market. Equally significant was the fact that relationships among managers on Eurobrand teams were built on interdependence rather than on independence, as in the old organization, or on dependence, as with the Pampers experiment. Different subsidiaries had the lead role for different brands, and the need for reciprocal cooperation was obvious to everyone.

Other companies have made similar discoveries about new ways to manage their international operations—at NEC and Philips, at L.M. Ericsson and Matsushita, at ITT and Unilever, we observed executives challenging the assumptions behind the traditional head office–subsidiary relationship. The various terms they used—lead-country concept, key-market subsidiary, global-market mandate, center of excellence—all suggested a new model based on a recognition that their organizational task was focused on a single problem: the need to resolve imbalances between market demands and constraints on the one hand and uneven subsidiary capabilities on the other. Top officers understand that the option of a zero-based organization is not open to an established multinational organization. But they seem to have hit on an approach that works.

BLACK HOLES, AND SO FORTH

The actions these companies have taken suggest an organizational model of differentiated rather than homogeneous subsidiary roles and of dispersed rather than concentrated responsibilities. As we analyzed the nature of the emerging subsidiary roles and responsibilities, we were able to see a pattern in their distribution and identify the criteria used to assign them. Exhibit I represents

Exhibit I. Roles for National Subsidiaries

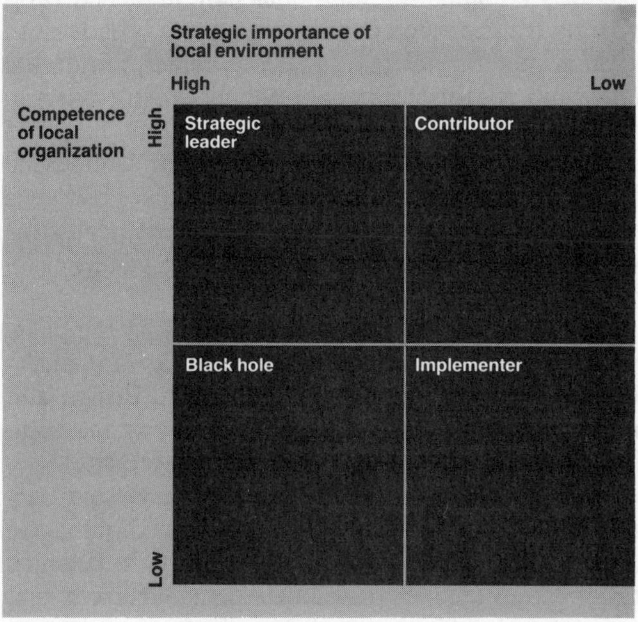

a somewhat oversimplified conceptualization of the criteria and roles, but it is true enough for discussion purposes.

The strategic importance of a specific country unit is strongly influenced by the significance of its national environment to the company's global strategy. A large market is obviously important, and so is a competitor's home market or a market that is particularly sophisticated or technologically advanced. The organizational competence of a particular subsidiary can, of course, be in technology, production, marketing, or any other area.

STRATEGIC LEADER.   This role can be played by a highly competent national subsidiary located in a strategically important market. In this role, the subsidiary serves as a partner of headquarters in developing and implementing strategy. It must not only be a sensor for detecting signals of change but also a help in analyzing the threats and opportunities and developing appropriate responses.

The part played by the U.K. subsidiary of Philips in building the company's strong leadership position in the teletext-TV business provides an illustration. In the early 1970s, the BBC and ITV (an independent British TV company) simultaneously launched projects to adapt existing transmission capacity to permit broadcast of text and simple diagrams. But teletext, as it was called, required a TV receiver that would accept and decode the modified transmissions. For TV set manufacturers, the market opportunity required a big investment in R&D and production facilities, but commercial possibilities of teletext were highly uncertain, and most producers decided against making the investment. They spurned teletext as a typical British toy—fancy and not very useful. Who would pay a heavy premium just to read text on a TV screen?

Philips' U.K. subsidiary, however, was convinced that the product had a future and decided to pursue its own plans. Its top officers persuaded Philips' component manufacturing unit to design and produce the integrated-circuit chip for receiving teletext and commissioned their Croydon plant to build the teletext decoder.

In the face of poor market acceptance (the company sold only 1,000 teletext sets in its first year), the U.K. subsidiary did not give up. It lent support to the British government's efforts to promote teletext and make it widely available. Meanwhile, management kept up pressure on the Croydon factory to find ways of reducing costs and improving reception quality—which it did.

In late 1979, teletext took off, and by 1982 half a million sets were being sold annually in the United Kingdom. Today almost three million teletext sets are in use in Britain, and the concept is spreading abroad. Philips has built up a dominant position in markets that have accepted the service. Corporate management has given the U.K. subsidiary formal responsibility to continue to exercise leadership in the development, manufacture, and marketing of teletext on a companywide basis. The Croydon plant is recognized as Philips' center of competence and international sourcing plant for teletext-TV sets.

CONTRIBUTOR.   Filling this role is a subsidiary operating in a small or strategically unimportant market but having a distinctive capability. A fine example is the Australian subsidiary of L.M. Ericsson, which played a crucial part in developing its successful AXE digital telecommunications switch. The down-under group gave impetus to the conversion of the system from its initial analog design to the digital form. Later its engineers helped construct several key components of the system.

This subsidiary had built up its superior technological capability when the Australian telephone authority became one of the first in the world to call for bids on electronic telephone switching equipment. The government in Canberra, however, had insisted on a strong local technical capability as a condition for access to the market. Moreover, heading this unit of the Swedish company was a willful, independent, and entrepreneurial country manager who strengthened the R&D team, even without full support from headquarters.

These various factors resulted in the local subsidiary having a technological capability and an R&D resource base that was much larger than subsidiaries in other markets of similar size or importance. Left to their own devices, management worried that such internal competencies would focus on local tasks and priorities that were unnecessary or even detrimental to the overall global strategy. But if the company inhibited the development activities of the local units, it risked losing these special skills. Under the circumstances, management saw the need to co-opt this valuable subsidiary expertise and channel it toward projects of corporate importance.

IMPLEMENTER.   In the third situation, a national organization in a less strategically important market has just enough competence to maintain its local operation. The market potential is limited, and the corporate resource commitment reflects it. Most national units of most companies are given this role. They might include subsidiaries in the developing countries, in Canada, and in the smaller European countries. Without access to critical information, and having to control scarce resources, these national organizations lack the potential to become contributors to the company's strategic planning. They are deliverers of the company's value added; they have the important task of generating the funds that keep the company going and underwrite its expansion.

The implementers' efficiency is as important as the creativity of the strategic leaders or contributors—and perhaps more so, for it is this group that provides the strategic leverage that affords MNCs their competitive advantage. The implementers produce the opportunity to capture economies of scale and scope that are crucial to most companies' global strategies.

In Procter & Gamble's European introduction of Vizir, the French company played an important contributing role by undertaking a second market test and later modifying the advertising approach. In the other launches during the first year, Austria, Spain, Holland, and Belgium were implementers; they took the defined strategy and made it work in their markets. Resisting any temptation to push for change in the formula, alteration of the package, or adjustment of the advertising theme, these national subsidiaries enabled P&G to extract profitable efficiencies.

THE BLACK HOLE.   Philips in Japan, Ericsson in the United States, and Matsushita in Germany are black holes. In each of these important markets, strong local presence is essential for maintaining the company's global position. And in each case, the local company hardly makes a dent.

The black hole is not an acceptable strategic position. Unlike the other roles we have described, the objective is not to manage it but to manage one's way out of it. But building a significant local presence in a national environment that is large, sophisticated, and competitive is extremely difficult, expensive, and time-consuming.

One common tack has been to create a sensory outpost in the black hole environment so as to exploit the learning potential, even if the local business potential is beyond reach. Many American and European companies have set up small establishments in Japan to monitor technologies, market trends, and competitors. Feedback to headquarters, so the thinking goes, will allow further analysis of the global implications of local developments and will at least help prevent erosion of the company's position in other markets. But this strategy has often been less fruitful than the company had hoped. Look at the case of Philips in Japan.

Although Philips had two manufacturing joint ventures with Matsushita, not until 1956 did it enter Japan by establishing a marketing organization. When Japan was emerging as a significant force in the consumer electronics market in the late 1960s, the company decided it had to get further into that market. After years of unsuccessfully trying to penetrate the captive distribution channels of the principal Japanese manufacturers, headquarters settled for a Japan "window" that would keep it informed of technical developments there. But results were disappointing. The reason, according to a senior manager of Philips in Japan, is that to sense effectively, eyes and ears are not enough. One must get "inside the bloodstream of the business," he said, with constant and direct access to distribution channels, component suppliers, and equipment manufacturers.

Detecting a new development after it has occurred is useless, for there is no time to play catch-up. One needs to know of developments as they emerge, and for that one must be a player, not a spectator. Moreover, being confined to window status, the local company is prevented from playing a strategic role. It is condemned to a permanent existence as a black hole.

So Philips is trying to get into the bloodstream of the Japanese market, moving away from the window concept and into the struggle for market share. The local organization now sees its task as winning market share rather than just monitoring local developments. But it is being very selective and focusing on areas where it has advantages over strong local competition. The Japanese unit started with coffee makers and electric shavers. Philips' acquisition of Marantz, a hi-fi equipment producer, gives it a bid to expand on its strategic base and build the internal capabilities that will enable the Japanese subsidiary to climb out of the black hole.

Another way to manage one's way out of the black hole is to develop a strategic alliance. Such coalitions can involve different levels of cooperation. Ericsson's joint venture with Honeywell in the United States and AT&T's with Philips in Europe are examples of attempts to fill up a black hole by obtaining resources and competence from a strong local organization in exchange for capabilities available elsewhere.

SHAPING, BUILDING, DIRECTING

Corporate management faces three big challenges in guiding the dispersion of responsibilities and differentiating subsidiaries' tasks. The first is in setting the strategic direction for the company by identifying its mission and its business objectives. The second is in building the differentiated organization, not only by designing the diverse roles and distributing the assignments but also by giving the managers responsible for filling them the legitimacy and power to do so. The final challenge is in directing the process to ensure that the several roles are coordinated and that the distributed responsibilities are controlled.

SETTING THE COURSE.   Any company (or any organization, for that matter) needs a strong, unifying sense of direction. But that need is particularly strong in an organization in which tasks are differentiated and responsibilities dispersed. Without it, the decentralized management process will quickly degenerate into strategic anarchy. A visitor to any NEC establishment in the world will see everywhere the company motto "C&C," which stands for computers and communications. This simple pairing of words is much more than a definition of NEC's product markets; top managers have made it the touchstone of a common global strategy. They emphasize it to focus the attention of employees on the key strategy of linking two technologies. And they employ it to help managers think how NEC can compete with larger companies like IBM and AT&T, which are perceived as vulnerable insofar as they lack a balance in the two technologies and markets.

Top management at NEC headquarters in Tokyo strives to inculcate its worldwide organization with an understanding of the C&C strategy and philosophy. It is this strong, shared understanding that permits greater differentiation of managerial processes and the decentralization of tasks.

But in addition to their role of developing and communicating a vision of the corporate mission, the top officers at headquarters also retain overall responsibility for the company's specific business strategies. While not abandoning this role at the heart of the company's strategic process, executives of many multinational companies are co-opting other parts of the organization (and particularly its diverse national organizations) into important business strategy roles, as we have already described. When it gives up its lead role, however, headquarters management always tracks that delegated responsibility.

BUILDING DIFFERENTIATION.   In determining which units should be given the lead, contributor, or follower roles, management must consider the motivational as well as the strategic impact of its decisions. If unfulfilled, the promise offered by the new organization model can be as demotivating as the symmetrical hierarchy, in which all foreign subsidiaries are assigned permanent secondary roles. For most national units, an organization in which lead and contributor roles are concentrated in a few favorite children represents little advance from old situations in which the parent dominated the decision making. In any units continually obliged to implement strategies developed elsewhere, skills atrophy, entrepreneurship dies, and any innovative spark that existed when it enjoyed more independence now sputters.

By dealing out lead or contributing roles to the smaller or less developed units, even if only for one or two strategically less important products, the headquarters group will give them a huge incentive. Although Philips N.V. had many other subsidiaries closer to large markets or with better access to corporate know-how and expertise, headquarters awarded the Taiwan unit the lead role in the small-screen monitor business. This vote of confidence gave the Taiwanese terrific motivation to do well and made them feel like a full contributing partner in the company's worldwide strategy.

But allocating roles isn't enough; the head office has to empower the units to exercise their voices in the organization by ensuring that those with lead positions particularly have access to and influence in the corporate decision-making process. This is not a trivial task, especially if strategic initiative and decision-making powers have long been concentrated at headquarters.

NEC discovered this truth about a decade ago when it was trying to transform itself into a global enterprise. Because NTT, the Japanese telephone authority, was dragging its feet in converting its exchanges to the new digital switching technology, NEC was forced to diverge from its custom of designing equipment mainly for its big domestic customer. The NEAC 61 digital switch was the first outgrowth of the policy shift; it was aimed primarily at the huge, newly deregulated U.S. telephone market.

Managers and engineers in Japan developed the product; the American subsidiary had little input. Although the hardware drew praise from customers, the switch had severe software deficiencies that hampered its penetration of the U.S. market.

Recognizing the need to change its administrative setup, top management committed publicly to becoming "a genuine world enterprise" rather than a Japanese company operating abroad. To permit the U.S. subsidiary a greater voice, headquarters helped it build a local software development capability. This plus the unit's growing knowledge about the Bell operating companies—NEC's target customers—gave the American managers legitimacy and power in Japan.

NEC's next-generation digital switch, the NEAC 61E, evolved quite differently. Exercising their new influence at headquarters, U.S. subsidiary managers took the lead in establishing its features and specifications and played a big part in the design.

Another path to empowerment takes the form of dislodging the decision-making process from the home office. Ericsson combats the headquarters hierarchy syndrome by appointing product and functional managers from headquarters to subsidiary boards. The give-and-take in board meetings is helpful for both subsidiary and parent. Matsushita holds an annual review of each major worldwide function (like manufacturing and human resource management) in the offices of a national subsidiary it considers to be a leading exponent of the particular function. In addition to the symbolic value for employees of the units, the siting obliges officials from Tokyo headquarters to consider issues that the front lines are experiencing and gives local managers the home-court advantage in seeking a voice in decision making.

Often the most effective means of giving strategy access and influence to national units is to create entirely new channels and forums. This approach permits roles, responsibilities, and relationships to be defined and developed with far less constraint than through modification of existing communication patterns or through shifting of responsibility boundaries. Procter & Gamble's Eurobrand teams are a case in point.

DIRECTING THE PROCESS. When the roles of operating units are differentiated and responsibility is more dispersed, corporate management must be prepared to deemphasize its direct control over the strategic content but develop an ability to manage the dispersed strategic process. Furthermore, headquarters must adopt a flexible administrative stance that allows it to differentiate the way it manages one subsidiary to the next and from business to business within a single unit, depending on the particular role it plays in each business.

In units with lead roles, headquarters plays an important role in ensuring that the business strategies developed fit the company's overall goals and priorities. But control in the classic sense is often quite loose. Corporate management's chief function is to support those with strategy leadership responsibility by giving them the resources and the freedom needed for the innovative and entrepreneurial role they have been asked to play.

With a unit placed in a contributor role, the head-office task is to redirect local resources to programs outside the unit's control. In so doing, it has to counter the natural hierarchy of loyalties that in most national organizations puts local interests above global ones. In such a situation, headquarters must be careful not to discourage the local managers and technicians so much that they stop contributing or leave in frustration. This has happened to many U.S. companies that have tried to manage their Canadian subsidiaries in a contributor role. Ericsson has solved the problem in its Australian subsidiary by attaching half the R&D team to headquarters, which farms out to these engineers projects that are part of the company's global development program.

The head office maintains tighter control over a subsidiary in an implementer role. Because such a group represents the company's opportunity to capture the benefits of scale and learning from which it gets and sustains its competitive advantage, headquarters stresses economy and efficiency in selling the products. Communication of strategies developed elsewhere and control of routine tasks can be carried out through systems, allowing headquarters to manage these units more efficiently than most others.

As for the black hole unit, the task for top executives is to develop its resources and capabilities to make it more responsive to its environment. Managers of these units depend heavily on headquarters for help and support, creating an urgent need for intensive training and transfer of skills and resources.

Firing the Spark Plugs

Multinational companies often build cumbersome and expensive infrastructures designed to control their widespread operations and to coordinate the diverse and often conflicting demands they make. As the coordination and control task expands, the typical headquarters organization becomes larger and more powerful, while the national subsidiaries are increasingly regarded as pipelines for centrally developed products and strategy.

But an international company enjoys a big advantage over a national one: It is exposed to a wider and more diverse range of environmental stimuli. The broader range of customer preferences, the wider spectrum of competitive behavior, the more serious array of government demands, and the more diverse sources of technological information represent potential triggers of innovation and thus a rich source of learning for the company. To capitalize on this advantage requires an organization that is sensitive to the environment and responsive in absorbing the information it gathers.

So national companies must not be regarded as just pipelines but recognized as sources of information and expertise that can build competitive advantage. The best way to exploit this resource is not through centralized direction and control but through a cooperative effort and co-option of dispersed capabilities. In such a relationship, the entrepreneurial spark plugs in the national units can flourish.

3
The Globalization of Markets

Theodore Levitt

A powerful force drives the world toward a converging commonality, and that force is technology. It has proletarianized communication, transport, and travel. It has made isolated places and impoverished peoples eager for modernity's allurements. Almost everyone everywhere wants all the things they have heard about, seen, or experienced via the new technologies.

The result is a new commercial reality—the emergence of global markets for standardized consumer products on a previously unimagined scale of magnitude. Corporations geared to this new reality benefit from enormous economies of scale in production, distribution, marketing, and management. By translating these benefits into reduced world prices, they can decimate competitors that still live in the disabling grip of old assumptions about how the world works.

Gone are accustomed differences in national or regional preference. Gone are the days when a company could sell last year's models—or lesser versions of advanced products—in the less-developed world. And gone are the days when prices, margins, and profits abroad were generally higher than at home.

The globalization of markets is at hand. With that, the multinational commercial world nears its end, and so does the multinational corporation.

The multinational and the global corporation are not the same thing. The multinational corporation operates in a number of countries, and adjusts its products and practices in each—at high relative costs. The global corporation operates with resolute constancy—at low relative cost—as if the entire world (or major regions of it) were a single entity; it sells the same things in the same way everywhere.

187

Which strategy is better is not a matter of opinion but of necessity. Worldwide communications carry everywhere the constant drumbeat of modern possibilities to lighten and enhance work, raise living standards, divert, and entertain. The same countries that ask the world to recognize and respect the individuality of their cultures insist on the wholesale transfer to them of modern goods, services, and technologies. Modernity is not just a wish but also a widespread practice among those who cling, with unyielding passion or religious fervor, to ancient attitudes and heritages.

Who can forget the televised scenes during the 1979 Iranian uprisings of young men in fashionable French-cut trousers and silky body shirts thirsting with raised modern weapons for blood in the name of Islamic fundamentalism?

In Brazil, thousands swarm daily from pre-industrial Bahian darkness into exploding coastal cities, there quickly to install television sets in crowded corrugated huts and, next to battered Volkswagens, make sacrificial offerings of fruit and fresh-killed chickens to Macumban spirits by candlelight.

During Biafra's fratricidal war against the Ibos, daily televised reports showed soldiers carrying bloodstained swords and listening to transistor radios while drinking Coca-Cola.

In the isolated Siberian city of Krasnoyarsk, with no paved streets and censored news, occasional Western travelers are stealthily propositioned for cigarettes, digital watches, and even the clothes off their backs.

The organized smuggling of electronic equipment, used automobiles, Western clothing, cosmetics, and pirated movies into primitive places exceeds even the thriving underground trade in modern weapons and their military mercenaries.

A thousand suggestive ways attest to the ubiquity of the desire for the most advanced things that the world makes and sells— goods of the best quality and reliability at the lowest price. The world's needs and desires have been irrevocably homogenized. This makes the multinational corporation obsolete and the global corporation absolute.

Living in the Republic of Technology

Daniel J. Boorstin, author of the monumental trilogy *The Americans,* characterized our age as driven by "the Republic of Technology [whose] supreme law . . . is convergence, the tendency for everything to become more like everything else."

In business, this trend has pushed markets toward global commonality. Corporations sell standardized products in the same way everywhere—autos, steel, chemicals, petroleum, cement, agricultural commodities and equipment, industrial and commercial construction, banking and insurance services, computers, semiconductors, transport, electronic instruments, pharmaceuticals, and telecommunications, to mention some of the obvious.

Nor is the sweeping gale of globalization confined to these raw material or high-tech products, where the universal language of customers and users facilitates standardization. The transforming winds whipped up by the proletarianization of communication and travel enter every crevice of life.

Commercially, nothing confirms this as much as the success of McDonald's from the Champs Elysées to the Ginza, of Coca-Cola in Bahrain and Pepsi-Cola in Moscow, and of rock music, Greek salad, Hollywood movies, Revlon cosmetics, Sony televisions, and Levi jeans everywhere. "High-touch" products are as ubiquitous as high-tech.

Starting from opposing sides, the high-tech and the high-touch ends of the commercial spectrum gradually consume the undistributed middle in their cosmopolitan orbit. No one is exempt and nothing can stop the process. Everywhere everything gets more and more like everything else as the world's preference structure is relentlessly homogenized.

Consider the cases of Coca-Cola and Pepsi-Cola, which are globally standardized products sold everywhere and welcomed by everyone. Both successfully cross multitudes of national, regional, and ethnic taste buds trained to a variety of deeply ingrained local preferences of taste, flavor, consistency, effervescence, and aftertaste. Everywhere both sell well. Cigarettes, too, especially American-made, make year-to-year global inroads on territories previously held in the firm grip of other, mostly local, blends.

These are not exceptional examples. (Indeed their global reach would be even greater were it not for artificial trade barriers.) They exemplify a general drift toward the homogenization of the world and how companies distribute, finance, and price products.[1] Nothing is exempt. The products and methods of the industrialized world play a single tune for all the world, and all the world eagerly dances to it.

Ancient differences in national tastes or modes of doing business disappear. The commonality of preference leads inescapably to the standardization of products, manufacturing, and the institutions of trade and commerce. Small nation-based markets transmogrify and expand. Success in world competition turns on efficiency in production, distribution, marketing, and management, and inevitably becomes focused on price.

The most effective world competitors incorporate superior quality and reliability into their cost structures. They sell in all national markets the same kind of products sold at home or in their largest export market. They compete on the basis of appropriate value— the best combinations of price, quality, reliability, and delivery for products that are globally identical with respect to design, function, and even fashion.

That, and little else, explains the surging success of Japanese companies dealing worldwide in a vast variety of products—both tangible products like steel, cars, motorcyles, hi-fi equipment, farm machinery, robots, microprocessors, carbon fibers, and now even textiles, and intangibles like banking, shipping, general contracting, and soon computer software. Nor are high-quality and low-cost operations incompatible, as a host of consulting organizations and data engineers argue with vigorous vacuity. The reported data are incomplete, wrongly analyzed, and contradictory. The truth is that low-cost operations are the hallmark of corporate cultures that require and produce quality in all that they do. High quality and low costs are not opposing postures. They are compatible, twin identities of superior practice.[2]

To say that Japan's companies are not global because they export cars with left-side drives to the United States and the European continent, while those in Japan have right-side drives, or because they sell office machines through distributors in the United States but directly at home, or speak Portuguese in Brazil is to mistake a difference for a distinction. The same is true of Safeway and Southland retail chains operating effectively in the Middle East, and to not only native but also imported populations from Korea, the Philippines, Pakistan, India, Thailand, Britain, and the United States. National rules of the road differ, and so do distribution channels and languages. Japan's distinction is its unrelenting push for economy and value enhancement. That translates into a drive for standardization at high quality levels.

VINDICATION OF THE MODEL T

If a company forces costs and prices down and pushes quality and reliability up—while maintaining reasonable concern for suitability—customers will prefer its world-standardized products. The theory holds, at this stage in the evolution of globalization, no matter what conventional market research and even common sense may suggest about different national and regional tastes, preferences, needs, and institutions. The Japanese have repeatedly vindicated this theory, as did Henry Ford with the Model T. Most important, so have their imitators, including companies from South Korea (television sets and heavy construction), Malaysia (personal calculators and microcomputers), Brazil (auto parts and tools), Colombia (apparel), Singapore (optical equipment), and yes, even from the United States (office copiers, computers, bicycles, castings), Western Europe (automatic washing machines), Rumania (housewares), Hungary (apparel), Yugoslavia (furniture), and Israel (pagination equipment).

Of course, large companies operating in a single nation or even a single city don't standardize everything they make, sell, or do. They have product lines instead of a single product version, and multiple distribution channels. There are neighborhood, local, regional, ethnic, and institutional differences, even within metropolitan areas. But although companies customize products for particular market segments, they know that success in a world with homogenized demand requires a search for sales opportunities in similar segments across the globe in order to achieve the economies of scale necessary to compete.

Such a search works because a market segment in one country is seldom unique; it has close cousins everywhere precisely because technology has homogenized the globe. Even small local segments have their global equivalents everywhere and become subject to global competition, especially on price.

The global competitor will seek constantly to standardize its offering everywhere. It will digress from this standardization only after exhausting all possibilities to retain it, and it will push for reinstatement of standardization whenever digression and divergence have occurred. It will never assume that the customer is a king who knows his or her own wishes.

Trouble increasingly stalks companies that lack clarified global focus and remain inattentive to the economics of simplicity and standardization. The most endangered companies in the rapidly evolving world tend to be those that dominate rather small domestic markets with high value-added products for which there are smaller markets elsewhere. With transportation costs proportionately low, distant competitors will enter the now-sheltered markets of those companies with goods produced more cheaply under scale-efficient conditions. Global competition spells the end of domestic territoriality, no matter how diminutive the territory may be.

When the global producer offers his lower costs internationally, his patronage expands exponentially. He not only reaches into distant markets, but also attracts customers who previously held to local preferences and now capitulate to the attractions of lesser prices. The strategy of standardization not only responds to world-wide homogenized markets but also expands those markets with aggressive low pricing. The new technological juggernaut taps an ancient motivation—to make one's money go as far as possible. This is universal—not simply a motivation but actually a need.

The Hedgehog Knows

The difference between the hedgehog and the fox, wrote Sir Isaiah Berlin in distinguishing between Dostoevski and Tolstoy, is that the fox knows a lot about a great many things, but the hedgehog knows everything about one great thing. The multinational corporation knows a lot about a great many countries and congenially adapts to supposed differences. It willingly accepts vestigial national differences, not questioning the possibility of their transformation, not recognizing how the world is ready and eager for the benefit of modernity, especially when the price is right. The multinational corporation's accommodating mode to visible national differences is medieval.

By contrast, the global corporation knows everything about one great thing. It knows about the absolute need to be competitive on a worldwide basis as well as nationally and seeks constantly to drive down prices by standardizing what it sells and how it operates. It treats the world as composed of few standardized markets rather than many customized markets. It actively seeks and vigorously works toward global convergence. Its mission is modernity and its mode, price competition, even when it sells top-of-the-line, high-end products. It knows about the one great thing all nations and people have in common: scarcity.

Nobody takes scarcity lying down; everyone wants more. This in part explains division of labor and specialization of production. They enable people and nations to optimize their conditions through trade. The median is usually money.

Experience teaches that money has three special qualities: scarcity, difficulty of acquisition, and transience. People understandably treat it with respect. Everyone in the increasingly homogenized world market wants products and features that everybody else wants. If the price is low enough, they will take highly standardized world products, even if these aren't exactly what mother said was suitable, what immemorial custom decreed was right, or what market-research fabulists asserted was preferred.

The implacable truth of all modern production—whether of tangible or intangible goods—is that large-scale production of standardized items is generally cheaper within a wide range of volume than small-scale production. Some argue that CAD/CAM will allow companies to manufacture customized products on a small scale— but cheaply. But the argument misses the point. If a company treats the world as one or two distinctive product markets, it can serve the world more economically than if it treats it as three, four, or five product markets.

WHY REMAINING DIFFERENCES?

Different cultural preferences, national tastes and standards, and business institutions are vestiges of the past. Some inheritances die gradually; others prosper and expand into mainstream global preferences. So-called ethnic markets are a good example. Chinese food, pita bread, country and western music, pizza, and jazz are everywhere. They are market segments that exist in worldwide proportions. They don't deny or contradict global homogenization but confirm it.

Many of today's differences among nations as to products and their features actually reflect the respectful accommodation of multinational corporations to what they believe are fixed local preferences. They *believe* preferences are fixed, not because they are but because of rigid habits of thinking about what actually is. Most executives in multinational corporations are thoughtlessly accommodating. They falsely presume that marketing means giving the customer what he says he wants rather than trying to understand exactly what he'd like. So they persist with high-cost, customized multinational products and practices instead of pressing hard and pressing properly for global standardization.

I do not advocate the systematic disregard of local or national differences. But a company's sensitivity to such differences does not require that it ignore the possibilities of doing things differently or better.

There are, for example, enormous differences among Middle Eastern countries. Some are socialist, some monarchies, some republics. Some take their legal heritage from the Napoleonic Code, some from the Ottoman Empire, and some from the British common law; except for Israel, all are influenced by Islam. Doing business means personalizing the business relationship in an obsessively intimate fashion. During the month of Ramadan, business discussions can start only after 10 o'clock at night, when people are tired and full of food after a day of fasting. A company must almost certainly have a local partner; a local lawyer is required (as, say, in New York), and irrevocable letters of credit are essential. Yet, as Coca-Cola's Senior Vice President Sam Ayoub noted, "Arabs are much more capable of making distinctions between cultural and religious purposes on the one hand and economic realities on the other than is generally assumed. Islam is compatible with science and modern times."

Barriers to globalization are not confined to the Middle East. The free transfer of technology and data across the boundaries of the European Common Market countries are hampered by legal and financial impediments. And there is resistance to radio and television interference ("pollution") among neighboring European countries.

But the past is a good guide to the future. With persistence and appropriate means, barriers against superior technologies and economics have always fallen. There is no recorded exception where reasonable effort has been made to overcome them. It is very much a matter of time and effort.

A Failure in Global Imagination

Many companies have tried to standardize world practice by exporting domestic products and processes without accommodation or change—and have failed miserably. Their deficiencies have been seized on as evidence of bovine stupidity in the face of abject impossibility. Advocates of global standardization see them as examples of failures in execution.

In fact, poor execution is often an important cause. More important, however, is failure of nerve—failure of imagination.

Consider the case for the introduction of fully automatic home laundry equipment in Western Europe at a time when few homes had even semiautomatic machines. Hoover, Ltd., whose parent company was headquartered in North Canton, Ohio, had a prominent presence in Britain as a producer of vacuum cleaners and washing machines. Because of insufficient demand in the home market and low exports to the European continent, the large washing machine plant in England operated far below capacity. The company needed to sell more of its semiautomatic or automatic machines.

Because it had a "proper" marketing orientation, Hoover conducted consumer preference studies in Britain and each major continental country. The results showed feature preferences clearly enough among several countries (see Exhibit I).

The incremental unit variable costs (in pounds sterling) of customizing to meet just a few of the national preferences were:

	£	s.	d.
Stainless steel vs. enamel drum	1	0	0
Porthole window		10	0
Spin speed of 800 rpm vs. 700 rpm		15	0
Water heater	2	15	0
6 vs. 5 kilos capacity	1	10	0
	£6	10s	0d

$18.20 at the exchange
rate of that time.

Considerable plant investment was needed to meet other preferences.

The lowest retail prices (in pounds sterling) of leading locally produced brands in the various countries were approximately:

U.K.	£110
France	114
West Germany	113
Sweden	134
Italy	57

Exhibit I.　Consumer Preferences as to Automatic Washing Machine Features in the 1960s

Features	Great Britain	Italy	West Germany	France	Sweden
Shell dimensions*	34" and narrow	Low and narrow	34" and wide	34" and narrow	34" and wide
Drum material	Enamel	Enamel	Stainless steel	Enamel	Stainless steel
Loading	Top	Front	Front	Front	Front
Front porthole	Yes/no	Yes	Yes	Yes	Yes
Capacity	5 kilos	4 kilos	6 kilos	5 kilos	6 kilos
Spin speed	700 rpm	400 rpm	850 rpm	600 rpm	800 rpm
Water-heating system	No†	Yes	Yes††	Yes	No†
Washing action	Agitator	Tumble	Tumble	Agitator	Tumble
Styling features	Inconspicuous appearance	Brightly colored	Indestructible appearance	Elegant appearance	Strong appearance

*34" height was (in the process of being adopted as) a standard work-surface height in Europe.

†Most British and Swedish homes had centrally heated hot water.

††West Germans preferred to launder at temperatures higher than generally provided centrally.

Product customization in each country would have put Hoover in a poor competitive position on the basis of price, mostly due to the higher manufacturing costs incurred by short production runs for separate features. Because Common Market tariff reduction programs were then incomplete, Hoover also paid tariff duties in each continental country.

HOW TO MAKE A CREATIVE ANALYSIS

In the Hoover case, an imaginative analysis of automatic washing machine sales in each country would have revealed that:

1. Italian automatics, small in capacity and size, low-powered, without built-in heaters, with porcelain enamel tubs, were priced aggressively low and were gaining large market shares in all countries, including West Germany.
2. The best-selling automatics in West Germany were heavily advertised (three times more than the next most promoted brand), were ideally suited to national tastes, and were also by far the highest priced machines available in that country.
3. Italy, with the lowest penetration of washing machines of any kind (manual, semiautomatic, or automatic) was rapidly going directly to automatics, skipping the pattern of first buying hand-wringer, manually assisted machines and then semiautomatics.
4. Detergent manufacturers were just beginning to promote the technique of cold-water and tepid-water laundering then used in the United States.

The growing success of small, low-powered, low-speed, low-capacity, low-priced Italian machines, even against the preferred but highly priced and highly promoted brand in West Germany, was significant. It contained a powerful message that was lost on managers confidently wedded to a distorted version of the marketing concept according to which you give the customer what he says he wants. In fact the customers *said* they wanted certain features, but their behavior demonstrated they'd take other features provided the price and the promotion were right.

In this case it was obvious that, under prevailing conditions, people preferred a low-priced automatic over any kind of manual or semiautomatic machine and certainly over higher-priced automatics, even though the low-priced automatics failed to fulfill all their expressed preferences. The supposedly meticulous and demanding German consumers violated all expectations by buying the simple, low-priced Italian machines.

It was equally clear that people were profoundly influenced by promotions of automatic washers; in West Germany, the most heavily promoted ideal machine also had the largest market share despite its high price. Two things clearly influenced customers to buy: low price regardless of feature preferences and heavy promotion regardless of price. Both factors helped homemakers get what they most wanted—the superior benefits bestowed by fully automatic machines.

Hoover should have aggressively sold a simple, standardized high-quality machine at a low price (afforded by the 17% variable cost reduction that the elimination of £6-10-0 worth of extra features made possible). The suggested retail prices could have been somewhat less than £100. The extra funds "saved" by avoiding unnecessary plant modifications would have supported an extended service network and aggressive media promotions.

Hoover's media message should have been: *This* is the machine that you, the homemaker, *deserve* to have to reduce the repetitive heavy daily household burdens, so that you may have more constructive time to spend with your children and your husband. The promotion should also have targeted the husband to give him, preferably in the presence of his wife, a sense of obligation to provide an automatic washer for her even before he bought an automobile for himself. An aggressively low price, combined with heavy promotion of this kind, would have overcome previously expressed preferences for particular features.

The Hoover case illustrates how the perverse practice of the marketing concept and the absence of any kind of marketing imagination let multinational attitudes survive when customers actually want the benefits of global standardization. The whole project got off on the wrong foot. It asked people what features they wanted in a washing machine rather than what they wanted out of life. Selling a line of products individually tailored to each nation is thoughtless. Managers who took pride in practicing the marketing concept to the fullest did not, in fact, practice it at all. Hoover asked the wrong questions, then applied neither thought nor imagination to the answers. Such companies are like the ethnocentricists in the Middle Ages who saw with everyday clarity the sun revolving around the earth and offered it as Truth. With no additional data but a more searching mind, Copernicus, like the hedgehog, interpreted a more compelling and accurate reality. Data do not yield information except with the intervention of the mind. Information does not yield meaning except with the intervention of imagination.

Accepting the Inevitable

The global corporation accepts for better or for worse that technology drives consumers relentlessly toward the same common goals—alleviation of life's burdens and the expansion of discretionary time and spending power. Its role is profoundly different from what it has been for the ordinary corporation during its brief, turbulent, and remarkably protean history. It orchestrates the twin vectors of technology and globalization for the world's benefit. Neither fate, nor nature, nor God but rather the necessity of commerce created this role.

In the United States two industries became global long before they were consciously aware of it. After over a generation of persistent and acrimonious labor shutdowns, the United Steelworkers of America have not called an industrywide strike since 1959; the United Auto Workers have not shut down General Motors since 1970. Both unions realize that they have become global—shutting down all or most of U.S. manufacturing would not shut out U.S. customers. Overseas suppliers are there to supply the market.

CRACKING THE CODE OF WESTERN MARKETS

Since the theory of the marketing concept emerged a quarter of a century ago, the more managerially advanced corporations have been eager to offer what customers clearly wanted rather than what was merely convenient. They have created marketing departments supported by professional market researchers of awesome and often costly proportions. And they have proliferated extraordinary numbers of operations and product lines—highly tailored products and delivery systems for many different markets, market segments, and nations.

Significantly, Japanese companies operate almost entirely without marketing departments or market research of the kind so prevalent in the West. Yet, in the colorful words of General Electric's chairman John F. Welch, Jr., the Japanese, coming from a small cluster of resource-poor islands, with an entirely alien culture and an almost impenetrably complex language, have cracked the code of Western markets. They have done it not by looking with mechanistic thoroughness at the way markets are different but rather by searching for meaning with a deeper wisdom. They have discovered the one great thing all markets have in common—an overwhelming desire for dependable, world-standard modernity in all things, at aggressively low prices. In response, they deliver irresistible value everywhere, attracting people with products that market-research technocrats described with superficial certainty as being unsuitable and uncompetitive.

The wider a company's global reach, the greater the number of regional and national preferences it will encounter for certain product features, distribution systems, or promotional media. There will always need to be some accommodation to differences. But the widely prevailing and often unthinking belief in the immutability of these differences is generally mistaken. Evidence of business failure because of lack of accommodation is often evidence of other shortcomings.

Take the case of Revlon in Japan. The company unnecessarily alienated retailers and confused customers by selling world-standardized cosmetics only in elite outlets; then it tried to recover with low-priced world-standardized products in broader distribution, followed by a change in the company president and cutbacks in distribution as costs rose faster than sales. The problem was not that Revlon didn't understand the Japanese market; it didn't do the job right, wavered in its programs, and was impatient to boot.

By contrast, the Outboard Marine Corporation, with imagination, push, and persistence, collapsed long-established three-tiered distribution channels in Europe into a more focused and controllable two-step system—and did so despite the vociferous warnings of local trade groups. It also reduced the number and types of retail outlets. The result was greater improvement in credit and product-installation service to customers, major cost reductions, and sales advances.

In its highly successful introduction of Contac 600 (the timed-release decongestant) into Japan, SmithKline Corporation used 35 wholesalers instead of the 1,000-plus that established practice required. Daily contacts with the wholesalers and key retailers, also in violation of established practice, supplemented the plan, and it worked.

Denied access to established distribution institutions in the United States, Komatsu, the Japanese manufacturer of lightweight farm machinery, entered the market through over-the-road construction equipment dealers in rural areas of the Sunbelt, where farms are smaller, the soil sandier and easier to work. Here inexperienced distributors were able to attract customers on the basis of Komatsu's product and price appropriateness.

In cases of successful challenge to prevailing institutions and practices, a combination of product reliability and quality, strong and sustained support systems, aggressively low prices, and sales-compensation packages, as well as audacity and implacability, circumvented, shattered, and transformed very different distribution systems. Instead of resentment, there was admiration.

Still, some differences between nations are unyielding, even in a world of microprocessors. In the United States almost all manufacturers of microprocessors check them for reliability through a so-called parallel system of testing. Japan prefers the totally different sequential testing system. So Teradyne Corporation, the world's largest producer of microprocessor test equipment, makes one line for the United States and one for Japan. That's easy.

What's not so easy for Teradyne is to know how best to organize and manage, in this instance, its marketing effort. Companies can organize by product, region, function, or by using some combination of these. A company can have separate marketing organizations for Japan and for the United States, or it can have separate product groups, one working largely in Japan and the other in the United States. A single manufacturing facility or marketing operation might service both markets, or a company might use separate marketing operations for each.

Questions arise if the company organizes by product. In the case of Teradyne, should the group handling the parallel system, whose major market is the United States, sell in Japan and compete with the group focused on the Japanese market? If the company organizes regionally, how do regional groups divide their efforts between promoting the parallel versus the sequential system? If the company organizes in terms of function, how does it get commitment in marketing, for example, for one line instead of the other?

There is no one reliably right answer—no one formula by which to get it. There isn't even a satisfactory contingent answer.[3] What works well for one company or one place may fail for another in precisely the same place, depending on the capabilities, histories, reputations, resources, and even the cultures of both.

The Earth Is Flat

The differences that persist throughout the world despite its globalization affirm an ancient dictum of economics—that things are driven by what happens at the margin, not at the core. Thus, in ordinary competitive analysis, what's important is not the average price but the marginal price; what happens not in the usual case but at the interface of newly erupting conditions. What counts in commercial affairs is what happens at the cutting edge. What is most striking today is the underlying similarities of what is happening now to national preferences at the margin. These similarities at the cutting edge cumulatively form an overwhelming, predominant commonality everywhere.

To refer to the persistence of economic nationalism (protective and subsidized trade practices, special tax aids, or restrictions for home market producers) as a barrier to the globalization of markets is to make a valid point. Economic nationalism does have a powerful persistence. But, as with the present almost totally smooth internationalization of investment capital, the past alone does not shape or predict the future.

Reality is not a fixed paradigm, dominated by immemorial customs and derived attitudes, heedless of powerful and abundant new forces. The world is becoming increasingly informed about the liberating and enhancing possibilities of modernity. The persistence of the inherited varieties of national preferences rests uneasily on increasing evidence of, and restlessness regarding, their inefficiency, costliness, and confinement. The historic past, and the national differences respecting commerce and industry it spawned and fostered everywhere, is now subject to relatively easy transformation.

Cosmopolitanism is no longer the monopoly of the intellectual and leisure classes; it is becoming the established property and defining characteristic of all sectors everywhere in the world. Gradually and irresistibly it breaks down the walls of economic insularity, nationalism, and chauvinism. What we see today as escalating commercial nationalism is simply the last violent death rattle of an obsolete institution.

Companies that adapt to and capitalize on economic convergence can still make distinctions and adjustments in different markets. Persistent differences in the world are consistent with fundamental underlying commonalities; they often complement rather than oppose each other—in business as they do in physics. There is, in physics, simultaneously matter and antimatter working in symbiotic harmony.

The earth is round, but for most purposes it's sensible to treat it as flat. Space is curved, but not much for everyday life here on earth.

Divergence from established practice happens all the time. But the multinational mind, warped into circumspection and timidity by years of stumbles and transnational troubles, now rarely challenges existing overseas practices. More often it considers any departure from inherited domestic routines as mindless, disrespectful, or impossible. It is the mind of a bygone day.

The successful global corporation does not abjure customization or differentiation for the requirements of markets that differ in product preferences, spending patterns, shopping preferences, and institutional or legal arrangements. But the global corporation accepts and adjusts to these differences only reluctantly, only after relentlessly testing their immutability, after trying in various ways to circumvent and reshape them as we saw in the cases of Outboard Marine in Europe, SmithKline in Japan, and Komatsu in the United States.

There is only one significant respect in which a company's activities around the world are important, and this is in what it produces and how it sells. Everything else derives from, and is subsidiary to, these activities.

The purpose of business is to get and keep a customer. Or, to use Peter Drucker's more refined construction, to *create* and keep a customer. A company must be wedded to the ideal of innovation—offering better or more preferred products in such combinations of ways, means, places, and at such prices that prospects *prefer* doing business with the company rather than with others.

Preferences are constantly shaped and reshaped. Within our global commonality enormous variety constantly asserts itself and thrives, as can be seen within the world's single largest domestic market, the United States. But in the process of world homogenization, modern markets expand to reach cost-reducing global proportions. With better and cheaper communication and transport, even small local market segments hitherto protected from distant competitors now feel the pressure of their presence. Nobody is safe from global reach and the irresistible economies of scale.

Two vectors shape the world—technology and globalization. The first helps determine human preferences; the second, economic realities. Regardless of how much preferences evolve and diverge, they also gradually converge and form markets where economies of scale lead to reduction of costs and prices.

The modern global corporation contrasts powerfully with the aging multinational corporation. Instead of adapting to superficial and even entrenched differences within and between nations, it will seek sensibly to force suitably standardized products and practices on the entire globe. They are exactly what the world will take, if they come also with low prices, high quality, and blessed reliability. The global company will operate, in this regard, precisely as Henry Kissinger wrote in *Years of Upheaval* about the continuing Japanese economic success—"voracious in its collection of information, impervious to pressure, and implacable in execution."

Given what is everywhere the purpose of commerce, the global company will shape the vectors of technology and globalization into its great strategic fecundity. It will systematically push these vectors toward their own convergence, offering everyone simultaneously high-quality, more or less standardized products at optimally low prices, thereby achieving for itself vastly expanded markets and profits. Companies that do not adapt to the new global realities will become victims of those that do.

Notes

1. In a landmark article, Robert D. Buzell pointed out the rapidity with which barriers to standardization were falling. In all cases they succumbed to more and cheaper advanced ways of doing things. See "Can You Standardize Multinational Marketing?," *Harvard Business Review* (November–December 1968), p. 102.

2. There is powerful new evidence for this, even though the opposite has been urged by analysis of PIMS data for nearly a decade. See "Product Quality: Cost Production and Business Performance—A Test of Some Key Hypotheses" by Lynn W. Phillips, Dae Chang, and Robert D. Buzzell, Harvard Business School Working Paper No. 83–13.

3. For a discussion of multinational reorganization, see Christopher A. Bartlett, "MNCs: Get Off the Reorganization Merry-Go Round," *Harvard Business Review* (March–April 1983), p. 138.

4
Managing in a Borderless World

Kenichi Ohmae

Most managers are nearsighted. Even though today's competitive landscape often stretches to a global horizon, they see best what they know best: the customers geographically closest to home. These managers may have factories or laboratories in a dozen countries. They may have joint ventures in a dozen more. They may source materials and sell in markets all over the world. But when push comes to shove, their field of vision is dominated by home-country customers and the organizational units that serve them. Everyone—and everything—else is simply part of "the rest of the world."

This nearsightedness is not intentional. No responsible manager purposefully devises or implements an astigmatic strategy. But by the same token, too few managers consciously try to set plans and build organizations as if they saw all key customers equidistant from the corporate center. Whatever the trade figures show, home markets are usually in focus; overseas markets are not.

Effective global operations require a genuine equidistance of perspective. But even with the best will in the world, managers find that kind of vision hard to develop—and harder to maintain. Not long ago, the CEO of a major Japanese capital-goods producer canceled several important meetings to attend the funeral of one of his company's local dealers. When I asked him if he would have done the same for a Belgian dealer, one who did a larger volume of business each year than his late counterpart in Japan, the unequivocal answer was no. Perhaps headquarters would have had the relevant European manager send a letter of condolence. No more than that. In Japan, however, tradition dictated the CEO's presence. But Japanese tradition isn't everything, I reminded him.

After all, he was the head of a global, not just a Japanese organization. By violating the principle of equidistance, his attendance underscored distinctions among dealers. He was sending the wrong signals and reinforcing the wrong values. Poor vision has consequences.

It may be unfamiliar and awkward, but the primary rule of equidistance is to see—and to think—global first. Honda, for example, has manufacturing divisions in Japan, North America, and Europe—all three legs of the Triad—but its managers do not think or act as if the company were divided between Japanese and overseas operations. Indeed, the very word "overseas" has no place in Honda's vocabulary because the corporation sees itself as equidistant from all its key customers. At Casio, the top managers gather information directly from each of their primary markets and then sit down together once a month to lay out revised plans for global product development.

There is no single best way to avoid or overcome nearsightedness. An equidistant perspective can take many forms. However managers do it, however they get there, building a value system that emphasizes seeing and thinking globally is the bottom-line price of admission to today's borderless economy.

A Geography Without Borders

On a political map, the boundaries between countries are as clear as ever. But on a competitive map, a map showing the real flows of financial and industrial activity, those boundaries have largely disappeared. What has eaten them away is the persistent, ever-speedier flow of information—information that governments previously monopolized, cooking it up as they saw fit and redistributing in forms of their own devising. Their monopoly of knowledge about things happening around the world enabled them to fool, mislead, or control the people because only the governments possessed real facts in anything like real time.

Today, of course, people everywhere are more and more able to get the information they want directly from all corners of the world. They can see for themselves what the tastes and preferences are in other countries, the styles of clothing now in fashion, the sports, the lifestyles. In Japan, for example, our leaders can no longer keep the people in substandard housing because we now know—

directly—how people elsewhere live. We now travel abroad. In fact, ten million Japanese travel abroad annually these days. Or we can sit in our living rooms at home, watch CNN, and know instantaneously what is happening in the United States. During 1988, nearly 90% of all Japanese honeymooners went abroad. This kind of fact is hard to ignore. The government now seriously recognizes that it has built plants and offices but has failed to meet the needs of its young people for relaxation and recreation. So, for the first time in 2,000 years, our people are revolting against their government and telling it what it must do for them. This would have been unthinkable when only a small, official elite controlled access to all information.

In the past, there were gross inefficiencies—some purposeful, some not—in the flow of information around the world. New technologies are eliminating those inefficiencies, and, with them, the opportunity for a kind of top-down information arbitrage—that is, the ability of a government to benefit itself or powerful special interests at the expense of its people by following policies that would never win their support if they had unfettered access to all relevant information. A government could, for example, protect weak industries for fear of provoking social unrest over unemployment. That is less easy to do now, for more of its people have become cosmopolitan and have their own sources of information. They know what such a policy would cost them.

In Korea, students demonstrate in front of the American embassy because the government allows the United States to export cigarettes to Korea and thus threaten local farmers. That's what happens when per capita GNP runs in the neighborhood of $5,000 a year and governments can still control the flow of information and mislead their people. When GNP gets up to around $10,000 a year, religion becomes a declining industry. So does government.

At $26,000 a year, where Japan is now, things are really different. People want to buy the best and the cheapest products—no matter where in the world they are produced. People become genuinely global consumers. We import beef and oranges from the United States, and everyone thinks it's great. Ten years ago, however, our students would have been the ones throwing stones at the American embassy. Our leaders used to tell us American and Australian beef was too lean and too tough to chew. But we've been there and tasted it and know for ourselves that it is cheap and good.

Through this flow of information, we've become global citizens, and so must the companies that want to sell us things. Black-and-white television sets extensively penetrated households in the United States nearly a dozen years before they reached comparable numbers of viewers in Europe and Japan. With color television, the time lag fell to about five or six years for Japan and a few more for Europe. With videocassette recorders, the difference was only three or four years—but this time, Europe and Japan led the way; the United States, with its focus on cable TV, followed. With the compact disk, household penetration rates evened up after only one year. Now, with MTV available by satellite across Europe, there is no lag at all. New music, styles, and fashion reach all European youngsters almost at the same time they are reaching their counterparts in America. We all share the same information.

More than that, we are all coming to share it in a common language. Ten years ago when I would speak in English to students at Bocconi, an Italian university, most of them would listen to me through a translator. Last year, they listened to me directly in English and asked me questions in English. (They even laughed when they should at what I said, although my jokes have not improved.) This is a momentous change. The preparation for 1992 has taken place in language much sooner than it has in politics. We can all talk to each other now, understand each other, and governments cannot stop us. "Global citizenship" is no longer just a nice phrase in the lexicon of rosy futurologists. It is every bit as real and concrete as measurable changes in GNP or trade flows. It is actually coming to pass.

The same is true for corporations. In the pharmaceutical industry, for example, the critical activities of drug discovery, screening, and testing are now virtually the same among the best companies everywhere in the world. Scientists can move from one laboratory to another and start working the next day with few hesitations or problems. They will find equipment with which they are familiar, equipment they have used before, equipment that comes from the same manufacturers.

The drug companies are not alone in this. Most people, for example, believed that it would be a very long time before Korean companies could produce state-of-the-art semiconductor chips—things like 256K NMOS DRAMs. Not so. They caught up with the rest of the Triad in only a few short years. In Japan, not that long ago, a common joke among the chip-making fraternity had to do with the "Friday Express." The Japanese engineers working for different companies on Kyushu, Japan's southwestern "Silicon Island" only 100 km or so away from Korea, would catch a late flight to Korea on Friday evenings. During the weekend, they would work privately for Korean semiconductor companies. This was illegal, of course, and violated the engineers' employment agreements in Japan. Nonetheless, so many took the flight that they had a tacit gentleman's agreement not to greet or openly recognize each other on the plane. Their trip would have made no sense, however, if semiconductor-related machines, methods, software, and workstations had not already become quite similar throughout the developed world.

Walk into a capital-goods factory anywhere in the developed world, and you will find the same welding machines, the same robots, the same machine tools. When information flows with relative freedom, the old geographic barriers become irrelevant. Global needs lead to global products. For managers, this universal flow of information puts a high premium on learning how to build the strategies and the organizations capable of meeting the requirements of a borderless world.

What Is a Universal Product?

Imagine that you are the CEO of a major automobile company reviewing your product plans for the years ahead. Your market data tell you that you will have to develop four dozen different models if you want to design separate cars for each distinct segment of the Triad market. But you don't have enough world-class engineers to design so many models. You don't have enough managerial talent or enough money. No one does. Worse, there is no single "global" car that will solve your problems for you. America, Europe, and Japan are quite different markets with quite different mixes of needs and preferences. Worse still, as head of a worldwide company, you cannot write off any of these Triad markets. You simply have to be in each of them—and with first-rate successful products. What do you do?

If you are the CEO of Nissan, you first look at the Triad region by region and identify each market's dominant requirements. In the United Kingdom, for example, tax policies make it essential that you develop a car suitable for corporate fleet sales. In the

United States, you need a sporty "Z" model as well as a four-wheel drive family vehicle. Each of these categories is what Nissan's president, Yutaka Kume, calls a "lead country" model—a product carefully tailored to the dominant and distinct needs of individual national markets. Once you have your short list of "lead-country" models in hand, you can ask your top managers in other parts of the Triad whether minor changes can make any of them suitable for local sales. But you start with the lead-country models.

"With this kind of thinking," says Mr. Kume, "we have been able to halve the number of basic models needed to cover the global markets and, at the same time, to cover 80% of our sales with cars designed for specific national markets. Not to miss the remaining 20%, however, we also provided each country manager with a range of additional model types that could be adapted to the needs of local segments. This approach," Mr. Kume reports, "allowed us to focus our resources on each of our largest core markets and, at the same time, provide a pool of supplemental designs that could be adapted to local preferences. We told our engineers to 'be American,' 'be European,' or 'be Japanese.' If the Japanese happened to like something we tailored for the American market, so much the better. Low-cost, incremental sales never hurt. Our main challenge, however, was to avoid the trap of pleasing no one well by trying to please everyone halfway."

Imagine, instead, if Nissan had taken its core team of engineers and designers in Japan and asked them to design only global cars, cars that would sell all over the world. Their only possible response would have been to add up all the various national preferences and divide by the number of countries. They would have had to optimize across markets by a kind of rough averaging. But when it comes to questions of taste and, especially, aesthetic preference, consumers do not like averages. They like what they like, not some mathematical compromise. Kume is emphatic about this particular point. "Our success in the U.S. with Maxima, 240 SX, and Pathfinder—all designed for the American market—shows our approach to be right."

In high school physics, I remember learning about a phenomenon called diminishing primaries. If you mix together the primary colors of red, blue, and yellow, what you get is black. If Europe says its consumers want a product in green, let them have it. If Japan says red, let them have red. No one wants the average. No one wants the colors all mixed together. Of course it makes sense to take advantage of, say, any technological commonalities in creating the paint. But local managers close to local customers have to be able to pick the color.

When it comes to product strategy, managing in a borderless world doesn't mean managing by averages. It doesn't mean that all tastes run together into one amorphous mass of universal appeal. And it doesn't mean that the appeal of operating globally removes the obligation to localize products. The lure of a universal product is a false allure. The truth is a bit more subtle.

Although the needs and tastes of the Triad markets vary considerably, there may well be market segments of different sizes in each part of the Triad that share many of the same preferences. In the hair-care market, for instance, Japanese companies know a lot more about certain kinds of black hair, which is hard and thick, than about blond or brown hair, which is often soft and thin. As a result, they have been able to capture a few segments of the U.S. market in, say, shampoos. That makes a nice addition to their sales, of course. But it does not position them to make inroads into the mainstream segments of that market.

Back to the automobile example: There is a small but identifiable group of Japanese consumers who want a "Z" model car like the one much in demand in the United States. Fair enough. During the peak season, Nissan sells about 5,000 "Z" cars a month in the United States and only 500 in Japan. Those 500 cars make a nice addition, of course, generating additional revenue and expanding the perceived richness of a local dealer's portfolio. But they are not—and cannot be—the mainstay of such portfolios.

There is no universal "montage" car—a rear axle from Japan, a braking system from Italy, a drive train from the United States—that will quicken pulses on all continents. Remember the way the tabloids used to cover major beauty contests? They would create a composite picture using the best features from all of the most beautiful entrants—this one's nose, that one's mouth, the other one's forehead. Ironically, the portrait that emerged was never very appealing. It always seemed odd, a bit off, lacking in distinctive character. But there will always be beauty judges—and car buyers—in, say, Europe, who, though more used to continental standards, find a special attractiveness in the features of a Japanese or a Latin American. Again, so much the better.

For some kinds of products, however, the kind of globalization that Ted Levitt talks about makes excellent sense. One of the most obvious is, oddly enough, battery-powered products like cameras, watches, and pocket calculators. These are all part of the "Japan game"—that is, they come from industries dominated by Japanese electronics companies. What makes these products successful across the Triad? Popular prices, for one thing, based on aggressive cost reduction and global economies of scale. Also important, however, is the fact that many general design choices reflect an in-depth understanding of the preferences of leading consumer segments in key markets throughout the Triad. Rigid model changes during the past decade have helped educate consumers about the "fashion" aspects of these products and have led them to base their buying decisions in large measure on such fashion-related criteria.

With other products, the same electronics companies use quite different approaches. Those that make stereophonic equipment, for example, offer products based on aesthetics and product concepts that vary by region. Europeans tend to want physically small, high-performance equipment that can be hidden in a closet; Americans prefer large speakers that rise from the floor of living rooms and dens like the structural columns of ancient temples. Companies that have been globally successful in white goods like kitchen appliances focus on close interaction with individual users; those that have prospered with equipment that requires installation (air conditioners, say, or elevators) focus on interactions with designers, engineers, and trade unions. To repeat: Approaches to global products vary.

Another important cluster of these global products is made up of fashion-oriented, premium-priced branded goods. Gucci bags are sold around the world, unchanged from one place to another. They are marketed in virtually the same way. They appeal to an upper-bracket market segment that shares a consistent set of tastes and preferences. By definition, not everyone in the United States or Europe or Japan belongs to that segment. But for those who do, the growing commonality of their tastes qualifies them as members of a genuinely cross-Triad, global segment. There is even such a segment for top-of-the-line automobiles like the Rolls-Royce and the Mercedes-Benz. You can—in fact, should—design such cars for select buyers around the globe. But you cannot do that with Nissans or Toyotas or Hondas. Truly universal products are few and far between.

Insiderization

Some may argue that my definition of universal products is unnecessarily narrow, that many such products exist that do not fit neatly into top-bracket segments: Coca-Cola, Levi's, things like that. On closer examination, however, these turn out to be very different sorts of things. Think about Coca-Cola for a moment. Before it got established in each of its markets, the company had to build up a fairly complete local infrastructure and do the ground-work to establish local demand.

Access to markets was by no means assured from day one; consumer preference was not assured from day one. In Japan, the long-established preference was for carbonated lemon drinks known as saida. Unlike Gucci bags, consumer demand did not "pull" Coke into these markets; the company had to establish the infrastructure to "push" it. Today, because the company has done its homework and done it well, Coke is a universally desired brand. But it got there by a different route: local replication of an entire business system in every important market over a long period of time.

For Gucci-like products, the ready flow of information around the world stimulates consistent primary demand in top-bracket segments. For relatively undifferentiated, commodity-like products, demand expands only when corporate muscle pushes hard. If Coke is to establish a preference, it has to build it, piece by piece.

Perhaps the best way to distinguish these two kinds of global products is to think of yourself browsing in a duty-free shop. Here you are in something of an oasis. National barriers to entry do not apply. Products from all over the world lie available to you on the shelves. What do you reach for? Do you think about climbing on board your jetliner with a newly purchased six-pack of Coke? Hardly. But what about a Gucci bag? Yes, of course. In a sense, duty-free shops are the precursor to what life will be like in a genuinely borderless environment. Customer pull, shaped by im-ages and information from around the world, determine your prod-uct choices. You want the designer handbag or the sneakers by Reebok, which are made in Korea and sold at three times the price of equivalent no-brand sneakers. And there are others like you in every corner of the Triad.

At bottom, the choice to buy Gucci or Reebok is a choice about fashion. And the information that shapes fashion-driven choices is different in kind from the information that shapes choices about commodity products. When you walk into the 7-Elevens of the world and look for a bottle of cola, the one you pick depends on its location on the shelf, its price, or perhaps the special in-store promotion going on at the moment. In other words, your preference is shaped by the effects of the cola company's complete business system in that country.

Now, to be sure, the quality of that business system will depend to some extent on the company's ability to leverage skills developed elsewhere or to exploit synergies with other parts of its operations—marketing competence, for example, or economies of scale in the production of concentrates. Even so, your choice as a consumer rests on the power with which all such functional strengths have been brought to bear in your particular local market—that is, on the company's ability to become a full-fledged insider in that local market.

With fashion-based items, where the price is relatively high and the purchase frequency low, insiderization does not matter all that much. With commodity items, however, where the price is low and the frequency of purchase high, the insiderization of functional skills is all-important. There is simply no way to be successful around the world with this latter category of products without replicating your business system in each key market.

Coke has 70% of the Japanese market for soft drinks. The reason is that Coke took the time and made the investments to build up a full range of local functional strengths, particularly in its route sales force and franchised vending machines. It is, after all, the Coke van or truck that replaces empty bottles with new ones, not the trucks of independent wholesalers or distributors. When Coke first moved into Japan, it did not understand the complex, many-layered distribution system for such products. So it used the capital of local bottlers to re-create the kind of sales force it has used so well in the United States. This represented a heavy, front-end, fixed investment, but it has paid off handsomely. Coke redefined the domestic game in Japan—and it did so, not from a distance, but with a deliberate "insiderization" of functional strengths. Once this sales force is in place, for example, once the company has become a full-fledged insider, it can move not only soft drinks but also fruit juice, sport drinks, vitamin drinks, and canned coffee through the same sales network. It can sell pretty much whatever it wants to. For Coke's competitors, foreign and domestic, the millions of dollars they are spending on advertising are like little droplets of water sprinkled over a desert. Nothing is going to bloom—at least, not if that is all they do. Not if they fail to build up their own distinctive "insider" strengths.

When global success rests on market-by-market functional strength, you have to play a series of domestic games against well-defined competitors. If the market requires a first-class sales force, you simply have to have one. If competition turns on dealer support programs, that's where you have to excel. Some occasions *do* exist when doing more, better, is the right, the necessary, course to follow. Still, there are usually opportunities to redefine these domestic games to your own advantage. Companies that fail to establish a strong insider position tend to mix up the strategies followed by the Cokes and the Guccis. The managers of many leading branded-goods companies are often loud in their complaints about how the Japanese market is closed to their products. Or, more mysteriously, about the inexplicable refusal of Japanese consumers to buy their products when they are obviously better than those of any competitor anywhere in the world. Instead of making the effort to understand Japanese distribution and Japanese consumers, they assume that something is wrong with the Japanese market. Instead of spending time in their plants and offices or on the ground in Japan, they spend time in Washington.

Not everyone, of course. There are plenty of branded-goods companies that *are* very well represented on the Japanese retailing scene—Coke, to be sure, but also Nestlé, Schick, Wella, Vicks, Scott, Del Monte, Kraft, Campbell, Unilever (its Timotei shampoo is number one in Japan), Twinings, Kellogg, Borden, Ragú, Oscar Mayer, Hershey, and a host of others. These have all become household names in Japan. They have all become insiders.

For industrial products companies, becoming an insider often poses a different set of challenges. Because these products are chosen largely on the basis of their performance characteristics, if they cut costs or boost productivity, they stand a fair chance of being accepted anywhere in the world. Even so, however, these machines do not operate in a vacuum. Their success may have to wait until the companies that make them have developed a full range of insider functions—engineering, sales, installation, finance, service, and so on. So, as these factors become more critical, it often makes sense for the companies to link up with local operations that already have these functions in place.

Financial services have their own special characteristics. Product globalization already takes place at the institutional investor level but much less so at the retail level. Still, many retail products now originate overseas, and the money collected from them is often invested across national borders. Indeed, foreign exchange, stock markets, and other trading facilities have already made money a legitimately global product.

In all these categories, then, as distinct from premium fashion-driven products like Gucci bags, insiderization in key markets is the route to global success. Yes, some top-of-the-line tastes and preferences have become common across the Triad. In many other cases, however, creating a global product means building the capability to understand and respond to customer needs and business system requirements in each critical market.

The Headquarters Mentality

By all reasonable measures, Coke's experience in Japan has been a happy one. More often than not, however, the path it took to insiderization—replicating a home-country business system in a new national market—creates many more problems than it solves. Managers back at headquarters, who have had experience with only one way to succeed, are commonly inclined to force that model on each new opportunity that arises. Of course, sometimes it will work. Sometimes it will be exactly the right answer. But chances are that the home-country reflex, the impulse to generalize globally from a sample of one, will lead efforts astray.

In the pharmaceutical industry, for example, Coke's approach would not work. Foreign entrants simply have to find ways to adapt to the Japanese distribution system. Local doctors will not accept or respond favorably to an American-style sales force. When the doctor asks a local detail man to take a moment and photocopy some articles for him, he has to be willing to run the errands. No ifs, ands, or buts.

One common problem with insiderization, then, is a misplaced home-country reflex. Another, perhaps more subtle, problem is what happens back at headquarters after initial operations in another market really start paying off. When this happens, in most companies everyone at home starts to pay close attention. Without really understanding why things have turned out as well as they have, managers at headquarters take an increasing interest in what is going on in Japan or wherever it happens to be.

Functionaries of all stripes itch to intervene. Corporate heavyweights decide they had better get into the act, monitor key decisions, ask for timely reports, take extensive tours of local activities. Every power-that-be wants a say in what has become a critical portion of the overall company's operations. When minor difficulties arise, no one is willing to let local managers continue to handle things themselves. Corporate jets fill the skies with impatient satraps eager to set things right.

We know perfectly well where all this is likely to lead. A cosmetics company, with a once-enviable position in Japan, went through a series of management shake-ups at home. As a result, the Japanese operation, which had grown progressively more important, was no longer able to enjoy the rough autonomy that made its success possible. Several times, eager U.S. hands reached in to change the head of activities in Japan, and crisp memos and phone calls kept up a steady barrage of challenges to the unlucky soul who happened to be in the hot seat at the moment. Relations became antagonistic, profits fell, the intervention grew worse, and the whole thing just fell apart. Overeager and overanxious managers back at headquarters did not have the patience to learn what really worked in the Japanese market. By trying to supervise things in the regular "corporate" fashion, they destroyed a very profitable business.

This is an all-too-familiar pattern. With dizzying regularity, the local top manager changes from a Japanese national to a foreigner, to a Japanese, to a foreigner. Impatient, headquarters keeps fitfully searching for a never-never ideal "person on the spot." Persistence and perseverance are the keys to long-term survival and success. Everyone knows it. But headquarters is just not able to wait for a few years until local managers—of whatever nationality—build up the needed rapport with vendors, employees, distributors, and customers. And if, by a miracle, they do, then headquarters is likely to see them as having become too "Japanized" to represent their interests abroad. They are no longer "one of us." If they do not, then obviously they have failed to win local acceptance.

This headquarters mentality is not just a problem of bad attitude or misguided enthusiasm. Too bad, because these would be relatively easy to fix. Instead, it rests on—and is reinforced by—a company's entrenched systems, structures, and behaviors. Dividend payout ratios, for example, vary from country to country. But most global companies find it hard to accept low or no payout from investment in Japan, medium returns from Germany, and larger returns from the United States. The usual wish is to get comparable levels of return from all activities, and internal benchmarks of performance reflect that wish. This is trouble waiting to happen. Looking for 15% ROI a year from new commitments in Japan is going to sour a company on Japan very quickly. The companies that have done the best there—the Coca-Colas and the IBMs—were willing to adjust their conventional expectations and settle in for the long term.

Or, for example, when top managers rely heavily on financial statements, they can easily lose sight of the value of operating globally—because these statements usually mask the performance of activities outside the home country. Accounting and reporting systems that are parent-company dominated—and remember, genuinely consolidated statements are still the exception, not the rule— merely confirm the lukewarm commitment of many managers to global competition. They may talk a lot about doing business globally, but it is just lip service. It sounds nice, and it may convince the business press to write glowing stories, but when things get tough, most of the talk turns out to be only talk.

Take a closer look at what actually happens. If a divisionalized Japanese company like Matsushita or Toshiba wants to build a plant to make widgets in Tennessee, the home-country division manager responsible for widgets often finds himself in a tough position. No doubt, the CEO will tell him to get that Tennessee facility up and running as soon as possible. But the division manager knows that, when the plant does come on-stream, his own operations are going to look worse on paper. At a minimum, his division is not going to get credit for American sales that he used to make by export from Japan. Those are now going to come out of Tennessee. The CEO tells him to collaborate, to help out, but he is afraid that the better the job he does, the worse it will be for him—and with good reason!

This is crazy. Why not change company systems? Have the Tennessee plant report directly to him, and consolidate all widget-making activities at the divisional level. Easier said than done. Most companies use accounting systems that consolidate at the corporate, not the divisional, level. That's traditional corporate practice. And every staff person since the time of Homer comes fully equipped with a thousand reasons not to make exceptions to time-honored institutional procedures. As a result, the division manager is going to drag his feet. The moment Tennessee comes on-line, he sees his numbers go down, he has to lay off people, and he has to worry about excess capacity. Who is going to remember his fine efforts in getting Tennessee started up? More to the point, who is going to care—when his Japanese numbers look so bad?

If you want to operate globally, you have to think and act globally, and that means challenging entrenched systems that work against collaborative efforts. Say our widget maker has a change of heart and goes to a division-level consolidation of accounts. This helps, but the problems are just beginning. The American managers of a sister division that uses these widgets look at the Tennessee plant as just another vendor, perhaps even a troublesome one because it is new and not entirely reliable. Their inclination is to treat the new plant as a problem, ignore it if possible, and to continue to buy from Japan where quality is high and delivery guaranteed. They are not going to do anything to help the new plant come on-stream or to plan for long-term capital investment. They are not going to supply technical assistance or design help or anything. All it represents is fairly unattractive marginal capacity.

If we solve this problem by having the plant head report to the division manager, then we are back where we started. If we do nothing, then this new plant is just going to struggle along. Clearly, what we need is to move toward a system of double counting of credits—so that both the American manager and the division head in Japan have strong reasons to make the new facility work. But this runs afoul of our entrenched systems, and they are very hard to change. If our commitment to acting globally is not terribly strong, we are not going to be inclined to make the painful efforts needed to make it work.

Under normal circumstances, these kinds of entrepreneurial decisions are hard enough to reach anyway. It is no surprise that many of the most globally successful Japanese companies—Honda, Sony, Matsushita, Canon, and the like—have been led by a strong owner-founder for at least a decade. They can override bureaucratic inertia; they can tear down institutional barriers. In practice, the managerial decision to tackle wrenching organizational and systems changes is made even more difficult by the way in which problems become visible. Usually, a global systems problem first comes into view in the form of explicitly local symptoms. Rarely do global problems show up where the real underlying causes are.

Troubled CEOs may say that their Japanese operations are not doing well, that the money being spent on advertising is just not paying off as expected. They will not say that their problems are really back at headquarters with its superficial understanding of what it takes to market effectively in Japan. They will not say that it lies in the design of their financial reporting systems. They will not say that it is part and parcel of their own reluctance to make long-term, front-end capital investments in new markets. They will not say that it lies in their failure to do well the central job of any headquarters operation: the development of good people at the local level. Or at least they are not likely to. They will diagnose the problems as local problems and try to fix them.

Thinking Global

Top managers are always slow to point the finger of responsibility at headquarters or at themselves. When global faults have local symptoms, they will be slower still. When taking corrective action means a full, zero-based review of all systems, skills, and structures, their speed will decrease even further. And when their commitment to acting globally is itself far from complete, it is a wonder there is any motion at all. Headquarters mentality is the prime expression of managerial nearsightedness, the sworn enemy of a genuinely equidistant perspective on global markets.

In the early days of global business, experts like Raymond Vernon of the Harvard Business School proposed, in effect, a United Nations model of globalization. Companies with aspirations to diversify and expand throughout the Triad were to do so by cloning the parent company in each new country of operation. If successful, they would create a mini-U.N. of clonelike subsidiaries repatriating profits to the parent company, which remained the dominant force at the center. We know that successful companies enter fewer countries but penetrate each of them more deeply. That is why this model gave way by the early 1980s to a competitor-focused approach to globalization. By this logic, if we were a European producer of medical electronics equipment, we had to take on General Electric in the United States so that it would not come over here and attack us on our home ground. Today, however, the pressure for globalization is driven not so much by diversification or competition as by the needs and preferences of customers. Their needs have globalized, and the fixed costs of meeting them have soared. That is why we must globalize.

Managing effectively in this new borderless environment does not mean building pyramids of cash flow by focusing on the discovery of new places to invest. Nor does it mean tracking your competitors to their lair and preemptively undercutting them in their own home market. Nor does it mean blindly trying to replicate home-country business systems in new colonial territories. Instead, it means paying central attention to delivering value to customers— and to developing an equidistant view of who they are and what they want. Before everything else comes the need to see your customers clearly. They—and only they—can provide legitimate reasons for thinking global.

PART
IV

Corporate Strategy and Firm Scope

1
From Competitive Advantage to Corporate Strategy

Michael E. Porter

Corporate strategy, the overall plan for a diversified company, is both the darling and the stepchild of contemporary management practice—the darling because CEOs have been obsessed with diversification since the early 1960s, the stepchild because almost no consensus exists about what corporate strategy is, much less about how a company should formulate it.

A diversified company has two levels of strategy: business unit (or competitive) strategy and corporate (or companywide) strategy. Competitive strategy concerns how to create competitive advantage in each of the businesses in which a company competes. Corporate strategy concerns two different questions: what businesses the corporation should be in and how the corporate office should manage the array of business units.

Corporate strategy is what makes the corporate whole add up to more than the sum of its business unit parts.

The track record of corporate strategies has been dismal. I studied the diversification records of 33 large, prestigious U.S. companies over the 1950–1986 period and found that most of them had divested many more acquisitions than they had kept. The corporate strategies of most companies have dissipated instead of created shareholder value.

The need to rethink corporate strategy could hardly be more

Author's note: the research for this article was done with the able assistance of my research associate Cheng G. Ong. Malcolm S. Salter, Andrall E. Pearson, A. Michael Keehner, and the Monitor Company also provided helpful comments.

urgent. By taking over companies and breaking them up, corporate raiders thrive on failed corporate strategy. Fueled by junk bond financing and growing acceptability, raiders can expose any company to takeover, no matter how large or blue chip.

Recognizing past diversification mistakes, some companies have initiated large-scale restructuring programs. Others have done nothing at all. Whatever the response, the strategic questions persist. Those who have restructured must decide what to do next to avoid repeating the past; those who have done nothing must awake to their vulnerability. To survive, companies must understand what good corporate strategy is.

A Sober Picture

While there is disquiet about the success of corporate strategies, none of the available evidence satisfactorily indicates the success or failure of corporate strategy. Most studies have approached the question by measuring the stock market valuation of mergers, captured in the movement of the stock prices of acquiring companies immediately before and after mergers are announced.

These studies show that the market values mergers as neutral or slightly negative, hardly cause for serious concern.[1] Yet the short-term market reaction is a highly imperfect measure of the long-term success of diversification, and no self-respecting executive would judge a corporate strategy this way.

Studying the diversification programs of a company over a long period of time is a much more telling way to determine whether a corporate strategy has succeeded or failed. My study of 33 companies, many of which have reputations for good management, is a unique look at the track record of major corporations. Each company entered an average of 80 new industries and 27 new fields. Just over 70% of the new entries were acquisitions, 22% were start-ups, and 8% were joint ventures. IBM, Exxon, Du Pont, and 3M, for example, focused on start-ups, while ALCO Standard, Beatrice, and Sara Lee diversified almost solely through acquisitions (Exhibit I has a complete rundown).

My data paint a sobering picture of the success ratio of these moves (see Exhibit II). I found that on average corporations divested more than half their acquisitions in new industries and more than 60% of their acquisitions in entirely new fields. Fourteen companies left more than 70% of all the acquisitions they had made in new fields. The track record in unrelated acquisitions is even worse—the average divestment rate is a startling 74% (see Exhibit III). Even a highly respected company like General Electric divested a very high percentage of its acquisitions, particularly those in new fields. Companies near the top of the list in Exhibit II achieved a remarkably low rate of divestment. Some bear witness to the success of well-thought-out corporate strategies. Others, however, enjoy a lower rate simply because they have not faced up to their problem units and divested them.

I calculated total shareholder returns (stock price appreciation plus dividends) over the period of the study for each company so that I could compare them with its divestment rate. While companies near the top of the list have above-average shareholder returns, returns are not a reliable measure of diversification success. Shareholder return often depends heavily on the inherent attractiveness of companies' base industries. Companies like CBS and General Mills had extremely profitable base businesses that subsidized poor diversification track records.

I would like to make one comment on the use of shareholder value to judge performance. Linking shareholder value quantitatively to diversification performance only works if you compare the shareholder value that is, with the shareholder value that might have been without diversification. Because such a comparison is virtually impossible to make, my own measure of diversification success—the number of units retained by the company—seems to be as good an indicator as any of the contribution of diversification to corporate performance.

My data give a stark indication of the failure of corporate strategies.[2] Of the 33 companies, 6 had been taken over as my study was being completed (see the note on Exhibit II). Only the lawyers, investment bankers, and original sellers have prospered in most of these acquisitions, not the shareholders.

Premises of Corporate Strategy

Any successful corporate strategy builds on a number of premises. These are facts of life about diversification. They cannot be altered, and when ignored, they explain in part why so many corporate strategies fail.

Exhibit I.   *Diversification Profiles of 33 Leading U.S. Companies*

Company	Number total entries	All entries into new industries	Percent acqui- sitions	Percent joint ventures
ALCO Standard	221	165	99 %	0 %
Allied Corp.	77	49	67	10
Beatrice	382	204	97	1
Borden	170	96	77	4
CBS	148	81	67	16
Continental Group	75	47	77	6
Cummins Engine	30	24	54	17
Du Pont	80	39	33	16
Exxon	79	56	34	5
General Electric	160	108	47	20
General Foods	92	53	91	4
General Mills	110	102	84	7
W.R.Grace	275	202	83	7
Gulf & Western	178	140	91	4
IBM	46	38	18	18
IC Industries	67	41	85	3
ITT	246	178	89	2
Johnson & Johnson	88	77	77	0
Mobil	41	32	53	16
Procter & Gamble	28	23	61	0
Raytheon	70	58	86	9
RCA	53	46	35	15
Rockwell	101	75	73	24
Sara Lee	197	141	96	1
Scovill	52	36	97	0
Signal	53	45	67	4
Tenneco	85	62	81	6
3M	144	125	54	2
TRW	119	82	77	10
United Technologies	62	49	57	18
Westinghouse	129	73	63	11
Wickes	71	47	83	0
Xerox	59	50	66	6
Total	**3,788**	**2,644**		
Average	**114.8**	**80.1**	**70.3 %**	**7.9 %**

Note:
Beatrice, Continental Group, General
Foods, RCA, Scovill, and Signal were
taken over as the study was being completed. Their data cover the period up
through takeover but not subsequent
divestments.

Percent start-ups	Entries into new industries that repre- sented entire- ly new fields	Percent acqui- sitions	Percent joint ventures	Percent start-ups
1 %	56	100 %	0 %	0 %
22	17	65	6	29
2	61	97	0	3
19	32	75	3	22
17	28	65	21	14
17	19	79	11	11
29	13	46	23	31
51	19	37	0	63
61	17	29	6	65
33	29	48	14	38
6	22	86	5	9
9	27	74	7	19
10	66	74	5	21
6	48	88	2	10
63	16	19	0	81
12	17	88	6	6
9	50	92	0	8
23	18	56	0	44
31	15	60	7	33
39	14	79	0	21
5	16	81	19	6
50	19	37	21	42
3	27	74	22	4
4	41	95	2	2
3	12	92	0	8
29	20	75	0	25
13	26	73	8	19
45	34	71	3	56
13	28	64	11	25
24	17	23	17	39
26	36	61	3	36
17	22	68	0	32
28	18	50	11	39
	906			
21.8 %	**27.4**	**67.9 %**	**7.0 %**	**25.9 %**

Note:
The percentage averages may not add up
to 100% because of rounding off.

Exhibit II.   Acquisition Track Records of Leading U.S. Diversifiers Ranked by Percent Divested

Company	All acquisitions in new industries	Percent made by 1980 and then divested	Percent made by 1975 and then divested	Acquisitions in new industries that represented entirely new fields	Percent made by 1980 and then divested	Percent made by 1975 and then divested
Johnson & Johnson	59	17%	12%	10	33%	14%
Procter & Gamble	14	17	17	11	17	17
Raytheon	50	17	26	13	25	33
United Technologies	28	25	13	10	17	0
3M	67	26	27	24	42	45
TRW	63	27	31	18	40	38
IBM	7	33	0*	3	33	0*
Du Pont	13	38	43	7	60	75
Mobil	17	38	57	9	50	50
Borden	74	39	40	24	45	50
IC Industries	35	42	50	15	46	44
Tenneco	50	43	47	19	27	33
Beatrice	198	46	45	59	52	51
ITT	159	52	52	46	61	61
Rockwell	55	56	57	20	71	71
Allied Corp.	33	57	45	11	80	67
Exxon	19	62	20*	5	80	50*
Sara Lee	135	62	65	39	80	76

Company						
General Foods	48	63	62	19	93	93
Scovill	35	64	77	11	64	70
Signal	30	65	63	15	70	67
ALCO Standard	164	65	70	56	72	76
W.R. Grace	167	65	70	49	71	70
General Electric	51	65	78	14	100	100
Wickes	38	67	72	15	73	70
Westinghouse	46	68	69	22	61	59
Xerox	33	71	79	9	100	100
Continental Group	36	71	72	15	60	60
General Mills	86	75	73	20	65	60
Gulf & Western	127	79	78	42	75	72
Cummins Engine	13	80	80	6	83	83
RCA	16	80	92	7	86	100
CBS	54	87	89	18	88	88
Total	**2,021**			**661**		
Average per company†	**61.2**	**53.4%**	**56.5%**	**20.0**	**61.2%**	**61.1%**

*Companies with three or fewer acquisitions by the cutoff year.

†Companies with three or fewer acquisitions by the cutoff year are excluded from the average to minimize statistical distortions.

Note:
Beatrice, Continental Group, General Foods, RCA, Scovill, and Signal were taken over as the study was being completed. Their data cover the period up through takeover but not subsequent divestments.

**Exhibit III.   *Diversification Performance in Joint Ventures,
Start-Ups, and Unrelated Acquisitions***
Companies in Same Order as in Exhibit II

Company	Joint ventures as a percent of new entries	Percent made by 1980 and then divested	Percent made by 1975 and then divested
Johnson & Johnson	0 %	†	†
Procter & Gamble	0	†	†
Raytheon	9	60 %	60 %
United Technologies	18	50	50
3M	2	100*	100*
TRW	10	20	25
IBM	18	100*	†
Du Pont	16	100*	†
Mobil	16	33	33
Borden	4	33	33
IC Industries	3	100*	100*
Tenneco	6	67	67
Beatrice	1	†	†
ITT	2	0*	†
Rockwell	24	38	42
Allied Corp.	10	100	75
Exxon	5	0	0
Sara Lee	1	†	†
General Foods	4	†	†
Scovill	0	†	†
Signal	4	†	†
ALCO Standard	0	†	†
W.R. Grace	7	33	38
General Electric	20	20	33
Wickes	0	†	†
Westinghouse	11	0*	0*
Xerox	6	100*	100*
Continental Group	6	67	67
General Mills	7	71	71
Gulf & Western	4	75	50
Cummins Engine	17	50	50
RCA	15	67	67
CBS	16	71	71
Average per company‡	**7.9 %**	**50.3 %**	**48.9 %**

*Companies with two or fewer entries.

†No entries in this category.

‡Average excludes companies with two or fewer entries to minimize statistical distortions.

Note:
Beatrice, Continental Group, General Foods, RCA, Scovill, and Signal were taken over as the study was being completed. Their data cover the period up through takeover but not subsequent divestments.

Start-ups as a percent of new entries	Percent made by 1980 and then divested	Percent made by 1975 and then divested	Acquisitions in unrelated new fields as a percent of total acquisitions in new fields	Percent made by 1980 and then divested	Percent made by 1975 and then divested
23 %	14 %	20 %	0 %	†	†
39	0	0	9	†	†
5	50	50	46	40 %	40 %
24	11	20	40	0*	0*
45	2	3	33	75	86
13	63	71	39	71	71
63	20	22	33	100*	100*
51	61	61	43	0*	0*
31	50	56	67	60	100
19	17	13	21	80	80
13	80	30	33	50	50
13	67	80	42	33	40
2	0	0	63	59	53
8	38	57	61	67	64
3	0	0	35	100	100
22	38	29	45	50	0
61	27	19	100	80	50*
4	75	100*	41	73	73
6	67	50	42	86	83
3	100	100*	45	80	100
29	20	11	67	50	50
1	†	†	63	79	81
10	71	71	39	65	65
33	33	44	36	100	100
17	63	57	60	80	75
26	44	44	36	57	67
28	50	56	22	100	100
17	14	0	40	83	100
9	89	80	65	77	67
6	100	100	74	77	74
29	0	0	67	100	100
50	99	55	36	100	100
17	86	80	39	100	100
21.8 %	**44.0 %**	**40.9 %**	**46.1 %**	**74.0 %**	**74.4 %**

COMPETITION OCCURS AT THE BUSINESS UNIT LEVEL.   Diversified companies do not compete; only their business units do. Unless a corporate strategy places primary attention on nurturing the success of each unit, the strategy will fail, no matter how elegantly constructed. Successful corporate strategy must grow out of and reinforce competitive strategy.

DIVERSIFICATION INEVITABLY ADDS COSTS AND CONSTRAINTS TO BUSINESS UNITS.   Obvious costs such as the corporate overhead allocated to a unit may not be as important or subtle as the hidden costs and constraints. A business unit must explain its decisions to top management, spend time complying with planning and other corporate systems, live with parent company guidelines and personnel policies, and forgo the opportunity to motivate employees with direct equity ownership. These costs and constraints can be reduced but not entirely eliminated.

SHAREHOLDERS CAN READILY DIVERSIFY THEMSELVES.   Shareholders can diversify their own portfolios of stocks by selecting those that best match their preferences and risk profiles.[3] Shareholders can often diversify more cheaply than a corporation because they can buy shares at the market price and avoid hefty acquisition premiums.

These premises mean that corporate strategy cannot succeed unless it truly adds value—to business units by providing tangible benefits that offset the inherent costs of lost independence and to shareholders by diversifying in a way they could not replicate.

Passing the Essential Tests

To understand how to formulate corporate strategy, it is necessary to specify the conditions under which diversification will truly create shareholder value. These conditions can be summarized in three essential tests:

1. **The attractiveness test.** The industries chosen for diversification must be structurally attractive or capable of being made attractive.
2. **The cost-of-entry test.** The cost of entry must not capitalize all the future profits.
3. **The better-off test.** Either the new unit must gain competitive advantage from its link with the corporation or vice versa.

Of course, most companies will make certain that their proposed strategies pass some of these tests. But my study clearly shows that when companies ignored one or two of them, the strategic results were disastrous.

HOW ATTRACTIVE IS THE INDUSTRY?

In the long run, the rate of return available from competing in an industry is a function of its underlying structure, which I have described in another *Harvard Business Review* article.[4] An attractive industry with a high average return on investment will be difficult to enter because entry barriers are high, suppliers and buyers have only modest bargaining power, substitute products or services are few, and the rivalry among competitors is stable. An unattractive industry like steel will have structural flaws, including a plethora of substitute materials, powerful and price-sensitive buyers, and excessive rivalry caused by high fixed costs and a large group of competitors, many of whom are state supported.

Diversification cannot create shareholder value unless new industries have favorable structures that support returns exceeding the cost of capital. If the industry doesn't have such returns, the company must be able to restructure the industry or gain a sustainable competitive advantage that leads to returns well above the industry average. An industry need not be attractive before diversification. In fact, a company might benefit from entering before the industry shows its full potential. The diversification can then transform the industry's structure.

In my research, I often found companies had suspended the attractiveness test because they had a vague belief that the industry "fit" very closely with their own businesses. In the hope that the corporate "comfort" they felt would lead to a happy outcome, the companies ignored fundamentally poor industry structures. Unless the close fit allows substantial competitive advantage, however, such comfort will turn into pain when diversification results in poor returns. Royal Dutch Shell and other leading oil companies have had this unhappy experience in a number of chemicals businesses, where poor industry structures overcame the benefits of vertical integration and skills in process technology.

Another common reason for ignoring the attractiveness test is a low entry cost. Sometimes the buyer has an inside track or the owner is anxious to sell. Even if the price is actually low, however, a one-shot gain will not offset a perpetually poor business. Almost always, the company finds it must reinvest in the newly acquired unit, if only to replace fixed assets and fund working capital.

Diversifying companies are also prone to use rapid growth or other simple indicators as a proxy for a target industry's attractiveness. Many that rushed into fast-growing industries (personal computers, video games, and robotics, for example) were burned because they mistook early growth for long-term profit potential. Industries are profitable not because they are sexy or high tech; they are profitable only if their structures are attractive.

WHAT IS THE COST OF ENTRY?

Diversification cannot build shareholder value if the cost of entry into a new business eats up its expected returns. Strong market forces, however, are working to do just that. A company can enter new industries by acquisition or start-up. Acquisitions expose it to an increasingly efficient merger market. An acquirer beats the market if it pays a price not fully reflecting the prospects of the new unit. Yet multiple bidders are commonplace, information flows rapidly, and investment bankers and other intermediaries work aggressively to make the market as efficient as possible. In recent years, new financial instruments such as junk bonds have brought new buyers into the market and made even large companies vulnerable to takeover. Acquisition premiums are high and reflect the acquired company's future prospects—sometimes too well. Philip Morris paid more than four times book value for Seven-Up Company, for example. Simple arithmetic meant that profits had to more than quadruple to sustain the preacquisition ROI. Since there proved to be little Philip Morris could add in marketing prowess to the sophisticated marketing wars in the soft-drink industry, the result was the unsatisfactory financial performance of Seven-Up and ultimately the decision to divest.

In a start-up, the company must overcome entry barriers. It's a real catch-22 situation, however, since attractive industries are attractive because their entry barriers are high. Bearing the full cost of the entry barriers might well dissipate any potential profits. Otherwise, other entrants to the industry would have already eroded its profitability.

In the excitement of finding an appealing new business, companies sometimes forget to apply the cost-of-entry test. The more attractive a new industry, the more expensive it is to get into.

WILL THE BUSINESS BE BETTER OFF?

A corporation must bring some significant competitive advantage to the new unit, or the new unit must offer potential for significant advantage to the corporation. Sometimes, the benefits to the new unit accrue only once, near the time of entry, when the parent instigates a major overhaul of its strategy or installs a first-rate management team. Other diversification yields ongoing competitive advantage if the new unit can market its product, through the well-developed distribution system of its sister units, for instance. This is one of the important underpinnings of the merger of Baxter Travenol and American Hospital Supply.

When the benefit to the new unit comes only once, the parent company has no rationale for holding the new unit in its portfolio over the long term. Once the results of the one-time improvement are clear, the diversified company no longer adds value to offset the inevitable costs imposed on the unit. It is best to sell the unit and free up corporate resources.

The better-off test does not imply that diversifying corporate risk creates shareholder value in and of itself. Doing something for shareholders that they can do themselves is not a basis for corporate strategy. (Only in the case of a privately held company, in which the company's and the shareholder's risk are the same, is diversification to reduce risk valuable for its own sake.) Diversification of risk should only be a by-product of corporate strategy, not a prime motivator.

Executives ignore the better-off test most of all or deal with it through arm waving or trumped-up logic rather than hard strategic analysis. One reason is that they confuse company size with shareholder value. In the drive to run a bigger company, they lose sight of their real job. They may justify the suspension of the better-off test by pointing to the way they manage diversity. By cutting corporate staff to the bone and giving business units nearly complete autonomy, they believe they avoid the pitfalls. Such thinking misses the whole point of diversification, which is to create shareholder value rather than to avoid destroying it.

Concepts of Corporate Strategy

The three tests for successful diversification set the standards that any corporate strategy must meet; meeting them is so difficult that most diversification fails. Many companies lack a clear concept of corporate strategy to guide their diversification or pursue a concept that does not address the tests. Others fail because they implement a strategy poorly.

My study has helped me identify four concepts of corporate strategy that have been put into practice—portfolio management, restructuring, transferring skills, and sharing activities. While the concepts are not always mutually exclusive, each rests on a different mechanism by which the corporation creates shareholder value and each requires the diversified company to manage and organize itself in a different way. The first two require no connections among business units; the second two depend on them (see Exhibit IV). While all four concepts of strategy have succeeded under the right circumstances, today some make more sense than others. Ignoring any of the concepts is perhaps the quickest road to failure.

PORTFOLIO MANAGEMENT

The concept of corporate strategy most in use is portfolio management, which is based primarily on diversification through acquisition. The corporation acquires sound, attractive companies with competent managers who agree to stay on. While acquired units do not have to be in the same industries as existing units, the best portfolio managers generally limit their range of businesses in some way, in part to limit the specific expertise needed by top management.

The acquired units are autonomous, and the teams that run them are compensated according to unit results. The corporation supplies capital and works with each to infuse it with professional management techniques. At the same time, top management provides objective and dispassionate review of business unit results. Portfolio managers categorize units by potential and regularly transfer resources from units that generate cash to those with high potential and cash needs.

In a portfolio strategy, the corporation seeks to create shareholder value in a number of ways. It uses its expertise and analytical resources to spot attractive acquisition candidates that the individual shareholder could not. The company provides capital on favorable terms that reflect corporatewide fund-raising ability. It introduces professional management skills and discipline. Finally, it provides high-quality review and coaching, unencumbered by conventional wisdom or emotional attachments to the business.

The logic of the portfolio management concept rests on a number of vital assumptions. If a company's diversification plan is to meet the attractiveness and cost-of-entry tests, it must find good but undervalued companies. Acquired companies must be truly undervalued because the parent does little for the new unit once it is acquired. To meet the better-off test, the benefits the corporation provides must yield a significant competitive advantage to acquired units. The style of operating through highly autonomous business units must both develop sound business strategies and motivate managers.

In most countries, the days when portfolio management was a valid concept of corporate strategy are past. In the face of increasingly well-developed capital markets, attractive companies with good managements show up on everyone's computer screen and attract top dollar in terms of acquisition premium. Simply contributing capital isn't contributing much. A sound strategy can easily be funded; small to medium-size companies don't need a munificent parent.

Other benefits have also eroded. Large companies no longer corner the market for professional management skills; in fact, more and more observers believe managers cannot necessarily run anything in the absence of industry-specific knowledge and experience. Another supposed advantage of the portfolio management concept—dispassionate review—rests on similarly shaky ground since the added value of review alone is questionable in a portfolio of sound companies.

The benefit of giving business units complete autonomy is also questionable. Increasingly, a company's business units are interrelated, drawn together by new technology, broadening distribution channels, and changing regulations. Setting strategies of units independently may well undermine unit performance. The companies in my sample that have succeeded in diversification have recognized the value of interrelationships and understood that a strong sense of corporate identity is as important as slavish adherence to parochial business unit financial results.

Exhibit IV.   Concepts of Corporate Strategy

	Portfolio management	Restructuring	Transferring skills	Sharing activities
Strategic prerequisites	Superior insight into identifying and acquiring undervalued companies	Superior insight into identifying restructuring opportunities	Proprietary skills in activities important to competitive advantage in target industries	Activities in existing units that can be shared with new business units to gain competitive advantage
	Willingness to sell off losers quickly or to opportunistically divest good performers when buyers are willing to pay large premiums	Willingness and capability to intervene to transform acquired units	Ability to accomplish the transfer of skills among units on an ongoing basis	Benefits of sharing that outweigh the costs
	Broad guidelines for and constraints on the types of units in the portfolio so that senior management can play the review role effectively	Broad similarities among the units in the portfolio	Acquisitions of beachhead positions in new industries as a base	Both start-ups and acquisitions as entry vehicles
	A private company or undeveloped capital markets	Willingness to cut losses by selling off units where restructuring proves unfeasible		Ability to overcome organizational resistance to business unit collaboration
	Ability to shift away from portfolio management as the capital markets get more efficient or the company gets unwieldy	Willingness to sell units when restructuring is complete, the results are clear, and market conditions are favorable		

Organizational prerequisites	Autonomous business units	Autonomous business units	Largely autonomous but collaborative business units	Strategic business units that are encouraged to share activities
	A very small, low-cost, corporate staff	A corporate organization with the talent and resources to oversee the turnarounds and strategic repositionings of acquired units	High-level corporate staff members who see their role primarily as integrators	An active strategic planning role at group, sector, and corporate levels
	Incentives based largely on business unit results	Incentives based largely on acquired units' results	Cross-business-unit committees, task forces, and other forums to serve as focal points for capturing and transferring skills	High-level corporate staff members who see their roles primarily as integrators
			Objectives of line managers that include skills transfer	Incentives based heavily on group and corporate results
			Incentives based in part on corporate results	
Common pitfalls	Pursuing portfolio management in countries with efficient capital marketing and a developed pool of professional management talent	Mistaking rapid growth or a "hot" industry as sufficient evidence of a restructuring opportunity	Mistaking similarity or comfort with new businesses as sufficient basis for diversification	Sharing for its own sake rather than because it leads to competitive advantage
	Ignoring the fact that industry structure is not attractive	Lacking the resolve or resources to take on troubled situations and to intervene in management	Providing no practical ways for skills transfer to occur	Assuming sharing will occur naturally without senior management playing an active role
		Ignoring the fact that industry structure is not attractive	Ignoring the fact that industry structure is not attractive	Ignoring the fact that industry structure is not attractive
		Paying lip service to restructuring but actually practicing passive portfolio management		

But it is the sheer complexity of the management task that has ultimately defeated even the best portfolio managers. As the size of the company grows, portfolio managers need to find more and more deals just to maintain growth. Supervising dozens or even hundreds of disparate units and under chain-letter pressures to add more, management begins to make mistakes. At the same time, the inevitable costs of being part of a diversified company take their toll and unit performance slides while the whole company's ROI turns downward. Eventually, a new management team is installed that initiates wholesale divestments and pares down the company to its core businesses. The experiences of Gulf & Western, Consolidated Foods (now Sara Lee), and ITT are just a few comparatively recent examples. Reflecting these realities, the U.S. capital markets today reward companies that follow the portfolio management model with a "conglomerate discount"; they value the whole less than the sum of the parts.

In developing countries, where large companies are few, capital markets are undeveloped, and professional management is scarce, portfolio management still works. But it is no longer a valid model for corporate strategy in advanced economies. Nevertheless, the technique is in the limelight today in the United Kingdom, where it is supported so far by a newly energized stock market eager for excitement. But this enthusiasm will wane—as well it should. Portfolio management is no way to conduct corporate strategy.

RESTRUCTURING

Unlike its passive role as a portfolio manager, when it serves as banker and reviewer, a company that bases its strategy on restructuring becomes an active restructurer of business units. The new businesses are not necessarily related to existing units. All that is necessary is unrealized potential.

The restructuring strategy seeks out undeveloped, sick, or threatened organizations or industries on the threshold of significant change. The parent intervenes, frequently changing the unit management team, shifting strategy, or infusing the company with new technology. Then it may make follow-up acquisitions to build a critical mass and sell off unneeded or unconnected parts and thereby reduce the effective acquisition cost. The result is a strengthened company or a transformed industry. As a coda, the parent sells off the stronger unit once results are clear because the parent is no longer adding value and top management decides that its attention should be directed elsewhere.

When well implemented, the restructuring concept is sound, for it passes the three tests of successful diversification. The restructurer meets the cost-of-entry test through the types of company it acquires. It limits acquisition premiums by buying companies with problems and lackluster images or by buying into industries with as yet unforeseen potential. Intervention by the corporation clearly meets the better-off test. Provided that the target industries are structurally attractive, the restructuring model can create enormous shareholder value. Some restructuring companies are Loew's, BTR, and General Cinema. Ironically, many of today's restructurers are profiting from yesterday's portfolio management strategies.

To work, the restructuring strategy requires a corporate management team with the insight to spot undervalued companies or positions in industries ripe for transformation. The same insight is necessary to actually turn the units around even though they are in new and unfamiliar businesses.

These requirements expose the restructurer to considerable risk and usually limit the time in which the company can succeed at the strategy. The most skillful proponents understand this problem, recognize their mistakes, and move decisively to dispose of them. The best companies realize they are not just acquiring companies but restructuring an industry. Unless they can integrate the acquisitions to create a whole new strategic position, they are just portfolio managers in disguise. Another important difficulty surfaces if so many other companies join the action that they deplete the pool of suitable candidates and bid their prices up.

Perhaps the greatest pitfall, however, is that companies find it very hard to dispose of business units once they are restructured and performing well. Human nature fights economic rationale. Size supplants shareholder value as the corporate goal. The company does not sell a unit even though the company no longer adds value to the unit. While the transformed units would be better off in another company that had related businesses, the restructuring company instead retains them. Gradually, it becomes a portfolio manager. The parent company's ROI declines as the need for reinvestment in the units and normal business risks eventually offset restructuring's one-shot gain. The perceived need to keep growing intensifies the pace of acquisition; errors result and standards fall.

The restructuring company turns into a conglomerate with returns that only equal the average of all industries at best.

TRANSFERRING SKILLS

The purpose of the first two concepts of corporate strategy is to create value through a company's relationship with each autonomous unit. The corporation's role is to be a selector, a banker, and an intervenor.

The last two concepts exploit the interrelationships between businesses. In articulating them, however, one comes face-to-face with the often ill-defined concept of synergy. If you believe the text of the countless corporate annual reports, just about anything is related to just about anything else! But imagined synergy is much more common than real synergy. GM's purchase of Hughes Aircraft simply because cars were going electronic and Hughes was an electronics concern demonstrates the folly of paper synergy. Such corporate relatedness is an ex post facto rationalization of a diversification undertaken for other reasons.

Even synergy that is clearly defined often fails to materialize. Instead of cooperating, business units often compete. A company that can define the synergies it is pursuing still faces significant organizational impediments in achieving them.

But the need to capture the benefits of relationships between businesses has never been more important. Technological and competitive developments already link many businesses and are creating new possibilities for competitive advantage. In such sectors as financial services, computing, office equipment, entertainment, and health care, interrelationships among previously distinct businesses are perhaps the central concern of strategy.

To understand the role of relatedness in corporate strategy, we must give new meaning to this often ill-defined idea. I have identified a good way to start—the value chain.[5] Every business unit is a collection of discrete activities ranging from sales to accounting that allow it to compete. I call them value activities. It is at this level, not in the company as a whole, that the unit achieves competitive advantage.

I group these activities in nine categories. *Primary* activities create the product or service, deliver and market it, and provide after-sale support. The categories of primary activities are inbound logistics, operations, outbound logistics, marketing and sales, and service. *Support* activities provide the input and infrastructure that allow the primary activities to take place. The categories are company infrastructure, human resource management, technology development, and procurement.

The value chain defines the two types of interrelationships that may create synergy. The first is a company's ability to transfer skills or expertise among similar value chains. The second is the ability to share activities. Two business units, for example, can share the same sales force or logistics network.

The value chain helps expose the last two (and most important) concepts of corporate strategy. The transfer of skills among business units in the diversified company is the basis for one concept. While each business unit has a separate value chain, knowledge about how to perform activities is transferred among the units. For example, a toiletries business unit, expert in the marketing of convenience products, transmits ideas on new positioning concepts, promotional techniques, and packaging possibilities to a newly acquired unit that sells cough syrup. Newly entered industries can benefit from the expertise of existing units and vice versa.

These opportunities arise when business units have similar buyers or channels, similar value activities like government relations or procurement, similarities in the broad configuration of the value chain (for example, managing a multisite service organization), or the same strategic concept (for example, low cost). Even though the units operate separately, such similarities allow the sharing of knowledge.

Of course, some similarities are common; one can imagine them at some level between almost any pair of businesses. Countless companies have fallen into the trap of diversifying too readily because of similarities; mere similarity is not enough.

Transferring skills leads to competitive advantage only if the similarities among businesses meet three conditions:

1. The activities involved in the businesses are similar enough that sharing expertise is meaningful. Broad similarities (marketing intensiveness, for example, or a common core process technology such as bending metal) are not a sufficient basis for diversification. The resulting ability to transfer skills is likely to have little impact on competitive advantage.
2. The transfer of skills involves activities important to competitive

advantage. Transferring skills in peripheral activities such as government relations or real estate in consumer goods units may be beneficial but is not a basis for diversification.

3. The skills transferred represent a significant source of competitive advantage for the receiving unit. The expertise or skills to be transferred are both advanced and proprietary enough to be beyond the capabilities of competitors.

The transfer of skills is an active process that significantly changes the strategy or operations of the receiving unit. The prospect for change must be specific and identifiable. Almost guaranteeing that no shareholder value will be created, too many companies are satisfied with vague prospects or faint hopes that skills will transfer. The transfer of skills does not happen by accident or by osmosis. The company will have to reassign critical personnel, even on a permanent basis, and the participation and support of high-level management in skills transfer is essential. Many companies have been defeated at skills transfer because they have not provided their business units with any incentives to participate.

Transferring skills meets the tests of diversification if the company truly mobilizes proprietary expertise across units. This makes certain the company can offset the acquisition premium or lower the cost of overcoming entry barriers.

The industries the company chooses for diversification must pass the attractiveness test. Even a close fit that reflects opportunities to transfer skills may not overcome poor industry structure. Opportunities to transfer skills, however, may help the company transform the structures of newly entered industries and send them in favorable directions.

The transfer of skills can be one-time or ongoing. If the company exhausts opportunities to infuse new expertise into a unit after the initial postacquisition period, the unit should ultimately be sold. The corporation is no longer creating shareholder value. Few companies have grasped this point, however, and many gradually suffer mediocre returns. Yet a company diversified into well-chosen businesses can transfer skills eventually in many directions. If corporate management conceives of its role in this way and creates appropriate organizational mechanisms to facilitate cross-unit interchange, the opportunities to share expertise will be meaningful.

By using both acquisitions and internal development, companies can build a transfer-of-skills strategy. The presence of a strong base of skills sometimes creates the possibility for internal entry instead of the acquisition of a going concern. Successful diversifiers that employ the concept of skills transfer may, however, often acquire a company in the target industry as a beachhead and then build on it with their internal expertise. By doing so, they can reduce some of the risks of internal entry and speed up the process. Two companies that have diversified using the transfer-of-skills concept are 3M and Pepsico.

SHARING ACTIVITIES

The fourth concept of corporate strategy is based on sharing activities in the value chains among business units. Procter & Gamble, for example, employs a common physical distribution system and sales force in both paper towels and disposable diapers. McKesson, a leading distribution company, will handle such diverse lines as pharmaceuticals and liquor through superwarehouses.

The ability to share activities is a potent basis for corporate strategy because sharing often enhances competitive advantage by lowering cost or raising differentiation. But not all sharing leads to competitive advantage, and companies can encounter deep organizational resistance to even beneficial sharing possibilities. These hard truths have led many companies to reject synergy prematurely and retreat to the false simplicity of portfolio management.

A cost-benefit analysis of prospective sharing opportunities can determine whether synergy is possible. Sharing can lower costs if it achieves economies of scale, boosts the efficiency of utilization, or helps a company move more rapidly down the learning curve. The costs of General Electric's advertising, sales, and after-sales service activities in major appliances are low because they are spread over a wide range of appliance products. Sharing can also enhance the potential for differentiation. A shared order-processing system, for instance, may allow new features and services that a buyer will value. Sharing can also reduce the cost of differentiation. A shared service network, for example, may make more advanced, remote servicing technology economically feasible. Often, sharing will allow an activity to be wholly reconfigured in ways that can dramatically raise competitive advantage.

Sharing must involve activities that are significant to competitive advantage, not just any activity. P&G's distribution system is such an instance in the diaper and paper towel business, where products are bulky and costly to ship. Conversely, diversification based on the opportunities to share only corporate overhead is rarely, if ever, appropriate.

Sharing activities inevitably involves costs that the benefits must outweigh. One cost is the greater coordination required to manage a shared activity. More important is the need to compromise the design or performance of an activity so that it can be shared. A salesperson handling the products of two business units, for example, must operate in a way that is usually not what either unit would choose were it independent. And if compromise greatly erodes the unit's effectiveness, then sharing may reduce rather than enhance competitive advantage.

Many companies have only superficially identified their potential for sharing. Companies also merge activities without consideration of whether they are sensitive to economies of scale. When they are not, the coordination costs kill the benefits. Companies compound such errors by not identifying costs of sharing in advance, when steps can be taken to minimize them. Costs of compromise can frequently be mitigated by redesigning the activity for sharing. The shared salesperson, for example, can be provided with a remote computer terminal to boost productivity and provide more customer information. Jamming business units together without such thinking exacerbates the costs of sharing.

Despite such pitfalls, opportunities to gain advantage from sharing activities have proliferated because of momentous developments in technology, deregulation, and competition. The infusion of electronics and information systems into many industries creates new opportunities to link businesses. The corporate strategy of sharing can involve both acquisition and internal development. Internal development is often possible because the corporation can bring to bear clear resources in launching a new unit. Start-ups are less difficult to integrate than acquisitions. Companies using the shared-activities concept can also make acquisitions as beachhead landings into a new industry and then integrate the units through sharing with other units. Prime examples of companies that have diversified via using shared activities include P&G, Du Pont, and IBM. The fields into which each has diversified are a cluster of tightly related units. Marriott illustrates both successes and failures in sharing activities over time.

Following the shared-activities model requires an organizational context in which business unit collaboration is encouraged and reinforced. Highly autonomous business units are inimical to such collaboration. The company must put into place a variety of what I call horizontal mechanisms—a strong sense of corporate identity, a clear corporate mission statement that emphasizes the importance of integrating business unit strategies, an incentive system that rewards more than just business unit results, cross-business-unit task forces, and other methods of integrating.

A corporate strategy based on shared activities clearly meets the better-off test because business units gain ongoing tangible advantages from others within the corporation. It also meets the cost-of-entry test by reducing the expense of surmounting the barriers to internal entry. Other bids for acquisitions that do not share opportunities will have lower reservation prices. Even widespread opportunities for sharing activities do not allow a company to suspend the attractiveness test, however. Many diversifiers have made the critical mistake of equating the close fit of a target industry with attractive diversification. Target industries must pass the strict requirement test of having an attractive structure as well as a close fit in opportunities if diversification is to ultimately succeed.

Choosing a Corporate Strategy

Each concept of corporate strategy allows the diversified company to create shareholder value in a different way. Companies can succeed with any of the concepts if they clearly define the corporation's role and objectives, have the skills necessary for meeting the concept's prerequisites, organize themselves to manage diversity in a way that fits the strategy, and find themselves in an appropriate capital market environment. The caveat is that portfolio management is only sensible in limited circumstances.

A company's choice of corporate strategy is partly a legacy of its past. If its business units are in unattractive industries, the company must start from scratch. If the company has few truly proprietary skills or activities it can share in related diversification, then its initial diversification must rely on other concepts. Yet corporate strategy should not be a once-and-for-all choice but a vision that can evolve. A company should choose its long-term preferred concept and then proceed pragmatically toward it from its initial starting point.

Both the strategic logic and the experience of the companies I studied over the last decade suggest that a company will create shareholder value through diversification to a greater and greater extent as its strategy moves from portfolio management toward sharing activities. Because they do not rely on superior insight or other questionable assumptions about the company's capabilities, sharing activities and transferring skills offer the best avenues for value creation.

Each concept of corporate strategy is not mutually exclusive of those that come before, a potent advantage of the third and fourth concepts. A company can employ a restructuring strategy at the same time it transfers skills or shares activities. A strategy based on shared activities becomes more powerful if business units can also exchange skills. A company can often pursue the two strategies together and even incorporate some of the principles of restructuring with them. When it chooses industries in which to transfer skills or share activities, the company can also investigate the possibility of transforming the industry structure. When a company bases its strategy on interrelationships, it has a broader basis on which to create shareholder value than if it rests its entire strategy on transforming companies in unfamiliar industries.

My study supports the soundness of basing a corporate strategy on the transfer of skills or shared activities. The data on the sample companies' diversification programs illustrate some important characteristics of successful diversifiers. They have made a disproportionately low percentage of unrelated acquisitions, *unrelated* being defined as having no clear opportunity to transfer skills or share important activities (see Exhibit III). Even successful diversifiers such as 3M, IBM, and TRW have terrible records when they have strayed into unrelated acquisitions. Successful acquirers diversify into fields, each of which is related to many others. Procter & Gamble and IBM, for example, operate in 18 and 19 interrelated fields, respectively, and so enjoy numerous opportunities to transfer skills and share activities.

Companies with the best acquisition records tend to make heavier-than-average use of start-ups and joint ventures. Most companies shy away from modes of entry besides acquisition. My results cast doubt on the conventional wisdom regarding start-ups. Exhibit III demonstrates that while joint ventures are about as risky as acquisitions, start-ups are not. Moreover, successful companies often have very good records with start-up units, as 3M, P&G, Johnson & Johnson, IBM, and United Technologies illustrate. When a company has the internal strength to start up a unit, it can be safer and less costly to launch a company than to rely solely on an acquisition and then have to deal with the problem of integration. Japanese diversification histories support the soundness of start-up as an entry alternative.

My data also illustrate that none of the concepts of corporate strategy works when industry structure is poor or implementation is bad, no matter how related the industries are. Xerox acquired companies in related industries, but the businesses had poor structures and its skills were insufficient to provide enough competitive advantage to offset implementation problems.

AN ACTION PROGRAM

To translate the principles of corporate strategy into successful diversification, a company must first take an objective look at its existing businesses and the value added by the corporation. Only through such an assessment can an understanding of good corporate strategy grow. That understanding should guide future diversification as well as the development of skills and activities with which to select further new businesses. The following action program provides a concrete approach to conducting such a review. A company can choose a corporate strategy by:

1. **Identifying the interrelationships among already existing business units.**

A company should begin to develop a corporate strategy by identifying all the opportunities it has to share activities or transfer skills in its existing portfolio of business units. The company will not only find ways to enhance the competitive advantage of existing units but also come upon several possible diversification avenues. The lack of meaningful interrelationships in the portfolio is an equally important finding, suggesting the need to justify the value added by the corporation or, alternately, a fundamental restructuring.

2. **Selecting the core businesses that will be the foundation of the corporate strategy.**

Successful diversification starts with an understanding of the core businesses that will serve as the basis for corporate strategy. Core businesses are those that are in an attractive industry, have the potential to achieve sustainable competitive advantage, have important interrelationships with other business units, and provide skills or activities that represent a base from which to diversify.

The company must first make certain its core businesses are on sound footing by upgrading management, internationalizing strategy, or improving technology. My study shows that geographic extensions of existing units, whether by acquisition, joint venture, or start-up, had a substantially lower divestment rate than diversification.

The company must then patiently dispose of the units that are not core businesses. Selling them will free resources that could be better deployed elsewhere. In some cases disposal implies immediate liquidation, while in others the company should dress up the units and wait for a propitious market or a particularly eager buyer.

3. **Creating horizontal organizational mechanisms to facilitate interrelationships among the core businesses and lay the groundwork for future related diversification.**

Top management can facilitate interrelationships by emphasizing cross-unit collaboration, grouping units organizationally and modifying incentives, and taking steps to build a strong sense of corporate identity.

4. **Pursuing diversification opportunities that allow shared activities.**

This concept of corporate strategy is the most compelling, provided a company's strategy passes all three tests. A company should inventory activities in existing business units that represent the strongest foundation for sharing, such as strong distribution channels or world-class technical facilities. These will in turn lead to potential new business areas. A company can use acquisitions as a beachhead or employ start-ups to exploit internal capabilities and minimize integrating problems.

5. **Pursuing diversification through the transfer of skills if opportunities for sharing activities are limited or exhausted.**

Companies can pursue this strategy through acquisition, although they may be able to use start-ups if their existing units have important skills they can readily transfer.

Such diversification is often riskier because of the tough conditions necessary for it to work. Given the uncertainties, a company should avoid diversifying on the basis of skills transfer alone. Rather it should also be viewed as a stepping-stone to subsequent diversification using shared activities. New industries should be chosen that will lead naturally to other businesses. The goal is to build a cluster of related and mutually reinforcing business units. The strategy's logic implies that the company should not set the rate of return standards for the initial foray into a new sector too high.

6. **Pursuing a strategy of restructuring if this fits the skills of management or no good opportunities exist for forging corporate interrelationships.**

When a company uncovers undermanaged companies and can deploy adequate management talent and resources to the acquired units, then it can use a restructuring strategy. The more developed the capital markets and the more active the market for companies, the more restructuring will require a patient search for that special opportunity rather than a headlong race to acquire as many bad apples as possible. Restructuring can be a permanent strategy, as it is with Loew's, or a way to build a group of businesses that supports a shift to another corporate strategy.

7. **Paying dividends so that the shareholders can be the portfolio managers.**

Paying dividends is better than destroying shareholder value through diversification based on shaky underpinnings. Tax considerations, which some companies cite to avoid dividends, are hardly legitimate reason to diversify if a company cannot demonstrate the capacity to do it profitably.

CREATING A CORPORATE THEME

Defining a corporate theme is a good way to ensure that the corporation will create shareholder value. Having the right theme helps unite the efforts of business units and reinforces the ways they interrelate as well as guides the choice of new businesses to enter. NEC Corporation, with its "C&C" theme, provides a good example. NEC integrates its computer, semiconductor, telecommunications, and consumer electronics businesses by merging computers and communication.

It is all too easy to create a shallow corporate theme. CBS wanted to be an "entertainment company," for example, and built a group of businesses related to leisure time. It entered such industries as toys, crafts, musical instruments, sports teams, and hi-fi retailing. While this corporate theme sounded good, close listening revealed its hollow ring. None of these businesses had any significant opportunity to share activities or transfer skills among themselves or with CBS's traditional broadcasting and record businesses. They were all sold, often at significant losses, except for a few of CBS's publishing-related units. Saddled with the worst acquisition record in my study, CBS has eroded the shareholder value created through its strong performance in broadcasting and records.

Moving from competitive strategy to corporate strategy is the business equivalent of passing through the Bermuda Triangle. The failure of corporate strategy reflects the fact that most diversified companies have failed to think in terms of how they really add value. A corporate strategy that truly enhances the competitive advantage of each business unit is the best defense against the corporate raider. With a sharper focus on the tests of diversification and the explicit choice of a clear concept of corporate strategy, companies' diversification track records from now on can look a lot different.

Notes

1. The studies also show that sellers of companies capture a large fraction of the gains from merger. See Michael C. Jensen and Richard S. Ruback, "The Market for Corporate Control: The Scientific Evidence," *Journal of Financial Economics* (April 1983), p. 5, and Michael C. Jensen, "Takeovers: Folklore and Science," *Harvard Business Review* (November–December 1984), p. 109.

2. Some recent evidence also supports the conclusion that acquired companies often suffer eroding performance after acquisition. See Frederick M. Scherer, "Mergers, Sell-Offs and Managerial Behavior," in *The Economics of Strategic Planning,* ed. Lacy Glenn Thomas (Lexington, Mass.: Lexington Books, 1986), p. 143, and

David A. Ravenscraft and Frederick M. Scherer, "Mergers and Managerial Performance," paper presented at the Conference on Takeovers and Contests for Corporate Control, Columbia Law School, 1985.

3. This observation has been made by a number of authors. See, for example, Malcolm S. Salter and Wolf A. Weinhold, *Diversification Through Acquisition* (New York: Free Press, 1979).

4. See Michael E. Porter, "How Competitive Forces Shape Strategy," *Harvard Business Review* (March–April 1979), p. 86. The article is Chapter 2, Part I of this volume.

5. Michael E. Porter, *Competitive Advantage* (New York: Free Press, 1985).

2
The Enduring Logic of Industrial Success

Alfred D. Chandler

In 1881, John D. Rockefeller combined Standard Oil and 39 allied companies to form the Standard Oil Trust. His aim was not monopoly. Linked by financial ties, the companies in the Trust already controlled close to 90% of the kerosene produced in the United States. Rockefeller's goal was the cost advantages that could only be realized by placing the companies' refining facilities under a single management.

Quickly, the Trust's management concentrated close to one-quarter of the world's production into three 6,000 barrel-a-day refineries. Thanks to economies of scale, the unit cost per gallon dropped from 2.5 cents in 1879 to 0.5 cents in 1884 and to 0.4 cents in 1885. With this fivefold reduction in costs, Standard Oil could undersell kerosene made from Russian oil in Europe and kerosene made from Southeast Asian oil in China and still generate profits that created at least three of the world's largest industrial fortunes. Its successor, Exxon, remains the nation's biggest oil company.

At the same time in Germany, Bayer, BASF, and Hoechst—the world's oldest and still largest chemical companies—were driving down the price of dyes and pharmaceuticals by using economies of scope to reduce their production costs. Alizarin, a new, manmade red dye widely used in yarns, fabrics, and leather products, is representative. When the German companies began producing the dye, its price was close to 200 marks per kilo. By 1878, the price per kilo had dropped to 23 marks, and by 1886, it had fallen even further, to 9 marks. By the end of the 1880s, the large German plants were producing more than 500 different dyes and pharmaceuticals at unit costs far below those of smaller competitors.

Over the next century, these stories were repeated in the other industries that have been most critical to the growth of modern economies. Whether we look at chemicals and electrical equipment in the 1880s and 1890s, motor vehicles in the 1920s, or computers today, the same pattern recurs. The dominant companies are those whose founders and senior executives understood what I call the logic of managerial enterprise, that is, the dynamic logic of growth and competition that drives modern industrial capitalism.

By conforming to this logic, entrepreneurs and managers helped to make Germany the most powerful industrial nation in Europe before World War I, the United States the most productive country in the world from the 1920s to the 1960s, and Japan their most successful competitor since that time. Conversely, ignoring the logic—departing from its basic principles—in large part explains why the United States lost its competitive capabilities in such vital industries as semiconductors, machine tools, and consumer electronics.

The term managerial enterprise refers to large industrial concerns in which operating and investment decisions are made by a hierarchy of salaried managers governed by a board of directors. Recently, such organizations have been roundly attacked for dissipating wealth and stifling innovation. In fact, they have been the engines of economic growth and social transformation in industrial nations for the past 100 years. This lesson emerges clearly from my 10-year study of the 200 largest manufacturing companies in the United States, Britain, and Germany from the 1880s, when the modern industrial corporation first appeared, until World War II. But we also see it reflected in the pages of the current business press. The logic that drives the creation and growth of large managerial enterprises is as relevant now as it was when John D. Rockefeller put together Standard Oil.

The Logic of Managerial Enterprise

The logic of managerial enterprise begins with economics—and the cost advantages that scale and scope provide in technologically advanced, capital-intensive industries. In these industries, large plants can produce products at a much lower cost than small ones because the cost per unit drops as the volume of output rises. (This is what is meant by economies of scale.) In addition, large plants can use many of the same raw and semifinished materials and intermediate production processes to make a variety of different products. (This is what is meant by economies of scope.) But these potential cost advantages can be fully realized only if the flow of materials through the plant can be kept constant to assure capacity utilization. That is why entrepreneurs like Rockefeller did not build giant industrial works until the 1880s, when integration of the railroad, the telegraph, the steamship, and the cable made it possible to speed goods and messages through an entire economy for the first time. It is also why large plants quickly became so common in chemicals, branded packaged foods, steel, agricultural machinery, and all the other "high-technology" industries of the late nineteenth century.

But size alone is not enough to fully exploit the cost advantages of scale and scope. To capitalize on their manufacturing investments, the entrepreneurs who built these large plants had to make two related sets of investments. They had to create national—and then international—marketing and distribution organizations. And they had to recruit teams of managers: lower and middle managers to coordinate the flow of products through production and distribution, and top managers to coordinate and monitor current operations and to plan and allocate resources for future activities. Those who first made these large investments—the companies I call first movers—quickly dominated their industries and continued to do so for decades.[1] Those who failed to make these investments rarely became competitive at home or in international markets, nor did the industries in which they operated.

The advantages of being a first mover were immense. To benefit from comparable costs, challengers had to build plants of comparable size—even as the first movers were working out the bugs in the new production processes. Challengers had to create distribution and sales organizations to capture markets where first movers were already established. They also had to recruit management teams to compete with those already well down the learning curve in their specialized activities of production, distribution, and research and development. Challengers did appear. But they were few.

First movers' investments also transformed the structure of the industries in which they competed. These soon came to be dominated by a small number of large companies that vied for market share and profit in new ways. In these competitive battles, innovation and strategy were more powerful weapons than price. As far back as the 1890s, companies like Singer Sewing Machine, Procter & Gamble, and National Cash Register were competing by improving quality and creating new markets as well as by lowering costs. They searched for ways to carry out production and distribution more capably. They engaged in systematic research and development to improve their products and processes. They located better sources of supply and provided more effective marketing services. They differentiated their products (in branded packaged products, primarily through advertising). And they moved rapidly into growing markets and out of declining ones. The test of such competition was market share—and in the new oligopolistic industries, market share and profits changed constantly.

Such competition sharpened the product-specific capabilities of both workers and managers, and these, in turn, became the basis for continuing growth. Companies did grow horizontally (by combining with competitors) and vertically (by moving backward to control materials and forward to control outlets). But such moves were usually responses to specific opportunities. Long term, management's strategy was to grow by moving into related product markets or by moving abroad. In 1913, for instance, the two largest commercial enterprises in Imperial Russia were Singer Sewing Machine and International Harvester (and these were not the largest of those companies' European operations).

Geographic expansion was usually based on economies of scale, while moves into related product markets more often rested on economies of scope. In both cases, however, organizational capabilities honed by oligopolistic competition provided the dynamic for continuing growth—of the companies themselves, the industries they dominated, and the national economies in which they operated.

Competitive Dynamics: Where Britain Went Wrong

The dynamics of the new competitive battles—and the costs of disregarding the logic of managerial enterprise—are evident in the history of British industry in the years before the Second World War. Chemicals is a case in point. Of all the industries developed in this period (which historians rightly call the Second Industrial

Revolution), chemicals was the most technologically advanced and provided the widest range of new industrial and consumer products. Among those products were medicines, fertilizers, textiles, film, and the industry's first major innovation—synthetic dyes.

An Englishman, William Perkin, invented the first man-made dyes in 1856, and in the 1860s and 1870s Britain had almost every comparative advantage in the new industry. Dyes are made from coal, and Britain had the largest supplies of high-quality coal in Europe. Its huge domestic textile industry constituted the world's largest market for the new dyes. All it lacked was experienced chemists, and British entrepreneurs had little trouble hiring trained German chemists for their factories. By any economic criteria, British entrepreneurs should soon have dominated the world in this new industry. Instead, German companies—Bayer, BASF, Hoechst, and three smaller enterprises—took the lead. Why? Because they made the essential investments in production, distribution, and management that the British industrialists failed to make.

Bayer's experience is representative. In the late 1870s, Friedrich Bayer & Co. was a relatively small pioneer. Under the guidance of Carl Duisberg, a chemist still in his twenties, the company began exploiting economies of scope—developing first new dyes and then pharmaceuticals. Then in 1891, it decided to expand by purchasing a dye maker on the Rhine at Leverkusen, near Cologne, a location that was better for receiving raw materials and shipping finished goods than Bayer's original works at Elberfeld. At first, plans called for enlarging the Leverkusen plant. But then Duisberg convinced his colleagues to scrap the existing facilities and build a giant new works that would meet the company's needs for the next half century. (Today, almost 100 years later, Leverkusen is still one of the most efficient chemical plants in the world.)

Duisberg designed the new works to assure a steady flow of material from arrival through production to storage and shipment of the final products. He also made sure that each of the five production departments had its own laboratories and engineering staff and that the offices of the production engineers were close to the chemical laboratories so that "works chemists can at any time get into direct communication with the works engineers." As a result, Leverkusen's laboratories became and remained among the most innovative in the world, producing a stream of new dyes, pharmaceuticals, films, pigments, resins, and other products.

At the same time, Bayer invested heavily in marketing, distribution, and management. By the time the Leverkusen works went into operation, Bayer's global sales force of experienced chemists was contacting and working with more than 20,000 customers, all of whom had to be taught how to apply the new synthetic dyes to their materials. And by the turn of the century, Bayer had created one of the largest and most carefully defined managerial hierarchies the world had yet seen.

The Germans' competitive advantages demolished Britain's economic comparative advantages. In 1913, 160,000 tons of dye were produced. German companies made 140,000 (with the big three accounting for 72% of that output); 10,000 more came from Swiss neighbors up the Rhine. Total British production—4,400 tons. Figures for pharmaceuticals, films, agricultural chemicals, and electrochemicals tell much the same story.

A similar scenario was played out in the electrical equipment industry after 1882, when the first central power station opened in New York City. The industry sparked by Thomas Edison's inventions transformed economic life in myriad ways: by providing sources of light and power that altered urban living and transportation; by changing the ways of the workplace; and by giving rise to new industrial methods such as electrolytic processes for producing copper and other materials. British pioneers were as active in this industry as any in Germany or the United States. Sir William Mather, the senior partner of Mather & Platt, one of the largest British textile machinery manufacturers, obtained the Edison patents at the same time that Emil Rathenau did at AEG. But in the 1880s and 1890s, it was AEG and Siemens—and General Electric and Westinghouse in the United States—that made the essential first-mover investments, not Mather & Platt.

Again, the German story is instructive. In 1903, after merging with a major competitor, Siemens embarked on a ten-year plan to ensure its global position, systematizing and rationalizing production by concentrating its operations under a single management. The result was the world's largest industrial complex, a giant set of works covering several square miles that Siemens financed largely from retained earnings. (The municipality of Berlin that the complex dominated soon became officially known as Siemensstadt.) Where Bayer had built a single works, Siemens constructed several in which more than 20,000 workers made telecommunications equipment and instruments, large machinery, small motors, dynamos, electrochemicals, and cables. Its domestic rival AEG built a similar though somewhat less massive set of works only a few miles away during these same years.

By 1913, two-thirds of the electrical equipment machinery made in British factories by British labor came from subsidiaries of GE, Westinghouse, and Siemens. AEG sold more products in Britain than the largest British company. Mather & Platt had become a minor producer of electrical equipment for factories. From the 1890s on, research and development to improve existing products and develop new ones was carried out in Schenectady, Pittsburgh, and Berlin—but not in Britain.

What was true of chemicals and electrical equipment was also true in heavy and light machinery, steel, and copper and other metals. In metals the British pioneered, but Germans and Americans made the essential investments that drove the British out of international markets. In machinery the British did not even try. German companies quickly took the lead in producing heavy processing machines and equipment for the new industries of the Second Industrial Revolution (as well as many of the old). Americans acquired a near-global monopoly in sewing, business, agricultural, and other light machinery produced by fabricating and assembling standardized parts. By the 1880s, this high-volume production process was already known as "the American system of manufacturing."

As these examples suggest, the opportunity to make first-mover investments and create a managerial enterprise is short-lived. And once the opportunity is lost, it is hard for an enterprise and its national industry to regain competitive capabilities, even in its own domestic market. The British did succeed in chemicals through the creation of Imperial Chemical Industries (ICI), as the Appendix relates. But that was the only major technologically advanced industry in which they ever regained a strong competitive edge.

Competitive Dynamics: What IBM Did Right

The passage of time has not made the logic of managerial enterprise obsolete. On the contrary, its principles were clearly at work in the development of the computer industry after World War II, and they drive competition in the industry today. But there is one striking historical difference: Most of the computer industry's pioneers were long-established managerial enterprises in closely related industries, not entrepreneurs.

U.S. business machine companies were the first to see the commercial possibilities of the costly giant computers initially developed for scientific and military purposes. In 1951, Remington Rand, the nation's leading typewriter company, began to develop UNIVAC, the first computer designed for business uses. Other leading business machine companies—IBM, Burroughs Adding Machine, National Cash Register, and Honeywell (all players in their industry for decades)—quickly followed. Still other pioneers were large, established enterprises with electronics capabilities—Raytheon, General Electric, RCA, and Philco. The only new company to enter the competition was Control Data, founded by William Norris in 1957.

All these pioneering companies made substantial investments in producing and distributing the new machine. But IBM was the first to make the investments that transformed it into the industry's first mover. The strategy of IBM's top managers, particularly Thomas Watson, Jr., was to pursue as wide a commercial market as possible. Several years of intensive investment in research and production led, in 1964, to the introduction of the System 360, a broad line of compatible mainframe computers with peripherals for a wide range of uses. IBM's massive investment in research and production, the swift expansion of its international marketing organization, and an impressive increase in its management ranks gave the company the dominant industry position it retains today.

With the single exception of Control Data, IBM's successful mainframe competitors continued to be business machine companies, all of which acquired electronics companies to improve their production and research competences. In contrast, the electronics companies dropped out of the business. Raytheon and General Electric sold their operations to Honeywell. RCA's computer activities were acquired by Sperry Rand. And Philco dropped its computer operations soon after it was taken over by the Ford Motor Company. These companies had as great a potential for success in computers as the business machine companies did. But by the 1960s, they had become widely diversified. Because computers were only one of many product lines, top management was unwilling to allocate the time and make the large investments necessary to build an effective competitive capability. (Much the same thing has happened more recently in consumer electronics.)

Entrepreneurial companies played a greater role in mini- and microcomputers where opportunities existed to design machines using different technologies for different markets. Nevertheless, the logic holds: The successful companies followed a first-mover strategy. At Digital Equipment, for example, heavy investments in manufacturing for the PDP-8 line of minicomputers were accompanied by the creation of a worldwide marketing network and a sharp rise in the number of managers. Edson de Castro, the engineer who headed the design team for the PDP-8, made a comparable set of investments when he left DEC in 1968 to form Data General. However, the third pioneer, Scientific Data Systems, failed to scale up and quickly disappeared from the scene after it was acquired by Xerox in 1969.

The most successful challengers to DEC and Data General were not entrepreneurial enterprises but managerial companies. By 1980, DEC ranked second and Data General fourth in revenues generated. IBM was first, Burroughs third, and Hewlett-Packard, an established producer of electronic measuring and testing instruments, fifth. The sixth was Wang Laboratories, a first mover with a new product for a different market—word processing and office systems. Together these six accounted for 75% of the revenues generated in the minicomputer branch of the industry.

Much the same pattern appears in personal (micro) computers. By 1980, the first entrepreneurial companies to make extensive three-pronged investments—Apple Computer, Tandy, and Commodore—accounted for 72% of U.S. dollar sales. (The three pioneers that accounted for 50% of sales in 1976 had already dropped by the wayside.) Two years later, however, three established companies—IBM, NEC, and Hewlett-Packard—moved in and captured 35% of the market, driving the entrepreneurial first movers' share down to 48%.

Like American machinery manufacturers in earlier years, these computer companies quickly moved abroad. IBM almost immediately became the leading producer of mainframe computers in Europe. DEC led in microcomputers. By the mid-1980s, Apple and IBM were already world leaders in personal computers. Long-established enterprises created all but one of the successful European or Japanese competitors. True to form, British pioneers failed to make the necessary investments in production, distribution, and management. By 1974, only a little over a quarter of all computer installations in Britain came from British producers.

Major players in the industry have changed little in the past decade. Of the 20 largest hardware producers in 1987, only two were founded in the 1980s. The single successful challenger in existing sectors was Compaq (ranked fourteenth in total revenues), whose management announced in its very first annual report that it thought of itself "as a major company in its formative stage rather than as a small company with big plans" and invested accordingly. The other new company, Sun Microsystems (ranked twentieth), followed the path entrepreneurial companies had traditionally taken and developed a new architecture for a new market, workstations.

Conforming to the logic of industrial growth kept U.S. computer companies competitive—even as they encountered hurdles like the rising cost of capital, the fluctuating dollar, and antitrust and other regulatory legislation that are often cited to explain the decline of other industries. In 1987, U.S. companies still enjoyed just under 60% of the European market in mainframe and minicomputers and just over 20% of the Japanese market. In Europe, IBM's market share was 35%, DEC's 7%, Unisys's (formed by the merger of Burroughs and Sperry Rand in 1986) 5%, and Hewlett-Packard's 3%. In Japan, IBM has 15%, Unisys 3%, and NCR 2%. In microcomputers, Apple and IBM (with Japan's NEC) accounted for 50% of the world market. Foreign competition in the United States remains limited except in some peripherals.

In semiconductors, the story has been very different. This industry, which supplies critical components for computers, telecommunications, factory automation, robotics, aerospace, and production controls, was created in the United States. In the mid-1970s, the pioneering American companies held 60% of the world market, 95% of the domestic market, half the European market, and a quarter of the Japanese market. By 1987, their world market share had fallen to 40%, while the Japanese share had risen to 50%. The United States had become a net importer, with the Japanese supplying 25% of its market. Japanese enterprises controlled over 80% of the world's sales of DRAMs invented by the U.S. company, Intel. IBM, the only world-class producer of semiconductors in the United States, is working with the Defense Department through Sematech to try to save the industry.

What happened? Again, the diversified electronics companies with the greatest capabilities for production and continuing research in semiconductors—RCA and GE—pulled out, while Ford's takeover of Philco destroyed the potential there. More serious, though, was the pioneering companies' failure to invest and grow. If IBM is the prototype of the giant managerial enterprise as first mover, surely the semiconductor companies in Silicon Valley epitomize entrepreneurial enterprise. Instead of making the long-term investments to create organizational capabilities and then continuing to reinvest, they remained small or sold out, often to the Japanese. Repeatedly, groups of engineers left their companies to start new ones. Too many companies—both old and new—ignored the logic of industrial growth. Those few that did not—Texas Instruments, Motorola (both established well before World War II), and Intel—remain significant players, America's major hope (with IBM) of staving off the Japanese challenge.

In Japan, on the other hand, makers of semiconductors followed the logic to its profitable conclusion. Like IBM, all made computers; unlike IBM, they produced semiconductors not only for themselves but also for the larger domestic and international markets. These companies—NEC, Hitachi, Toshiba, Mitsubishi Electric, Oki Electric, Fujitsu, and Matsushita—were long-established producers of electrical and telecommunications equipment. They had diversified but only into closely related product lines. Moreover, all belonged to *keiretsu*—groups of allied, independent enterprises with their own bank and trading companies—and these allies provided further financial, marketing, and research benefits.

By aggressively exploiting the cost advantages of scale and scope, these Japanese companies easily drove entrepreneurial American competitors and the large, more widely diversified electronics companies out of the business or into specialized niches. Efforts by the very few remaining U.S. semiconductor companies may permit them to win back market share. But if the experience of British entrepreneurs in the chemical, electrical, and machinery industries is any indication, such restructuring is difficult and the opportunity to regain competitiveness, fleeting.

When Large Is Not Logical

If size makes sense, as I have been arguing, why have so many large U.S. companies done so poorly in the past few decades? Why is size so often a disadvantage rather than an asset? One answer is that like any human institution, managerial enterprises can stagnate. In the 1920s, Henry Ford destroyed his company's first-mover advantages with a series of wrongheaded decisions, including the firing of his most effective executives. Both GM and Chrysler seized the opportunity to challenge Ford's dominance, first by investing in mid- and high-priced cars and then by moving into the low-price range where Ford had held a worldwide monopoly. Only after Henry Ford died—and his son had hired a group of GM managers to restructure the company—did the automaker begin to regain competitive strength and profits. A similar tale is unfolding today, of course, as the Big Three struggle to regain market share and profitability lost to foreign competitors in the 1970s.

More serious to the long-term health of American companies and industries was the diversification movement of the 1960s—and the chain of events it helped to set off. When senior managers chose to grow through diversification—to acquire businesses in which they had few if any organizational capabilities to give them a competitive edge—they ignored the logic of managerial enterprise. Under these circumstances, bigger was worse, not better.

The catalyst for this diversification was unprecedented competitive pressure. Growth has always been a basic goal of managerial enterprises. And as I have already pointed out, growth came primarily by moving abroad or into new markets in related industries. But until the 1960s, the full impact of this international and inter-industry competition was held back by world events.

World War I and the massive inflation and military occupation of the Ruhr and the Rhineland that followed kept German companies out of international markets for almost a decade. They returned with impressive strength between 1925 and 1929, only to be reined in again by the coming of the Great Depression, Hitler's command economy, and the disastrous Second World War. Depression, global war, and postwar recovery also dampened or redirected the growth of U.S. enterprises and those in other European nations. As a result, the international competition that had been developing before 1914 only became a full-fledged reality in the 1960s, once the economic health of the European nations was fully restored and Japan (following a massive technology transfer) was rapidly industrializing. At the same time, unprecedented investments in research and development were intensifying interindustry competition in the United States and Europe.

This new competition challenged many American companies as they had not been challenged since their founding decades earlier.

The challenge was particularly unexpected because the American economy was so prosperous. Even so, markets became saturated. And with capacity underutilized, costs rose.

Many U.S. managers responded as the business machinery executives did, by reinvesting to improve their capabilities in their own and closely related industries. But others began to grow by moving into industries in which their enterprises had no particular competitive advantage. Because they had had little competition abroad since well before World War II—and because they were being told by academics that management was a general skill— many of these executives had come to believe that if they were successful in their own industries they could be just as successful in others. Moreover, their companies were cash-ladened precisely because the postwar years of American hegemony had been so prosperous. So they sought to invest retained earnings in industries that appeared to show a greater profit potential than their own, even though those industries were only distantly related or even unrelated to their companies' core capabilities. And because they lacked knowledge of their targets' operations, they obtained these plants and personnel not through direct investment as in the past but through acquisitions or, occasionally, mergers.

The Tangled Logic of Diversification

By the late 1960s, acquisitions and mergers had become almost a mania. The number rose from just over 2,000 in 1965 to over 6,000 in 1969. From 1963 to 1972, close to three-fourths of the assets acquired were for product diversification, and one-half of these were in unrelated product lines. From 1973 to 1977, one-half of all assets acquired through merger and acquisition came from unrelated industries.

Such unprecedented diversification led to another new phenomenon: the separation of top management at the corporate office from the middle managers who were responsible for running the operating divisions and battling for profits and market share. This separation occurred for two reasons. First, top managers often had little specific knowledge of or experience with the technological processes and markets of the divisions or subsidiaries they had acquired. The second was simply that the large number of acquired businesses created an extraordinary overload in decision making at the corporate office. Before World War II, the corporate executives of large, diversified international enterprises rarely managed more than 10 divisions, and only the largest companies had as many as 25. By 1969, many companies were operating with 40 to 70 divisions, and a few had even more.

Because few senior executives had either the training or the experience to evaluate the proposals and monitor the performance of so many different divisions, they had to rely more and more heavily on financial data. But as H. Thomas Johnson and Robert S. Kaplan point out in *Relevance Lost: The Rise and Fall of Management Accounting,* such data were no longer very helpful for understanding the complexities of competitive battles. The reason was simple: Accounting methods developed by Carnegie, Brown of Du Pont and General Motors, and other industrialists to manage costs had been replaced by financial reporting techniques devised by professional independent public accountants (imported from Britain) that focused on defining profits.[2]

Managerial weaknesses arising from the separation of top and operating management quickly led to another new phenomenon— the sale of operating units in unheard-of numbers. Before the mid-1960s, divestitures were rare. By the early 1970s, they had become commonplace. In 1965, there was only one divestiture for every 11 mergers; by 1970, it was 1 to 2.4; and from 1974 to 1977, the ratio was close to or even under 1 to 2.

All these mergers, acquisitions, and divestitures established the buying and selling of corporations as a business—and a lucrative one at that. While the industrialists pioneered in this business, the financial community prospered most from it. Many financial institutions (particularly investment banks) turned away from what had been their basic function for almost a century: providing funds to supplement retained earnings to keep people and plants competitive. (Financial institutions in Japan and continental Europe still perform this function effectively.)

The new business was further encouraged by another unprecedented change—this one in the ownership of U.S. industrial companies. Before World War II, most securities were held by relatively wealthy individuals and families. Even as late as 1952, only 4.2% of the American population held corporate securities (and this includes owners of mutual funds). The major institutional investors were insurance companies and the trust departments of commercial banks, which normally invested for growth and assets rather than for short-term gains in share prices and dividends.

After World War II, however, growing numbers of shares were held by pension and mutual funds. Begun in the 1920s, these funds grew little during the depressed years of the 1930s. But by the 1960s, they had come into their own, and their managers were being measured by how well their portfolios performed against the Standard & Poor's indexes. To succeed they had constantly to buy and sell securities. As time passed, they increasingly traded securities in large blocks of 10,000 shares or more.

As the number of such funds and the volume of the securities traded increased, both block sales and turnover rose rapidly. And this made possible still another new phenomenon—the coming of an institutionalized market for corporate control. For the first time, individuals, groups, and companies could obtain control of well-established companies in industries in which the buyers had no previous connections simply by purchasing their shares on the stock exchange. Large blocks of stock were being traded regularly and such buyers had little trouble raising funds for their purchases from financial institutions and financiers.

By the mid-1970s, widespread restructuring was clearly required. Continuing intense competition made it imperative that senior managers reinvest in reshaping and rationalizing operations to maintain —or regain—competitiveness. The same was true for enterprises that had grown huge and unwieldy through unbridled diversification. But the desire of investment banks and other financial institutions to maintain their new and profitable business and the need of pension and mutual fund managers to maintain the current value of their portfolios clearly affected how managers could proceed.

Restructuring for Competitiveness

Taken together, these phenomena have greatly facilitated corporate restructuring. Large companies can be bought, sold, split up, and recombined in ways that would have been impossible before the acquisition wave of the 1960s. Such restructuring can be destructive. It contributed greatly to the dissolution of powerful U.S. companies such as International Harvester and Singer Sewing Machine, to the loss of others like B.F. Goodrich and Uniroyal to foreign control, and to the destruction of the U.S. machine-tool industry. Nevertheless, this flexibility has not been all bad. On the contrary, it can help enhance competitive capabilities *if* it is used in the service of a carefully considered long-term strategy. Again, the chemicals industry provides a case in point.

The intensified interindustry and international competition of the 1960s hit chemical companies especially hard. Forced to restructure, the managerial enterprises that had long dominated their national industries—Du Pont, Union Carbide, Dow, and Monsanto in the United States—as well as BASF, Bayer, and Hoechst in Germany, Ciba-Geigy in Switzerland, and ICI in Britain—reshaped their product lines and organizational strategies. In the process, they also restructured the industry.

These companies narrowed their product lines, spinning off many of the commodity products, particularly petrochemicals. (At Dow, for example, commodities dropped from 63% of sales to 35% in five years.) They expanded output in existing higher value-added specialties. And they moved into new areas such as pharmaceuticals, biotechnology, and advanced materials, often through acquisitions of pioneering companies. In other words, they stuck to the same basic strategy they had followed for a century—pursuing growth through economies of scope and developing markets that best fit their distinctive core production and research technologies.

New entrepreneurial companies played almost no role in the restructured industry, although some smaller businesses did appear to operate and occasionally consolidate the petrochemical activities the giants had spun off. Today the United States remains an exporter of chemicals. Japanese companies have yet to become serious competitors in U.S. or international markets.

Other manifestations of the market for corporate control can also build competitiveness. Take conglomerates. As long as their executives concentrate on a relatively small number of divisions (as, for example, those at Tenneco do), they can often provide a more effective and immediate discipline over managerial inertia than the product markets can. Similarly, outside directors representing financial institutions or large stockholders can play an important role in reviving stagnant companies by bringing in outsiders to turn the company around. But the basic task of conglomerate managers, outside directors, and new CEOs must be to recruit managers with the experience and skills to understand the enterprise's complex technological products and processes, the intricacies of its many markets, and the activities of its competitors.

Individual financiers, managers, and shareholders have often profited from ignoring the dynamics of managerial enterprise in capital-intensive industries. But the consequences of their actions have hurt the long-term health of the enterprises and industries involved. The development, production, and distribution of goods for national and global markets require a wide variety of activities calling for many different facilities and skills. Only when all these activities are carefully coordinated can they be integrated in ways that reduce price, assure quality, and provide essential services. Such cooperative efforts are so profitable that if entrepreneurial enterprises fail to become managerial and managerial enterprises fail to maintain and nourish their competitive capabilities, they will lose markets and profits to those in other nations and other industries that do. At least that has been the experience of the industries that have done most to transform the world since the coming of modern transportation and communication networks more than a century ago.

Appendix

REGAINING COMPETITIVE CAPABILITIES

By 1900, the German chemical companies had driven nearly all the pioneering companies in Britain out of business. Earlier, the dye makers had petitioned Parliament for tariff or other protective legislation. But the British textile manufacturers—the most powerful industrial group in England—were delighted with the low price and high quality of the German products, while British scholars and policymakers had come to accept free trade as both an economic theory and an article of faith. (The fact that in the 1890s Britain was still the world's largest exporter of machine-made goods doubtless deepened their commitment.) So the dye makers had little hope of government protection, and their enterprises failed.

Then came World War I. To meet acute shortages, the British producer expanded its output. The government set up another enterprise, British Dyestuffs Corporation, and then, in 1918, acquired the private company. This expansion of capacity plus the greatly enlarged output of the Swiss producers (Ciba, Geigy, and Sandoz) permitted Britain to obtain essential dyes at high cost.

Once the war was over, however, the German companies came back quickly. By 1921, the newly appointed head of British Dyestuffs told the Board of Trade that he saw little hope of making the company competitive unless it acquired technical skills from the Germans. The latter were willing enough to strike a deal, but their proposal would give them de facto control. British Dyestuffs would become little more than their selling agents in Britain. Neither the Conservative nor the Labour party could accept such terms.

In 1925, the government pulled out, but British Dyestuffs did little better in private hands. As 1926 opened, Reginald McKenna, head of the Midland Bank, former Chancellor of the Exchequer, and former chairman of the Board of Trade's committee to supervise British Dyestuffs, began to plead with one and then the other of the two largest British chemical companies, Nobel Industries and Brunner, Mond, to take British Dyestuffs under their wing. His pleas set off a series of complex negotiations that led to the formation of Imperial Chemical Industries (ICI) in the fall of 1926. (By then, both industry and government saw the merger as an essential response to the creation of I.G. Farben, which consolidated Bayer, BASF, Hoechst, and five smaller German chemical companies.)

Nobel Industries and Brunner, Mond were the *only* two chemical companies in Britain that had recruited a substantial set of top and middle managers. And both had strengthened their organizational capabilities after the war. Nobel Industries had acquired several small explosives producers and then become one of the first companies in Britain to do what had become standard practice in the United States—reorganize and rationalize the merged companies. Explicitly following the example of its American ally, E.I. du Pont de Nemours, Nobel Industries centralized its administrative structure, created functional departments, closed down 44 older factories, sold off obsolete plants and equipment, and invested in up-to-date machines.

Brunner, Mond, the other merger partner, had grown more by direct investment in plant and personnel than by acquisitions. Of these investments, by far the most costly and important was one to produce synthetic nitrates for fertilizers through a process acquired from the Germans as a spoil of war. By 1926, Brunner, Mond had invested £3 million in the project (undertaken at the urging of the British government) and had yet to show a profit. Once fully in operation, however, it assured Britain a strong position in international markets.

More reorganization and rationalization followed the formation of ICI. Eventually, managament created a multidivisional structure with autonomous integrated divisions, or "groups," for explosives, synthetic alkalis, dyestuffs, nitrates and fertilizers, and chemicals, among others. By the 1930s, ICI was becoming an effective global competitor in all these products. Agreements struck by international cartels during the depression years reflect its growing strength. In the nitrate agreement of 1932, for example, ICI received a quota of close to 20% and exclusive marketing rights in several large markets. That same year, it obtained close to 10% in comparable agreements on dyes—a far cry from the outcome of the British Dyestuffs negotiations in the early 1920s. As one ICI executive observed, "the only way BDG [ICI's Dyestuff Group] could get into the dye business was to invent its way in. The I.G. [Farben] never took much notice of BDG until they found that BDG could invent."

As this comment indicates, capabilities developed in exploiting economies of scale and scope encouraged process and product innovation. From 1933 through 1935, the dyestuffs laboratory came up with 87 new products including rubber goods, chemicals, synthetic resins and lacquers, detergents, pesticides, and pharmaceuticals.

The moral? Through management's decisions and actions, ICI and its two predecessors were able to achieve what too few British industrial enterprises have ever done: develop the product-specific facilities and skills essential to obtain and maintain a competitive position in world markets.

Notes

1. It is important to distinguish first movers from the inventors of a product or process and from the pioneers that first commercialize an innovation. In mainframe computers, for example, several pioneers invested in marketing the new machines on a national scale. But it was IBM's massive investments in the production, distribution, and management of the System 360 that made it the industry's first mover. Often there is more than one first mover in an industry: BASF, Hoechst, and Bayer were all first movers in chemicals.

2. Boston: Harvard Business School Press, 1987.

3
The Core Competence of the Corporation

C.K. Prahalad and Gary Hamel

The most powerful way to prevail in global competition is still invisible to many companies. During the 1980s, top executives were judged on their ability to restructure, declutter, and delayer their corporations. In the 1990s, they'll be judged on their ability to identify, cultivate, and exploit the core competencies that make growth possible—indeed, they'll have to rethink the concept of the corporation itself.

Consider the past ten years of GTE and NEC. In the early 1980s, GTE was well positioned to become a major player in the evolving information technology industry. It was active in telecommunications. Its operations spanned a variety of businesses including telephones, switching and transmission systems, digital PABX, semiconductors, packet switching, satellites, defense systems, and lighting products. And GTE's Entertainment Products Group, which produced Sylvania color TVs, had a position in related display technologies. In 1980, GTE's sales were $9.98 billion, and net cash flow was $1.73 billion. NEC, in contrast, was much smaller, at $3.8 billion in sales. It had a comparable technological base and computer businesses, but it had no experience as an operating telecommunications company.

Yet look at the positions of GTE and NEC in 1988. GTE's 1988 sales were $16.46 billion, and NEC's sales were considerably higher at $21.89 billion. GTE has, in effect, become a telephone operating company with a position in defense and lighting products. GTE's other businesses are small in global terms. GTE has divested Sylvania TV and Telenet, put switching, transmission, and digital

PABX into joint ventures, and closed down semiconductors. As a result, the international position of GTE has eroded. Non-U.S. revenue as a percent of total revenue dropped from 20% to 15% between 1980 and 1988.

NEC has emerged as the world leader in semiconductors and as a first-tier player in telecommunications products and computers. It has consolidated its position in mainframe computers. It has moved beyond public switching and transmission to include such lifestyle products as mobile telephones, facsimile machines, and laptop computers—bridging the gap between telecommunications and office automation. NEC is the only company in the world to be in the top five in revenue in telecommunications, semiconductors, and mainframes. Why did these two companies, starting with comparable business portfolios, perform so differently? Largely because NEC conceived of itself in terms of "core competencies," and GTE did not.

Rethinking the Corporation

Once, the diversified corporation could simply point its business units at particular end-product markets and admonish them to become world leaders. But with market boundaries changing ever more quickly, targets are elusive and capture is at best temporary. A few companies have proven themselves adept at inventing new markets, quickly entering emerging markets, and dramatically shifting patterns of customer choice in established markets. These are the ones to emulate. The critical task for management is to create an organization capable of infusing products with irresistible functionality or, better yet, creating products that customers need but have not yet even imagined.

This is a deceptively difficult task. Ultimately, it requires radical change in the management of major companies. It means, first of all, that top managements of Western companies must assume responsibility for competitive decline. Everyone knows about high interest rates, Japanese protectionism, outdated antitrust laws, obstreperous unions, and impatient investors. What is harder to see, or harder to acknowledge, is how little added momentum companies actually get from political or macroeconomic "relief." Both the theory and practice of Western management have created a drag on our forward motion. It is the principles of management that are in need of reform.

NEC versus GTE, again, is instructive and only one of many such comparative cases we analyzed to understand the changing basis for global leadership. Early in the 1970s, NEC articulated a strategic intent to exploit the convergence of computing and communications, what it called "C&C."[1] Success, top management reckoned, would hinge on acquiring *competencies,* particularly in semiconductors. Management adopted an appropriate "strategic architecture," summarized by C&C, and then communicated its intent to the whole organization and the outside world during the mid-1970s.

NEC constituted a "C&C Committee" of top managers to oversee the development of core products and core competencies. NEC put in place coordination groups and committees that cut across the interests of individual businesses. Consistent with its strategic architecture, NEC shifted enormous resources to strengthen its position in components and central processors. By using collaborative arrangements to multiply internal resources, NEC was able to accumulate a broad array of core competencies.

NEC carefully identified three interrelated streams of technological and market evolution. Top management determined that computing would evolve from large mainframes to distributed processing, components from simple ICs to VLSI, and communications from mechanical cross-bar exchange to complex digital systems we now call ISDN. As things evolved further, NEC reasoned, the computing, communications, and components businesses would so overlap that it would be very hard to distinguish among them, and that there would be enormous opportunities for any company that had built the competencies needed to serve all three markets.

NEC top management determined that semiconductors would be the company's most important "core product." It entered into myriad strategic alliances—over 100 as of 1987—aimed at building competencies rapidly and at low cost. In mainframe computers, its most noted relationship was with Honeywell and Bull. Almost all the collaborative arrangements in the semiconductor-component field were oriented toward technology access. As they entered collaborative arrangements, NEC's operating managers understood the rationale for these alliances and the goal of internalizing partner skills. NEC's director of research summed up its competence acquisition during the 1970s and 1980s this way: "From an investment standpoint, it was much quicker and cheaper to use foreign tech-nology. There wasn't a need for us to develop new ideas."

No such clarity of strategic intent and strategic architecture ap-peared to exist at GTE. Although senior executives discussed the implications of the evolving information technology industry, no commonly accepted view of which competencies would be required to compete in that industry were communicated widely. While significant staff work was done to identify key technologies, senior line managers continued to act as if they were managing indepen-dent business units. Decentralization made it difficult to focus on core competencies. Instead, individual businesses became increas-ingly dependent on outsiders for critical skills, and collaboration became a route to staged exits. Today, with a new management team in place, GTE has repositioned itself to apply its competencies to emerging markets in telecommunications services.

The Roots of Competitive Advantage

The distinction we observed in the way NEC and GTE conceived of themselves—a portfolio of competencies versus a portfolio of businesses—was repeated across many industries. From 1980 to 1988, Canon grew by 264%, Honda by 200%. Compare that with Xerox and Chrysler. And if Western managers were once anxious about the low cost and high quality of Japanese imports, they are now overwhelmed by the pace at which Japanese rivals are in-venting new markets, creating new products, and enhancing them. Canon has given us personal copiers; Honda has moved from mo-torcycles to four-wheel off-road buggies. Sony developed the 8mm camcorder, Yamaha, the digital piano. Komatsu developed an un-derwater remote-controlled bulldozer, while Casio's latest gambit is a small-screen color LCD television. Who would have anticipated the evolution of these vanguard markets?

In more established markets, the Japanese challenge has been just as disquieting. Japanese companies are generating a blizzard of features and functional enhancements that bring technological sophistication to everyday products. Japanese car producers have been pioneering four-wheel steering, four-valve-per-cylinder en-gines, in-car navigation systems, and sophisticated electronic en-gine-management systems. On the strength of its product features, Canon is now a player in facsimile transmission machines, desktop laser printers, even semiconductor manufacturing equipment.

In the short run, a company's competitiveness derives from the price/performance attributes of current products. But the survivors of the first wave of global competition, Western and Japanese alike, are all converging on similar and formidable standards for product cost and quality—minimum hurdles for continued competition, but less and less important as sources of differential advantage. In the long run, competitiveness derives from an ability to build, at lower cost and more speedily than competitors, the core competencies that spawn unanticipated products. The real sources of advantage are to be found in management's ability to consolidate corporate-wide technologies and production skills into competencies that empower individual businesses to adapt quickly to changing opportunities.

Senior executives who claim that they cannot build core competencies either because they feel the autonomy of business units is sacrosanct or because their feet are held to the quarterly budget fire should think again. The problem in many Western companies is not that their senior executives are any less capable than those in Japan nor that Japanese companies possess greater technical capabilities. Instead, it is their adherence to a concept of the corporation that unnecessarily limits the ability of individual businesses to fully exploit the deep reservoir of technological capability that many American and European companies possess.

The diversified corporation is a large tree. The trunk and major limbs are core products, the smaller branches are business units; the leaves, flowers, and fruit are end products. The root system that provides nourishment, sustenance, and stability is the core competence. You can miss the strength of competitors by looking only at their end products, in the same way you miss the strength of a tree if you look only at its leaves (see Exhibit I).

Core competencies are the collective learning in the organization, especially how to coordinate diverse production skills and integrate multiple streams of technologies. Consider Sony's capacity to miniaturize or Philips's optical-media expertise. The theoretical knowledge to put a radio on a chip does not in itself assure a company the skill to produce a miniature radio no bigger than a business card. To bring off this feat, Casio must harmonize know-how in miniaturization, microprocessor design, material science, and ultrathin precision casing—the same skills it applies in its miniature card calculators, pocket TVs, and digital watches.

If core competence is about harmonizing streams of technology, it is also about the organization of work and the delivery of value.

Exhibit I.

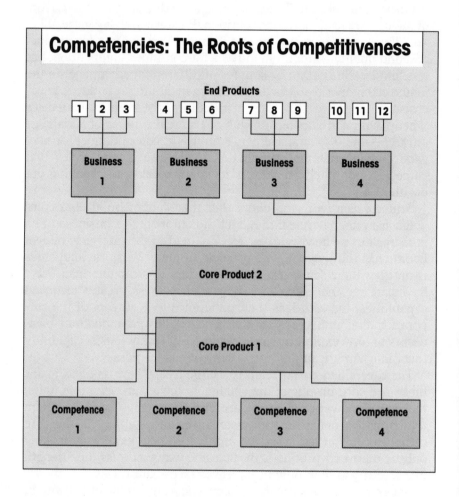

Competencies: The Roots of Competitiveness

Among Sony's competencies is miniaturization. To bring miniaturization to its products, Sony must ensure that technologists, engineers, and marketers have a shared understanding of customer needs and of technological possibilities. The force of core competence is felt as decisively in services as in manufacturing. Citicorp was ahead of others investing in an operating system that allowed it to participate in world markets 24 hours a day. Its competence in systems has provided the company the means to differentiate itself from many financial services institutions.

Core competence is communication, involvement, and a deep commitment to working across organizational boundaries. It involves many levels of people and all functions. World-class research in, for example, lasers or ceramics can take place in corporate laboratories without having an impact on any of the businesses of the company. The skills that together constitute core competence must coalesce around individuals whose efforts are not so narrowly focused that they cannot recognize the opportunities for blending their functional expertise with those of others in new and interesting ways.

Core competence does not diminish with use. Unlike physical assets, which do deteriorate over time, competencies are enhanced as they are applied and shared. But competencies still need to be nurtured and protected; knowledge fades if it is not used. Competencies are the glue that binds existing businesses. They are also the engine for new business development. Patterns of diversification and market entry may be guided by them, not just by the attractiveness of markets.

Consider 3M's competence with sticky tape. In dreaming up businesses as diverse as "Post-it" notes, magnetic tape, photographic film, pressure-sensitive tapes, and coated abrasives, the company has brought to bear widely shared competencies in substrates, coatings, and adhesives and devised various ways to combine them. Indeed, 3M has invested consistently in them. What seems to be an extremely diversified portfolio of businesses belies a few shared core competencies.

In contrast, there are major companies that have had the potential to build core competencies but failed to do so because top management was unable to conceive of the company as anything other than a collection of discrete businesses. GE sold much of its consumer electronics business to Thomson of France, arguing that it was becoming increasingly difficult to maintain its competitiveness in this sector. That was undoubtedly so, but it is ironic that it sold several key businesses to competitors who were already competence leaders—Black & Decker in small electrical motors, and Thomson, which was eager to build its competence in microelectronics and had learned from the Japanese that a position in consumer electronics was vital to this challenge.

Management trapped in the strategic business unit (SBU) mindset almost inevitably finds its individual businesses dependent on external sources for critical components, such as motors or compressors. But these are not just components. They are core products that contribute to the competitiveness of a wide range of end products. They are the physical embodiments of core competencies.

How Not to Think of Competence

Since companies are in a race to build the competencies that determine global leadership, successful companies have stopped imagining themselves as bundles of businesses making products. Canon, Honda, Casio, or NEC may seem to preside over portfolios of businesses unrelated in terms of customers, distribution channels, and merchandising strategy. Indeed, they have portfolios that may seem idiosyncratic at times: NEC is the only global company to be among leaders in computing, telecommunications, and semiconductors *and* to have a thriving consumer electronics business.

But looks are deceiving. In NEC, digital technology, especially VLSI and systems integration skills, is fundamental. In the core competencies underlying them, disparate businesses become coherent. It is Honda's core competence in engines and power trains that gives it a distinctive advantage in car, motorcycle, lawn mower, and generator businesses. Canon's core competencies in optics, imaging, and microprocessor controls have enabled it to enter, even dominate, markets as seemingly diverse as copiers, laser printers, cameras, and image scanners. Philips worked for more than 15 years to perfect its optical-media (laser disk) competence, as did JVC in building a leading position in video recording. Other examples of core competencies might include mechantronics (the ability to marry mechanical and electronic engineering), video displays, bioengineering, and microelectronics. In the early stages of its competence building, Philips could not have imagined all the products that would be spawned by its optical-media competence, nor could JVC have anticipated miniature camcorders when it first began exploring videotape technologies.

Unlike the battle for global brand dominance, which is visible in the world's broadcast and print media and is aimed at building global "share of mind," the battle to build world-class competencies is invisible to people who aren't deliberately looking for it. Top management often tracks the cost and quality of competitors' products, yet how many managers untangle the web of alliances their Japanese competitors have constructed to acquire competencies at low cost? In how many Western boardrooms is there an explicit, shared understanding of the competencies the company must build for world leadership? Indeed, how many senior executives discuss the crucial distinction between competitive strategy at the level of a business and competitive strategy at the level of an entire company?

Let us be clear. Cultivating core competence does *not* mean outspending rivals on research and development. In 1983, when Canon surpassed Xerox in worldwide unit market share in the copier business, its R&D budget in reprographics was but a small fraction of Xerox's. Over the past 20 years, NEC has spent less on R&D as a percentage of sales than almost all of its American and European competitors.

Nor does core competence mean shared costs, as when two or more SBUs use a common facility—a plant, service facility, or sales force—or share a common component. The gains of sharing may be substantial, but the search for shared costs is typically a post hoc effort to rationalize production across existing businesses, not a premeditated effort to build the competencies out of which the businesses themselves grow.

Building core competencies is more ambitious and different than integrating vertically, moreover. Managers deciding whether to make or buy will start with end products and look upstream to the efficiencies of the supply chain and downstream toward distribution and customers. They do not take inventory of skills and look forward to applying them in nontraditional ways. (Of course, decisions about competencies *do* provide a logic for vertical integration. Canon is not particularly integrated in its copier business, except in those aspects of the vertical chain that support the competencies it regards as critical.)

Identifying Core Competencies—And Losing Them

At least three tests can be applied to identify core competencies in a company. First, a core competence provides potential access to a wide variety of markets. Competence in display systems, for example, enables a company to participate in such diverse businesses as calculators, miniature TV sets, monitors for laptop computers, and automotive dashboards—which is why Casio's entry into the hand-held TV market was predictable. Second, a core competence should make a significant contribution to the perceived customer benefits of the end product. Clearly, Honda's engine expertise fills this bill.

Finally, a core competence should be difficult for competitors to imitate. And it *will* be difficult if it is a complex harmonization of individual technologies and production skills. A rival might acquire some of the technologies that comprise the core competence, but it will find it more difficult to duplicate the more or less comprehensive pattern of internal coordination and learning. JVC's decision in the early 1960s to pursue the development of a videotape competence passed the three tests outlined here. RCA's decision in the late 1970s to develop a stylus-based video turntable system did not.

Few companies are likely to build world leadership in more than five or six fundamental competencies. A company that compiles a list of 20 to 30 capabilities has probably not produced a list of core competencies. Still, it is probably a good discipline to generate a list of this sort and to see aggregate capabilities as building blocks. This tends to prompt the search for licensing deals and alliances through which the company may acquire, at low cost, the missing pieces.

Most Western companies hardly think about competitiveness in these terms at all. It is time to take a tough-minded look at the risks they are running. Companies that judge competitiveness, their own and their competitors', primarily in terms of the price/performance of end products are courting the erosion of core competencies—or making too little effort to enhance them. The embedded skills that give rise to the next generation of competitive products cannot be "rented in" by outsourcing and OEM-supply relationships. In our view, too many companies have unwittingly surrendered core competencies when they cut internal investment in what they mistakenly thought were just "cost centers" in favor of outside suppliers.

Consider Chrysler. Unlike Honda, it has tended to view engines and power trains as simply one more component. Chrysler is becoming increasingly dependent on Mitsubishi and Hyundai: Between 1985 and 1987, the number of outsourced engines went from 252,000 to 382,000. It is difficult to imagine Honda yielding manufacturing responsibility, much less design, of so critical a part of a car's function to an outside company—which is why Honda has made such an enormous commitment to Formula One auto racing.

Honda has been able to pool its engine-related technologies: It has parlayed these into a corporatewide competency from which it develops world-beating products, despite R&D budgets smaller than those of GM and Toyota.

Of course, it is perfectly possible for a company to have a competitive product line up but be a laggard in developing core competencies—at least for a while. If a company wanted to enter the copier business today, it would find a dozen Japanese companies more than willing to supply copiers on the basis of an OEM private label. But when fundamental technologies changed or if its supplier decided to enter the market directly and become a competitor, that company's product line, along with all of its investments in marketing and distribution, could be vulnerable. Outsourcing can provide a shortcut to a more competitive product, but it typically contributes little to building the people-embodied skills that are needed to sustain product leadership.

Nor is it possible for a company to have an intelligent alliance or sourcing strategy if it has not made a choice about where it will build competence leadership. Clearly, Japanese companies have benefited from alliances. They've used them to learn from Western partners who were not fully committed to preserving core competencies of their own. As we've argued in these pages before, learning within an alliance takes a positive commitment of resources— travel, a pool of dedicated people, test-bed facilities, time to internalize and test what has been learned.[2] A company may not make this effort if it doesn't have clear goals for competence building.

Another way of losing is forgoing opportunities to establish competencies that are evolving in existing businesses. In the 1970s and 1980s, many American and European companies—like GE, Motorola, GTE, Thorn, and GEC—chose to exit the color television business, which they regarded as mature. If by "mature" they meant that they had run out of new product ideas at precisely the moment global rivals had targeted the TV business for entry, then yes, the industry was mature. But it certainly wasn't mature in the sense that all opportunities to enhance and apply video-based competencies had been exhausted.

In ridding themselves of their television businesses, these companies failed to distinguish between divesting the business and destroying their video media-based competencies. They not only got out of the TV business but they also closed the door on a whole stream of future opportunities reliant on video-based competencies.

The television industry, considered by many U.S. companies in the 1970s to be unattractive, is today the focus of a fierce public policy debate about the inability of U.S. corporations to benefit from the $20-billion-a-year opportunity that HDTV will represent in the mid- to late 1990s. Ironically, the U.S. government is being asked to fund a massive research project—in effect, to compensate U.S. companies for their failure to preserve critical core competencies when they had the chance.

In contrast, one can see a company like Sony reducing its emphasis on VCRs (where it has not been very successful and where Korean companies now threaten), without reducing its commitment to video-related competencies. Sony's Betamax led to a debacle. But it emerged with its videotape recording competencies intact and is currently challenging Matsushita in the 8mm camcorder market.

There are two clear lessons here. First, the costs of losing a core competence can be only partly calculated in advance. The baby may be thrown out with the bath water in divestment decisions. Second, since core competencies are built through a process of continuous improvement and enhancement that may span a decade or longer, a company that has failed to invest in core competence building will find it very difficult to enter an emerging market, unless, of course, it will be content simply to serve as a distribution channel.

American semiconductor companies like Motorola learned this painful lesson when they elected to forgo direct participation in the 256k generation of DRAM chips. Having skipped this round, Motorola, like most of its American competitors, needed a large infusion of technical help from Japanese partners to rejoin the battle in the 1-megabyte generation. When it comes to core competencies, it is difficult to get off the train, walk to the next station, and then reboard.

From Core Competencies to Core Products

The tangible link between identified core competencies and end products is what we call the core products—the physical embodiments of one or more core competencies. Honda's engines, for example, are core products, linchpins between design and development skills that ultimately lead to a proliferation of end-products. Core products are the components or subassemblies that actually contribute to the value of the end products. Thinking in terms of core products forces a company to distinguish between the brand share it achieves in end-product markets (for example, 40% of the U.S. refrigerator market) and the manufacturing share it achieves in any particular core product (for example, 5% of the world share of compressor output).

Canon is reputed to have an 84% world manufacturing share in desktop laser printer "engines," even though its brand share in the laser printer business is minuscule. Similarly, Matsushita has a world manufacturing share of about 45% in key VCR components, far in excess of its brand share (Panasonic, JVC, and others) of 20%. And Matsushita has a commanding core product share in compressors worldwide, estimated at 40%, even though its brand share in both the air-conditioning and refrigerator businesses is quite small.

It is essential to make this distinction between core competencies, core products, and end products because global competition is played out by different rules and for different stakes at each level. To build or defend leadership over the long term, a corporation will probably be a winner at each level. At the level of core competence, the goal is to build world leadership in the design and development of a particular class of product functionality—be it compact data storage and retrieval, as with Philips's optical-media competence, or compactness and ease of use, as with Sony's micromotors and microprocessor controls.

To sustain leadership in their chosen core competence areas, these companies *seek to maximize their world manufacturing share in core products*. The manufacture of core products for a wide variety of external (and internal) customers yields the revenue and market feedback that, at least partly, determines the pace at which core competencies can be enhanced and extended. This thinking was behind JVC's decision in the mid-1970s to establish VCR supply relationships with leading national consumer electronics companies in Europe and the United States. In supplying Thomson, Thorn, and Telefunken (all independent companies at that time) as well as U.S. partners, JVC was able to gain the cash and the diversity of market experience that ultimately enabled it to outpace Philips and Sony. (Philips developed videotape competencies in parallel with JVC, but it failed to build a worldwide network of OEM relationships that would have allowed it to accelerate the refinement of its videotape competence through the sale of core products.)

JVC's success has not been lost on Korean companies like Goldstar, Sam Sung, Kia, and Daewoo, which are building core product leadership in areas as diverse as displays, semiconductors, and automotive engines through their OEM-supply contracts with Western companies. Their avowed goal is to capture investment initiative away from potential competitors, often U.S. companies. In doing so, they accelerate their competence-building efforts while "hollowing out" their competitors. By focusing on competence and embedding it in core products, Asian competitors have built up advantages in component markets first and have then leveraged off their superior products to move downstream to build brand share. And they are not likely to remain the low-cost suppliers forever. As their reputation for brand leadership is consolidated, they may well gain price leadership. Honda has proven this with its Acura line, and other Japanese car makers are following suit.

Control over core products is critical for other reasons. A dominant position in core products allows a company to shape the evolution of applications and end markets. Such compact audio disk-related core products as data drives and lasers have enabled Sony and Philips to influence the evolution of the computer-peripheral business in optical-media storage. As a company multiplies the number of application arenas for its core products, it can consistently reduce the cost, time, and risk in new product development. In short, well-targeted core products can lead to economies of scale *and* scope.

The Tyranny of the SBU

The new terms of competitive engagement cannot be understood using analytical tools devised to manage the diversified corporation of 20 years ago, when competition was primarily domestic (GE versus Westinghouse, General Motors versus Ford) and all the key players were speaking the language of the same business schools and consultancies. Old prescriptions have potentially toxic side effects. The need for new principles is most obvious in companies organized exclusively according to the logic of SBUs. The implications of the two alternate concepts of the corporation are summarized in Exhibit II.

Exhibit II.

Two Concepts of the Corporation: SBU or Core Competence

	SBU	Core Competence
Basis for competition	Competitiveness of today's products	Interfirm competition to build competencies
Corporate structure	Portfolio of businesses related in product-market terms	Portfolio of competencies, core products, and businesses
Status of the business unit	Autonomy is sacrosanct; the SBU "owns" all resources other than cash	SBU is a potential reservoir of core competencies
Resource allocation	Discrete businesses are the unit of analysis; capital is allocated business by business	Businesses and competencies are the unit of analysis: top management allocates capital and talent
Value added of top management	Optimizing corporate returns through capital allocation trade-offs among businesses	Enunciating strategic architecture and building competencies to secure the future

Obviously, diversified corporations have a portfolio of products and a portfolio of businesses. But we believe in a view of the company as a portfolio of competencies as well. U.S. companies do not lack the technical resources to build competencies, but their top management often lacks the vision to build them and the administrative means for assembling resources spread across multiple businesses. A shift in commitment will inevitably influence patterns of diversification, skill deployment, resource allocation priorities, and approaches to alliances and outsourcing.

We have described the three different planes on which battles for global leadership are waged: core competence, core products, and end products. A corporation has to know whether it is winning or losing on each plane. By sheer weight of investment, a company might be able to beat its rivals to blue-sky technologies yet still lose the race to build core competence leadership. If a company is winning the race to build core competencies (as opposed to building leadership in a few technologies), it will almost certainly outpace rivals in new business development. If a company is winning the race to capture world manufacturing share in core products, it will probably outpace rivals in improving product features and the price/performance ratio.

Determining whether one is winning or losing end-product battles is more difficult because measures of product market share do not necessarily reflect various companies' underlying competitiveness. Indeed, companies that attempt to build market share by relying on the competitiveness of others, rather than investing in core competencies and world core-product leadership, may be treading on quicksand. In the race for global brand dominance, companies like 3M, Black & Decker, Canon, Honda, NEC, and Citicorp have built global brand umbrellas by proliferating products out of their core competencies. This has allowed their individual businesses to build image, customer loyalty, and access to distribution channels.

When you think about this reconceptualization of the corporation, the primacy of the SBU—an organizational dogma for a generation—is now clearly an anachronism. Where the SBU is an article of faith, resistance to the seductions of decentralization can seem heretical. In many companies, the SBU prism means that only one plane of the global competitive battle, the battle to put competitive products on the shelf *today,* is visible to top management. What are the costs of this distortion?

UNDERINVESTMENT IN DEVELOPING CORE COMPETENCIES AND CORE PRODUCTS

When the organization is conceived of as a multiplicity of SBUs, no single business may feel responsible for maintaining a viable position in core products nor be able to justify the investment required to build world leadership in some core competence. In the absence of a more comprehensive view imposed by corporate management, SBU managers will tend to underinvest. Recently, companies such as Kodak and Philips have recognized this as a potential problem and have begun searching for new organizational forms that will allow them to develop and manufacture core products for both internal and external customers.

SBU managers have traditionally conceived of competitors in the same way they've seen themselves. On the whole, they've failed to note the emphasis Asian competitors were placing on building leadership in core products or to understand the critical linkage between world manufacturing leadership and the ability to sustain development pace in core competence. They've failed to pursue OEM-supply opportunities or to look across their various product divisions in an attempt to identify opportunities for coordinated initiatives.

IMPRISONED RESOURCES

As an SBU evolves, it often develops unique competencies. Typically, the people who embody this competence are seen as the sole property of the business in which they grew up. The manager of another SBU who asks to borrow talented people is likely to get a cold rebuff. SBU managers are not only unwilling to lend their competence carriers but they may actually hide talent to prevent its redeployment in the pursuit of new opportunites. This may be compared to residents of an underdeveloped country hiding most of their cash under their mattresses. The benefits of competencies, like the benefits of the money supply, depend on the velocity of their circulation as well as on the size of the stock the company holds.

Western companies have traditionally had an advantage in the stock of skills they possess. But have they been able to reconfigure them quickly to respond to new opportunities? Canon, NEC, and Honda have had a lesser stock of the people and technologies that compose core competencies but could move them much quicker from one business unit to another. Corporate R&D spending at Canon is not fully indicative of the size of Canon's core competence stock and tells the casual observer nothing about the velocity with which Canon is able to move core competencies to exploit opportunities.

When competencies become imprisoned, the people who carry the competencies do not get assigned to the most exciting opportunities, and their skills begin to atrophy. Only by fully leveraging core competencies can small companies like Canon afford to compete with industry giants like Xerox. How strange that SBU managers, who are perfectly willing to compete for cash in the capital budgeting process, are unwilling to compete for people—the company's most precious asset. We find it ironic that top management devotes so much attention to the capital budgeting process yet typically has no comparable mechanism for allocating the human skills that embody core competencies. Top managers are seldom able to look four or five levels down into the organization, identify the people who embody critical competencies, ·and move them across organizational boundaries.

BOUNDED INNOVATION

If core competencies are not recognized, individual SBUs will pursue only those innovation opportunities that are close at hand—marginal product-line extensions or geographic expansions. Hybrid opportunities like fax machines, laptop computers, hand-held televisions, or portable music keyboards will emerge only when managers take off their SBU blinkers. Remember, Canon appeared to be in the camera business at the time it was preparing to become a world leader in copiers. Conceiving of the corporation in terms of core competencies widens the domain of innovation.

Developing Strategic Architecture

The fragmentation of core competencies becomes inevitable when a diversified company's information systems, patterns of communication, career paths, managerial rewards, and processes of strategy development do not transcend SBU lines. We believe that senior management should spend a significant amount of its time developing a corporatewide strategic architecture that establishes objectives for competence building. A strategic architecture is a road map of the future that identifies which core competencies to build and their constituent technologies.

By providing an impetus for learning from alliances and a focus for internal development efforts, a strategic architecture like NEC's C&C can dramatically reduce the investment needed to secure future market leadership. How can a company make partnerships intelligently without a clear understanding of the core competencies it is trying to build and those it is attempting to prevent from being unintentionally transferred?

Of course, all of this begs the question of what a strategic architecture should look like. The answer will be different for every company. But it is helpful to think again of that tree, of the corporation organized around core products and, ultimately, core competencies. To sink sufficiently strong roots, a company must answer some fundamental questions: How long could we preserve our competitiveness in this business if we did not control this particular core competence? How central is this core competence to perceived customer benefits? What future opportunities would be foreclosed if we were to lose this particular competence?

The architecture provides a logic for product and market diversification, moreover. An SBU manager would be asked: Does the new market opportunity add to the overall goal of becoming the best player in the world? Does it exploit or add to the core competence? At Vickers, for example, diversification options have been judged in the context of becoming the best power and motion control company in the world.

The strategic architecture should make resource allocation priorities transparent to the entire organization. It provides a template for allocation decisions by top management. It helps lower-level managers understand the logic of allocation priorities and disciplines senior management to maintain consistency. In short, it yields a definition of the company and the markets it serves. 3M, Vickers, NEC, Canon, and Honda all qualify on this score. Honda *knew* it was exploiting what it had learned from motorcycles—how to make high-revving, smooth-running, lightweight engines—when it entered the car business. The task of creating a strategic architecture forces the organization to identify and commit to the technical and production linkages across SBUs that will provide a distinct competitive advantage.

It is consistency of resource allocation and the development of an administrative infrastructure appropriate to it that breathes life into a strategic architecture and creates a managerial culture, teamwork, a capacity to change, and a willingness to share resources, to protect proprietary skills, and to think long term. That is also the reason the specific architecture cannot be copied easily or overnight by competitors. Strategic architecture is a tool for communicating with customers and other external constituents. It reveals the broad direction without giving away every step.

Redeploying to Exploit Competencies

If the company's core competencies are its critical resource and if top management must ensure that competence carriers are not held hostage by some particular business, then it follows that SBUs should bid for core competencies in the same way they bid for capital. We've made this point glancingly. It is important enough to consider more deeply.

Once top management (with the help of divisional and SBU managers) has identified overarching competencies, it must ask businesses to identify the projects and people closely connected with them. Corporate officers should direct an audit of the location, number, and quality of the people who embody competence.

This sends an important signal to middle managers: Core competencies are *corporate* resources and may be reallocated by corporate management. An individual business doesn't own anybody. SBUs are entitled to the services of individual employees so long as SBU management can demonstrate that the opportunity it is pursuing yields the highest possible payoff on the investment in their skills. This message is further underlined if each year in the strategic planning or budgeting process, unit managers must justify their hold on the people who carry the company's core competencies.

Elements of Canon's core competence in optics are spread across businesses as diverse as cameras, copiers, and semiconductor lithographic equipment and are shown in "Core Competencies at Canon." When Canon identified an opportunity in digital laser printers, it gave SBU managers the right to raid other SBUs to pull together the required pool of talent. When Canon's reprographics products division undertook to develop microprocessor-controlled copiers, it turned to the photo products group, which had developed the world's first microprocessor-controlled camera.

Also, reward systems that focus only on product-line results and career paths that seldom cross SBU boundaries engender patterns of behavior among unit managers that are destructively competitive. At NEC, divisional managers come together to identify next-generation competencies. Together they decide how much investment needs to be made to build up each future competency and the contribution in capital and staff support that each division will need to make. There is also a sense of equitable exchange. One division may make a disproportionate contribution or may benefit less from the progress made, but such short-term inequalities will balance out over the long term.

Incidentally, the positive contribution of the SBU manager should be made visible across the company. An SBU manager is unlikely to surrender key people if only the other business (or the general manager of that business who may be a competitor for promotion) is going to benefit from the redeployment. Cooperative SBU managers should be celebrated as team players. Where priorities are clear, transfers are less likely to be seen as idiosyncratic and politically motivated.

Transfers for the sake of building core competence must be recorded and appreciated in the corporate memory. It is reasonable to expect a business that has surrendered core skills on behalf of corporate opportunities in other areas to lose, for a time, some of its competitiveness. If these losses in performance bring immediate censure, SBUs will be unlikely to assent to skills transfers next time.

Finally, there are ways to wean key employees off the idea that they belong in perpetuity to any particular business. Early in their careers, people may be exposed to a variety of businesses through a carefully planned rotation program. At Canon, critical people move regularly between the camera business and the copier business and between the copier business and the professional optical-products business. In mid-career, periodic assignments to cross-divisional project teams may be necessary, both for diffusing core competencies and for loosening the bonds that might tie an individual to one business even when brighter opportunities beckon elsewhere. Those who embody critical core competencies should know that their careers are tracked and guided by corporate human resource professionals. In the early 1980s at Canon, all engineers under 30 were invited to apply for membership on a seven-person committee that was to spend two years plotting Canon's future direction, including its strategic architecture. See Exhibit III for a list of Canon's core competencies.

Competence carriers should be regularly brought together from across the corporation to trade notes and ideas. The goal is to build

Exhibit III.

Core Competencies at Canon

	Precision Mechanics	Fine Optics	Micro-electronics
Basic camera	☐	☐	
Compact fashion camera	☐	☐	
Electronic camera	☐	☐	
EOS autofocus camera	☐	☐	☐
Video still camera	☐	☐	☐
Laser beam printer	☐	☐	☐
Color video printer	☐		☐
Bubble jet printer	☐		☐
Basic fax	☐		☐
Laser fax	☐		☐
Calculator			☐
Plain paper copier	☐	☐	☐
Battery PPC	☐	☐	☐
Color copier	☐	☐	☐
Laser copier	☐	☐	☐
Color laser copier	☐	☐	☐
NAVI	☐	☐	☐
Still video system	☐	☐	☐
Laser imager	☐	☐	☐
Cell analyzer	☐	☐	☐
Mask aligners	☐		☐
Stepper aligners	☐		☐
Excimer laser aligners	☐	☐	☐

a strong feeling of community among these people. To a great extent, their loyalty should be to the integrity of the core compe- tence area they represent and not just to particular businesses. In traveling regularly, talking frequently to customers, and meeting with peers, competence carriers may be encouraged to discover new market opportunities.

Core competencies are the wellspring of new business development. They should constitute the focus for strategy at the corporate level. Managers have to win manufacturing leadership in core products and capture global share through brand-building programs aimed at exploiting economies of scope. Only if the company is conceived of as a hierarchy of core competencies, core products, and market-focused business units will it be fit to fight.

Nor can top management be just another layer of accounting consolidation, which it often is in a regime of radical decentralization. Top management must add value by enunciating the strategic architecture that guides the competence acquisition process. We believe an obsession with competence building will characterize the global winners of the 1990s. With the decade underway, the time for rethinking the concept of the corporation is already overdue.

Notes

1. For a fuller discussion, see our article, "Strategic Intent," *Harvard Business Review* (May–June 1989), p. 63.
2. With Yves L. Doz, "Collaborate with Your Competitors and Win," *Harvard Business Review* (January–February 1989), p. 133.

4
Beyond Products: Services-Based Strategy

James Brian Quinn, Thomas L. Doorley, and Penny C. Paquette

When communication was limited to telephones and letters, and transportation took weeks or months instead of hours or days, concentrating on a few products—and the vertical integration that let managers control every step of their production processes—made real sense. Now such traditional strategic formulas no longer hold.

Thanks to new technologies, executives can divide up their companies' value chains, handle the key strategic elements internally, outsource others advantageously anywhere in the world with minimal transaction costs, and yet coordinate all essential activities more effectively to meet customers' needs. Under these circumstances, moving to a less-integrated but more focused organization is not just feasible but imperative for competitive success.

Companies that understand this new approach—Honda, Apple, and Merck among them—build their strategies not around products but around deep knowledge of a few highly developed core service skills. In such companies, the organization is kept as lean as possible. The company strips itself down to the essentials necessary to deliver to customers the greatest possible value from its core skills—and outsources as much of the rest as possible. As a result, management focuses on what it does best, avoids distractions, and leverages its organizational and financial resources far beyond what traditional strategies allow.

The Power of Services

To rethink their strategies objectively, managements need to break out of the mind-set that considers manufacturing (or goods production) as separate from (and somehow superior to) the service activities that make such production possible and effective. In fact, most companies—product manufacturers and service providers alike—are largely service operations. U.S. employment and output statistics reflect this clearly, as do internal company cost figures. Upon analysis, so do most manufacturers' value chains.

First consider some numbers. Approximately 76% of all U.S. workers are employed in industries commonly thought of as services: communications, transportation, health care, wholesale and retail distribution, financial services, and professional firms. Of those working in manufacturing industries, 65% to 75% perform service tasks ranging from critical production-related activities like research, logistics, maintenance, and product and process design to indirect staff services like accounting, law, financing, and personnel. Overall, services account for over three-fourths of all costs in most U.S. industries.

The role of services in providing value is ever more important. Not long ago, most of a product's value added came from the production processes that converted raw material into useful forms (steel into auto bodies, for example, or grain into edible cereals). Now, however, value added is increasingly likely to come from technological improvements, styling features, product image, and other attributes that only services can create.

This occurs in part because systemization and automation have driven production costs steadily downward, thus diminishing their relative importance in most companies' value chains. More and more companies are beginning to look like those in the personal computer industry, where producing the actual "box" is a low-margin activity, and software and service-support activities create most of a product's value to customers. In fact, nonmanufacturing services are so preeminent in many pharmaceutical, clothing, food, and sports equipment companies (to name just a few) that even classifying them as manufacturers seems open to question.

In pharmaceuticals, for example, value is added primarily by service activities like drug development in R&D, carefully constructed patent and legal defenses, thorough clinical and regulatory clearances, and effective drug retailing and distribution systems.

With production costs a trivial portion of a drug's value, leading companies' strategies concentrate on specialized activities within the value chain. Merck, for example, focuses on a powerful research-based patent position, while Glaxo targets rapid regulatory clearance of drugs.

SCI Systems, the world's largest electronics subcontractor, is a less obvious case in point. SCI produces a wide variety of communications, computer, and advanced instrumentation equipment that it sells both to value-added resellers and on an OEM basis. The company has been growing at a rate of 35% per year in its cutthroat business by outsourcing as much of its production processes and nonessential services as possible. Management concentrates its resources on design and development, logistics management, quality control, and the company's special expertise—low-cost assembly technologies for surface mounting components on both sides of the circuit board. The thin overhead structure such outsourcing allows (130 managers for 7,000 employees) lets SCI respond flexibly, rapidly, and precisely, with lower bureaucratic costs than its competitors or its customers themselves would incur.

In addition to enhancing the leverage of services inside companies, new technologies have significantly increased the relative power of service enterprises. For both manufacturers and service companies, this presents important opportunities and challenges.

On the one hand, services technologies offer astute managers new options for lowering costs, restructuring their organizations, and redefining their strategic focus. On the other hand, those who ignore the opportunities that services technologies create will surely sacrifice competitive advantages to their more farsighted rivals. Our three-year study of technology's impacts provided us with examples of both phenomena time and time again.

At the most basic level, technology has made it possible for independent companies to specialize in particular service activities, automate them, and create higher value added at lower costs than all but a few integrated companies can attain. Automatic Data Processing provides a good example.

ADP developed a flexible payroll-handling system that is so low cost it now processes payrolls for more than 10% of its potential client base. From this initial service, ADP expanded into routine bank accounting and tax filings for its customers and their employees, then into ERISA reporting, personnel records, and financial analyses, and finally into personalized communications like printing slogans, messages, or logos on checks and including notes with employees' paychecks. ADP's customers get expertise they could not afford in-house, lower overhead costs thanks to ADP's substantial economies of scale, and an objective check on their own costs for these services.

Similarly, the $1.5 billion ServiceMaster uses its system economies and specialized management skills to raise the quality of its customers' maintenance services while at the same time lowering their costs. ServiceMaster's data base, which covers 14 years of maintenance history on 17 million pieces of equipment at thousands of locations, enables the company to determine objectively how its customers' facilities should be maintained, when equipment purchases and preventive maintenance will pay off, and when parts should be replaced. So effective are its systems that ServiceMaster and its customers often invest jointly in new equipment and share the resulting productivity gains.

As these examples suggest, many service companies have become large, capital-intensive, technology-dominated organizations on which companies from almost every industry depend for specialized knowledge and assistance. Service companies are now among the most important suppliers, customers, market innovators, coalition partners, and repositories of market knowledge available to manufacturers.[1] A prime illustration is Toys "R" Us, which sells at year-round discount prices the largest selection of toys available nationwide.

To maintain inventories of 18,000 items in each store at lowest cost, Toys "R" Us must make huge off-season purchases, respond rapidly to developing fads, yet minimize systemwide storage and handling costs. It does this through what is perhaps the most detailed materials management and movement system in retailing, combining daily updates from its electronic point-of-sale system with an expert system linked to its sophisticated supplier information models.

The power of this system does not stop with Toys "R" Us. The 350-store system is so effective that the company knows more about toy sales than any of its manufacturer-suppliers, that often use their spring and summer Toys "R" Us sales to gauge production levels and to redesign products for their Christmas lines. With its market share approaching 20%, Toys "R" Us is so powerful that it can strongly influence product offerings and require manufacturers to meet its needs (for example, providing special packaging and four-sided product markings for its open, high-stack displays).

Shifting Strategic Focus

True strategic focus means that a company can concentrate more power in its chosen markets than anyone else can. Once, this meant owning the largest resource base, manufacturing plants, research labs, or distribution channels to support product lines. Now physical facilities—including a seemingly superior product—seldom provide a sustainable competitive edge. They are too easily bypassed, reverse engineered, cloned, or slightly surpassed. Instead, a maintainable advantage usually derives from outstanding depth in selected human skills, logistics capabilities, knowledge bases, or other service strengths that competitors cannot reproduce and that lead to greater demonstrable value for the customer.

Recognizing this, smart strategists no longer analyze market shares and their associated cost positions ad infinitum, nor do they build integrated companies to exploit them. Instead, they concentrate on identifying those few core service activities where their company has—or can develop—unique capabilities. Then they aggressively seek ways to eliminate, limit, or outsource activities where the company cannot attain superiority, unless those activities are essential to its chosen areas of strategic focus.

Apple Computer illustrates the value of this kind of activity-based focus. Like many other now-large companies, Apple initially succeeded by organizing itself as an intellectual holding company that purposely manufactured as little internally as possible. Because its business strength lay in creating the friendly look and feel of its software and hardware, Apple's management concentrated on designing and controlling its products' concepts, appearance, and key software, especially Apple DOS, which was not even made available for license. Other components and activities were outsourced wherever possible.

Apple bought microprocessors from Synertek, other chips from Hitachi, Texas Instruments, and Motorola, video monitors from Hitachi, power supplies from Astec, and printers from Tokyo Electric and Qume. (The Apple II was estimated to cost less than $500 to build, of which $350 was for purchased components.[2]) Similarly, Apple kept its internal service activities and investments to a minimum by outsourcing application software development to Microsoft, promotion to Regis McKenna, product styling to Frogdesign, and distribution to ITT and ComputerLand.

While this strategy may have been essential in Apple's early days, when it lacked both the time and the capital to build factories or hire a sales force, even today it is structured less like a traditional manufacturing company and more like a $4 billion service company that happens to have limited manufacturing facilities. Yet it has produced spectacular employee productivity and profitability: In 1988, Apple had $377,000 in sales per employee and $57,400 in profits per employee, outperforming the more vertically integrated IBM ($154,200 and $22,600) and DEC ($101,900 and $10,600).

To develop an activity-focused strategy, management needs to concentrate its competitive analyses not on market share but on the relative potency of the services undergirding its own and its competitors' product positions. Too much attention has been paid to high market share, especially since it often is bought by inappropriate pricing and short-term marketing strategies. High market share and high profitability together come from having a high activity share, or the most effective presence in selected services that the market truly desires.

Defining each activity in the value chain as a service that can be either produced internally or sourced externally is the first step in this new competitive analysis. Next management must ask a series of questions about each activity: Do we have or can we achieve best-in-the-world capabilities for this service? If so, should we make it a part of our core strategy? If not, what possibilities exist for outsourcing the activity or forming a strategic alliance with someone who does have superior capabilities? Finally, management needs to focus the organization's energies on two sets of activities: those where it can create unique value and those it must control to maintain its supremacy in the critical elements of its value chain.

In recent years, outsourcing has been disparaged for "hollowing out" companies and making them uncompetitive. Approached strategically, as we suggest, the effects of outsourcing are just the opposite. Whenever a company produces something internally that others can buy or produce more efficiently and effectively, it sacrifices competitive advantage. Conversely, the key to strategic success for many companies has been a carefully developed coalition with one or more of the world's best suppliers, product designers, advertising agencies, distributors, financial houses, or other service providers. Apple is one company that profits from such an approach. Honda Motor Company is another.

Soichiro Honda's personal commitment and engineering skills led him to create the world's finest team for designing small, efficient engines, first for bicycles, then for motorcycles. In the company's early years, limited capital resources and the cost-competitiveness of the motorcycle market forced Honda to develop very small, efficient assembly operations and to outsource as much of its nonengine fabrication work as possible. At the same time, Honda's president, Takeo Fujisawa, used innovative financing to build the strongest motorcycle distribution network in Japan.

Once Honda's motorcycles had succeeded at home, the company parlayed these same core service capabilities into building a steadily broader line of motorcycles, automobiles, and household machines sold worldwide. Its successes in the United States and elsewhere are still based on its unique depth in small engine design, moderate-scale assembly management, superb outsourcing logistics, and creative marketing and distribution coalitions. It has avoided many of the investments and inflexibilities that its major competitors have been saddled with, while building itself a number one share of the U.S. foreign car market and a number three share of all cars sold in Japan.

While both Apple and Honda began by outsourcing critical activities, other companies have adopted this strategy later in life. Intel Corporation, for example, at first relied heavily on its internal production prowess to lower costs, increase reliability, and open new markets. Now it focuses primarily on its extraordinary competencies in chip design and development. When its chips move toward commodity status, Intel often withdraws from the manufacturing process, subcontracting that to silicon foundries and other producers that concentrate on volume manufacturing and may have inherent cost advantages.

Similarly, in a lower-tech industry, E&J Gallo Winery shifted to outsourcing an activity many vintners consider the core of their business—growing the specialized grapes for its wines. Gallo devotes its resources and management attention to maintaining the legendary marketing and sales strengths that give the company its volume advantages and to using the deep knowledge base its 31% market share can provide to purchase grapes with the precise qualities its wines require. An important side benefit is that Gallo has avoided the investments and risks inherent in growing grapes.

What Stays, What Goes?

The great part of most companies' costs (other than those for purchased materials) typically occur in overhead categories. Even in manufacturing, more than two-thirds of all nonmaterial costs tend to be indirect or overhead expenses. Yet most overhead is merely services that the company began to buy internally. Reconceptualizing internal staffs and overhead costs as services that could be bought externally exposes a powerful, unexploited source of competitive advantage for most companies. Management can ask activity by activity: Are we really competitive with the world's best here? If not, can intelligent outsourcing or coalitions improve our productivity and long-term competitive position?

Competitive analyses should consider not just competitors in the company's own industry or the exclusive providers of a service (like insurance companies or communications companies) but *all* the potential providers and industries that might cross-compete in the activity, using "best in the activity" as the relevant benchmark. This approach broadens the analytical process and gives it a much more external, market-driven orientation. It also introduces new objectivity into the evaluation process and, at a minimum, generates strong pressures for productivity gains if management decides to continue sourcing internally. In many cases, managers discover that specialized sources are so much more cost-effective than their internal groups that they outsource activities long considered integral to their business.

Clearly, however, not all overhead is worthless—and therefore to be eliminated. Many of the most essential activities that modern companies perform are in what could be considered overhead categories. The objective is not to slash costs simplistically but rather to produce or buy needed services most effectively.

By limiting or shedding activities that provide no strategic advantage, a company can increase the value it delivers to both customers and shareholders and, in the process, lower its costs and investments. Conversely, if a company performs activities that it could buy more effectively, costs tend to balloon, and it loses competitive advantage. The company may also become more vulnerable to takeovers by outsiders who see in these activities the potential for margin gains.

Determining which core activities to emphasize is not always easy or obvious. Often a company's true strengths are obscured by management's tendency to think in divisional or product terms and by each functional group's need to see itself as the main source of the enterprise's success. But careful analysis will identify the few critical activities that drive (or could drive) the company's strategy and that it therefore must dominate.

Consider recent developments in the credit card industry. Processing customer charges and transactions is obviously an important activity in this business. Yet both MasterCard and Visa have clearly decided that their distinctive advantage lies not in this costly and complicated activity—which they often outsource to arch-competitor American Express—but in their large customer bases, retail networks, and ability to market effectively to both.

Managers must, of course, plan and control outsourcing so that the company does not become overly dependent on—and hence dominated by—its partners. In most cases, this means consciously developing and maintaining alternative competitive sources. It also means the company may have to perform activities at certain critical stages of its value creation process that it would otherwise outsource if efficiency were the sole criterion.

As Apple demonstrates, a company need not fabricate many components itself to control manufacturing. But it must dominate the strategic steps in the manufacturing process and develop technological knowledge, logistics systems, and commercial intelligence networks about the other steps that are second to none. That is why Honda still manufactures key engine parts in Japan and does all of its critical engine-related R&D there, although it outsources body parts overseas and shares responsibility for body design with its affiliates worldwide.

One way to avoid becoming too dependent on critical suppliers is to seek alliances with outstanding but noncompeting enterprises. Seagate Technology, the world's leading manufacturer of hard disk drives for personal computers, provides a good example. To gain competitive advantage against Japanese rivals, Seagate decided to absorb the cost of delivering its products to customers and to guarantee delivery within four days. To handle this crucial service, the company developed a special relationship with Skyway Freight Systems to make deliveries from its California distribution center to customers all over the United States. On a per unit basis, Seagate's payments to Skyway amounted to less than 1% of each disk drive's total cost. Yet in six months and thousands of shipments, only three deliveries arguably were late.

On rare occasions, companies can even outsource some strategic components to potential competitors—as Apple did with its microprocessor chips—provided that they develop and protect other key elements in the value creation process and control the critical information linkages between their various suppliers and customers—as Apple did by controlling Apple DOS and its marketing interfaces.

This kind of refocusing and strategic hollowing out goes well beyond mere tactical redeployment for efficiency's sake. By avoiding investments in vertical integration and by managing "intellectual systems" instead of workers and machines, companies decrease total investment and leverage resources substantially. They also minimize certain unavoidable risks.

For example, if one unit in an outsourced system underperforms, management can substitute another competitor's components or services more quickly than it could shut down an internal operation or develop an alternative itself. Similarly, if new technologies suddenly appear, it is easier to switch among outside sources than to forsake internal investments. Lastly, if there is a cyclical or temporary drop in demand, the coordinating company is not saddled with all the idle capacity and inventory losses.

With strategic outsourcing, companies have at their disposal the world's best talent, offering both higher quality and greater flexibility than internal groups could provide. For this reason, many large manufacturers now rely on smaller, state-of-the-art product and service suppliers to shorten product-development cycle times. While the larger company must typically maintain strong R&D efforts in its core technologies—and be willing to share its longer-term plans with suppliers to ensure that its new products make the best use of suppliers' designs—it can substantially leverage its R&D funds through inputs from specialized technical vendors. Dramatic savings, totaling some 70% to 80% of the cost of key components or designs, are common when joint development is managed properly.

In the early 1980s, General Motors, like many other large companies, realized that the rigidities and costs of its internal suppliers were not only raising its cost per unit against its competitors' but also cutting off the company from the R&D support and innovations that outside suppliers could provide. In a policy reversal, GM began to encourage more extensive outsourcing and, among other initiatives, turned to PPG Industries to handle the painting of auto bodies. Today PPG manages and operates the paint shops in GM assembly plants, lowering GM's cost per unit and offering the latest advances in robotics and materials research related to painting.

Perhaps most important, strategic outsourcing allows a company to focus all its attention on the areas in which it adds the most value per unit of input. This creates entry barriers for would-be competitors in a variety of ways. Because they are leaner, these companies can respond faster to customers and move more easily to form the cross-functional teams that best provide innovative products for new market needs. Because they have fewer management levels, less bureaucracy, and more opportunities for employees' personal and entrepreneurial development, they can often attract better people. Finally, they can leverage managerial talent—their most limited and most crucial resource—because their executives no longer need to waste time and attention on peripheral activities.

Service-Driven Competition

Global sourcing, volatile currency fluctuations, fast-changing communications and information technologies, and the increased leverage of services are combining to restructure entire industries as well as individual companies. As an example, consider biotechnology.

The industry is becoming a loosely structured network of service enterprises built around specialized core competencies and joined together (often temporarily) for one undertaking, while remaining suppliers, competitors, and customers in others. Many research groups and companies focus only on identifying and patenting biological organisms (often proteins) at the laboratory level. Others develop and license cell lines that can reproduce these organisms. Still others have developed processes for using these cell lines to make particular proteins in sufficient quantities for clinical tests and commercialization. Some enterprises specialize in running clinical trials, others concentrate on having the marketing expertise and distribution channels to bring new products to market, and so on.

Because of the high risks involved, the scarcity of expensive expertise, and the relatively small scale required at each of these stages, it is hard for a single company to support the full chain of activities in-house. As a result, the industry is developing a series of multilevel consortia in which each enterprise—and each new product introduced—has its own network of contract relationships with research, clinical, production, and marketing groups around the world.

The semiconductor and electronics industries are becoming similarly structured, with independent design, foundry, packaging, assembly, industrial distribution, kitting, configuration, systems analysis, networking, and value-added distributor groups essentially acting as service units that perform specialized tasks for one another. Because of services' high value added and extremely low shipping costs, the most powerful consortia now seek and coordinate the world's best suppliers on a truly global basis.

In another set of major restructurings, large service companies are exploiting their technological power and size in ways that have erased many traditional industry boundaries and distribution patterns. This process is most apparent in banking and financial services, where specialists of all sorts have captured important segments of familiar value chains and cross-competition is rampant. But this process is very much alive in other service and manufacturing sectors.

For example, retailing, wholesaling, and manufacturing companies now partner and cross-compete on many levels. Many large retailers like Sears, K mart, and Wal-Mart design or produce their own products worldwide, run their own distribution operations, and compete directly with wholesalers, drugstores, and supermarkets. Wholesalers like McKesson are also large manufacturers of private brands, and they support extensive independent retail networks with electronic accounting, billing, merchandising, planning, and control systems. Broad-line manufacturers like Matsushita control thousands of wholesale and retail outlets, which they use both to gather better market information and to assure rapid market access for new products.

Similarly, boundaries between transportation, communications, and travel-service industries are disappearing as airlines begin to provide direct reservations, tours, conferences, auto and hotel arrangements, in-flight telephone service, electronic retailing, and package delivery services in competition—and coalition—with thousands of other service units. Accounting, software, and professional service firms are also breaking all traditional industry boundaries as they openly compete and cooperate to develop and supply new and better products and services to each other and to a wide variety of common customers.

The bottom line is simple but powerful: Whenever a company outsources, sets up a joint venture, or enters into a strategic partnership with a major service company—as most will—it is likely to encounter a totally new set of potential competitors and competitive interests. Under these circumstances, an activity-focused competitive analysis, which includes all possible cross-competitors, provides a much clearer basis for assessing the opportunities, relationships, and threats these complex new situations offer. Conversely, defining the company's industry and competitors in product rather than in service-activity terms can lead to strategic disasters.

The capacity to command and coordinate services activities, supplier networks, and contract relations across the globe has become perhaps the most important strategic weapon and scale economy for many of today's most successful enterprises. Indeed, our study suggests that one reason large Japanese export manufacturers have been so successful is that they have avoided the controlled vertical integration of U.S. companies. Instead, they have moved directly to a kind of quasi-integration similar to what we are describing here: coordinating many independent suppliers through strong contractual and strategic relationships. U.S. industry, with its more efficient service sector, now has an opportunity to jump to a higher level of coordinated disaggregation and thus to regain its strategic advantage.

Notes

1. James Brian Quinn, Jordan J. Baruch, and Penny C. Paquette, "Exploiting the Manufacturing-Services Interface," *Sloan Management Review* (Summer 1988), p. 45.
2. William H. Davidson, and Edward F. Colby, Jr., "Apple Computer, Inc.," University of Virginia Darden Graduate Business School Foundation Case Study, 1983 (UVA-BP219).

5
The Strategic Benefits of
Logistics Alliances

Donald J. Bowersox

In early 1990, American President Companies started double-stack container rail service from Woodhaven, Michigan, to Ford Motor Company's auto assembly plant in Hermosillo, Mexico. APC coordinates all the information, transportation, and inventory handling necessary to pick up parts and components from vendors and sequence-load them into containers for delivery on a just-in-time basis to Hermosillo. The movement includes coordination over four railroads and with Mexican customs officials for delay-free clearance. At the plant, Ford has built a state-of-the-art stack train terminal to smooth the flow of sequenced parts into assembly operations. APC provides cranes and management to break down the containers. The partners collaborate to return containers to the United States carrying components produced in the Maquiladora region and specialized part racks.

A warehouse service venture of Lever Brothers and Distribution Centers, Inc. is bearing fruit. DCI has built, staffed, and operates a high-tech dedicated distribution warehouse for the toiletries maker in Columbus, Ohio. The companies share the benefits and risks: If warehouse utilization falls below a certain point, Lever helps cover the overhead; in return, DCI shares the productivity benefits when utilization approaches full-capacity economies of scale. A similar arrangement exists between Lever Brothers and Dry Storage Corporation in Atlanta.

Schneider National furnished initial computerized scheduling and electronic data interchange for 90 Minnesota Mining & Manufacturing Company shipping locations that were revamping their transportation operations in the late 1980s. The service included coordination of freight transit and associated documentation for all motor carriers 3M was using. 3M got the benefits of the latest information technology, and Schneider gained and still enjoys the position of nationwide core carrier for 3M.

These examples illustrate logistics alliances that are becoming commonplace business arrangements. Virtually unheard of a decade ago, such agreements are now spreading as a way of lowering distribution and storage operating costs. For many manufacturers and vendors, these ventures offer opportunities to dramatically improve the quality of customer service.

The principals in a typical agreement are a provider of customized logistics services and a producer of goods that jointly engineer and launch a system to speed goods to customers. But there are other forms too, like arrangements between two service providers and between two product marketers (see the Appendix).

Outsourcing of transportation or warehousing requirements to a specialist is, of course, an everyday matter. What is unusual about the relationships described here is the innovative manner in which the parties commingle their operations to obtain mutual benefits. A prime example is Drug Transport, Inc., which has carved out a niche in less-than-truckload distribution in the pharmaceutical and office supply fields.

To permit wholesalers to offer daily delivery to retail customers at specified times, the Atlanta-based carrier has established an array of services and pricing. The rates are based on guaranteed delivery, at a fixed charge, to the retailer of whatever product quantity is required. The charge is based on average shipment weight at a rate negotiated in advance of each 30-day planning period; it remains the same throughout the period regardless of the quantity of freight shipped. The result is a dependable daily service at a fixed cost that the wholesalers and retailers know in advance. For Drug Transport, the arrangement means guaranteed revenue and stable operations for route planning and equipment scheduling.

Another feature of these arrangements is the cooperation they engender that replaces the sometimes adversarial stance separating buyers and sellers. Many of these relationships endure for five or more years, and many operate with informal understandings rather than formal contracts.

The level of involvement of specialists ranges from the routine services they perform as a matter of course to complete responsibility for the logistics requirements of a customer or a customer's unit. Informal partnerships are common in the transport sector. For instance, CenTra, Inc.'s Central Transport Division provides time-phased delivery of components and parts to General Motors's BOC Group plants in Lansing, Michigan. No specialized equipment is needed, and the arrangement is subject to annual review. At the other end of the spectrum is the long-term contract between NYK Line (Nippon Yusen Kaisha) and Pioneer Electronic, whereby NYK is handling all logistics aspects, from importing to customer distribution of mixed shipments of products, from a network of over one million square feet of warehouse space in the Los Angeles area.

Often these compacts call for the service provider to perform highly customized activity. Not long ago, Southern Bonded Warehouse agreed to combine U.S.-made bubble gum and Portuguese-made soccer balls into a point-of-sale promotion package. The Georgia company had to (1) take three pounds of gum from a bulk container, weigh it, and put it in a heat-sealed, tamperproof package; (2) inflate and inspect the soccer ball; (3) place the gum bag in the ball box; (4) place the ball on top of the box and stretch-wrap the package; and (5) put a certain number of units in a master carton and label and seal it.

In these alliances, the service provider usually assumes a certain amount of risk through an agreement calling for a penalty, such as an automatic reduction in revenues, when performance is poorer than specified. On the other hand, the agreements often include rewards for superior performance, such as a greater than expected percentage of on-time delivery. As indicated, the risk also may include a capital investment on the provider's part.

Sometimes, however, the synergy obtained involves *less* risk for one of the partners. Owens-Corning Fiberglas, to boost productivity and gain competitive advantage, has taken on some tasks that traditionally are the carriers' burden. Once a trucker delivers ready-to-use trailers to an Owens-Corning plant, its on-site responsibility ends. The manufacturer positions the trailers at docks and does the loading according to destination. Timing shipments for off-peak traffic periods helps to cut cost and boost driver productivity. The over-the-road movement direct from Owens-Corning plants to customer construction sites avoids costly pickup and origin terminal routing cost. Gaining lower operating costs and predictable equipment location, the carriers can reduce their freight rates. They share the savings with Owens-Corning. For the manufacturer, however, the great benefit is the competitive advantage it gains by supplying dependable job-site delivery within very tight time windows.

The benefits of these alliances are tangible enough and often big enough to attract quite a few players—many of them strangers to the logistics service industry. A very fast-growing segment of the field is the fulfillment or full-support company that specializes in turnkey services, from order processing to customer order delivery. By the mid-1990s, such value-added logistics business is expected to surpass $20 billion in volume. A few of these integrated providers pursuing full-service work are Roadway Logistics, Trammell Crow Distribution Corporation, KLS Logistics, CSL Logistics (part of CSX), USCO, Itel Distribution Systems, and Caterpillar Logistics Services.

Forces of Impetus

What accounts for this surge of enterprise in an activity that has often been a corporate stepchild? Among the multiplicity of forces creating a favorable environment for logistics alliances, four dominate.

1. The political-legal terrain of the 1980s stimulated the development of integrated service practices. Deregulation of transportation and communications, coupled with relaxed antitrust enforcement—intended to give productivity a charge—generated an atmosphere conducive to innovation. Washington is looking benignly at business alliances as long as they do not inhibit the prevailing level of competition in end-user markets. The National Cooperative Research Act of 1984, permitting some cooperation among competitors, is being construed to apply to logistics coalitions.

2. The explosion in information technology has made computerization cheap, and computers hold logistics alliances together. Schneider National, for example, has put satellite communications in all its over-the-road trucks so it can keep real-time track of vehicle location and on-board shipment data from headquarters in Wisconsin. Other late technological advances, like cellular phones, laser-based bar codes, and radio frequency transmissions, are in standard use at diverse haulers like Roadway, UPS, the Union Pacific Railroad, and Sea-Land.

3. Today's emphasis on leaner organization makes managers more likely to turn to external specialists to solve problems or perform tasks outside the organization's sphere of expertise. The objective of competing more effectively—through greater asset utilization, higher leverage, and faster responsiveness—is a prime stimulant toward logistics collaboration.

4. An escalating competitive environment forces the players to do all they can to become lowest-cost competitors. Efficiency in logistics is particularly important for companies that are doing business abroad. Distribution costs, as a percentage of revenue, are greater for international companies than for their domestic counterparts. Complexity, long order lead times, unusual product-service requirements, and differing legal and cultural factors in foreign countries combine to create a much more challenging operating environment. Consequently, headquarters is willing to use qualified external support.

Strategic Vision

For companies successful with logistics partnerships, a common factor overriding all others is a recognition that this business activity is an important part of marketing strategy. Product, promotion, and price are the traditional competitive ingredients, while time and place competencies have taken a back seat. That relative neglect is changing. Those companies forming alliances are seeking to exploit their logistical competencies—not weaknesses. During the course of conducting research into the practices of more than 1,000 manufacturers, retailers, and wholesalers, it was clearly shown that some companies stand head and shoulders above their competitors in logistics performance, and they use this superiority to gain and keep customer loyalty.[1]

Superiority over the competition means placing a premium on being easy to do business with. All top managers "feel" they know what customers want. But fewer than one out of five companies establish rigid customer service standards, regularly measure performance to standards, or systematically digest feedback to improve operations.

Logistically speaking, being easy to do business with means that suppliers meet commitments and shipments arrive when and where promised. When problems crop up, progressive companies develop work-arounds that smoothly take care of the difficulty. Most note-worthy is the way that top performers use electronically conveyed information to gain competitive advantage. They specialize in elim-inating surprises and in providing same-call responses to customer inquiries.

Strategic vision, however, calls for more than readiness to serve the customer; it calls for a willingness to offer extra, value-adding services. The object, of course, is to become a preferred supplier of key customers. Companies committed to strategic use of logistics usually outperform the competition in speed and consistency of order cycle. They normally have standards they intend customers to rely on and expect employees to adhere to. For Federal Express, the standard is delivery of all premium-service packages within 24 hours.

Often difficult to apply, reasonable but effective standards are also not always easy to set. A product marketer may feel comfort-able promising the trade a 95% case-fill rate, supported by a five-to seven-day delivery that it expects to achieve 98% of the time. This goal, even if met, means that at least 5% of customers will always be disappointed in what they receive and at least 2% in when they receive it. Such statistically based performance, while once acceptable, does not fit a business strategy based on just-in-time or quick-response inventory replenishment.

A shrewd marketer will strive not only to consistently deliver complete orders to customers at the time and location requested but also to expand the scope and upgrade the level of service to keep a customer's loyalty. At Atlanta-based Genuine Parts, the logistics staff is authorized to procure a critical out-of-stock part from a competitor rather than fail to deliver a key customer's order. Leading companies recognize that while perfection in service may be unattainable, a culture based on an acceptable rate of failure *will* fail. By developing a high level of standard performance, they reduce the number of less-than-standard situations that have to be resolved. Moreover, high-quality logistics service compliance is almost invariably less expensive than a procedure based on an expected percentage of failure that demands frequent correction.

The drive to secure and hold customers reaches its peak in the leveraging of resources in the form of strategic alliances. Procter & Gamble, with its outstanding product supply network, can divert a customer's shipment from a warehouse directly to a store on short notice. Drug wholesalers Bergen Brunswig, McKesson, and

Alco Health Services offer their customers complete electronic inventory replenishment and merchandising control. Wal-Mart Stores has alliances with important suppliers of merchandise through which they manage their inventory levels and resupply in Wal-Mart warehouses.

In these alliances, specialization through a dedicated resource base generates economies of scale. For example, Dauphin Distribution Services Company, a warehouse specialist, can furnish consolidated inbound delivery for Shaw's Supermarkets. In a single truck, Shaw's outlet gets a mix of products from a combination of suppliers. Similarly, Continental Freezers of Illinois provides inbound staging and frozen food assortment service for Jewel Food Stores supermarkets. Normal distribution arrangements are more expensive and much less efficient.

The spread of risk is another attraction of these ventures; meshed operations between a product marketer and a service provider offer what amounts to risk insurance. Not only is the chance of error much less because each party is focusing on its specialty but also the partners share the consequences of failure if the compact includes performance guarantees. In the Hermosillo plant situation, Ford, American President Companies, and the four railroads share the risk.

The synergy stimulated by the joint effort can create a coalition of great strength. One reason for the synergy is the focus generated by a reduction in suppliers by the product marketer and a limit on the service provider's number of customers (normal by-products of an alliance). Once focused, the two organizations often begin to seek growth opportunities for each other—to their mutual benefit. The fact that each views the logistics process from a different vantage point inspires creativity.

What They Bring to the Party

Because the core business of an enterprise is the focal point or target of the logistics partnership, the players must be economically and managerially strong. The typical alliance is a long-term arrangement that is expected to survive the fluctuations characteristic of most businesses. To support an alliance, the service provider and marketer must have the staying power to weather the downs as well as exploit the ups.

To justify using customized logistics services, the marketer needs an opportunity with a key customer or in a niche market for a rich return in market share improvement or competitive superiority. For Wal-Mart, the criterion is the volume of potential business at stake. Moreover, the potential supplier's technological sophistication must be advanced enough to permit direct electronic connection with Wal-Mart's satellite communications network. Otherwise, sharing the assortment of information required to make the alliance work is impractical.

As I have noted, information sharing is the glue that holds these ventures together. Synchronization of activities and progress toward shared goals require open disclosure, from operating details to strategic planning. Technology has kept pace to provide such capability. Some service providers have full-disclosure information systems in place.

Systems are available that permit real-time tracking of shipments at case-level or stockkeeping-unit detail throughout the distribution process. In some instances, as at Skyway Freight and Systems, a traffic manager wanting to know the projected arrival time can get a computer screen view of the in-transit status of a shipment. Estimated time of arrival (ETA) projections supply the information for evaluating the cost versus benefit of expediting a shipment to meet a required delivery time. Such in-transit control is a feature of a double-stack container service, operated by the Union Pacific Railroad and American President Companies, that links Pacific Rim garment manufacturers with the interior of North America. The service offers containerized delivery of goods on hangers that are size- and color-sequenced to particular retailers' specifications before loading in Asia.

To perform effectively, each partner must operate on two levels. One level is performance of a specified role in a well-understood operating domain. The logistics process may take place across an enormous geographical playing field in what amounts to a 24-hour, 7-day-a-week, 52-week-a-year engagement. There is no room for ambiguity regarding who is responsible for doing what. Effectiveness depends on near error-free task completion and meshing of tasks.

The meshing of tasks is the second level of operation. Each party must see its assignment in terms of its contribution to the alliance and the way it adds value for customers. Otherwise, it may develop role myopia. The service provider and the marketer have to understand each other's culture. The provider must appreciate the value system that drives the marketer's decision-making process. The marketer must grasp how the provider approaches the marketer's business. (Cultural absorption admittedly gets tricky when a service provider is simultaneously engaged in multiple alliances.)

A grasp of the whole distribution channel is necessary but sometimes difficult, especially for service providers. Moving damaged goods or product recalls back to the source is a headache for retailers and wholesalers. On their part, manufacturers do not want damaged goods for which they have already given credit to reappear on sale somewhere. The carrier, if it is not considering the entire channel, might treat its partners' serious concerns too lightly.

Robin Transport's understanding of GM's parts delivery needs and of the total distribution channel led the Lansing, Michigan, company to an innovation that benefited all parties. Robin designed trailers with fabric walls that made the trailers capable of being unloaded from the sides as well as from the rear. The trailers could load and unload in places where the standard trailer could not go, and they could be unloaded from three sides at once, near points of assembly. Robin loads the trailers in sequence for ease of components handling and delivers at certain specified times when GM is ready to take the shipments. To justify its investment in special handling equipment in the trailers and the dedication of part of its over-the-road fleet, Robin sought and got status as a preferred carrier at a premium rate. GM set up its production assembly to benefit from the different mode of materials handling. The manufacturer benefited from Robin's understanding of the distribution channel by realizing productivity improvement through inventory reduction, JIT delivery, and more efficient materials handling.

The hallmark of these ventures is cooperation. An effective way to signal willingness to work together is to establish ground rules at the outset. These rules should include a procedure for conflict resolution so that any friction that arises is smoothed over before it harms the arrangement. Negotiation of roles before operations start, with clear ground rules for the parties, helps perpetuate alliance longevity.

Even so, partnerships often evolve or are modified for good reasons, especially changing business conditions. Signal Freight's operation that supports the Sears-Whirlpool alliance has shifted significantly over the years to accommodate the customers. Sears's recent decision to stock a variety of national-brand appliances (its

"Brand Central" promotion) has meant one more adjustment for this Leaseway Transportation Division.

A provision allowing for changed circumstances, negotiated before start-up, is especially important for the service provider, since in a typical logistics alliance the marketing organization holds the power. Carriers and other service providers have usually been at the mercy of product marketers because transportation can always be purchased on a trip-by-trip basis and warehouse agreements can be limited to 30-day commitments. Provision for an exit from the agreement is a sensitive matter, but in fairness to the service provider it should be negotiated. (Where special-purpose equipment or facilities are involved, it is the practice to incorporate buy-sell agreements in the alliance documents.)

Exel Logistics, a subsidiary of the U.K.-based conglomerate NFC, has rules regarding this issue. It requires that all contracts signed by Exel affiliates include a framework outlining the dissolution procedure and an agenda of exit negotiation items. Although several of these contracts have operating horizons of a decade or more, Exel management is convinced that such a framework is essential to establish a sound platform for the alliance up front and that, in fact, spelling everything out strengthens the relationship.

Why Alliances Fail

While simulation of alternatives is sometimes possible, many operations represent a leap of faith; the parties are obliged to forge ahead, full of hope. When Procter & Gamble decided to consolidate its West Coast distribution facilities into one giant 400,000-plus square-foot facility in Sacramento, the company obviously could not test the idea. Without the benefit of complete information, P&G and its warehouse partner hammered out agreements concerning goals, expected benefits, and contingent responsibilities. The warehouse installation proceeded without major problems.

Such a plunge into the unknown complicates the all-important business of establishing relationships and developing a clear vision of mutual expectations. In such situations, the managers involved often are simply incapable of overcoming the limits of their different cultures. Given people's natural resistance to change, it is reasonable to expect clashes of culture and styles when employees of two or more companies commence working together toward common objectives. Often they are working side by side more or less permanently.

Developing the trust that makes the alliance work requires an open door and an open mind. This attitude is not easy for managers schooled in an adversarial tradition. For example, the belief that carriers and warehouse-based service companies promote the alliance concept as a subterfuge for selling the same old service is widespread among shipper executives. (One category of service providers actually tries to exploit this suspicion. The entry strategy of Global Logistics Venture, a joint venture of AMR and CSX, calls for provision of information technology to coordinate the purchase of services from a number of specialists, in contrast to actual provision of the services.)

In the traditional kind of negotiation of a service agreement, the tone is adversarial and the parties rely on a host of competitive checks and balances to ensure buyers that they are getting a good deal. In an alliance, trust has to substitute for many of the perceived benefits of competitive bidding. The partners' reluctance to share ideas can abort an agreement, once entered into, if they also have to share information they consider to be confidential.

Then how do you build trust in situations where no track record exists? One way to resolve this dilemma is through a procedure used by Union Pacific Logistics for building trust progressively during the evaluation and negotiation of an alliance. The instrument is a facilitator acceptable to all the parties and connected with none of them. This person tries to put the negotiations on an objective basis by acting as the neutral focal point during the bargaining.

As the alliance matures, trust level and operational success become inseparable. Failure to develop trust during the early stages spells trouble. One supplier of multiple logistics services recently ended negotiations with a consortium of shippers because the supplier decided that the group was not truly seeking a total system solution for their joint requirements. Early on, the supplier became convinced that the consortium was really trying to leverage its purchasing power to get a low price from the supplier, and so trust never developed.

As in this case, the reality is that one of the parties usually has more at stake than the others. There is often an imbalance of power as well. The result: uneven commitment to the welfare of the arrangement.

Sometimes an alliance is forged at high levels of the companies involved, but little attention is paid to getting the lower echelons, which will be charged to make it work, to sign on. The middle managers who play a key role in the operation may see the prospects as jeopardizing their careers, particularly if their areas of expertise become the focus of outsourcing. Moreover, if they remain unacquainted with the goals of the program, they may perceive the objective as simply to cut costs. Why then, they say, throw out the old, proven techniques? Why do we need all these people from the other company around?

But business cannot be operations as usual under the umbrella of a logistics alliance. At one retailer, a warehouse traditionally granted delivery appointments no earlier than 24 hours in advance, and then on a first-come, first-unloaded basis. The practice frustrated a fully integrated, quick-response inventory replenishment system arranged with a carrier. Dedicated equipment loaded with time-sensitive merchandise was left undelivered at the warehouse.

In traditional operations, it is unnecessary to separate ownership from control. But in an alliance, the separation has to be part of daily practice because ownership spreads across the joint process and at all the levels concerned. Control is recognized in a framework of interorganizational operating principles expressing what the alliance is supposed to do and how it will get done. Included are measures to be taken by each party when things go wrong, as they inevitably will.

The operating framework will falter if it omits mutually accepted yardsticks for gauging performance and progress. Conflict will arise if all the parties do not fully understand the score.

The appropriate accounting for total costs and asset-driven activity is not easy to establish when two or more organizations are involved. From a service supplier's viewpoint, the key to accurate measurement may be an understanding of the client's critical business success factors. For example, price margins based on average cost have little, if any, usefulness in specialized service situations. In an alliance, selling margins may be much lower but utilization of assets much higher. Bergen Brunswig recently reported a sharp improvement in pretax income despite big gross margin reductions. This improvement comes from a disciplined approach to distribution and an improved return on net assets produced by alliances with druggists.

For a product marketer, the major benefit of an alliance could be as basic as improved reliability. The partners must see to it that measurement of this factor gets translated into numbers that can be put on paper and compared with some prior period. The reliability improvement may start with the fact that the same truck drivers are visiting key customers continually and thus forming relationships with them. Eventually this intangible gets translated into something more tangible and thus measurable.

Making a Partnership Work

Logistics alliances are making U.S. industry more efficient and thus more competitive. Logistics costs in 1990 are expected to exceed $525 billion, or about 10.5% of GNP. In 1981, the proportion was 15.4%. In terms of comparative assets to GNP, the distribution system is operating this year on $100 billion less average inventory than it did in 1981. Some of these improvements can be attributed to logistics partnerships.

While cost reductions are, of course, very desirable, they are not an end in themselves. The main rationale for orchestrating an alliance is to increase competitive advantage. As one executive put it, "For us, the reason for this venture is market impact. Cost reduction is important but secondary."

To make a partnership work, experience provides these guidelines:

View the arrangement as the implementation of a strategic plan. Encourage the participants involved to consider their roles in terms of a value-added process.

Seek an arrangement that achieves scale-economy benefits while spreading risk.

Recognizing that the benefits can be gained only through a long-term relationship in which the parties are interdependent, make sure that the information necessary to function well is shared between them.

Build trust between the organizations by setting unambiguous goals, establishing clear roles, laying down firm rules, and measuring performance rigorously.

Start the venture on a realistic course by acknowledging that eventually the alliance may have to be terminated.

Appendix

ANATOMY OF ALLIANCES

Three characteristics distinguish logistics partnerships from run-of-the-mill cooperative business arrangements. First is a far more extensive link that makes the venture almost an extended organization with its own role, rules, values, and objectives. In the traditional purchasing situation, outsourcing is a make versus buy decision guided mostly by cost considerations. The logistics alliance is a special business compact in which the parties seek to benefit from the synergy of working together.

The second characteristic is concentration on a relationship continuum instead of a series of single transactions. A high degree of dependency develops, which stimulates further cooperation. Trust builds as the parties focus on customer satisfaction and loyalty.

Of the forms these ventures take, the most common involves a product marketer and a service provider like a warehousing company or a rail carrier. For example, look at the joint operation of Sears Business Systems and Itel Distribution Systems in Alsip, Illinois. Sears runs a reconfiguration room in Itel's warehouse for modifying equipment to customers' specifications. Itel supplies full-service logistics tying into Sears's information network. Itel assembles basic orders, positioning equipment requiring modification in the reconfiguration room. Itel then assembles the complete order and performs the tasks necessary for timely delivery to the customer.

Some alliances combine the resources of service providers seeking to bolster their competitive positions. The Santa Fe Railway and J.B. Hunt Transport Services recently established intermodal freight transport whereby the former provides line-haul service and the latter, pickup and delivery. To stabilize the service—scheduled to run daily between Chicago and Los Angeles—the partners snared freight business from UPS and Ralston Purina. Some ventures between service companies may involve joint provision of service to a product marketer.

A common format for an alliance is a vertical alignment between two or more product marketers, usually marked by transfer of inventory ownership. (Some of these include a service supplier.) A simple instance is a distribution link between Procter & Gamble and Wal-Mart. A more complicated version is a projected consortium of four companies in the women's ready-to-wear apparel business: Du Pont, which makes the fiber, Milliken, which converts the fiber into fabric; Leslie Fay, which produces women's garments; and Dillard Department Stores, which sells them. The arrangement makes the use of resources more efficient in the face of volatile fashion demand. The arrangement is geared to speed inventory replenishment and to reduce the time elapsing from fiber to retail rack.

Yet another type is horizontal alignment of product marketers selling to the same customer base. (It may include a service company as coordinator.) In the hospital supply business, such an alliance offers frequent joint delivery of member-company products—all facilitated by electronic data interchange. Formed in 1987 by Abbott Laboratories and the 3M Company, the group has expanded to include Standard Register (business forms), IBM (computer network services), Kimberly-Clark (nonwoven disposable products), and C.R. Bard (urological products). Abbott and 3M made their move initially to compete more effectively against rivals Baxter Healthcare and Johnson & Johnson Hospital Supply.

Note

1. The research is reported in Donald J. Bowersox et al., *Leading Edge Logistics—Competitive Positioning for the 1990s* (Oak Brook, Ill.: Council of Logistics Management, 1989).

PART

V

The Process of
Making Strategy

1
Many Best Ways to Make Strategy

Michael Goold and Andrew Campbell

"The shoe that fits one person pinches another; there is no recipe for living that suits all cases," observed Carl Jung in *Modern Man in Search of a Soul*. Jung wasn't thinking about strategic management when he wrote that passage. But he could have been.

Managing a multibusiness organization means managing the relationship between executives in the central office and those who run the business units or divisions. And strategy gurus notwithstanding, there is no one best way to do that. Rather, the best way always depends on the nature and needs of the businesses in a company's portfolio, on the styles of the people in the corporate office, on the company's strategy and goals.

At British Petroleum, headquarters is involved in all the important strategy decisions; it leaves the operating decisions to division managers. And BP flourishes. BTR wears a different shoe. At BTR, strategy issues are determined by managers in close touch with their markets. Top management concentrates on the operating ratios and financial controls. BTR also thrives.

In a study of 16 large, diversified British companies, we identified three successful styles of managing strategy, which we call "strategic planning," "financial control," and "strategic control." Each is characterized by a particular way of organizing the relationships between headquarters and the business units. The secret to choosing among them is to find the style that suits the circumstances best. Then keep a sharp eye out for its inevitable drawbacks.

Bolder Strategies, Slower Decisions

In many companies headquarters is deeply involved in strategy. Unit managers formulate proposals, but headquarters reserves the right to have the final say. The rationale is simple. As one senior manager commented to us, "There are two or three decisions each decade that make or break a business. Do you really want to leave the business manager alone to make them?" BP, the BOC Group, Cadbury Schweppes, Lex Service Group, STC, and United Biscuits (UB) are among the companies that do not.

One strength of this "strategic planning" style is that it builds checks and balances into the process of determining each business unit's strategy. Responsibilities typically overlap, so business unit managers and corporate staffers are forced to communicate. This exchange of ideas stretches the thinking and improves strategy proposals by the exposure to a variety of views. Unit managers also have a strong incentive to produce good proposals. They will be challenged by managers from headquarters. Although the corporate leaders will ultimately rely on their own judgment, unit managers know that their views will be carefully examined.

A second strength of this style is that it encourages strategies that are well integrated across business units. The close involvement of central managers, strong staff functions, and overlapping responsibilities make it possible for the units to coordinate their plans. Doing so is especially important when business areas are linked through shared resources, for instance, or common distribution networks. As Dominic Cadbury, chief executive of Cadbury Schweppes, noted: "I'm trying to ensure that we maximize our opportunities for synergy in our core businesses, confectionery and soft drinks. We must make sure we are transferring skills and product knowledge and sharing assets." Or as Sir Kenneth Corfield, former chairman of STC, remarked: "In businesses like electronics, the divisions have to help each other. One may have to forgo things so another can get on better."

Perhaps the greatest strength of the strategic planning style is that it fosters the creation of ambitious business strategies. Strategic planning companies are most effective in helping business units strive to gain advantage over competitors. Once headquarters establishes the direction in which the business should be going, unit managers are free to develop bold plans to achieve whatever goal has been set. "We would never have been able to pursue such an ambitious strategy if we were an independent company," one business unit manager in a strategic planning company told us. And that statement characterizes the thinking of many similarly situated unit managers.

Moreover, because the strategic objectives come from the top, the units can support those objectives without great concern for the short-term financial impact of their actions. They are, in a sense, buffered from capital market pressures. Finally, at its best, the agreement between the corporate office and the business unit creates a shared purpose that helps motivate those who must carry out the plan.

Proof of these strengths is evident in the records of the strategic planning companies, which experience more expansion of their existing businesses than the strategic control or financial control companies (see Exhibit I). They also make more investments with long paybacks. As Sir Kenneth Corfield of STC commented, "Sometimes you need to go along with a development for five to seven years before getting any business." As Sir Hector Laing, chairman of UB, explained: "In my experience, it takes about seven years to build a viable business in today's competitive environment."

The strategic planning style is most effective, then, in organizations that are searching for a broad, integrated strategy for developing the business units, where the focus is on long-term competitive advantage. BP, for example, has invested heavily in minerals, coal, nutrition, electronics, and a number of other areas that yield low immediate returns. BOC has plowed resources into strengthening its worldwide position in gases. It has also directed large amounts of capital to its health-care and carbon-graphite electrode businesses. Cadbury, Lex, STC, and UB have all made important investments in the United States. Each company believes that a U.S. presence is essential to the long-term strength of its core businesses, even though it knows that returns may be temporarily low or volatile.

In a given business, strategic planning companies are more likely to choose an ambitious, expansive option than a cautious one. For example, STC, the Plessey Company, and General Electric Company (GEC) have all competed in manufacturing electronic components for defense and telecommunications systems. But only STC (the strategic planning company) made the decision to compete in the international market by building businesses in Europe and the United States and moving into the production of integrated circuits.

Exhibit I.   Which Management Style Is Best for Growth?

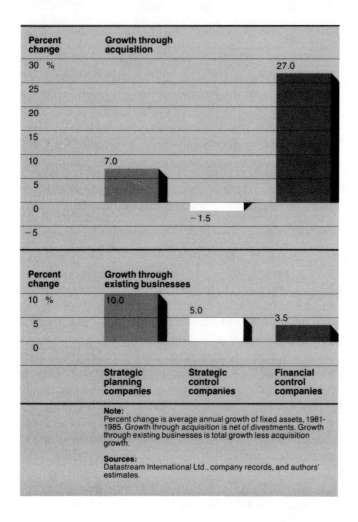

	Strategic planning companies	Strategic control companies	Financial control companies
Growth through acquisition (Percent change)	7.0	−1.5	27.0
Growth through existing businesses (Percent change)	10.0	5.0	3.5

Note:
Percent change is average annual growth of fixed assets, 1981-1985. Growth through acquisition is net of divestments. Growth through existing businesses is total growth less acquisition growth.

Sources:
Datastream International Ltd., company records, and authors' estimates.

Plessey chose to specialize rather than expand, while GEC essentially turned its back on the business because the profit returns in the industry were cyclical and low overall.

Good as this management style may sound, however, it is not without drawbacks. Chief among them are the motivation problems that often plague line managers. Because so many people are involved in planning, with each trying to stamp his or her own view on the outcome, the process can be cumbersome, frustrating, and costly. Line managers may become demoralized when their strategy choices are rejected or changed. They may possess little ownership of the decisions being made about the business ostensibly in their charge, and they may resent superiors for being bossy. The comment of a division manager in one strategic planning company is typical: "In this organization, if you ask the CEO for advice, you'll get instruction." In response, business managers often become protective of their decisions and try to avoid situations in which they have to defend their policies and methods.

The loss of autonomy at the business unit level is particularly troublesome when the distance between headquarters and the market is great. If central managers misunderstand the environment or lose touch with the business, bold investments can become risky ventures that impose harsh consequences on the company. Cadbury, Lex, and STC have all experienced setbacks in their expansion strategies, and each company saw its aggregate earnings decline as a result. BP, BOC, and UB have suffered heavy losses from some of their unsuccessful ventures.

Diminished flexibility is another characteristic weakness of the strategic planning style. The extensive decision-making process inhibits the company's ability to respond quickly to changing market needs or environmental conditions. Business units do not easily jump into emerging markets or close unprofitable operations.

Companies that use this style support losing strategies for too long. Headquarters can be slow to change its mind because it is invested in a particular plan or doesn't fully understand the factors involved. We encountered businesses or divisions that have performed poorly for five or even ten years and yet are still asking headquarters for one more chance to get the long-term strategy right. This problem is particularly acute in highly diversified corporations, because it's so hard to fully understand each business. For this reason, successful strategic planning companies tend to focus on a few core businesses, divesting those that don't fit into their main areas.

Better Financials, Less Innovation

The "financial control" style is almost a reverse image of the strategic planning style. Responsibility for strategy development rests squarely on the shoulders of business unit managers. Headquarters does not formally review strategic plans. Instead, it exerts influence through short-term budgetary control. The objective is to get the business units to put forward tough but achievable profit targets that will provide both a high return on capital and year-to-year growth.

The greatest value of the financial control style is the motivation it gives managers to improve financial performance immediately. Targets are clear and unequivocal. Investment paybacks are short. Performance is monitored carefully. Variances against plan invoke penetrating questions from the top and speedy action from the bottom. Companies set up this way don't buffer managers from financial pressures. Rather, they impose a more demanding and penetrating discipline than the capital market itself. All of this leads to strong profit performance, at least in the short term.

The results of our study support this assertion. As Exhibit II shows, the financial control companies—BTR, Ferranti, GEC, Hanson Trust, Tarmac—have, on average, higher profitability ratios (return on sales, return on capital) than the other companies. They are also better at rationalizing poor performing businesses quickly and turning around new acquisitions.

Other strong points of the financial control style are less obvious. First, it has a way of shaking managers loose from ineffective strategies. By setting demanding targets and strictly enforcing them, corporate management constantly challenges plans that are producing poor results. Corporate doesn't go so far as to suggest alternatives, but it provides the impetus for business managers to break away from strategies that aren't working.

Second, the financial control style is good for developing executives. Assigning profit responsibility to the lowest possible level gives potential high fliers general management experience early in their careers. Those who succeed have years of experience and results to call on by the time they reach the top. Those less suited to general management tasks are identified early and weeded out before they do damage to the company.

Survivors in the financial control system know they have been tested against the toughest benchmarks of performance. This knowledge gives them a great sense of achievement and self-confidence to push their businesses forward as they see fit. This "winner's psychology" creates decisive, ambitious leadership. As Graeme Odgers, former group managing director at Tarmac, com-

Exhibit II. Which Style Is Most Profitable?

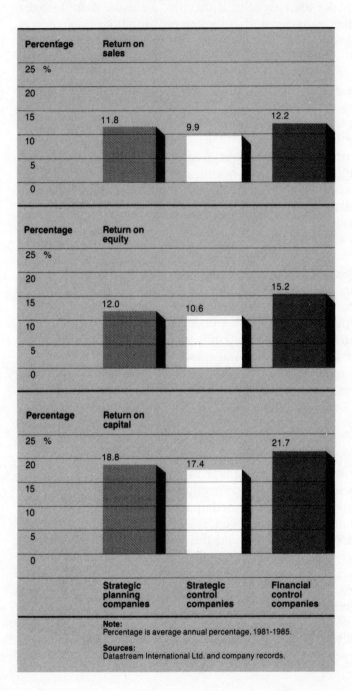

mented, "Pure logic would argue that managers will set a low budget, to make life easy. But if they do, we make them feel that they've let the team down, that they're not ambitious enough to be part of the group. For the most part, our problem lies in the other direction. The managers have so much faith in themselves that they think they can do anything."

This winner's psychology improves the quality of the dialogue between headquarters and the business general managers. Business managers with a track record of delivering will argue their views more forcefully and with less concern about pleasing the boss. They understand that their progress in the company depends on the results they achieve, not on their eloquence in meetings. "It's their business, their budget—and their heads that are on the block," explained one manager.

One final strength of the financial control style is its effectiveness with highly diversified portfolios. Corporate executives need not have an intimate knowledge of each unit's competitors and marketplace. Because the business units develop their own strategies, headquarters can manage through the relevant ratios by comparing performance among different businesses. "We peer at the businesses through the numbers," explained a manager at GEC.

One shortcoming of this system is its bias against strategies and investments with long lead times and paybacks. At a minimum, this makes financial control companies vulnerable to aggressive, committed competitors that can tolerate a long-term view. In essence, that's what happened to BTR, which gave up a strong position in the belting business because it was reluctant to invest aggressively in new technology. Rather than follow the trend to plastic belting (which captured more than 50% of the market), BTR chose to develop a niche position in steel cord belting and thus forfeited its market share to competitors.

Similarly, Hanson Trust passed up a proposal from one business unit to produce a promising generation of new products because corporate decision makers found the seven- to eight-year payback too hard to deal with. (Indeed, they sold the business shortly thereafter.) Pushed to extremes, therefore, the financial control style can lead to milking businesses for purely short-term gains and to excessive risk aversion that prevents healthy business development. When we asked managers from Hanson and BTR how they respond to Japanese competitors, they replied almost in unison, "They are good competitors to avoid."

The failure to back aggressive strategies means that growth in financial control companies comes more from acquisition than from internal development (see Exhibit I). Despite the highly successful record of companies like Hanson and BTR, there are limits to how far acquisition-based growth can be taken. Given Hanson's current size, for instance, few potential targets would make much impact on the company's overall financial performance.

Another drawback to this system is the difficulty decentralized strategy has in exploiting potential synergies between business units. In theory, of course, this problem can be solved by redefining the business units so that two linked businesses are viewed as one. But in fact, it's much more common for financial control companies to tear businesses apart in the quest to weed out low-profit activities. Moreover, few units in financial control companies try to build coordinated global positions. More often, they focus on segments or niches and avoid integrated strategies across a broad business area.

Finally, rigorous control systems limit the flexibility of financial control organizations. Blind adherence to last year's budget targets can preclude adaptive strategies and advantageous moves. Particularly in businesses where circumstances change rapidly, controls can become a straitjacket, and opportunities can be missed.

More Balance, Less Clarity

Companies that follow a "strategic control" style aim to capture the advantages of the other two while avoiding their weaknesses. In practice, however, the tensions involved in balancing control and decentralization make this style of management the hardest to execute because it creates ambiguity.

At best, a strategic control system accommodates both the need to build a business and the need to maximize financial performance. Responsibility for strategy rests with the business and division managers. But strategies must be approved by headquarters. For this purpose, there is an elaborate planning process. Corporate executives use the planning reviews to test logic, to pinpoint weak arguments, and to encourage businesses to raise the quality of their strategic thinking. They also judge whether or not the appropriate balance is being struck between investing to build a business and pushing for short-term financial performance, often with the use of portfolio planning systems.

Financial targets are set in a separate budgeting process. The strategic plan and the budget sometimes pull in opposite directions, and one or the other may have to give. One manager commented, "It's normal for risky investments to drop out of the plan as it gets turned into the budget." It is this tension between the plan and the budget that helps to maintain a balance between new development ideas and cash generation.

Once headquarters has approved a plan and a budget, it attempts to monitor businesses against strategic milestones, such as market share, as well as budgeted performance. The tension between strategic milestones and financial ratios, along with that between the planning and budgeting systems, creates uncertainty and ambiguity. Every business in the portfolio wants to be viewed as a growth prospect. Yet some must be cash cows. As a result, objectives can become confused and the planning process can be a political platform.

The performance of the strategic control companies we studied—Courtaulds, Imperial Chemical Industries (ICI), Imperial Group, Plessey, Vickers—shows the results of this balanced approach. As Exhibits I and III display, these companies had, in general, less internal growth than strategic planning companies, but they achieved substantial improvement in their profitability ratios. Long-term development is traded for short-term financial gains.

Some business units do, of course, pursue long-term strategies aimed at building major positions. The pharmaceutical division of ICI and the international paints division of Courtaulds made systematic, long-term investments and are among the greatest success stories in British industry. For the most part, however, the strategic control companies are focused on cleaning up the portfolio. Large investments and acquisitions, so important to the business-building strategies of strategic planning companies, are rare, ICI's recent acquisition of Stauffer being an exception. These companies have investigated many acquisitions, but few have come to fruition.

Further, although headquarters cares about financial results, it is less ruthless than with financial control in driving to raise performance. As with strategic planning companies, "strategic" arguments (or excuses) have allowed less profitable businesses to operate at unsatisfactory levels of return for too long. For example, Imperial Group took more than five years to bite the bullet and

Exhibit III. **Which Style Has the Most Improved Profits?**

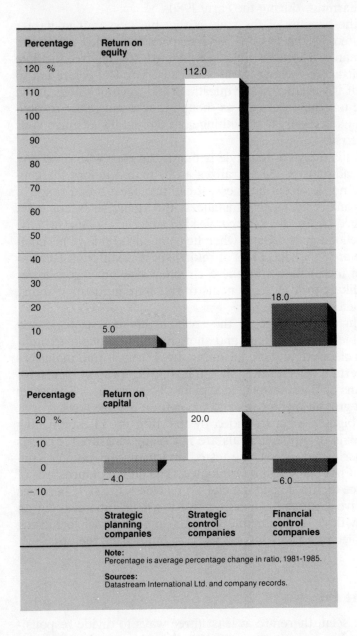

Percentage	Return on equity		
120 %		112.0	
110			
100			
90			
80			
70			
60			
50			
40			
30			
20			18.0
10	5.0		
0			

Percentage	Return on capital		
20 %		20.0	
10			
0			
	− 4.0		− 6.0
− 10			

Strategic planning companies	Strategic control companies	Financial control companies

Note:
Percentage is average percentage change in ratio, 1981-1985.

Sources:
Datastream International Ltd. and company records.

dispose of the Howard Johnson chain, which severely depressed corporate earnings during the early 1980s.

One of the benefits of the style is that business unit managers are motivated by the freedom and responsibility they are given. The chairman of a Vickers division explained: "Giving freedom like this is a bit nerve-racking at times because you feel you're not in control. But if you always ask questions and monitor things at the center, the unit managers act as though they're not really responsible for the decisions. If something goes wrong, it's as much your fault as theirs."

Another advantage of the style is that it can cope with diversity. Because headquarters decentralizes strategy and tailors the controls to the needs of the business, it can manage a broad range of businesses in different circumstances. But doing so is not easy. And managed badly, diversity can lead to superficial planning. One manager echoed many others when he complained that in his company there are "a whole series of rakings-over at different levels— all of them too shallow." In these circumstances managers lower down are likely to lose the benefits of freedom and responsibility and become demotivated.

The main disadvantage of the style is that the strategic and financial objectives, the long- and short-term goals, make accountability less clear-cut and create ambiguity. Business unit managers can be uncertain whether they should be putting forward aggressive growth plans or tight performance plans. They can be too cautious about high-growth businesses and too soft on mature lines.

This ambiguity is compounded by the difficulty of establishing strategic goals. If strategic goals are not easily measured, excuses for poor performance can't be tested and managers become confused about how they will be evaluated. The only real measures of performance then become financial. At its worst, the style becomes an ineffective form of financial control in which time is spent on planning without any tangible benefits and in which achieving planned objectives takes second place to impressing the boss.

The Right Fit

As we've seen, there are at least three ways to divide responsibility between corporate executives and business unit managers. We believe these different styles exist because of certain tensions implicit in the role of corporate management. Virtually all executives want strong leadership from the center, coordinated strategies that build in a variety of viewpoints, careful analysis of decisions, long-term thinking, and flexibility. But they also want autonomy for unit managers, clear accountability, the freedom to respond entrepreneurially to opportunities, superior short-term results, and tight controls.

The two sets of wishes are contradictory. Central leadership, if it has any teeth, inhibits business autonomy. Coordinated strategies detract from personal accountability. Thorough reviews preclude quick entrepreneurial responses. Long-term plans compromise short-term performance. Flexibility is at odds with precise adherence to planned objectives.

Successful corporations make trade-offs between these choices and draw on the combination that best fits the businesses in their portfolios. Is it worth sacrificing tight control and individual responsibility to build up core businesses? Do the benefits of clear goals and devolved responsibility outweigh the dangers of risk aversion and short-term thinking? Can managers cope with the ambiguity needed to achieve a balanced approach across a diverse portfolio? The answers depend on the very things top management knows best—the characteristics of its businesses and the people who make them work.

2
Scenarios: Uncharted Waters Ahead

Pierre Wack

Few companies today would say they are happy with the way they plan for an increasingly fluid and turbulent business environment. Traditional planning was based on forecasts, which worked reasonably well in the relatively stable 1950s and 1960s. Since the early 1970s, however, forecasting errors have become more frequent and occasionally of dramatic and unprecedented magnitude.

Forecasts are not always wrong; more often than not, they can be reasonably accurate. And that is what makes them so dangerous. They are usually constructed on the assumption that tomorrow's world will be much like today's. They often work because the world does not always change. But sooner or later forecasts will fail when they are needed most: in anticipating major shifts in the business environment that make whole strategies obsolete.

Most managers know from experience how inaccurate forecasts can be. On this point, there is probably a large consensus.

My thesis—on which agreement may be less general—is this: The way to solve this problem is not to look for better forecasts by perfecting techniques or hiring more or better forecasters. Too many forces work against the possibility of getting *the* right forecast. The future is no longer stable; it has become a moving target. No single "right" projection can be deduced from past behavior.

The better approach, I believe, is to accept uncertainty, try to understand it, and make it part of our reasoning. Uncertainty today is not just an occasional, temporary deviation from a reasonable predictability; it is a basic structural feature of the business environment. The method used to think about and plan for the future must be made appropriate to a changed business environment.

Royal Dutch/Shell believes that decision scenarios are such a method. As Shell's former group managing director, André Bénard, commented: "Experience has taught us that the scenario technique is much more conducive to forcing people to think about the future than the forecasting techniques we formerly used."[1]

Many strategic planners may claim they know all about scenarios: They have tried but do not like them. I would respond to their skepticism with two points:

Most scenarios merely quantify alternative outcomes of obvious uncertainties (for example, the price of oil may be $20 or $40 per barrel in 1995). Such scenarios are not helpful to decision makers. We call them "first-generation" scenarios. Shell's decision scenarios are quite different, as we shall see.

Even good scenarios are not enough. To be effective, they must involve top and middle managers in understanding the changing business environment more intimately than they would in the traditional planning process. Scenarios help managers structure uncertainty when (1) they are based on a sound analysis of reality, and (2) they change the decision makers' assumptions about how the world works and compel them to reorganize their mental model of reality. This process entails much more than simply designing good scenarios. A willingness to face uncertainty and to understand the forces driving it requires an almost revolutionary transformation in a large organization. This transformation process is as important as the development of the scenarios themselves.

My discussion will be in two parts. In this first article I will describe the development of scenarios in the early 1970s as they evolved out of the more traditional planning process. As you will see, the concept and the technique we arrived at are very different from that with which we began—mainly because there were some highly instructive surprises along the way for all concerned. The art of scenarios is not mechanistic but organic; whatever we had learned after one step advanced us to the next.

In a forthcoming article ["Scenarios: Shooting the Rapids," *Harvard Business Review* (November–December 1985)], I will examine a short-term application of the technique and conclude by discussing key aspects that make the discipline creative.

The First Steps

For ten years after World War II, Shell concentrated on physical planning: The company had to expand its production capacity and build tankers, depots, pipelines, and refineries. Its biggest challenge, like that of many companies, was to coordinate the scheduling of new facilities. Then from 1955 to 1965, financial considerations became more important but primarily on a project basis.

In 1965, Shell introduced a new system called "Unified Planning Machinery" (UPM) to provide planning details for the whole chain of activity—from moving oil from the ground, to the tanker, to the refinery, all the way to the gas station on the corner. UPM was a sophisticated, worldwide system that looked ahead six years: the first year in detail, the next five in broader lines. Unconsciously, managers designed the system to develop Shell's businesses in a familiar, predictable world of "more of the same."

Given the long lead times for new projects in an oil company, however, it was soon decided that the six-year horizon was too limited. Shell therefore undertook experimental studies to explore the business environment of the year 2000. One of them revealed that expansion simply could not continue and predicted that the oil market would switch from a buyers' to a sellers' market, with major discontinuities in the price of oil and changing interfuel competition. The study also signaled that major oil companies could become huge, heavily committed, and much less flexible—almost like dinosaurs. And dinosaurs, as we all know, did not adjust well to sudden environmental changes.

In view of the study's findings, Shell believed it had to find a new way to plan. It asked a dozen of its largest operating companies and business sectors to experiment and look ahead 15 years in an exercise called "Horizon Year Planning."

At the time, I worked for Shell Française. We were familiar with the late Herman Kahn's scenario approach and were intrigued by its possibilities for corporate planning.

Two important uncertainties made France a perfect testing ground for a corporate experiment with the technique: the availability of natural gas (then recently developed in France and the Netherlands), the only fuel that could compete with oil, and the political uncertainty surrounding the way France would manage energy. France's oil regime of that time favored national companies and severely limited Shell's market share.

But France, as a member of the European Community, might have had to change its oil regime at some point to conform to EC policy. The two options—no change or liberalization—combined

Exhibit I.   1970 Scenarios

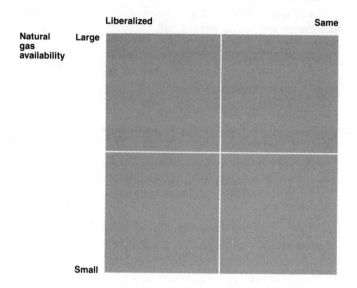

Liberalized   **Same**

Natural   **Large**
gas
availability

Small

with two alternatives, large or small availability of gas, gave us four potential scenarios, as illustrated in Exhibit I.

How far to go in describing each? We discovered quickly that we would almost quadruple our work load if we made each scenario as detailed as a normal plan under the UPM system. Just as the logistics of supply for an army have to be adapted to the type of war being fought, the logistics of scenario planning require a capacity to deal easily and quickly with alternatives. Without it, the whole process can be paralyzed by a bottleneck. In practice, this realization led later to our developing flexible simulation models and having a number of specialists in key areas who could rapidly assess the consequences of different alternatives.

More important, we realized that simply combining obvious uncertainties did not help much with decision making. That exercise brought us only to a set of obvious, simplistic, and conflicting strategic solutions. In fact, many companies are doing just that in their approach to scenarios—quantifying the obvious and not gaining any help in making decisions. Yet this negative realization led to discovery of a positive search tool. By carefully studying some uncertainties, we gained a deeper understanding of their interplay, which, paradoxically, led us to learn what was certain and inevitable and what was not.

We began to appreciate the importance of sorting out "predetermined elements" and "uncertainties." In emphasizing only uncertainties, and obvious ones at that, the scenarios we had developed were merely first-generation scenarios. They were useful in gaining a better understanding of the situation in order to ask better questions and develop better second-generation scenarios—that is, decision scenarios. This dawning intuition—confirmed by all later experience—was an awareness of the critical importance of design. Scenarios will either help decision makers or be of little use to them, depending on how they are constructed and presented, not just on the outcome they focus on. In the same way, two architects can create a well- or a poorly designed building, even though they both use the same construction materials.

The results of the horizon study across the company confirmed the conclusions of the year 2000 study. The most important findings were:

The oil market—long characterized by oversupply—was due to switch to a sellers' market.

Soon there would be virtually no spare crude oil supply capacity.

Inevitably, the Middle East and, in particular, the Arabian Gulf would be the balancing source of oil supply.

The great demand on Middle East production would bring a sharp reduction in the Middle East reserve-production ratio, if met.

The sharp peak in Middle East production would not be allowed to occur. Intervening factors would include a desire by Arab countries to extend the lifetime of their one valuable resource and a cornering of the world energy market by Gulf producers for perhaps 10 to 15 years by limiting production.

Only something approaching a sustained worldwide depression could reduce the growth of demand for Middle East oil to levels where the anticipated sellers' market would be too weak to command substantially higher oil prices.

The magnitude of the changes anticipated cast doubt on the ability of the UPM system to provide realistic planning assumptions. How could it provide the right answer if the forecasts on which it was based were likely to be wrong? In 1971, Shell therefore decided to try scenario planning as a potentially better framework for thinking about the future than forecasts—which were now perceived as a dangerous substitute for real thinking in times of uncertainty and potential discontinuity. But Shell, like many large organizations, is cautious. During the first year, when scenario analysis was done on an experimental basis, the company continued to employ the UPM system. In 1972, scenario planning was extended to central offices and certain large Shell national operating companies. In the following year, it was finally recommended throughout the group and UPM was then phased out.

The Next Step

The scenario process started with the construction of a set of exploratory first-generation scenarios. As we have learned, it is almost impossible to jump directly to proper decision scenarios.

Scenario I was surprise-free, virtually lifted whole from the work done under the old UPM system. The surprise-free scenario is one that rarely comes to pass but, in my experience, is essential in the package. It builds on the implicit views of the future shared by most managers, making it possible for them to recognize their outlook in the scenario package. If the package only contains possibilities that appear alien to the participants, they will likely find the scenario process threatening and reject it out of hand.

Scenario II postulated a tripling of host-government tax take in view of the 1975 renegotiation of the Teheran Agreement (which set the take for OPEC) and anticipated lower economic growth and depressed energy and oil demand as a consequence.

Scenario III treated the other obvious uncertainty: low growth. Based on the 1970–1971 recession model, a proliferation of "me-first" values, and a growing emphasis on leisure, it assumed an economic growth rate only half of that projected under Scenario I, with a slowdown in international trade, economic nationalism, and protective tariffs. Low oil demand would limit oil price rises and lower producer government take.

Scenario IV assumed increased demand for coal and nuclear energy—at the expense of oil.

All four scenarios assumed that the tax take of the producer governments would be increased at the 1975 Teheran renegotiation (see Exhibit II).

OK AS NUMBERS BUT—

This set of scenarios seemed reasonably well designed and would fit most definitions of what scenarios should be. It covered a wide span of possible futures, and each scenario was internally consistent.

When the set was presented to Shell's top management, the problem was the same as in the French scenarios: No strategic thinking or action could be taken from considering this material.

Many companies reach this same point in planning scenarios. Management reaction? "So what! What do I do with scenarios?" And planners abandon the effort, often because they believe the problem is, in part, management's inability to deal with uncertainty.

Yet this group of Shell managers was highly experienced in dealing with risk and uncertainty. For example, many of the decisions they make deal with exploratory drilling, a true uncertainty since you never know what you'll find until you drill. They must often decide whether to risk $5 million or $50 million on exploration projects and distinguish the risks, say, in Brazil or the North Sea. What was so different about the uncertainties of scenarios? Quite simply, they needed structuring. In oil exploration, there were theories to call on, concepts to use, an organized body of geological and geophysical analyses, comparisons with similar geological structures, and ways to spread the risk that were familiar to the decision maker. The first-generation scenarios presented the raw uncertainties but they offered no basis on which managers could exercise their judgment. Our next task was to provide that basis so that executives could understand the nature of these uncertainties and come to grips with them.

The goal of these exploratory first-generation scenarios is not action but understanding. Their purpose is to give insight into the system, to identify the predetermined elements, and to perceive connections among various forces and events driving the system. As the system's interrelatedness became clear, we realized that

Exhibit II.   Producer Government Take*
1970–1985

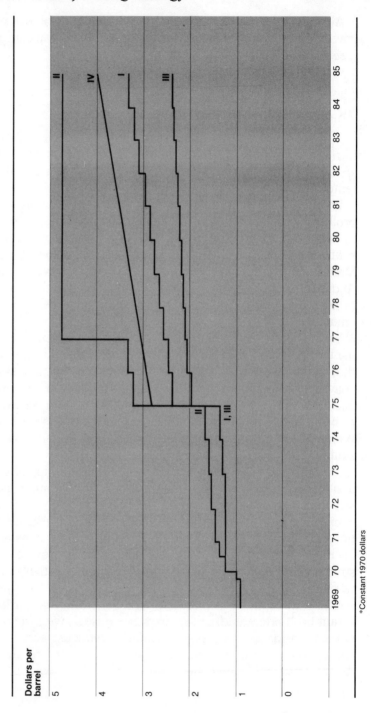

Dollars per
barrel

*Constant 1970 dollars

what may appear in some cases to be uncertain might actually be predetermined—that many outcomes were simply *not* possible.

These exploratory scenarios were not effective planning devices. Without them, however, we could not have developed the next generation of scenarios.

What Will Happen—What Cannot

To understand the fluctuations that give the oil system its character and determine its future, we had to understand the forces that drive it. Work on the next set of scenarios began with a closer look at the principal actors in Shell's business environment: oil producers, consumers, and companies. Because self-interest determined the fundamental concerns of these groups, significant behavioral differences existed. So we began to study the characters on the stage and how they would behave as the drama unfolded.

In analyzing the major oil-producing countries one by one, for example, it was clear that Iran's interests differed from Saudi Arabia's or Nigeria's and that their strategies would reflect these differences. The lower panel of Exhibit III shows Iran's oil production as its share of projected oil demand under each of the 1971 scenarios, as well as discovery rates and additions to reserves. For the first five years, we expected that Iran's reserves would grow as the industry found more new oil than it would produce. For the second five years, we expected the situation to reverse and reserves to fall.

As the upper panel of Exhibit III shows, reserve-production ratios would drop rapidly under all scenarios. Our conclusion was that Iran would then strive to change its oil policy from one of expanding production to one of increasing prices and possibly curbing production. Such a policy change would stem not from an anti-Western attitude but simply from the logic of national interest. If we were Iranian, we would behave the same way.

Saudi Arabia's situation was different. Except in the low-growth scenario, production would generate more revenue than the government could purposefully spend, even allowing for some "manageable" surplus. We concluded that even though oil company logic would have the Saudis producing 20 million barrels per day by 1985, the government could not do so in good political conscience. It was no surprise when Sheikh Zhaki Ahmed Yamani, Saudi Ara-

Exhibit III. Iran's Production Scenarios

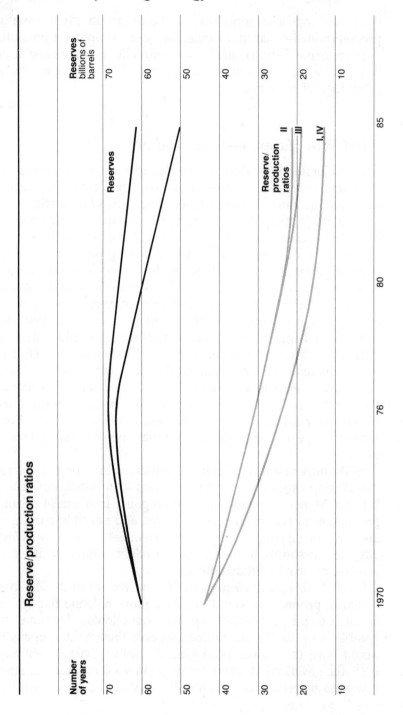

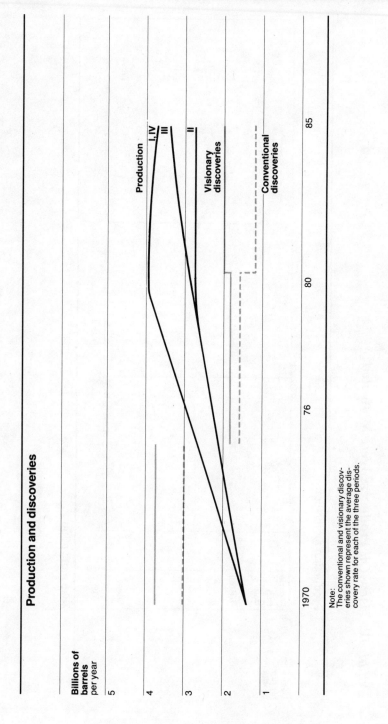

Production and discoveries

Billions of barrels per year

Production

I,IV
III

II

Visionary discoveries

Conventional discoveries

1970   76   80   85

Note:
The conventional and visionary discoveries shown represent the average discovery rate for each of the three periods.

Exhibit IV.   How Oil Producers Were Motivated

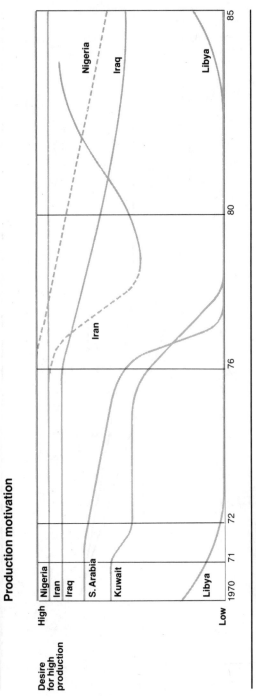

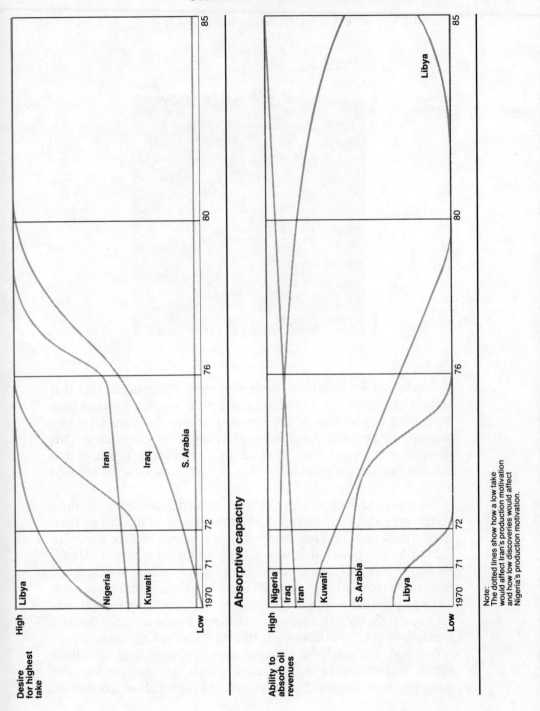

Desire for highest take

High — Libya, Nigeria, Iran, Iraq, Kuwait, S. Arabia — Low

1970 71 72 76 80 85

Absorptive capacity

Ability to absorb oil revenues

High — Nigeria, Iraq, Iran, Kuwait, S. Arabia, Libya — Low

1970 71 72 76 80 85

Note:
The dotted lines show how a low take
would affect Iran's production motivation
and how low discoveries would affect
Nigeria's production motivation.

Exhibit V.   The Major Oil Exporters

Reserves

	Limited	Ample
Absorptive capacity — Limited	**Group I** Libya Qatar	**Group III** Saudi Arabia Abu Dhabi Kuwait
Absorptive capacity — Ample	**Group II** Algeria Nigeria Venezuela Iraq Indonesia Iran	**Group IV**

bia's minister for oil affairs, later remarked: "We should find that leaving our crude in the ground is by far more profitable than depositing our money in the banks, particularly if we take into account the periodic devaluation of many of the currencies. This reassessment would lead us to adopt a production program that ensures that we get revenues which are only adequate for our real needs."[2]

We analyzed each of the producer countries according to their oil reserves and their need and ability to spend oil income productively (Exhibit IV). When arrayed in the simple matrix shown in Exhibit V, the power that was to become OPEC emerged clearly: No nation had both ample reserves and ample absorptive capacity, that is, the motivation to produce these reserves. If Indonesia, with its large population and enormous need for funds, had Saudi Arabia's reserves, then the growth of demand foreseen under the first scenario might have developed. But such was not the case.

We then analyzed the oil-consuming countries and saw their annual increments in import requirements (see Exhibit VI). For many years, oil imports had increased at a rate of about one million barrels per day; then for a long time the rate was about two million barrels per day.

Suddenly, in the mid-1970s, oil imports were expected to increase annually at much higher rates. This change can be understood by looking at Exhibit VII, which shows the sources of energy supply in the United States, Western Europe, and Japan. In the United States, oil supply had peaked early, and the incremental demand for energy had been satisfied by natural gas. Because of its regulated price, however, natural gas production plateaued in 1972. Coal production might have increased, but in light of the forecasts of future nuclear power generation, coal resources were not being developed. Nuclear plants, however, were not functioning in sufficient numbers to meet the demand, which was increasing annually at a rapid pace. Since the base was so large to begin with, even a 3% or 4% increase in the U.S. energy demand would in turn demand a great deal of the only available incremental energy source—imported oil.

In Japan—then like a new continent emerging on the world economic map—circumstances were different. In 1953, as the U.S. occupation ended, Japanese industrial production was 40% of the United Kingdom's; in 1970, it was more than double. With the economy growing by 11% or 12% a year, annual demand for oil increased by some 20%. The result: huge increases in oil imports.

Beyond the need to view each participant individually and as part of a group, we discovered that "soft" data were as important to us as "hard" data in analyzing outcomes. For example, because the Japanese become anxious when faced with a possible denial of imports, any tension over oil supply would be especially trying. Furthermore, they would project on multinational oil companies the type of behavior they expect from their own companies in a crisis: giving loyalty to the home country and ignoring the rest of the world. This attitude would add to the probable tension over oil supplies. Having collected and analyzed hard and soft data, and in order to expand the number of predetermined elements and get at the core of what remained uncertain, we looked at:

Oil demand by market class and at different rates of growth.

The implications of high oil prices for each nation's balance of payments and inflation.

The possible reactions of consumer governments to higher oil prices.

Interfuel competition and the impact of higher oil prices.

Exhibit VI. Annual Growth in Import Requirements

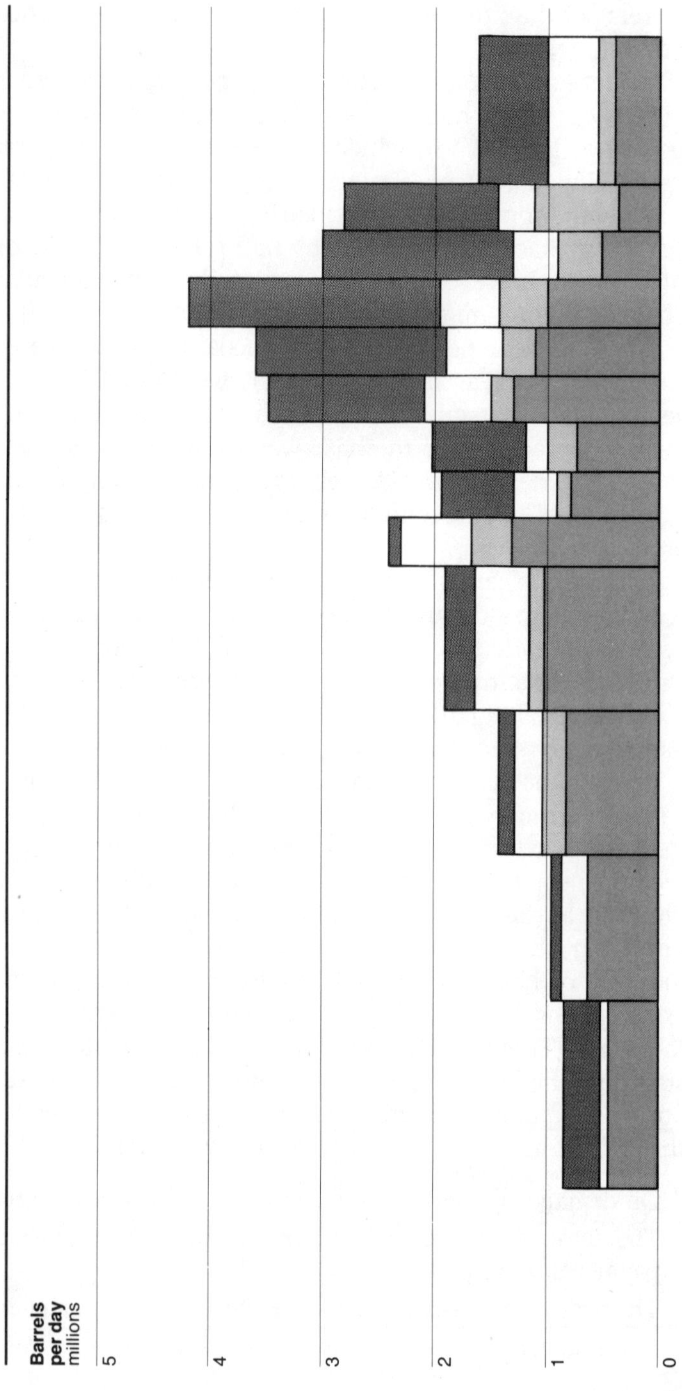
Barrels per day millions
5
4
3
2
1
0

1957-60   61-63   64-66   67-69   70 71 72 73 74 75 76 77 78-80

North America   **Japan**   **Rest**   **Western Europe**

Note:
The import requirements shown for 1957
through 1972 are actual; requirements
shown for 1973 through 1980 represent
the surprise-free consensus forecast.
Data for the years 1957-1960, 1961-1963,
1964-1966, 1967-1969, and 1978-1980
represent averages.

Exhibit VII.　Energy Demand by Sources

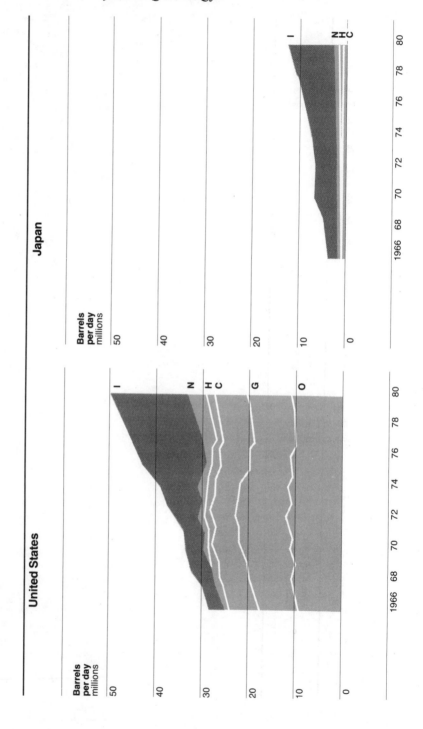

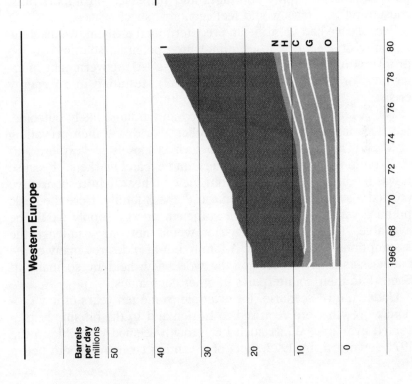

Western Europe

Barrels
per day
millions

I = Imported energy

Indigenous

N = nuclear
H = hydroelectricity
C = coal
G = natural gas
O = oil

Note:
The energy demand shown for 1966
through 1972 is actual; demand shown for
1974 through 1980 represents the
surprise-free consensus forecast.

The changing "cut of the barrel."
Construction of refinery, marine, and market facilities.

The 1972 Scenarios

Having all these building blocks, we could begin to understand the forces driving the system. In response, we presented the revamped scenarios to Shell's top management as an array of possible futures, gathered in two families, A and B, in September 1972. The A-group timed an oil supply disruption to coincide with the scheduled renegotiation of the Teheran price agreement in 1975. (In reality, it came, of course, in the fall of 1973—after the imposition of the oil embargo.)

Most oil-producing countries would be reaching the technical limit of their capacities by 1976, while others would be reluctant to increase output further because of their inability to absorb the additional revenues. Accordingly, producer countries' oil prices would increase substantially by the end of 1975. Confronted with possible energy supply shortages and increased oil import bills, consuming countries would feel economic shock waves.

Because we had identified a predetermined element, we used the A-family of scenarios to examine three potential solutions to the problems it presented: private enterprise (A1); government intervention, or *dirigiste* (A2); or none (A3), resulting in an energy crisis.

The A-family of scenarios emerged as the most likely outcome, but it varied sharply from the implicit worldview then prevailing at Shell. That view can be characterized loosely as "explore and drill, build refineries, order tankers, and expand markets." Because it was so different, how could our view be heard? In response, we created a set of "challenge scenarios," the B-family. Here the basic premise was that somehow, a sufficient energy supply would be available. The B-family scenarios would not only challenge the assumptions underlying the A-family but also destroy many of the business-as-usual aspects of the worldview held by so many at Shell (like their counterparts in other companies).

Under the B1 scenario, for example, some ten years of low economic growth were required to fit demand to the oil supply presumed available. While such low growth seemed plausible in the 1971 downturn, by 1972 signs of a coming economic boom began to show. B1 was also implausible since governments and citizens of industrialized countries viewed rising unemployment as unacceptable and would consciously seek growth no matter what. The implausibilities under B1 made the inevitability of a major disruption more plain to managers.

B3 was also an important educational tool because it postulated a very high supply of oil as a way to avoid major change. We called it the "three-miracles" scenario because it required the simultaneous occurrence of three extremely unlikely situations. The first was a miracle in exploration and production. The Shell exploration and production staff estimated a 30% chance that the reserves necessary to meet 1985 demand would be found in each of the oil provinces individually, but only a very small chance that these high reserves would be found in all areas simultaneously. Meeting the forecast 1985 demand under B3 would require not only 24 million barrels daily from Saudi Arabia, but also 13 million barrels from Africa and 6 million barrels from Alaska and Canada—clearly an impossibility.

The second miracle was sociopolitical: B3 foresaw that all major producing countries would happily deplete their resources at the will of the consumer. Countries with low capacities to absorb the excess revenue would agree to produce huge amounts of oil and put their money in the bank, exposed to the erosion of inflation, rather than keep it in the ground. That miracle projected the values of consuming countries onto oil producers—a kind of Western cultural imperialism that was extremely unconvincing, even to the most expansion-minded manager.

The final miracle started with the recognition that no capacity would be left above projected demand. Previously, when minor crises developed, additional oil was always available to meet sudden short-term needs. Under B3, however, there would be no spare production capacity. The miracle then was that there would be no need for it—no wars in the region, no acts of God, no cyclical peaks of demand higher than anticipated. Again, this was nothing short of miraculous. The improbability of B3 forced Shell management to realize how disruptive the change in their world would be.

B2 was a totally artificial construct. It premised that—despite all the problems—the world would muddle through. This reflects the sentiment that, as William Ogburn said, "There is much stability in society. . . . Social trends seldom change their directions quickly and sharply. . . . Revolutions are rare and evolution is the rule."

We couldn't rationally justify this scenario, but we realized that the worst outcome does not always develop. So we imagined a B2 scenario in which everything positive was possible. Oil producers would live and let live to obtain concessions from the consumers who, in turn and with great foresight, would immediately curb oil consumption.

We quantified both the A- and B-family scenarios in terms of volume, price, impact on individual oil producers and consumers, and interfuel competition. Our presentation gained the attention of top management principally because the B-family of scenarios destroyed the ground many of them had chosen to stand on. Management then made two decisions: to use scenario planning in the central offices and the larger operating companies and to informally advise governments of the major oil-consuming countries about what we saw coming.

We made a series of presentations to the governments of the major consuming countries and stressed the coming disruption by tracing its impact on their balance of payments, rates of inflation, and resource allocation.

BANGING THE DRUM QUICKLY

Shell first asked its major downstream operating companies to evaluate current strategies against two A-type scenarios, using the B2 scenario as a sensitivity check. By asking "what if," the B2 checked strategies already conceived in another conceptual framework (the A-family).

To this intent, we presented the A and B scenarios to the second echelon of Shell's management—its first exposure to scenarios. The meetings stood in stark contrast to traditional UPM planning sessions, which dealt out forecasts, trends, and premises—all under an avalanche of numbers. The scenarios focused less on predicting outcomes and more on understanding the forces that would eventually compel an outcome; less on figures and more on insight. The meetings were unusually lengthy and the audience clearly appreciative. We thought we had won over a large share of these managers.

The following months would show, however, that no more than a third of Shell's critical decision centers were really acting on the insights gained through the scenarios and actively preparing for the A-family of outcomes. The scenario package had sparked some intellectual interest but had failed to change behavior in much of the Shell organization. This reaction came as a shock and compelled us to rethink how to design scenarios geared for decision making.

Reality was painful: Most studies dealing with the future business environment, including these first scenarios, have a low "existential effectiveness." (We can define existential effectiveness as single-mindedness, but the Japanese express it much better: "When there is no break, not even the thickness of a hair, between a man's vision and his action.") A vacuum cleaner is mostly heat and noise; its actual effectiveness is only around 40%. Studies of the future, particularly when they point to an economic disruption, are less effective than a vacuum cleaner.

If your role is to be a corporate lookout and you clearly see a discontinuity on the horizon, you had better learn what makes the difference between a more or a less effective study. One of the differences involves the basic psychology of decision making.

Every manager has a mental model of the world in which he or she acts based on experience and knowledge. When a manager must make a decision, he or she thinks of behavior alternatives within this mental model. When a decision is good, others will say the manager has good judgment. In fact, what has really happened is that his or her mental map matches the fundamentals of the real world. We call this mental model the decision maker's "microcosm"; the real world is the "macrocosm."

There is also a corporate view of the world, a corporate microcosm. During a sabbatical year in Japan, for example, I found that Nippon Steel did not "see" the steel market in the same way as Usinor, the French steel giant. As a result, there were marked differences in the behavior and priorities of the two corporations. Each acted rationally, given its worldview. A company's perception of its business environment is as important as its investment infrastructure because its strategy comes from this perception. I cannot overemphasize this point: Unless the corporate microcosm changes, managerial behavior will not change; the internal compass must be recalibrated.

From the moment of this realization, we no longer saw our task as producing a documented view of the future business environment five or ten years ahead. Our real target was the microcosms of our decision makers: Unless we influenced the mental image, the picture of reality held by critical decision makers, our scenarios would be like water on a stone. This was a different and much more demanding task than producing a relevant scenario package.

We had first tried to produce scenarios that we would not be ashamed of when we subsequently compared them with reality. After our initiation with these first sets of scenarios, we changed our goal. We now wanted to design scenarios so that managers would question their own model of reality and change it when necessary, so as to come up with strategic insights beyond their minds' previous reach. This change in perspective—from producing a "good" document to changing the image of reality in the heads of critical decision makers—is as fundamental as that experienced when an organization switches from selling to marketing.

The 1973 Scenarios—the Rapids

More than 20 centuries ago, Cicero noted, "It was ordained at the beginning of the world that certain signs should prefigure certain events." As we prepared the 1973 scenarios, all economic signs pointed to a major disruption in oil supply. New analyses foretold a tight supply-demand relationship in the coming years. Now we saw the discontinuity as predetermined. No matter what happened in particular, prices would rise rapidly in the 1970s, and oil production would be constrained—not because of a real shortage of oil but for political reasons, with producers taking advantage of the very tight supply-demand relationship. Our next step was to make the disruption into our surprise-free scenario. We did not know how soon it would occur, how high the price increase would be, and how the various players would react. But we knew it would happen. Shell was like a canoeist who hears white water around the bend and must prepare to negotiate the rapids.

To help reframe our managers' outlook, we charted the 1973 scenarios (Exhibit VIII). From the calm upriver of the traditional environment, the company would plunge into the turbulence of the rapids and have to learn to live in a new habitat.

We could eliminate some of the original scenarios. We could dam off the alternate branch of the river (the B-family scenarios of 1972). The no-growth-no-problem scenario (B1) was clearly implausible as economies, fully recovered from the 1971 recession, boomed. The three-miracles scenario (B3) remained just that—three supply

Exhibit VIII. 1973 Scenarios

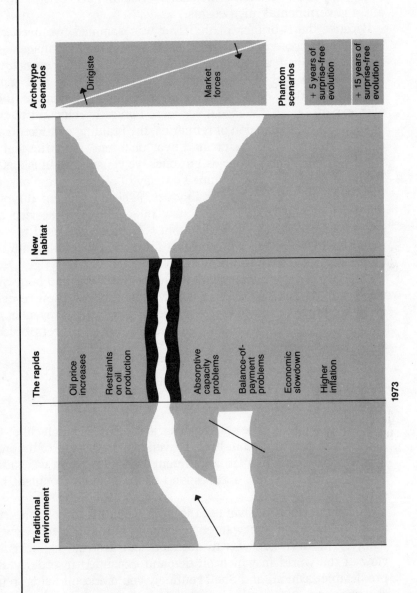

miracles. Finally, our discussions with governments about the impending crisis had allowed us to conclude that their reaction would occur only after the fact. (Obviously, we hadn't yet learned how to affect governmental microcosms.)

Because the B-branch of the river was dammed, we needed to explore other potential streams that dovetailed with management's current optimism, an optimism based on the booming economy of late 1972 and early 1973—in which growth exceeded that of any period since the Korean War. In an oil company having an affair with expansion, many executives were naturally reluctant to slow or suspend the expansion of refineries, the building of tankers, and so forth. In response, we created two "phantom" scenarios—alternatives to our main scenarios but ones we considered illusions. In Phantom Scenario I, we assumed a delay of 5 years in the onset of the disruption; in Phantom II, 15 years. (These represented typical times needed to first, bring a new oil facility into service and second, amortize it.) These phantom scenarios were used to measure the "regret" Shell would feel if it planned for a discontinuity that never occurred for 5 or even 15 more years.

Only two developments could delay the inevitable and both were ruled out: (1) the discovery of new Middle East-sized oil reserves in an area that would have no problem in absorbing revenues, or (2) political or military seizure and control of producers by consuming countries.

MORE THAN WATER ON A STONE

On the surface, the 1973 scenarios seemed much like the A scenarios constructed in 1972. Driven by a new sense of urgency, however, we saw them in a different light. The time we had to anticipate, prepare for, and respond to the new environment had shrunk greatly.

More important, we wanted the 1973 scenarios to be more than water on a stone: We wanted to change our managers' view of reality. The first step was to question and destroy their existing view of the world in which oil demand expanded in orderly and predictable fashion, and Shell routinely could add oil fields, refineries, tankers, and marketing outlets. In fact, we had been at this job of destruction now for several years.

But exposing and invalidating an obsolete worldview is not where scenario analysis stops. Reconstructing a new model is the most important job and is the responsibility of the managers themselves. The planners' job is to engage the decision makers' interest and participation in this reconstruction. We listen carefully to their needs and give them the highest quality materials to use in making decisions. The planners will succeed, however, only if they can securely link the new realities of the outside world—the unfolding business environment—to the managers' microcosm. Good scenarios supply this vital "bridge"; they must encompass both managers' concerns and external reality. Otherwise, no one will bother to cross the bridge.

If the planners design the package well, managers will use scenarios to construct a new model of reality by selecting from them those elements they believe relevant to their business world. Because they have been making decisions—and have a long track record to show that they're good at it—they may, of course, not see any relevant elements. Or they may go with what their "gut" tells them. But that should not discourage the planner who is drawing up the scenario.

Just as managers had to change their worldview, so planners had to change the way they viewed the planning process. So often, planning is divorced from the managers for whom it is intended. We came to understand that making the scenarios relevant required a keener knowledge of decision makers and their microcosm than we had ever imagined. In later years, we built some bridges that did not get used. The reason for this failure was always that we did not design scenarios that responded to managers' deepest concerns.

BUILDING BLOCKS FOR NEW MICROCOSMS

In developing the 1973 scenarios, we realized that if managers were to reframe their view of reality, they would need a clear overview of a new model. Exhibit IX, one way to portray that model, summarizes the anticipated business environment and its key elements: the predetermined events, which are shown on the left, and the major discontinuities, which are shown in the center.

We focused attention on the following features of the business environment (shown in Exhibit IX).

Exhibit IX.   A New Worldview

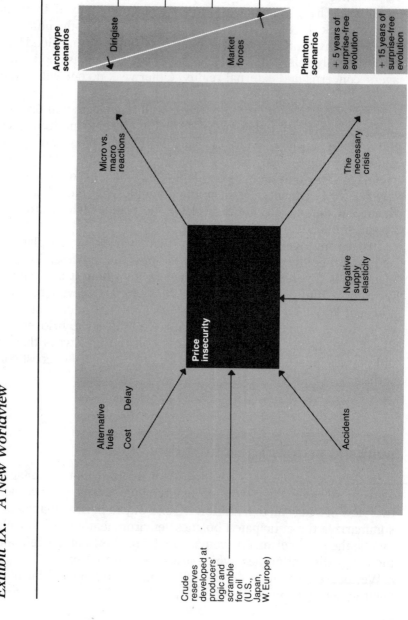

Alternative fuels, which we could develop only very slowly. Even under a wartime crash development program, none could be available before the 1980s. We analyzed the cost in three stages. First, even though other fuels might replace oil for generating power and steam in large industrial settings, the oil-producing nations would not be impressed. On the contrary, they welcomed the alternative of coal and nuclear power in what they considered low-value markets. Second, oil used for heating was a different story. Burning coal was not a satisfactory alternative. You would have to gasify or transform coal into electricity, with accompanying thermodynamic loss. The price for this alternative was high; the price for oil would not exceed this threshold in the near future. The third possibility, oil used in transport, had an even higher fuel cost than oil used for heating and was obviously irrelevant.

Accidents, which included both political and internal and physical incidents, are events that any oil executive considers a matter of course. In the same way, a Filipino knows that a roof must be built carefully; even though the weather in the Philippines is usually balmy, typhoons are frequent enough that the only uncertainty is when the roof's strength will be tested.

Negative supply elasticity, which means that unlike other commodities the supply of oil does not increase with increases in its price, at least for a number of years. On the contrary, the higher the price, the lower the volume of oil it would be in the interest of the major exporting countries to produce.

As planners at the center of a diverse group of companies, we faced a special problem beyond the construction of a new worldview. We had to make its message useful not only to managing directors but also to operating companies from Canada to Germany, Japan to Australia. And yet the dramatic changes we anticipated would affect each differently. What basic message could we convey to all of them?

To construct a framework for the message, we borrowed the concept of archetypes from psychology. Just as we often view individuals as composites of archetypes (for example, part introvert and part extrovert), so we developed governmental archetypes to help us examine differing national responses. In our view, nations would favor either a market-force or government-intervention *(dirigiste)* approach. No country would follow one path exclusively. We expected, for example, that West Germany's response would be more market oriented, whereas France's would be more *diri-*

giste. We analyzed the actions anticipated under each archetypal response in terms of price increases, taxes, alternative fuel development, and regulations by market class.

We Led the Managers to Water . . .

While we didn't fully comprehend that influencing managers required a tailor-made fit between the scenarios and their deepest concerns, we knew intuitively that events in 1973 gave us this fit in several ways. The arrows on the right side of Exhibit IX symbolize four of the implications stressed.

We told our upstream managers, engaged in exploration and production, that the unthinkable was going to happen: "Be careful! You are about to lose the major part of your concessions and mining rents." The traditional profit base in the upstream world would be lost and new relationships would have to be developed between the company and producing nations.

To the downstream world of refiners, transporters, and marketers, we said something equally alarming: "Prepare! You are about to become a low-growth industry." Oil demand had always grown more rapidly than GNP, something Shell's management took for granted. In the past, we did not have to consider the consequences of overinvestment; one or two years of normal market growth would cure any premature moves. Now oil consumption in industrial countries would increase at rates less than the increase in GNP, and Shell would have to develop new instincts and reflexes to function in a low-growth world.

A third serious implication was the need to further decentralize the decision-making and strategic process. One basic strategy would no longer be valid for operating companies in most parts of the world. Shell companies had generally—and successfully—aimed for a higher share of conversion in refineries than did the competition. Now we understood that the energy shock would affect each nation so differently that each would have to respond independently. Shell, which was already decentralized compared with other oil majors, did in fact decentralize further, enabling it to adjust faster to the turbulence experienced later. (For some time now, it has been the most decentralized of all the major oil companies.)

Finally, we made managers see that because we didn't know

when the disruption would come, they should prepare for it in different phases of the business cycle. We developed three simulations. In the first, the oil shock occurred before the cyclical downturn; in the second, the events were simultaneous; and in the third, the oil shock followed the downturn. These simulations led us to prepare for a far more serious economic decline than might otherwise have been expected.

. . . AND MOST FINALLY DRANK

We hit planning pay dirt with the 1973 scenarios because they met the deepest concerns of managers. If any managers were not fully convinced, the events of October soon made them believers. We had set out to produce not a scenario booklet simply summarizing views but a change in the way managers view their world. Only when the oil embargo began could we appreciate the power of scenarios—power that becomes apparent when the world overturns, power that has immense and immediate value in a large, decentralized organization.

Strategies are the product of a worldview. When the world changes, managers need to share some common view of the new world. Otherwise, decentralized strategic decisions will result in management anarchy. Scenarios express and communicate this common view, a shared understanding of the new realities to all parts of the organization.

Decentralized management in worldwide operating companies can adapt and use that view for strategic decisions appropriate to its varied circumstances. Its initiative is not limited by instructions dictated from the center but facilitated and freed by a broad framework; all will speak the same language in adapting their operations to a new business environment. Companies from Finland to New Zealand now knew what "the rapids" meant, were alert to the implications of producer logic, and recognized the need to prepare for a new environment.

From studying evolution, we learn how an animal suited to one environment must become a new animal to survive when the environment undergoes severe change. We believed that Shell would have to become a new animal to function in a new world. Business-as-usual decisions would no longer suffice.

In the next article, I will discuss how we adapted the technique to develop scenarios for the short term. As the time span between decisions steadily became shorter, this refinement became necessary.

Notes

1. André Bénard, "World Oil and Cold Reality," *Harvard Business Review* (November–December 1980), p. 91.
2. Quoted in *Platt's Oilgram,* February 10, 1972.

3
Selecting Strategies That Create Shareholder Value

Alfred Rappaport

In today's fast-changing, often bewildering business environment, formal systems for strategic planning have become one of top management's principal tools for evaluating and coping with uncertainty. Corporate board members are also showing increasing interest in ensuring that the company has adequate strategies and that these are tested against actual results. While the organizational dynamics and the sophistication of the strategic planning process vary widely among companies, the process almost invariably culminates in projected (commonly five-year) financial statements.

This accounting format enables top managers and the board to review and approve strategic plans in the same terms that the company reports its performance to shareholders and the financial community. Under current practice the projected financial statements, particularly projected earnings per share performance, commonly serve as the basis for judging the attractiveness of the strategic or long-term corporate plan.

The conventional accounting-oriented approach for evaluating the strategic plan does not, however, provide reliable answers to such basic questions as:

Will the corporate plan create value for shareholders? If so, how much?

Which business units are creating value and which are not?

How would alternative strategic plans affect shareholder value?

Author's note: I wish to thank Carl M. Noble, Jr. and Robert C. Statius Muller for their many helpful suggestions.

My chief objective here is to provide top management and board members with a theoretically sound, practical approach for assessing the contributions of strategic business units (SBU) plans and overall corporate strategic plans toward creating economic value for shareholders.

Limitations of EPS

A principal objective of corporate strategic planning is to create value for shareholders. By focusing systematically on strategic decision making, such planning helps management allocate corporate resources to their most productive and profitable use. It is commonly assumed that if the strategic plan provides for "satisfactory" growth in EPS, then the market value of the company's shares will increase as the plan materializes, thus creating value for shareholders. Unfortunately, EPS growth does not necessarily lead to an increase in the market value of the stock. This phenomenon can be observed empirically and explained on theoretical grounds as well.

Of the Standard & Poor's 400 industrial companies, 172 achieved compounded EPS growth rates of 15% or better during 1974–1979. In 27, or 16%, of these companies stockholders realized *negative* rates of return from dividends plus capital losses. For 60, or 35%, of the 172 companies, stockholders' returns were inadequate to compensate them just for inflation. The returns provided no compensation for risk. Exhibit I gives a more complete set of statistics. Additional evidence of the uncertain relationship between EPS growth and returns to shareholders is offered by the 1980 *Fortune* "500" survey of the largest industrial corporations. Forty-eight, or almost 10%, of the companies achieved positive EPS growth rates, while their stockholders realized negative rates of return for the 1969–1979 period. Thirteen of these companies had EPS growth rates in excess of 10% during this period.

EPS and related accounting ratios, such as return on investment and return on equity, have shortcomings as financial standards by which to evaluate corporate strategy for the following six reasons:

1. Alternative and equally acceptable determinations are possible for the EPS figure. Prominent examples are the differences that arise

Exhibit I.   EPS Growth Rates Versus Rates of Return to Shareholders for Standard & Poor's 400 Industrial Companies

	1976-1979	1975-1979‡	1974-1979
Companies with annual EPS growth of 10% or greater*			
Total	259 (100 %)	268 (100 %)	232 (100 %)
Negative rates of return to share-holders	32 (12 %)	7 (3 %)	39 (17 %)
Rates of return inadequate to compensate shareholders for inflation†	65 (25 %)	36 (13 %)	89 (38 %)
Companies with annual EPS growth of 15% or greater*			
Total	191 (100 %)	205 (100 %)	172 (100 %)
Negative rates of return to share-holders	14 (7 %)	2 (1 %)	27 (16 %)
Rates of return inadequate to compensate shareholders for inflation†	33 (17 %)	20 (10 %)	60 (35 %)

*Restated primary EPS excluding extraordinary items and discontinued operations.

†The annual growth rates in the consumer price index for 1976-1979, 1975-1979, and 1974-1979 are 7.7%, 7.6%, and 8%, respectively.

‡The small number of companies with negative rates of return to shareholders for this period is due to low level of market at the end of 1974. Standard & Poor's stock index at the close of 1974 was 76.47 and, in subsequent years, 100.88, 119.46, 104.71, 107.21, and 121.02.

Note: EPS growth and rate-of-return calculations prepared by CompuServe, Inc. using Standard & Poor's Compustat data base.

from LIFO and FIFO approaches to computing cost of sales and various methods of computing depreciation.

2. Earnings figures do not reflect differences in risk among strategies and SBUs. Risk is conditioned both by the nature of the business investment and by the relative proportions of debt and equity used to finance investments.

3. Earnings do not take into account the working capital and fixed investment needed for anticipated sales growth.

4. While projected earnings, of course, incorporate estimates of future revenues and expenses, they ignore potential changes in a company's cost of capital both because of inflation and because of shifting business and financial risk.

5. The EPS approach to strategy ignores dividend policy. If the objective were to maximize EPS, one could argue that the company should never pay any dividends as long as it expected to achieve a positive return on new investment. But we know that if the company invested shareholders' funds at below the minimum acceptable market rate, the value of the company would be bound to decrease.

6. The EPS approach does not specify a time preference rate for the EPS stream, i.e., it does not establish the value of a dollar of EPS this year compared with a year from now, two years from now, and so forth.

Shareholder Value Approach

The economic value of any investment is simply the anticipated cash flow discounted by the cost of capital. An essential feature of the discounted cash flow technique, of course, is that it takes into account that a dollar of cash received today is worth more than a dollar received a year from now, because today's dollar can be invested to earn a return during the intervening time.

While many companies employ the shareholder value approach using DCF analysis in capital budgeting, they use it more often at the project level than at the corporate strategy level. Thus, we sometimes see a situation where capital projects regularly exceed the minimum acceptable rate of return, while the business unit itself is a "problem" and creates little or no value for shareholders. The DCF criterion can be applied not only to internal investments such as additions to existing capacity but also is useful in analysis of opportunities for external growth such as corporate mergers and acquisitions.

Companies can usefully extend this approach from piecemeal applications to the entire strategic plan. An SBU is commonly defined as the smallest organizational unit for which integrated strategic planning, related to a distinct product that serves a well-defined market, is feasible. A strategy for an SBU may then be seen as a collection of product—market-related investments and the company itself may be characterized as a portfolio of these investment-requiring strategies. By estimating the future cash flows associated with each strategy, a company can assess the economic value to shareholders of alternative strategies at the business unit and corporate levels.

STEPS IN ANALYSIS

The analysis for a shareholder value approach to strategic planning involves the following sequential steps:

Estimation for each business unit and the corporation of the minimum pretax operating return on incremental sales needed to create value for shareholders.

Comparison of minimum acceptable rates of return on incremental sales with rates realized during the past five years and initial projections for the next year and the five-year plan.

Estimation of the contribution to shareholder value of alternative strategies at the business unit and corporate levels.

Evaluation of the corporate plan to determine whether the projected growth is financially feasible in light of anticipated return on sales, investment requirements per dollar of sales, target capital structure, and dividend policy.

A financial self-evaluation at the business unit and corporate levels.

(Before proceeding to the case illustration in the next section, the reader may wish to refer to the Appendix to examine the basis for estimating the minimum pretax operating return on incremental sales needed to increase shareholder value, as well as the calculation of the absolute shareholder value contributed by various strategies.)

Case of Econoval

Econoval, a diversified manufacturing company, divides its operations into three lines of business—semiconductors, energy, and automotive parts (see Exhibit II).

Before beginning their detailed analysis, Econoval managers must choose appropriate time horizons for calculating the value contributed by each business unit's strategy. The product life cycle stages of the various units will ordinarily determine this choice. If we were to measure value creation for all businesses arbitrarily in

Exhibit II.   *Strategic Overview of Econoval's Lines of Business*

Business unit	Product life cycle stage	Strategy	Risk	Current year's sales in $ millions
Semi-conductors	Embryonic	Invest aggressively to achieve dominant market position	High	$ 50
Energy	Expanding	Invest to improve market position	Medium	75
Automotive parts	Mature	Maintain market position	Low	125

a common time horizon, say 5 years, then embryonic businesses with large capital requirements in early years and large payoffs in later years would be viewed as poor prospects even if they were expected to yield exceptional value over the life cycle. Therefore, in this case, I have extended the projections for the semiconductor unit to 10 years and have limited projections for the energy and auto parts units to 5 years in the company's long-term financial plan.

STEP 1—ESTIMATION OF MINIMUM RETURN ON INCREMENTAL SALES NEEDED TO CREATE VALUE FOR SHAREHOLDERS.   The basis for calculating the minimum acceptable return on incremental sales appears as Equation (4) in the Appendix. For each business unit, four parameters need to be estimated: capital expenditures per dollar of sales increase, cash required for working capital per dollar of sales increase, the income tax rate, and the weighted average cost of capital. Exhibit III summarizes the results.

Before proceeding, I should comment on how to estimate these variables. To estimate the recent values for capital investment required per dollar of sales increase, one simply takes the sum of all capital expenditures less depreciation over the preceding 5 or 10 years and divides this amount by the sales increase during the period. Note that if a business continues to replace existing facilities in kind and if the prices of these facilities remain constant, then the numerator (i.e., capital expenditures less depreciation) approximates the cost of real growth in productive capacity.

Exhibit III. **Minimum Pretax Operating Return on Incremental Sales Based on Initial Planning Projections**

Business unit	Investment requirements per dollar of sales increase		Cost of capital	Minimum return on incremental sales
	Capital expenditures	Working capital		
Semiconductors	.40	.20	.15	.145
Energy	.20	.20	.14	.091
Automotive parts	.15	.20	.13	.075

However, the costs for capital expenditures usually rise each year owing to inflationary forces and regulatory requirements such as environmental control. These cost increases may be partially offset by advances in technology. Thus the numerator reflects not only the cost of real growth but price changes in facilities as well as the impact of product mix changes, regulation, and technological improvements. Whether the historical value of this variable is a reasonable basis for the projection period depends significantly on how quickly and to what extent the company can offset increased fixed capital costs by higher future selling prices, given the competitive structure of the industry.

The increase in required working capital should reflect the cash flow consequences of changes in (1) minimum required cash balance, (2) accounts receivable, (3) inventory, and (4) accounts payable and accruals.

The appropriate rate for discounting the company's cash flow stream is the weighted average of the costs of debt and equity capital. For example, suppose a company's aftertax cost of debt is 6% and its estimated cost of equity 16%. Further, it plans to raise capital in the following proportion—20% by way of debt and 80% by equity. It computes the average cost of capital at 14% as follows:

	Weight	Cost	Weighted Cost
Debt	.20	.06	.012
Equity	.80	.16	.128
Average cost of capital			.140

Is the company's cost of capital the appropriate rate for discounting the cash flow projections of individual business units? The use of a single discount rate for all parts of the company is valid only in the unlikely event that they are identically risky.

Executives who use a single discount rate companywide are likely to have a consistent bias in favor of funding higher-risk businesses at the expense of less risky businesses. To provide a consistent framework for dealing with different investment risks and thereby increasing shareholder value, management should allocate funds to business units on a risk-adjusted return basis.

The process of estimating a business unit's cost of capital inevitably involves a substantial degree of executive judgment. Unlike the company as a whole, ordinarily the business unit has no posted market price that would enable the analyst to estimate systematic or market-related risk. Moreover, it is often difficult to assign future financing (debt and equity) weights to individual business units.

One approach to estimating a business unit's cost of equity is to identify publicly traded stocks in the same line of business that might be expected to have about the same degree of systematic or market risk as the business unit. After establishing the cost of equity and cost of debt, the analyst can calculate a weighted-average cost of capital for the business unit in the same fashion as for the company.

The cost of equity or minimum return expected by investors is the risk-free rate (including the expected long-term rate of inflation) as reflected in current yields available in long-term government bonds plus a premium for accepting equity risk. The overall market risk premium for the past 40 years has averaged 5.7%.[1] The risk premium for an individual security can be estimated as the product of the market risk premium and the individual security's systematic risk, or beta coefficient.[2]

Following is the estimate for Econoval's semiconductor unit's cost of equity:

Risk-free rate + average beta coefficient for selected similarly financed semiconductor companies x market risk premiun for equity investments = cost of equity

9.25% + 1.5 (5.7%) = 17.8%

Assuming an aftertax cost of debt of 6.5% and financing proportions of 25% debt and 75% equity, the semiconductor unit's risk-adjusted

Exhibit IV. *Econoval's Rates of Return on Incremental Sales*

| Business unit | Historical | | Minimum acceptable | Initial forecast |
	Last year	Past five years		
Semiconductors	.115	.110	.145	.155
Energy	.100	.120	.091	.110
Automotive parts	.070	.080	.075	.080

cost of capital is estimated to be 15%. Risk-adjusted rates for the energy and auto parts units are 14% and 13%, respectively.

STEP 2—COMPARISON OF MINIMUM ACCEPTABLE RATES OF RETURN ON INCREMENTAL SALES WITH RECENTLY REALIZED RATES AND INITIAL PLANNING PROJECTIONS. Having developed some preliminary estimates of minimum return on incremental sales, Econoval now wishes to compare those rates with past and initially projected rates for each business unit's planning period. This comparison (Exhibit IV) provides both a reasonable check on the projections and insights into the potential of the various business units for creating shareholder value.

From Exhibit IV, we can determine that the semiconductor unit is projecting substantial improvement over historical margins on the basis of a continuing product mix shift toward higher-margin proprietary items and substantial R&D expenditures to maintain competitiveness in the learning curve race.

If the planned margins materialize, the semiconductor unit will contribute to shareholder value. At this initial stage, the company is concerned with the reasonableness of the projections and the small distance between projected and minimum acceptable margins. The energy unit is projecting a rate of return on incremental sales in line with its recent experience, and this 11% rate is comfortably over the 9.1% minimum acceptable rate.

The problem business unit is the automotive parts division. Margins have been eroding steadily, and the projected five-year margin is just above the acceptable minimum. Econoval managers are thus committed to investigating a full range of strategic alternatives for the automotive unit.

STEP 3—ESTIMATION OF SHAREHOLDER VALUE CONTRIBUTION FOR
ALTERNATIVE STRATEGIES AT THE BUSINESS UNIT AND CORPORATE
LEVELS. Once the company has developed and analyzed its initial
planning projections, SBU managers and the corporate planning
group can prepare more detailed analyses for evaluating alternative
planning scenarios. Exhibit V shows the semiconductor unit's planning parameters for conservative, most likely, and optimistic scenarios.

The worst case or conservative scenario assumes significant market penetration by Japanese producers via major technological
advances coupled with aggressive price cutting. The most likely
scenario assumes the semiconductor group's continued dominance
in the metal-oxide-semiconductor (MOS) market, substantial R&D
expenditures to enable the semiconductor group to maintain its
competitiveness in the learning curve race, and gradual Japanese
technological parity, which will place pressure on sales margins.
The optimistic scenario projects more rapid industry growth and
great success in the unit's effort to carve out high-margin proprietary niches.

Exhibit VI presents the shareholder value contribution for each
of these three scenarios and for a range of discount rates.

Econoval expects the semiconductor unit's 10-year plan for the
most likely scenario to contribute $10.60 million to shareholder
value. The range of shareholder values from conservative to optimistic scenarios is from $4.87 million to $29.93 million for the
estimated cost of capital or discount rate of 15%.

An assessment of the likelihood of each scenario will provide
further insight into the relative riskiness of business unit investment strategies. For example, if all three scenarios are equally
likely, the situation would be riskier than if the most likely scenario
is 60% probable and the other two are each 20% probable.

Econoval performed similar analyses for the energy and automotive parts units. Exhibit VII summarizes the results for most
likely scenarios. To ensure consistency in comparing or consolidating scenarios of various business units, it is important that the
corporate planning group establish that such scenarios share common assumptions about critical environmental factors such as inflation and energy prices.

On closer inspection, we see that the analysis in Exhibit VII
provides support for management's concern about the automotive
unit's performance. While the unit now accounts for 50% of Econ-

Exhibit V. Semiconductor Unit's Planning Projections for Various Scenarios

	Year									
	1	2	3	4	5	6	7	8	9	10
Conservative										
Sales growth rate	.25	.25	.20	.20	.18	.18	.18	.18	.18	.18
EBIT/sales	.115	.12	.125	.13	.135	.135	.135	.135	.135	.135
Working capital per dollar of sales increase	.20	.20	.20	.20	.20	.20	.20	.20	.20	.20
Capital expenditures per dollar of sales increase	.42	.42	.42	.40	.40	.35	.35	.35	.35	.35
Cash income tax rate	.41	.41	.41	.41	.41	.41	.41	.41	.41	.41
Most likely										
Sales growth rate	.30	.28	.25	.22	.20	.20	.20	.20	.20	.20
EBIT/sales	.12	.125	.13	.135	.14	.145	.15	.15	.15	.145
Working capital per dollar of sales increase	.20	.20	.20	.20	.20	.20	.20	.20	.20	.20
Capital expenditures per dollar of sales increase	.45	.45	.44	.42	.42	.40	.38	.38	.35	.35
Cash income tax rate	.40	.40	.40	.40	.40	.40	.40	.40	.40	.40
Optimistic										
Sales growth rate	.32	.30	.30	.25	.25	.25	.25	.25	.25	.25
EBIT/sales	.125	.13	.14	.145	.15	.15	.15	.15	.15	.15
Working capital per dollar of sales increase	.18	.18	.18	.18	.18	.18	.18	.18	.18	.18
Capital expenditures per dollar of sales increase	.40	.38	.38	.36	.36	.35	.35	.35	.35	.35
Cash income tax rate	.39	.39	.39	.39	.39	.39	.39	.39	.39	.39

*Exhibit VI. Semiconductor Unit's Shareholder Value
Contribution for Different Scenarios and
Discount Rates*
in $ millions

Scenario	Discount rate				
	.140	.145	.150	.155	.160
Conservative	$ 9.30	$ 6.96	$ 4.87	$ 2.99	$ 1.30
Most likely	16.92	13.59	10.60	7.91	5.48
Optimistic	39.64	34.53	29.93	25.79	22.05

oval's sales, the company expects it to contribute only $3.57 million, or about 15% of the total increase in shareholder value.

On the basis of traditional criteria such as sales and earnings growth rates, the semiconductor unit clearly emerges as the star performer. However, its high investment requirements and risk vis-à-vis its sales margins combine to limit its value-creating potential. Despite the fact that the semiconductor unit's sales and earnings growth rates are substantially greater than those of the energy unit, the semiconductor unit is expected to contribute only marginally more shareholder value in 10 years than the energy unit in 5 years.

The shareholder value increase per discounted dollar of investment provides management with important information about where it is realizing the greatest benefits per dollar of investment. Indeed, this *value* return on investment (VROI), rather than the traditional accounting ROI, enables management to rank various business units on the basis of a substantive economic criterion.

The numerator of the VROI is simply the shareholder value increase of a strategy and the denominator, the present cost or investment. When the VROI ratio is equal to zero, the strategy yields exactly the risk-adjusted cost of capital, and when VROI is positive, the strategy yields a rate greater than its cost of capital. Note that the semiconductor unit ranks last, even behind the auto parts unit, in this all-important performance measure.

Ranking units on the basis of VROI can be particularly helpful to corporate headquarters in capital-rationing situations where the various parts of the business are competing for scarce funds. In

Exhibit VII. *Shareholder Value, Sales Growth, and Earnings Growth Rates by Business Unit for Most Likely Scenarios*

Business unit	Years in plan	Shareholder value increase			Growth rates	
		$ millions	Per discounted $ of sales increase	Per discounted $ of investment	Sales	Earnings
Semiconductors	10	10.60	.077	.128	22.4 %	26.1 %
Energy	5	8.79	.175	.438	15	17.7
Automotive parts	5	3.57	.068	.194	10	11.9
Consolidated		**22.96**				

the final analysis, however, corporate resources should be allocated to units so as to maximize the shareholder value of the company's total product-market portfolio.

STEP 4—EVALUATION OF THE FINANCIAL FEASIBILITY OF THE STRATEGIC PLAN. Once the company has established a preliminary plan, it should test its financial feasibility and whether it is fundable. This involves integrating the company's planned investment growth strategies with its dividend and financing policies. A particularly effective starting point is to estimate the company's maximum affordable dividend payout rate and its sensitivity to varying assumptions underlying the strategic plan.

To illustrate, Econoval calculates the maximum dividend payout for the first year of the five-year plan. On a consolidated basis, Econoval projects sales growth of 15.5%, earnings before interest and taxes (EBIT) to sales of 9.56%, an investment of $.481 per dollar of incremental sales, a cash income tax rate of 42.2%, and a current and target debt-to-equity ratio of 45.2% and 44.3%, respectively. Econoval can pay out no more than 6.3% of its net income as dividends. At the 6.3% payout rate, the earnings retained, plus added debt capacity, are just equal to the investment dollars required to support the 15.5% growth in sales from $250 million to $288.75 million.

It is easy to demonstrate this result. At $.481 per dollar of incremental sales, investment requirements (net of depreciation) on the projected $38.75 million sales increase will total $18.63 million. This amount will be financed as follows:

Aftertax earnings on sales of $288.75 million	$13.34 million
Less 6.3% dividend payout	.84
Earnings retained, i.e., increase in equity	12.50
Added debt capacity	5.08
Increase in deferred taxes	1.05
	$18.63 million

The maximum affordable dividend payout rate table (Exhibit VIII) shows how sensitive this rate is to changes in growth, profitability, investment intensity, and financial leverage. Note, for example, that if sales growth is increased from 15.5% to 16.5%, the maximum affordable dividend payout rate decreases from 6.3% to 1.1%, while a 1% increase in EBIT/sales raises the maximum affordable rate from 6.3% to 16.6%.

Exhibit VIII. Maximum Dividend Payout Rate Analysis

Sales growth		Investment requirements per dollar of sales increase								
		.431			.481			.531		
		Debt/equity			Debt/equity			Debt/equity		
EBIT/sales		.393	.443	.493	.393	.443	.493	.393	.443	.493
.145										
	.086	−9.6%	10.1%	28.5%	−20.8%	−0.7%	18.1%	−31.9%	−11.5%	7.6%
	.096	3.8	21.2	37.4	−6.1	11.7	28.2	−15.9	2.2	19.0
	.106	14.4	29.9	44.4	5.6	21.4	36.2	−3.2	12.9	28.0
.155										
	.086	−15.1	4.7	23.1	−26.9	−6.7	12.1	−38.7	−18.1	1.1
	.096	−1.0	16.4	32.6	−11.4	6.3	22.9	−21.9	−3.7	13.2
	.106	10.1	25.7	40.2	0.7	16.6	31.5	−8.6	7.6	22.8
.165										
	.086	−20.4	−0.6	17.8	−32.8	−12.6	6.2	−45.3	−24.7	−5.4
	.096	−5.7	11.7	28.0	−16.7	1.1	17.7	−27.7	−9.5	7.5
	.106	5.8	21.4	36.0	−4.0	11.9	26.8	−13.8	2.4	17.6

Book tax rate = .460, cash tax rate = .422

Current debt/equity = .452

Current equity = $53.550 million

Exhibit IX.   *Econoval Strategic Funds Statement for
Five-Year Planning Period*
in $ millions

	Year					
	1	2	3	4	5	Total
Net income	13.34	15.74	18.54	21.75	25.44	94.81
Depreciation	3.84	4.74	5.82	7.03	8.32	29.74
Increase in deferred taxes	1.05	1.29	1.56	1.88	2.23	8.02
Sources of funds	**18.23**	**21.77**	**25.92**	**30.66**	**35.99**	**132.57**
Capital expenditures	14.71	17.58	20.22	22.55	25.66	100.72
Increase in working capital	7.76	8.97	10.16	11.33	12.66	50.88
Uses of funds	**22.47**	**26.55**	**30.38**	**33.88**	**38.32**	**151.60**
Net cash provided (required)	(4.24)	(4.78)	(4.46)	(3.22)	(2.33)	(19.03)
Increase in debt capacity	5.08	5.89	6.60	7.20	8.02	32.79
Maximum affordable dividend	**0.84**	**1.11**	**2.14**	**3.98**	**5.69**	**13.76**
Maximum affordable dividend payout rate	6.3%	7.1%	11.5%	18.3%	22.3%	14.5%

Exhibit IX presents Econoval's strategic funds statement for its
five-year planning period. The cash required for investment in
working capital and fixed capital exceeds the cash sources from
operations in each year. This difference is reflected in the "net cash
required" line. Another source of funds is, of course, debt financing.

The increase in debt capacity is established by reference to the
target debt-to-equity ratios of Econoval's three principal businesses. Adding the increase in debt capacity to the net cash required provides the maximum affordable dividend, which, as seen
earlier, is $.84 million or 6.3% in the first year and rises annually
to 22.3% in the fifth year.

In Exhibit X, strategic funds statements for each of Econoval's
main lines of business provide improved insights into product
portfolio balancing opportunities. The semiconductor group places

Exhibit X.   **Strategic Funds Statement for Five-Year**
Planning Period by Business Units
in $ millions

	Semicon-ductors	Energy	Auto-motive parts	Con-solidated
Net income	$ 34.53	$ 30.92	$ 29.36	$ 94.81
Depreciation	17.95	6.07	5.72	29.74
Increase in deferred income taxes	4.21	2.55	1.26	8.02
	56.69	**39.54**	**36.34**	**132.57**
Capital expenditures	62.31	21.24	17.17	100.72
Increase in working capital	20.45	15.17	15.26	50.88
	82.76	**36.41**	**32.43**	**151.60**
Net cash provided (required)	(26.07)	3.13	3.91	(19.03)
Increase in debt capacity	15.05	9.26	8.48	32.79
Maximum affordable dividend	**($ 11.02)**	**$ 12.39**	**$ 12.39**	**$ 13.76**

a substantial burden on corporate funds. Over the next five years it will require more than $26 million of cash while the energy and auto parts units will throw off about $7 million in cash. Even after taking into account the estimated debt capacity contribution of semiconductors, corporate headquarters will still have to transfer $11 million to the unit.

After some further analysis, Econoval managers concluded that the strategic plan was financially feasible. The analysis did, however, raise two concerns. First, Econoval had a low affordable dividend payout rate and was vulnerable to sales margins lower than those projected. Of immediate concern was that the current year's dividend is larger than next year's projected affordable dividend.

Also, the strategic funds statement underscored the risk associated with the semiconductor group's aggressive competitive positioning and the related high level of investment requirements. This group's large cash requirements, coupled with its modest VROI, prompted Econoval managers to launch a study of alternative product portfolio strategies.

STEP 5—A FINANCIAL SELF-EVALUATION AT THE BUSINESS UNIT AND CORPORATE LEVELS.   Increasingly, companies are adding financial self-evaluation to their strategic financial planning process.[3] A financial evaluation poses two fundamental questions: How much are the company and each of its major lines of business worth? How much would each of several plausible scenarios involving various combinations of future environments and management strategies affect the value of the company and its business units?

The following types of companies would especially benefit from conducting a financial evaluation:

Companies that wish to sell and need to establish a minimum acceptable selling price for their shares.

Companies that are potential takeover targets.

Companies considering selective divestments.

Companies evaluating the attractiveness of repurchasing their own shares.

Private companies wanting to establish the proper price at which to go public.

Acquisition-minded companies wanting to assess the advantages of a cash versus a stock offer.

The present equity or shareholder value of any business unit, or the entire company, is the sum of the estimated shareholder value contribution from its strategic plan and the current cash flow level discounted at the risk-adjusted cost of capital less the market value of outstanding debt. Exhibit XI summarizes these values for Econoval and its three major business units. For example, the semiconductor unit's current cash flow perpetuity level is $2.97 million, which, when discounted at its risk-adjusted rate of 15%, produces a value of $19.8 million. Subtracting the $5 million of debt outstanding provides the $14.8 million prestrategy equity value. To obtain the total equity or shareholder value of $25.40 million for the semiconductor unit, simply add the $10.60 million value contributed by the strategic plan.

The sum of the three business unit values is $83.79 million. Combining the cash flows of the individual businesses and discounting them at the 14% risk-adjusted corporate cost of capital

Exhibit XI. **Business Unit and Corporate Financial Evaluation Summary—For Most Likely Scenario**
in $ millions

	Semicon-ductors	Energy	Auto-motive parts	Con-solidated
Risk-adjusted pre-strategy equity value	$ 14.80	$ 20.93	$ 25.10	$ 60.83
Shareholder value contribution from strategic plan (see *Exhibit VII*)	10.60	8.79	3.57	22.96
Total equity value	**$ 25.40**	**$ 29.72**	**$ 28.67**	**$ 83.79**
Percent of total equity value	30.3 %	35.5 %	34.2 %	
Econoval equity value at corporate cost of capital of 14 %				$ 87.57

yields a value of $87.57 million. In this case, the difference between the value of the whole and the sum of the parts is minor. However, this may not always be true.

Aggregating the values of the company's business units is consistent with the assumption that the riskiness of each unit must be considered separately. If, however, the company's entry into unrelated businesses reduces the overall variability of its cash flows, then the lower expected probability of bankruptcy can decrease its cost of debt and increase its debt capacity.

What happens to the company's overall cost of capital naturally depends on any changes in the cost of equity capital as well as on the cost of debt. Analysis of the impact of business units on the total risk of the company is at best extremely difficult and subjective.

A more attractive alternative is to (1) assume risk independence in establishing cost of capital for business units and (2) interpret the difference between the value of the company and the aggregate value of its individual businesses as a broad approximation of the benefits or costs associated with the company's product portfolio balancing activities.

Econoval's corporate financial evaluation gave management not only an improved understanding of the relative contribution to shareholder value coming from each business but also the basis for structuring the purchase of an acquisition currently being negotiated. Econoval's market value was then about 25% less than its own estimate of value. Because the cash and exchange-of-shares price demanded by the selling shareholders was not materially different, Econoval management decided to offer cash rather than what it believed to be its undervalued shares.

Meeting the Fiduciary Duty

A fundamental fiduciary responsibility of corporate managers and boards of directors is to create economic value for their shareholders. Despite increasing sophistication in strategic planning applications, companies almost invariably evaluate the final product, the strategic plan, in terms of earnings per share or other accounting ratios such as return on investment or return on equity.

Surprisingly, the conventional accounting-oriented approach persists despite compelling theoretical and empirical evidence of the failings of accounting numbers as a reliable index for estimating changes in economic value. How should the board member of a company that has reported a decade of 15% annual EPS growth and no increase in its stock price respond when asked to approve yet another five-year business plan with projected EPS growth of 15%? The shareholder value approach to strategic planning would enable the board to recognize that despite impressive earnings growth projections, the company's increasing cost of capital, rising investment requirements per dollar of sales, and lower margins on sales are clear signs of value erosion.

A number of major companies are now using the shareholder value approach to strategic planning. The method requires virtually no data not already developed under current financial planning systems; moreover, an interactive computer program such as the "strategy valuator" (used in preparing the numerical illustrations) can help implement all of the steps I have outlined. Use of this approach should improve companies' prospects of creating value for their shareholders and thereby contribute to the long-run interests of the companies and of the economy.

Notes

1. Roger G. Ibbotson and Rex A. Sinquefield, "Stocks, Bonds, Bills and Inflation: Updates," *Financial Analysts Journal* (July–August 1979), p. 40.
2. For a method of predicting beta, see Barr Rosenberg and James Guy, "Prediction of Beta from Investment Fundamentals," *Financial Analysts Journal* (May–June 1976), p. 60 and (July–August 1976), p. 62.
3. For a more detailed description of how to conduct a corporate financial self-evaluation, see my article, "Do You Know the Value of Your Company?," *Mergers & Acquisitions* (Spring 1979).

Appendix:
Calculation of value contributed by strategy

The present value of a business is defined simply as the anticipated aftertax operating cash flows discounted by the weighted average cost of capital. The present value of the equity claims or shareholder value is then the value of the company (or business unit) less the market value of currently outstanding debt. The value of equity for a business that expects no further real sales growth and also expects annual cost increases to be offset by selling price increases is given by the following formula:

$$E_t = \frac{p(1-T)S}{k} - D_t \quad (1)$$

where:

E_t = value of the equity at time t

p = earnings before interest and taxes divided by sales

T = income tax rate

S = sales

assets are discounted by $(1 + k)$ to obtain the present value. There is neither an increase nor a decrease in shareholder value for a specified sales increase whenever the value of the inflows and outflows is identical. Specifically, when

$$\frac{p_t'(1-T)}{k} = \frac{(f_t + w_t)}{(1+k)} \quad (3)$$

From Equation (3) the break-even operating return on sales or the minimum pretax operating return on incremental sales (p'_{min}) needed to create value for shareholders is derived as:

$$p'_{min} = \frac{(f+w)k}{(1-T)(1+k)} \quad (4)$$

Minimum acceptable returns on incremental sales for a range of investment requirements per dollar of sales and costs of capital are presented below.

Minimum pretax operating return on incremental sales to create value for shareholders*

	Investment requirements per dollar of incremental sales						
Cost of capital	.20	.30	.40	.50	.60	.70	.80
.12	.040	.059	.079	.099	.119	.139	.159
.14	.045	.068	.091	.114	.136	.159	.182
.16	.051	.077	.102	.128	.153	.179	.204
.18	.056	.085	.113	.141	.169	.198	.226
.20	.062	.093	.123	.154	.185	.216	.247

*Assumed income tax rate, 46%.

Appendix (continued)

k = weighted average cost of capital

D_t = market value of debt outstanding at time t

The change in shareholder value (ΔE) for a given level of sales increase (ΔS) is then:

$$\Delta E_t = \frac{P_t'(1 - T)\Delta S_t}{k} - \frac{(f_t + w_t)\Delta S_t}{(1 + k)} \quad (2)$$

where:

p' = ΔEBIT/Δ sales, i.e., incremental operating margin on incremental sales

f = capital expenditures minus depreciation per dollar of sales increase

w = cash required for net working capital per dollar of sales increase

The change in equity or shareholder value is the difference between the aftertax operating cash flow perpetuity and the required investment outlay for fixed and working capital. Since all cash flows are assumed to occur at the end of the period, the outlays for working capital and fixed

The shareholder value contributed by any strategy can be estimated by taking the capitalized value of the difference between the projected and the minimum acceptable operating return on incremental sales. More specifically, the change in shareholder value for time t is given by the following equation, which assumes book and cash income tax rates are identical. If they are not, another term must be added.

$$\Delta E_t = \frac{(p_t' - p_{t\,min}')(1 - T_t)\Delta S_t}{k(1 + k)^{t-1}} \quad (5)$$

To illustrate, consider a business with sales of $50 million for its most recent year and the following assumptions for its five-year plan: sales growth rate = 15%; pretax operating margins on incremental sales = 13.5% for the first two years and 14.5% for the remaining three years; book and cash tax rate = 46%; working capital per dollar of sales = .20; capital expenditures per dollar of sales = .35; and cost of capital = 14%. Applying equation (4) for the minimum return on incremental sales (p_{min}), we obtain 12.5%. A summary of the shareholder value contributed by the five-year plan is presented below.

Shareholder value contributed by five-year plan (in $ millions)

	Years					
	1	2	3	4	5	Total
Sales	$57.50	$66.12	$76.04	$87.45	$100.57	$387.68
Sales increase	7.50	8.62	9.92	11.41	13.12	50.57
Projected return on incremental sales minus minimum return	.01	.01	.02	.02	.02	
Shareholder present value increase*	$.29	$.29	$.59	$.59	$.60	$2.36

*Computed by using equation (5).

Note: The present value of the five-year plan is $2.36 million.

4
Crafting Strategy

Henry Mintzberg

Imagine someone planning strategy. What likely springs to mind is an image of orderly thinking: a senior manager, or a group of them, sitting in an office formulating courses of action that everyone else will implement on schedule. The keynote is reason—rational control, the systematic analysis of competitors and markets, of company strengths and weaknesses, the combination of these analyses producing clear, explicit, full-blown strategies.

Now imagine someone *crafting* strategy. A wholly different image likely results, as different from planning as craft is from mechanization. Craft evokes traditional skill, dedication, perfection through the mastery of detail. What springs to mind is not so much thinking and reason as involvement, a feeling of intimacy and harmony with the materials at hand, developed through long experience and commitment. Formulation and implementation merge into a fluid process of learning through which creative strategies evolve.

My thesis is simple: The crafting image better captures the process by which effective strategies come to be. The planning image, long popular in the literature, distorts these processes and thereby misguides organizations that embrace it unreservedly.

In developing this thesis, I shall draw on the experiences of a single craftsman, a potter, and compare them with the results of a research project that tracked the strategies of a number of corporations across several decades. Because the two contexts are so obviously different, my metaphor, like my assertion, may seem farfetched at first. Yet if we think of a craftsman as an organization of one, we can see that he or she must also resolve one of the great challenges the corporate strategist faces: knowing the organization's capabilities well enough to think deeply enough about its strategic direction. By considering strategy making from the perspective of one person, free of all the paraphernalia of what has been called the strategy industry, we can learn something about the formation of strategy in the corporation. For much as our potter has to manage her craft, so too managers have to craft their strategy.

At work, the potter sits before a lump of clay on the wheel. Her mind is on the clay, but she is also aware of sitting between her past experiences and her future prospects. She knows exactly what has and has not worked for her in the past. She has an intimate knowledge of her work, her capabilities, and her markets. As a craftsman, she senses rather than analyzes these things; her knowledge is "tacit." All these things are working in her mind as her hands are working the clay. The product that emerges on the wheel is likely to be in the tradition of her past work, but she may break away and embark on a new direction. Even so, the past is no less present, projecting itself into the future.

In my metaphor, managers are craftsmen and strategy is their clay. Like the potter, they sit between a past of corporate capabilities and a future of market opportunities. And if they are truly craftsmen, they bring to their work an equally intimate knowledge of the materials at hand. That is the essence of crafting strategy.

In the pages that follow, we will explore this metaphor by looking at how strategies get made as opposed to how they are supposed to get made. Throughout, I will be drawing on the two sets of experiences I've mentioned. One is a research project on patterns in strategy formation that has been going on at McGill University under my direction since 1971. The second is the stream of work of a successful potter, my wife, who began her craft in 1967.

Ask almost anyone what strategy is, and they will define it as a plan of some sort, an explicit guide to future behavior. Then ask them what strategy a competitor or a government or even they themselves have actually pursued. Chances are they will describe consistency in *past* behavior—a pattern in action over time. Strategy, it turns out, is one of those words that people define in one way and often use in another, without realizing the difference.

The reason for this is simple. Strategy's formal definition and its Greek military origins notwithstanding, we need the word as much to explain past actions as to describe intended behavior. After all, if strategies can be planned and intended, they can also be pursued and realized (or not realized, as the case may be). And pattern in action, or what we call realized strategy, explains that pursuit. Moreover, just as a plan need not produce a pattern (some strategies that are intended are simply not realized), so too a pattern need not result from a plan. An organization can have a pattern (or realized strategy) without knowing it, let alone making it explicit.

Patterns, like beauty, are in the mind of the beholder, of course. But anyone reviewing a chronological lineup of our craftsman's work would have little trouble discerning clear patterns, at least in certain periods. Until 1974, for example, she made small, decorative ceramic animals and objects of various kinds. Then this "knickknack strategy" stopped abruptly, and eventually new patterns formed around waferlike sculptures and ceramic bowls, highly textured and unglazed.

Finding equivalent patterns in action for organizations isn't that much more difficult. Indeed, for such large companies as Volkswagenwerk and Air Canada, in our research, it proved simpler! (As well it should. A craftsman, after all, can change what she does in a studio a lot more easily than a Volkswagenwerk can retool its assembly lines.) Mapping the product models at Volkswagenwerk from the late 1940s to the late 1970s, for example, uncovers a clear pattern of concentration on the Beetle, followed in the late 1960s by a frantic search for replacements through acquisitions and internally developed new models, to a strategic reorientation around more stylish, water-cooled, front-wheel-drive vehicles in the mid-1970s.

But what about intended strategies, those formal plans and pronouncements we think of when we use the term *strategy?* Ironically, here we run into all kinds of problems. Even with a single craftsman, how can we know what her intended strategies really were? If we could go back, would we find expressions of intention? And if we could, would we be able to trust them? We often fool ourselves, as well as others, by denying our subconscious motives. And remember that intentions are cheap, at least when compared with realizations.

READING THE ORGANIZATION'S MIND

If you believe all this has more to do with the Freudian recesses of a craftsman's mind than with the practical realities of producing automobiles, then think again. For who knows what the intended strategies of a Volkswagenwerk really mean, let alone what they are? Can we simply assume in this collective context that the company's intended strategies are represented by its formal plans or by other statements emanating from the executive suite? Might these be just vain hopes or rationalizations or ploys to fool the competition? And even if expressed intentions exist, to what extent do others in the organization share them? How do we read the collective mind? Who is the strategist anyway?

The traditional view of strategic management resolves these problems quite simply, by what organizational theorists call attribution. You see it all the time in the business press. When General Motors acts, it's because Roger Smith has made a strategy. Given realization, there must have been intention, and that is automatically attributed to the chief.

In a short magazine article, this assumption is understandable. Journalists don't have a lot of time to uncover the origins of strategy, and GM is a large, complicated organization. But just consider all the complexity and confusion that gets tucked under this assumption—all the meetings and debates, the many people, the dead ends, the folding and unfolding of ideas. Now imagine trying to build a formal strategy-making system around that assumption. Is it any wonder that formal strategic planning is often such a resounding failure?

To unravel some of the confusion—and move away from the artificial complexity we have piled around the strategy-making process—we need to get back to some basic concepts. The most basic of all is the intimate connection between thought and action. That is the key to craft, and so also to the crafting of strategy.

Virtually everything that has been written about strategy making depicts it as a deliberate process. First we think, then we act. We formulate, then we implement. The progression seems so perfectly sensible. Why would anybody want to proceed differently?

Our potter is in the studio, rolling the clay to make a waferlike sculpture. The clay sticks to the rolling pin, and a round form appears. Why not make a cylindrical vase? One idea leads to another, until a new pattern forms. Action has driven thinking: A strategy has emerged.

Out in the field, a salesman visits a customer. The product isn't quite right, and together they work out some modifications. The salesman returns to his company and puts the changes through; after two or three more rounds, they finally get it right. A new product emerges, which eventually opens up a new market. The company has changed strategic course.

In fact, most salespeople are less fortunate than this one or than our craftsman. In an organization of one, the implementor is the formulator, so innovations can be incorporated into strategy quickly and easily. In a large organization, the innovator may be ten levels removed from the leader who is supposed to dictate strategy and may also have to sell the idea to dozens of peers doing the same job.

Some salespeople, of course, can proceed on their own, modifying products to suit their customers and convincing skunkworks in the factory to produce them. In effect, they pursue their own strategies. Maybe no one else notices or cares. Sometimes, however, their innovations do get noticed, perhaps years later, when the company's prevalent strategies have broken down and its leaders are groping for something new. Then the salesperson's strategy may be allowed to pervade the system, to become organizational.

Is this story farfetched? Certainly not. We've all heard stories like it. But since we tend to see only what we believe, if we believe that strategies have to be planned, we're unlikely to see the real meaning such stories hold.

Consider how the National Film Board of Canada (NFB) came to adopt a feature-film strategy. The NFB is a federal government agency, famous for its creativity and expert in the production of short documentaries. Some years back, it funded a filmmaker on a project that unexpectedly ran long. To distribute his film, the NFB turned to theaters and so inadvertently gained experience in marketing feature-length films. Other filmmakers caught onto the idea, and eventually the NFB found itself pursuing a feature-film strategy—a pattern of producing such films.

My point is simple, deceptively simple: Strategies can *form* as well as be *formulated*. A realized strategy can emerge in response to an evolving situation, or it can be brought about deliberately, through a process of formulation followed by implementation. But when these planned intentions do not produce the desired actions, organizations are left with unrealized strategies.

Today we hear a great deal about unrealized strategies, almost always in concert with the claim that implementation has failed. Management has been lax, controls have been loose, people haven't been committed. Excuses abound. At times, indeed, they may be valid. But often these explanations prove too easy. So some people look beyond implementation to formulation. The strategists haven't been smart enough.

While it is certainly true that many intended strategies are ill conceived, I believe that the problem often lies one step beyond, in the distinction we make between formulation and implementation, the common assumption that thought must be independent of (and precede) action. Sure, people could be smarter—but not only by conceiving more clever strategies. Sometimes they can be smarter by allowing their strategies to develop gradually, through the organization's actions and experiences. Smart strategists appreciate that they cannot always be smart enough to think through everything in advance.

HANDS AND MINDS

No craftsman thinks some days and works others. The craftsman's mind is going constantly, in tandem with her hands. Yet large organizations try to separate the work of minds and hands. In so doing, they often sever the vital feedback link between the two. The salesperson who finds a customer with an unmet need may possess the most strategic bit of information in the entire organization. But that information is useless if he or she cannot create a strategy in response to it or else convey the information to someone who can—because the channels are blocked or because the formulators have simply finished formulating. The notion that strategy is something that should happen way up there, far removed from the details of running an organization on a daily basis, is one of the great fallacies of conventional strategic management. And it explains a good many of the most dramatic failures in business and public policy today.

We at McGill call strategies like the NFB's that appear without clear intentions—or in spite of them—emergent strategies. Actions simply converge into patterns. They may become deliberate, of course, if the pattern is recognized and then legitimated by senior management. But that's after the fact.

All this may sound rather strange, I know. Strategies that emerge? Managers who acknowledge strategies already formed? Over the years, our research group at McGill has met with a good deal of resistance from people upset by what they perceive to be our passive definition of a word so bound up with proactive behavior and free will. After all, strategy means control—the ancient Greeks used it to describe the art of the army general.

STRATEGIC LEARNING

But we have persisted in this usage for one reason: learning. Purely deliberate strategy precludes learning once the strategy is formulated; emergent strategy fosters it. People take actions one by one and respond to them, so that patterns eventually form.

Our craftsman tries to make a freestanding sculptural form. It doesn't work, so she rounds it a bit here, flattens it a bit there. The result looks better, but still isn't quite right. She makes another and another and another. Eventually, after days or months or years, she finally has what she wants. She is off on a new strategy.

In practice, of course, all strategy making walks on two feet, one deliberate, the other emergent. For just as purely deliberate strategy making precludes learning, so purely emergent strategy making precludes control. Pushed to the limit, neither approach makes much sense. Learning must be coupled with control. That is why the McGill research group uses the word *strategy* for both emergent and deliberate behavior.

Likewise, there is no such thing as a purely deliberate strategy or a purely emergent one. No organization—not even the ones commanded by those ancient Greek generals—knows enough to work everything out in advance, to ignore learning en route. And no one—not even a solitary potter—can be flexible enough to leave everything to happenstance, to give up all control. Craft requires control just as it requires responsiveness to the material at hand. Thus deliberate and emergent strategy form the end points of a continuum along which the strategies that are crafted in the real world may be found. Some strategies may approach either end, but many more fall at intermediate points.

Effective strategies can show up in the strangest places and develop through the most unexpected means. There is no one best way to make strategy.

The form for a cat collapses on the wheel, and our potter sees a bull taking shape. Clay sticks to a rolling pin, and a line of cylinders results. Wafers come into being because of a shortage of clay and limited kiln space in a studio in France. Thus errors become opportunities, and limitations stimulate creativity. The natural propensity to experiment, even boredom, likewise stimulate strategic change.

Organizations that craft their strategies have similar experiences. Recall the National Film Board with its inadvertently long film. Or consider its experiences with experimental films, which made special use of animation and sound. For 20 years, the NFB produced a bare but steady trickle of such films. In fact, every film but one in that trickle was produced by a single person, Norman McLaren, the NFB's most celebrated filmmaker. McLaren pursued a *personal strategy* of experimentation, deliberate for him perhaps (though who can know whether he had the whole stream in mind or simply planned one film at a time?) but not for the organization. Then 20 years later, others followed his lead and the trickle widened, his personal strategy becoming more broadly organizational.

Conversely, in 1952, when television came to Canada, a *consensus strategy* quickly emerged at the NFB. Senior management was not keen on producing films for the new medium. But while the arguments raged, one filmmaker quietly went off and made a single series for TV. That precedent set, one by one his colleagues leapt in, and within months the NFB—and its management—found themselves committed for several years to a new strategy with an intensity unmatched before or since. This consensus strategy arose spontaneously, as a result of many independent decisions made by the filmmakers about the films they wished to make. Can we call this strategy deliberate? For the filmmakers perhaps; for senior management certainly not. But for the organization? It all depends on your perspective, on how you choose to read the organization's mind.

While the NFB may seem like an extreme case, it highlights behavior that can be found, albeit in muted form, in all organizations. Those who doubt this might read Richard Pascale's account of how Honda stumbled into its enormous success in the American motorcycle market. Brilliant as its strategy may have looked after the fact, Honda's managers made almost every conceivable mistake until the market finally hit them over the head with the right formula. The Honda managers on site in America, driving their products themselves (and thus inadvertently picking up market reaction), did only one thing right: They learned, firsthand.[1]

GRASS-ROOTS STRATEGY MAKING

These strategies all reflect, in whole or part, what we like to call a grass-roots approach to strategic management. Strategies grow like weeds in a garden. They take root in all kinds of places, wherever people have the capacity to learn (because they are in touch with the situation) and the resources to support that capacity. These strategies become organizational when they become collective, that is, when they proliferate to guide the behavior of the organization at large.

Of course, this view is overstated. But it is no less extreme than the conventional view of strategic management, which might be labeled the hothouse approach. Neither is right. Reality falls between the two. Some of the most effective strategies we uncovered in our research combined deliberation and control with flexibility and organizational learning.

Consider first what we call the *umbrella strategy*. Here senior management sets out broad guidelines (say, to produce only high-margin products at the cutting edge of technology or to favor products using bonding technology) and leaves the specifics (such as what these products will be) to others lower down in the organization. This strategy is not only deliberate (in its guidelines) and emergent (in its specifics), but it is also deliberately emergent in that the process is consciously managed to allow strategies to emerge en route. IBM used the umbrella strategy in the early 1960s with the impending 360 series, when its senior management approved a set of broad criteria for the design of a family of computers later developed in detail throughout the organization.[2]

Deliberately emergent, too, is what we call the *process strategy*. Here management controls the process of strategy formation—concerning itself with the design of the structure, its staffing, procedures, and so on—while leaving the actual content to others.

Both process and umbrella strategies seem to be especially prevalent in businesses that require great expertise and creativity—a 3M, a Hewlett-Packard, a National Film Board. Such organizations can be effective only if their implementors are allowed to be formulators because it is people way down in the hierarchy who are in touch with the situation at hand and have the requisite technical expertise. In a sense, these are organizations peopled with craftsmen, all of whom must be strategists.

The conventional view of strategic management, especially in the planning literature, claims that change must be continuous: The organization should be adapting all the time. Yet this view proves to be ironic because the very concept of strategy is rooted in stability, not change. As this same literature makes clear, organizations pursue strategies to set direction, to lay out courses of action, and to elicit cooperation from their members around common, established guidelines. By any definition, strategy imposes stability on an organization. No stability means no strategy (no course to the future, no pattern from the past). Indeed, the very fact of having a strategy, and especially of making it explicit (as the conventional literature implores managers to do), creates resistance to strategic change!

What the conventional view fails to come to grips with, then, is how and when to promote change. A fundamental dilemma of strategy making is the need to reconcile the forces for stability and for change—to focus efforts and gain operating efficiencies on the one hand, yet adapt and maintain currency with a changing external environment on the other.

QUANTUM LEAPS

Our own research and that of colleagues suggest that organizations resolve these opposing forces by attending first to one and then to the other. Clear periods of stability and change can usually be distinguished in any organization: While it is true that particular strategies may always be changing marginally, it seems equally true that major shifts in strategic orientation occur only rarely.

In our study of Steinberg Inc., a large Quebec supermarket chain headquartered in Montreal, we found only two important reorientations in the 60 years from its founding to the mid-1970s: a shift to self-service in 1933 and the introduction of shopping centers and public financing in 1953. At Volkswagenwerk, we saw only one between the late 1940s and the 1970s, the tumultuous shift from the traditional Beetle to the Audi-type design mentioned earlier.

And at Air Canada, we found none over the airline's first four decades, following its initial positioning.

Our colleagues at McGill, Danny Miller and Peter Friesen, found this pattern of change so common in their studies of large numbers of companies (especially the high-performance ones) that they built a theory around it, which they labeled the quantum theory of strategic change.[3] Their basic point is that organizations adopt two distinctly different modes of behavior at different times.

Most of the time they pursue a given strategic orientation. Change may seem continuous, but it occurs in the context of that orientation (perfecting a given retailing formula, for example) and usually amounts to doing more of the same, perhaps better as well. Most organizations favor these periods of stability because they achieve success not by changing strategies but by exploiting the ones they have. They, like craftsmen, seek continuous improvement by using their distinctive competencies in established courses.

While this goes on, however, the world continues to change, sometimes slowly, occasionally in dramatic shifts. Thus gradually or suddenly, the organization's strategic orientation moves out of sync with its environment. Then what Miller and Friesen call a strategic revolution must take place. That long period of evolutionary change is suddenly punctuated by a brief bout of revolutionary turmoil in which the organization quickly alters many of its established patterns. In effect, it tries to leap to a new stability quickly to reestablish an integrated posture among a new set of strategies, structures, and culture.

But what about all those emergent strategies, growing like weeds around the organization? What the quantum theory suggests is that the really novel ones are generally held in check in some corner of the organization until a strategic revolution becomes necessary. Then as an alternative to having to develop new strategies from scratch or having to import generic strategies from competitors, the organization can turn to its own emerging patterns to find its new orientation. As the old, established strategy disintegrates, the seeds of the new one begin to spread.

This quantum theory of change seems to apply particularly well to large, established, mass-production companies. Because they are especially reliant on standardized procedures, their resistance to strategic reorientation tends to be especially fierce. So we find long periods of stability broken by short disruptive periods of revolutionary change.

Volkswagenwerk is a case in point. Long enamored of the Beetle and armed with a tightly integrated set of strategies, the company ignored fundamental changes in its markets throughout the late 1950s and 1960s. The bureaucratic momentum of its mass-production organization combined with the psychological momentum of its leader, who institutionalized the strategies in the first place. When change finally did come, it was tumultuous: The company groped its way through a hodgepodge of products before it settled on a new set of vehicles championed by a new leader. Strategic reorientations really are cultural revolutions.

CYCLES OF CHANGE

In more creative organizations, we see a somewhat different pattern of change and stability, one that's more balanced. Companies in the business of producing novel outputs apparently need to fly off in all directions from time to time to sustain their creativity. Yet they also need to settle down after such periods to find some order in the resulting chaos.

The National Film Board's tendency to move in and out of focus through remarkably balanced periods of convergence and divergence is a case in point. Concentrated production of films to aid the war effort in the 1940s gave way to great divergence after the war as the organization sought a new raison d'être. Then the advent of television brought back a very sharp focus in the early 1950s, as noted earlier. But in the late 1950s, this dissipated almost as quickly as it began, giving rise to another creative period of exploration. Then the social changes in the early 1960s evoked a new period of convergence around experimental films and social issues.

We use the label "adhocracy" for organizations, like the National Film Board, that produce individual, or custom-made, products (or designs) in an innovative way, on a project basis.[4] Our craftsman is an adhocracy of sorts too, since each of her ceramic sculptures is unique. And her pattern of strategic change was much like that of the NFB's, with evident cycles of convergence and divergence: a focus on knickknacks from 1967 to 1972; then a period of exploration to about 1976, which resulted in a refocus on ceramic sculptures; that continued to about 1981, to be followed by a period of searching for new directions. More recently, a focus on ceramic murals seems to be emerging.

Whether through quantum revolutions or cycles of convergence and divergence, however, organizations seem to need to separate in time the basic forces for change and stability, reconciling them by attending to each in turn. Many strategic failures can be attributed either to mixing the two or to an obsession with one of these forces at the expense of the other.

The problems are evident in the work of many craftsmen. On the one hand, there are those who seize on the perfection of a single theme and never change. Eventually the creativity disappears from their work and the world passes them by—much as it did Volkswagenwerk until the company was shocked into its strategic revolution. And then there are those who are always changing, who flit from one idea to another and never settle down. Because no theme or strategy ever emerges in their work, they cannot exploit or even develop any distinctive competence. And because their work lacks definition, identity crises are likely to develop, with neither the craftsmen nor their clientele knowing what to make of it. Miller and Friesen found this behavior in conventional business too; they label it "the impulsive firm running blind."[5] How often have we seen it in companies that go on acquisition sprees?

The popular view sees the strategist as a planner or as a visionary, someone sitting on a pedestal dictating brilliant strategies for everyone else to implement. While recognizing the importance of thinking ahead and especially of the need for creative vision in this pedantic world, I wish to propose an additional view of the strategist—as a pattern recognizer, a learner if you will—who manages a process in which strategies (and visions) can emerge as well as be deliberately conceived. I also wish to redefine that strategist, to extend that someone into the collective entity made up of the many actors whose interplay speaks an organization's mind. This strategist *finds* strategies no less than creates them, often in patterns that form inadvertently in its own behavior.

What, then, does it mean to craft strategy? Let us return to the words associated with craft: dedication, experience, involvement with the material, the personal touch, mastery of detail, a sense of harmony and integration. Managers who craft strategy do not spend much time in executive suites reading MIS reports or industry analyses. They are involved, responsive to their materials, learning about their organizations and industries through personal touch. They are also sensitive to experience, recognizing that while individual vision may be important, other factors must help determine strategy as well.

MANAGE STABILITY. Managing strategy is mostly managing stability, not change. Indeed, most of the time senior managers should not be formulating strategy at all; they should be getting on with making their organizations as effective as possible in pursuing the strategies they already have. Like distinguished craftsmen, organizations become distinguished because they master the details.

To manage strategy, then, at least in the first instance, is not so much to promote change as to know *when* to do so. Advocates of strategic planning often urge managers to plan for perpetual instability in the environment (for example, by rolling over five-year plans annually). But this obsession with change is dysfunctional. Organizations that reassess their strategies continuously are like individuals who reassess their jobs or their marriages continuously—in both cases, people will drive themselves crazy or else reduce themselves to inaction. The formal planning process repeats itself so often and so mechanically that it desensitizes the organization to real change, programs it more and more deeply into set patterns, and thereby encourages it to make only minor adaptations.

So-called strategic planning must be recognized for what it is: a means, not to create strategy, but to program a strategy already created—to work out its implications formally. It is essentially analytic in nature, based on decomposition, while strategy creation is essentially a process of synthesis. That is why trying to create strategies through formal planning most often leads to extrapolating existing ones or copying those of competitors.

This is not to say that planners have no role to play in strategy formation. In addition to programming strategies created by other means, they can feed ad hoc analyses into the strategy-making process at the front end to be sure that the hard data are taken into consideration. They can also stimulate others to think strategically. And of course people called planners can be strategists too, so long as they are creative thinkers who are in touch with what is relevant. But that has nothing to do with the technology of formal planning.

DETECT DISCONTINUITY. Environments do not change on any regular or orderly basis. And they seldom undergo continuous dramatic change, claims about our "age of discontinuity" and environmental "turbulence" notwithstanding. (Go tell people who lived through the Great Depression or survivors of the siege of Leningrad during World War II that ours are turbulent times.) Much of the time, change is minor and even temporary and requires no strategic response. Once in a while there is a truly significant discontinuity or, even less often, a gestalt shift in the environment, where everything important seems to change at once. But these events, while critical, are also easy to recognize.

The real challenge in crafting strategy lies in detecting the subtle discontinuities that may undermine a business in the future. And for that, there is no technique, no program, just a sharp mind in touch with the situation. Such discontinuities are unexpected and irregular, essentially unprecedented. They can be dealt with only by minds that are attuned to existing patterns yet able to perceive important breaks in them. Unfortunately, this form of strategic thinking tends to atrophy during the long periods of stability that most organizations experience (just as it did at Volkswagenwerk during the 1950s and 1960s). So the trick is to manage within a given strategic orientation most of the time yet be able to pick out the occasional discontinuity that really matters.

The Steinberg chain was built and run for more than half a century by a man named Sam Steinberg. For 20 years, the company concentrated on perfecting a self-service retailing formula introduced in 1933. Installing fluorescent lighting and figuring out how to package meat in cellophane wrapping were the "strategic" issues of the day. Then in 1952, with the arrival of the first shopping center in Montreal, Steinberg realized he had to redefine his business almost overnight. He knew he needed to control those shopping centers and that control would require public financing and other major changes. So he reoriented his business. The ability to make that kind of switch in thinking is the essence of strategic management. And it has more to do with vision and involvement than it does with analytic technique.

KNOW THE BUSINESS. Sam Steinberg was the epitome of the entrepreneur, a man intimately involved with all the details of his business, who spent Saturday mornings visiting his stores. As he told us in discussing his company's competitive advantage, "Nobody knew the grocery business like we did. Everything has to do with your knowledge. I knew merchandise, I knew cost, I knew selling, I knew customers. I knew everything, and I passed on all my knowledge; I kept teaching my people. That's the advantage we had. Our competitors couldn't touch us."

Note the kind of knowledge involved: not intellectual knowledge, not analytical reports or abstracted facts and figures (though these can certainly help), but personal knowledge, intimate understanding, equivalent to the craftsman's feel for the clay. Facts are available to anyone; this kind of knowledge is not. Wisdom is the word that captures it best. But wisdom is a word that has been lost in the bureaucracies we have built for ourselves, systems designed to distance leaders from operating details. Show me managers who think they can rely on formal planning to create their strategies, and I'll show you managers who lack intimate knowledge of their businesses or the creativity to do something with it.

Craftsmen have to train themselves to see, to pick up things other people miss. The same holds true for managers of strategy. It is those with a kind of peripheral vision who are best able to detect and take advantage of events as they unfold.

MANAGE PATTERNS. Whether in an executive suite in Manhattan or a pottery studio in Montreal, a key to managing strategy is the ability to detect emerging patterns and help them take shape. The job of the manager is not just to preconceive specific strategies but also to recognize their emergence elsewhere in the organization and intervene when appropriate.

Like weeds that appear unexpectedly in a garden, some emergent strategies may need to be uprooted immediately. But management cannot be too quick to cut off the unexpected, for tomorrow's vision may grow out of today's aberration. (Europeans, after all, enjoy salads made from the leaves of the dandelion, America's most notorious weed.) Thus some patterns are worth watching until their effects have more clearly manifested themselves. Then those that prove useful can be made deliberate and be incorporated into the formal strategy, even if that means shifting the strategic umbrella to cover them.

To manage in this context, then, is to create the climate within which a wide variety of strategies can grow. In more complex organizations, this may mean building flexible structures, hiring creative people, defining broad umbrella strategies, and watching for the patterns that emerge.

RECONCILE CHANGE AND CONTINUITY.   Finally, managers considering radical departures need to keep the quantum theory of change in mind. As Ecclesiastes reminds us, there is a time to sow and a time to reap. Some new patterns must be held in check until the organization is ready for a strategic revolution, or at least a period of divergence. Managers who are obsessed with either change or stability are bound eventually to harm their organizations. As pattern recognizer, the manager has to be able to sense when to exploit an established crop of strategies and when to encourage new strains to displace the old.

While strategy is a word that is usually associated with the future, its link to the past is no less central. As Kierkegaard once observed, life is lived forward but understood backward. Managers may have to live strategy in the future, but they must understand it through the past.

Like potters at the wheel, organizations must make sense of the past if they hope to manage the future. Only by coming to understand the patterns that form in their own behavior do they get to know their capabilities and their potential. Thus crafting strategy, like managing craft, requires a natural synthesis of the future, present, and past.

Notes

1. Richard T. Pascale, "Perspective on Strategy: The Real Story Behind Honda's Success," *California Management Review* (May–June 1984), p. 47.

2. James Brian Quinn, IBM (A) case, in James Brian Quinn, Henry Mintzberg, and Robert M. James, *The Strategy Process: Concepts, Contexts, Cases* (Englewood Cliffs, N.J.: Prentice-Hall, 1987).

3. See Danny Miller and Peter H. Friesen, *Organizations: A Quantum View* (Englewood Cliffs, N.J.: Prentice-Hall, 1984).

4. See my article "Organization Design: Fashion or Fit?," *Harvard Business Review* (January–February 1981), p. 103; also see my book *Structure in Fives: Designing Effective Organizations* (En-

glewood Cliffs, N.J.: Prentice-Hall, 1983). The term *adhocracy* was coined by Warren G. Bennis and Philip E. Slater in *The Temporary Society* (New York: Harper & Row, 1964).

5. Danny Miller and Peter H. Friesen, "Archetypes of Strategy Formulation," *Management Science* (May 1978), p. 921.

PART
VI

Corporate Governance

1
Eclipse of the Public Corporation

Michael C. Jensen

New organizations are emerging in its place—organizations that are corporate in form but have no public shareholders and are not listed or traded on organized exchanges. These organizations use public and private debt, rather than public equity, as their major source of capital. Their primary owners are not households but large institutions and entrepreneurs that designate agents to manage and monitor on their behalf and bind those agents with large equity interests and contracts governing the use and distribution of cash.

Takeovers, corporate breakups, divisional spinoffs, leveraged buyouts, and going-private transactions are the most visible manifestations of a massive organizational change in the economy. These transactions have inspired criticism, even outrage, among many business leaders and government officials, who have called for regulatory and legislative restrictions. The backlash is understandable. Change is threatening; in this case, the threat is aimed at the senior executives of many of our largest companies.

Despite the protests, this organizational innovation should be encouraged. By resolving the central weakness of the public corporation—the conflict between owners and managers over the control and use of corporate resources—these new organizations are making remarkable gains in operating efficiency, employee productivity, and shareholder value. Over the long term, they will enhance U.S. economic performance relative to our most formidable international competitor, Japan, whose companies are moving in the opposite direction. The governance and financial structures of Japan's public companies increasingly resemble U.S. companies of the mid-1960s and early 1970s—an era of gross corporate waste and mismanagement that triggered the organizational transformation now under way in the United States.

Consider these developments in the 1980s:

The capital markets are in transition. The total market value of equity in publicly held companies has tripled over the past decade—from $1 trillion in 1979 to more than $3 trillion in 1989. But newly acquired capital comes increasingly from private placements, which have expanded more than ten times since 1980, to a rate of $200 billion in 1988. Private placements of debt and equity now account for more than 40% of annual corporate financings. Meanwhile, in every year since 1983, at least 5% of the outstanding value of corporate equity has disappeared through stock repurchases, takeovers, and going-private transactions. Finally, households are sharply reducing their stock holdings.[1]

The most widespread going-private transaction, the leveraged buyout, is becoming larger and more frequent. In 1988, the total value of the 214 public-company and divisional buyouts exceeded $77 billion—nearly one-third of the value of all mergers and acquisitions. The total value of the 75 buyouts in 1979 was only $1.3 billion (in constant 1988 dollars), while the 175 buyouts completed in 1983 had a total value of $16.6 billion. This process is just getting started; the $77 billion of LBOs in 1988 represented only 2.5% of outstanding public-company equity (see Exhibit I).

Entire industries are being reshaped. Just five years ago, the leading U.S. truck and automobile tire manufacturers were independent and diversified public companies. Today each is a vastly different enterprise. Uniroyal went private in 1985 and later merged its tire-making operations with those of B.F. Goodrich to form a new private company called Uniroyal Goodrich. In late 1986, Goodyear borrowed $2.6 billion and repurchased nearly half its outstanding shares to fend off a hostile tender offer by Sir James Goldsmith. It retained its core tire and rubber business while moving to divest an array of unrelated operations, including its Celeron oil and gas subsidiary, California-to-Texas oil pipeline, aerospace operation, and Arizona resort hotel. In 1987, GenCorp issued $1.75 billion of debt to repurchase more than half its outstanding shares. It divested several operations, including its General Tire subsidiary, to pay down the debt and focus on aerospace and defense. Last year, Firestone was sold to Bridgestone, Japan's largest tiremaker, for $2.6 billion, a transaction that created shareholder gains of $1.6 billion.

Developments as striking as the restructuring of our financial markets and major industries reflect underlying economic forces more fundamental and powerful than financial manipulation, management greed, reckless speculation, and the other colorful epithets used by defenders of the corporate status quo. The forces behind the decline of the public corporation differ from industry to industry. But its decline is real, enduring, and highly productive. It is not merely a function of the tax deductibility of interest. Nor does it reflect a transitory LBO phase through which companies pass before investment bankers and managers cash out by taking them public again. Nor, finally, is it premised on a systematic fleecing of shareholders and bondholders by managers and other insiders with superior information about the true value of corporate assets.

The current trends do not imply that the public corporation has no future. The conventional twentieth-century model of corporate governance—dispersed public ownership, professional managers without substantial equity holdings, a board of directors dominated by management-appointed outsiders—remains a viable option in some areas of the economy, particularly for growth companies whose profitable investment opportunities exceed the cash they generate internally. Such companies can be found in industries like computers and electronics, biotechnology, pharmaceuticals, and financial services. Companies choosing among a surplus of profitable projects are unlikely to invest systematically in unprofitable ones, especially when they must regularly turn to the capital markets to raise investment funds.

The public corporation is not suitable in industries where long-term growth is slow, where internally generated funds outstrip the opportunities to invest them profitably, or where downsizing is the most productive long-term strategy. In the tire industry, the shift to radials, which last three times longer than bias-ply tires, meant that manufacturers needed less capacity to meet world demand. Overcapacity inevitably forced a restructuring. The tenfold increase in oil prices from 1973 to 1981, which triggered worldwide conservation measures, forced oil producers into a similar retrenchment.[2]

Industries under similar pressure today include steel, chemicals, brewing, tobacco, television and radio broadcasting, wood and paper products. In these and other cash-rich, low-growth or declining sectors, the pressures on management to waste cash flow through organizational slack or investments in unsound projects is often irresistible. It is in precisely these sectors that the publicly held corporation has declined most rapidly. Barring regulatory interference, the public corporation is also likely to decline in industries such as aerospace, automobiles and auto parts, banking,

Exhibit 1.

Rise of the LBO

	Public-Company Buyouts			Divisional Buyouts			
Year	Number	Average Value (In millions of 1988 dollars)		Number	Average Value (In millions of 1988 dollars)		Total Value of Buyouts (In billions of 1988 dollars)
1979	16	$ 64.9		59	$ 5.4		$ 1.4
1980	13	106.0		47	34.5		3.0
1981	17	179.1		83	21.0		4.8
1982	31	112.2		115	40.7		8.2
1983	36	235.8		139	58.2		16.6
1984	57	473.6		122	104.0		39.7
1985	76	349.4		132	110.1		41.0
1986	76	303.3		144	180.7		49.0
1987	47	488.7		90	144.2		36.0
1988	125	487.4		89	181.3		77.0

Source: George P. Baker, "Management Compensation and Divisional Leveraged Buyouts," unpublished dissertation, Harvard Business School, 1986. Updates from W.T. Grimm, *Mergerstat Review 1988*. Transactions with no public data are valued at the average price of public transactions.

electric power generation, food processing, industrial and farm implements, and transportation equipment.

The public corporation is a social invention of vast historical importance. Its genius is rooted in its capacity to spread financial risk over the diversified portfolios of millions of individuals and institutions and to allow investors to customize risk to their unique circumstances and predilections. By diversifying risks that would otherwise be borne by owner-entrepreneurs and by facilitating the creation of a liquid market for exchanging risk, the public corporation lowered the cost of capital. These tradable claims on corporate ownership (common stock) also allowed risk to be borne by investors best able to bear it, without requiring them to manage the corporations they owned.

From the beginning, though, these risk-bearing benefits came at a cost. Tradable ownership claims create fundamental conflicts of interest between those who bear risk (the shareholders) and those who manage risk (the executives). The genius of the new organizations is that they eliminate much of the loss created by conflicts between owners and managers, without eliminating the vital functions of risk diversification and liquidity once performed exclusively by the public equity markets.

In theory, these new organizations should not be necessary. Three major forces are said to control management in the public corporation: the product markets, internal control systems led by the board of directors, and the capital markets. But product markets often have not played a disciplining role. For most of the past 60 years, a large and vibrant domestic market created for U.S. companies economies of scale and significant cost advantages over foreign rivals. Recent reversals at the hands of the Japanese and others have not been severe enough to sap most companies of their financial independence. The idea that outside directors with little or no equity stake in the company could effectively monitor and discipline the managers who selected them has proven hollow at best. In practice, only the capital markets have played much of a control function—and for a long time they were hampered by legal constraints.

Indeed, the fact that takeover and LBO premiums average 50% above market price illustrates how much value public-company managers can destroy before they face a serious threat of disturbance. Takeovers and buyouts both create new value and unlock value destroyed by management through misguided policies. I estimate that transactions associated with the market for corporate control unlocked shareholder gains (in target companies alone) of more than $500 billion between 1977 and 1988—more than 50% of the cash dividends paid by the entire corporate sector over this same period.

The widespread waste and inefficiency of the public corporation and its inability to adapt to changing economic circumstances have generated a wave of organizational innovation over the past 15 years—innovation driven by the rebirth of "active investors." By active investors I mean investors who hold large equity or debt positions, sit on boards of directors, monitor and sometimes dismiss management, are involved with the long-term strategic direction of the companies they invest in, and sometimes manage the companies themselves.

Active investors are creating a new model of general management. These investors include LBO partnerships such as Kohlberg Kravis Roberts and Clayton & Dubilier; entrepreneurs such as Carl Icahn, Ronald Perelman, Laurence Tisch, Robert Bass, William Simon, Irwin Jacobs, and Warren Buffett; the merchant banking arms of Wall Street houses such as Morgan Stanley, Lazard Frères, and Merrill Lynch; and family funds such as those controlled by the Pritzkers and the Bronfmans. Their model is built around highly leveraged financial structures, pay-for-performance compensation systems, substantial equity ownership by managers and directors, and contracts with owners and creditors that limit both cross-subsidization among business units and the waste of free cash flow. Consistent with modern finance theory, these organizations are not managed to maximize earnings per share but rather to maximize *value,* with a strong emphasis on cash flow.

More than any other factor, these organizations' resolution of the owner-manager conflict explains how they can motivate the same people, managing the same resources, to perform so much more effectively under private ownership than in the publicly held corporate form.

In effect, LBO partnerships and the merchant banks are rediscovering the role played by active investors prior to 1940, when Wall Street banks such as J.P. Morgan & Company were directly involved in the strategy and governance of the public companies they helped create. At the height of his prominence, Morgan and his small group of partners served on the boards of U.S. Steel, International Harvester, First National Bank of New York, and a host of railroads, and were a powerful management force in these and other companies.

Morgan's model of investor activism disappeared largely as a result of populist laws and regulations approved in the wake of the Great Depression. These laws and regulations—including the Glass-Steagall Banking Act of 1933, the Securities Act of 1933, the Securities Exchange Act of 1934, the Chandler Bankruptcy Revision Act of 1938, and the Investment Company Act of 1940—may have once had their place. But they also created an intricate web of restrictions on company "insiders" (corporate officers, directors, or investors with more than a 10% ownership interest), restrictions on bank involvement in corporate reorganizations, court precedents, and business practices that raised the cost of being an active investor. Their long-term effect has been to insulate management from effective monitoring and to set the stage for the eclipse of the public corporation.

Indeed, the high cost of being an active investor has left financial institutions and money management firms, which control more than 40% of all corporate equity in the United States, almost completely uninvolved in the major decisions and long-term strategies of the companies their clients own. They are almost never represented on corporate boards. They use the proxy mechanism rarely and usually ineffectively, notwithstanding recent efforts by the Council of Institutional Investors and other shareholder activists to gain a larger voice in corporate affairs.

All told, institutional investors are remarkably powerless; they have few options to express dissatisfaction with management other than to sell their shares and vote with their feet. Corporate managers criticize institutional selloffs as examples of portfolio churning and short-term investor horizons. One guesses these same managers much prefer churning to a system in which large investors on the boards of their companies have direct power to monitor and correct mistakes. Managers really want passive investors who can't sell their shares.

The absence of effective monitoring led to such large inefficiencies that the new generation of active investors arose to recapture the lost value. These investors overcome the costs of the outmoded legal constraints by purchasing entire companies—and using debt and high equity ownership to force effective self-monitoring.

A central weakness and source of waste in the public corporation is the conflict between shareholders and managers over the payout of free cash flow—that is, cash flow in excess of that required to fund all investment projects with positive net present values when discounted at the relevant cost of capital. For a company to operate efficiently and maximize value, free cash flow must be distributed to shareholders rather than retained. But this happens infrequently; senior management has few incentives to distribute the funds, and there exist few mechanisms to compel distribution.

A vivid example is the senior management of Ford Motor Company, which sits on nearly $15 billion in cash and marketable securities in an industry with excess capacity. Ford's management has been deliberating about acquiring financial services companies, aerospace companies, or making some other multibillion-dollar diversification move—rather than deliberating about effectively distributing Ford's excess cash to its owners so they can decide how to reinvest it.

Ford is not alone. Corporate managers generally don't disgorge cash unless they are forced to do so. In 1988, the 1,000 largest public companies (by sales) generated total funds of $1.6 trillion. Yet they distributed only $108 billion as dividends and another $51 billion through share repurchases.[3]

Managers have incentives to retain cash in part because cash reserves increase their autonomy vis-à-vis the capital markets. Large cash balances (and independence from the capital markets) can serve a competitive purpose, but they often lead to waste and inefficiency. Consider a hypothetical world in which companies distribute excess cash to shareholders and then must convince the capital markets to supply funds as sound economic projects arise. Shareholders are at a great advantage in this world, where management's plans are subject to enhanced monitoring by the capital markets. Wall Street's analytical, due diligence, and pricing disciplines give shareholders more power to quash wasteful projects.

Managers also resist distributing cash to shareholders because retaining cash increases the size of the companies they run—and managers have many incentives to expand company size beyond that which maximizes shareholder wealth. Compensation is one of the most important incentives. Many studies document that increases in executive pay are strongly related to increases in corporate size rather than value.[4]

The tendency of companies to reward middle managers through promotions rather than annual performance bonuses also creates a cultural bias toward growth. Organizations must grow in order to generate new positions to feed their promotion-based reward systems.

Finally, corporate growth enhances the social prominence, public prestige, and political power of senior executives. Rare is the CEO who wants to be remembered as presiding over an enterprise that makes fewer products in fewer plants in fewer countries than when he or she took office—even when such a course increases productivity and adds hundreds of millions of dollars of shareholder value. The perquisites of the executive suite can be substantial, and they usually increase with company size.

The struggle over free cash flow is at the heart of the role of debt in the decline of the public corporation. Bank loans, mezzanine securities, and high-yield bonds have fueled the wave of takeovers, restructurings, and going-private transactions. The combined borrowings of all nonfinancial corporations in the United States approached $2 trillion in 1988, up from $835 billion in 1979. The interest charges on these borrowings represent more than 20% of corporate cash flows, high by historical standards.[5]

This perceived "leveraging of corporate America" is perhaps the central source of anxiety among defenders of the public corporation and critics of the new organizational forms. But most critics miss three important points. First, the trebling of the market value of public-company equity over the last decade means that corporate borrowing had to increase to avoid a major deleveraging.

Second, debt creation *without retention of the proceeds of the issue* helps limit the waste of free cash flow by compelling managers to pay out funds they would otherwise retain. Debt is in effect a substitute for dividends—a mechanism to force managers to disgorge cash rather than spend it on empire-building projects with low or negative returns, bloated staffs, indulgent perquisites, and organizational inefficiencies.

By issuing debt in exchange for stock, companies bond their managers' promise to pay out future cash flows in a way that simple dividend increases do not. "Permanent" dividend increases or multiyear share repurchase programs (two ways public companies can distribute excess cash to shareholders) involve no contractual commitments by managers to owners. It's easy for managers to cut dividends or scale back share repurchases.

Take the case of General Motors. On March 3, 1987, several months after the departure of GM's only active investor, H. Ross Perot, the company announced a program to repurchase up to 20%

of its common stock by the end of 1990. As of mid-1989, GM had purchased only 5% of its outstanding common shares, even though its $6.8 billion cash balance was more than enough to complete the program. Given management's poor performance over the past decade, shareholders would be better off making their own investment decisions with the cash GM is retaining. From 1977 to 1987, the company made capital expenditures of $77.5 billion while its U.S. market share declined by 10 points.

Borrowing allows for no such managerial discretion. Companies whose managers fail to make promised interest and principal payments can be declared insolvent and possibly hauled into bankruptcy court. In the imagery of G. Bennett Stewart and David M. Glassman, "Equity is soft, debt hard. Equity is forgiving, debt insistent. Equity is a pillow, debt a sword."[6] Some may find it curious that a company's creditors wield far more power over managers than its public shareholders, but it is also undeniable.

Third, debt is a powerful agent for change. For all the deeply felt anxiety about excessive borrowing, "overleveraging" can be desirable and effective when it makes economic sense to break up a company, sell off parts of the business, and refocus its energies on a few core operations. Companies that assume so much debt they cannot meet the debt service payments out of operating cash flow force themselves to rethink their entire strategy and structure. Overleveraging creates the crisis atmosphere managers require to slash unsound investment programs, shrink overhead, and dispose of assets that are more valuable outside the company. The proceeds generated by these overdue restructurings can then be used to reduce debt to more sustainable levels, creating a leaner, more efficient and competitive organization.

In other circumstances, the violation of debt covenants creates a board-level crisis that brings new actors onto the scene, motivates a fresh review of top management and strategy, and accelerates response. The case of Revco D.S., Inc., one of the handful of leveraged buyouts to reach formal bankruptcy, makes the point well.

Critics cite Revco's bankruptcy petition, filed in July 1988, as an example of the financial perils associated with LBO debt. I take a different view. The $1.25 billion buyout, announced in December 1986, did dramatically increase Revco's annual interest charges. But several other factors contributed to its troubles, including management's decision to overhaul pricing, stocking, and merchandise layout in the company's drugstore chain. This mistaken strategic redirection left customers confused and dissatisfied, and Revco's performance suffered. Before the buyout, and without the burden of interest payments, management could have pursued these policies for a long period of time, destroying much of the company's value in the process. Within six months, however, debt served as a brake on management's mistakes, motivating the board and creditors to reorganize the company before even more value was lost.[7]

Developments at Goodyear also illustrate how debt can force managers to adopt value-creating policies they would otherwise resist. Soon after his company warded off Sir James Goldsmith's tender offer, Goodyear chairman Robert Mercer offered his version of the raiders' creed: "Give me your undervalued assets, your plants, your expenditures for technology, research and development, the hopes and aspirations of your people, your stake with your customers, your pension funds, and I will enhance myself and the dealmakers."[8]

What Mr. Mercer failed to note is that Goodyear's forced restructuring dramatically increased the company's value to shareholders by compelling him to disgorge cash and shed unproductive assets. Two years after this bitter complaint, Tom Barrett, who succeeded Mercer as Goodyear's CEO, was asked whether the company's restructuring had hurt the quality of its tires or the efficiency of its plants. "No," he replied. "We've been able to invest and continue to invest and do the things we've needed to do to be competitive."[9]

Robert Mercer's harsh words are characteristic of the business establishment's response to the eclipse of the public corporation. What explains such vehement opposition to a trend that clearly benefits shareholders and the economy? One important factor, as my Harvard Business School colleague Amar Bhide suggests, is that Wall Street now competes directly with senior management as a steward of shareholder wealth. With its vast increases in data, talent, and technology, Wall Street can allocate capital among competing businesses and monitor and discipline management more effectively than the CEO and headquarters staff of the typical diversified company. KKR's New York offices and Irwin Jacobs' Minneapolis base are direct substitutes for corporate headquarters in Akron or Peoria. CEOs worry that they and their staffs will lose lucrative jobs in favor of competing organizations. Many are right to worry; the performance of active investors versus the public corporation leaves little doubt as to which is superior.

Active investors are creating new models of general management, the most widespread of which I call the LBO Association. A typical LBO Association consists of three main constituencies: an LBO partnership that sponsors going-private transactions and counsels and monitors management in an ongoing cooperative relationship; company managers who hold substantial equity stakes in an LBO division and stay on after the buyout; and institutional investors (insurance companies, pension funds, and money management firms) that fund the limited partnerships that purchase equity and lend money (along with banks) to finance the transactions.

Much like a traditional conglomerate, LBO Associations have many divisions or business units, companies they have taken private at different points in time. KKR, for example, controls a diverse collection of 19 businesses including all or part of Beatrice, Duracell, Motel 6, Owens-Illinois, RJR Nabisco, and Safeway. But LBO Associations differ from publicly held conglomerates in at least four important respects (see Exhibit II).

MANAGEMENT INCENTIVES ARE BUILT AROUND A STRONG RELATION-SHIP BETWEEN PAY AND PERFORMANCE. Compensation systems in LBO Associations usually have higher upper bounds than do public companies (or no upper bounds at all), tie bonuses much more closely to cash flow and debt retirement than to accounting earnings, and otherwise closely link management pay to divisional performance. Unfortunately, because these companies are private, little data are available on salaries and bonuses.

Public data are available on stock ownership, however, and equity holdings are a vital part of the reward system in LBO Associations. The University of Chicago's Steven Kaplan studied all public-company buyouts from 1979 through 1985 with a purchase price of at least $50 million.[10] Business unit chiefs hold a median equity position of 6.4% in their unit. Even without considering bonus and incentive plans, a $1,000 increase in shareholder value triggers a $64 increase in the personal wealth of business unit chiefs. The median public-company CEO holds only .25% of the company's equity. Counting all sources of compensation—including salary, bonus, deferred compensation, stock options, and dismissal penalties—the personal wealth of the median public-company CEO increases by only $3.25 for a $1,000 increase in shareholder value.[11]

Thus the salary of the typical LBO business-unit manager is almost 20 times more sensitive to performance than that of the typical public-company manager. This comparison understates the

Exhibit II.

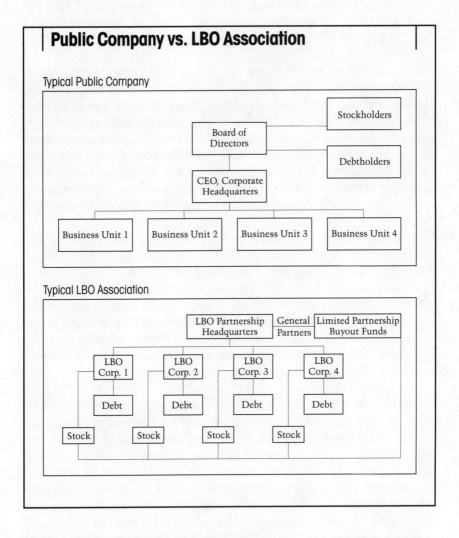

Public Company vs. LBO Association

Typical Public Company

Typical LBO Association

true differences in compensation. The personal wealth of managing partners in an LBO partnership (in effect, the CEOs of the LBO Associations) is tied almost exclusively to the performance of the companies they control. The general partners in an LBO Association typically receive (through overrides and direct equity holdings) 20% or more of the gains in the value of the divisions they help manage. This implies a pay-for-performance sensitivity of $200 for every $1,000 in added shareholder value. It's not hard to understand why an executive who receives $200 for every $1,000 increase in shareholder value will unlock more value than an executive who receives $3.25.

LBO ASSOCIATIONS ARE MORE DECENTRALIZED THAN PUBLICLY HELD CONGLOMERATES. The LBO Association substitutes compensation incentives and ownership for direct monitoring by headquarters. The headquarters of KKR, the world's largest LBO partnership, has only 16 professionals and 44 additional employees. In contrast, the Atlanta headquarters of RJR Nabisco employed 470 people when KKR took it private last year in a $25 billion transaction. At the time of the Goldsmith tender offer for Goodyear, the company's Akron headquarters had more than 5,000 people on its salaried payroll.

It is physically impossible for KKR and other LBO partnerships to become intimately involved in the day-to-day decisions of their operating units. They rely instead on stock ownership, incentive pay that rewards cash flow, and other compensation techniques to motivate managers to maximize value without bureaucratic oversight. My survey of 7 LBO partnerships found an average headquarters staff of 13 professionals and 19 nonprofessionals that oversees almost 24 business units with total annual sales of more than $11 billion (see Exhibit III).

LBO ASSOCIATIONS RELY HEAVILY ON LEVERAGE. The average debt ratio (long-term debt as a percentage of debt plus equity) for public companies prior to a buyout is about 20%. The Kaplan study shows the average debt ratio for an LBO is 85% on completion of the buyout.

Intensive use of debt dramatically shrinks the amount of equity in a company. This allows the LBO general partners and divisional managers to control a large fraction of the total ownership without requiring huge investments they would be unable to make or large grants of free equity. For example, in a company with $1 billion in assets and a debt ratio of 20%, management would have to raise $80 million to buy 10% of the equity. If that same company had a debt ratio of 90%, management would have to raise only $10 million to control a 10% stake. By concentrating equity holdings among managers and LBO partners, debt intensifies the ownership incentives that are so important to efficiency.

Exhibit III.

LBO Partnerships Keep Staff Lean

LBO Partnership	Year Started	Number of Professionals	Number of Nonprofessionals	Number of Business Units	Combined Annual Revenues (In billions of dollars)
Berkshire Partners	1986	14	6	15	$ 1
Butler Capital	1979	8	14	33	2.3
Clayton & Dubilier	1976	10	11	8	4.8
Gibbons Green van Amerongen	1969	6	7	12	5.3
Kohlberg Kravis Roberts	1976	16	44	19	58.7
Thomas H. Lee Co.	1974	15	12	25	8
Odyssey Partners	1950	19	39	53	N.A.

High debt also allows LBO Associations and other private organizations to tap the benefits of risk diversification once provided only by the public equity market. Intensive use of debt means much of it must be in the form of public, high-yield, noninvestment-grade securities, better known as junk bonds. This debt, which was pioneered by Drexel Burnham Lambert, reflects more of the risk borne by shareholders in the typical public company. Placing this public debt in the well-diversified portfolios of large financial institutions spreads equitylike risk among millions of investors, who are the ultimate beneficiaries of mutual funds and pension funds—without requiring those risks to be held as equity. Indeed, high-yield debt is probably the most important and productive capital market innovation in the last 40 years.

LBO ASSOCIATIONS HAVE WELL-DEFINED OBLIGATIONS TO THEIR CREDITORS AND RESIDUAL CLAIMANTS.   Most buyout funds are organized as limited partnerships in which the partners of the sponsoring LBO firm serve as general partners. The buyout fund purchases most of the equity and sometimes provides debt financing. The limited partnership agreement denies the general partner the right to transfer cash or other resources from one LBO division to another. That is, all returns from a business must be distributed to the limited partners and other equity holders of that business. Such binding agreements reduce the risk of unproductive reinvestment by prohibiting cross-subsidization among LBO units. In effect, the LBO sponsor must ask its institutional investors for permission to reinvest funds, a striking difference from the power of public-company managers to freely shift resources among business units.

The management, compensation, and financial structures of the LBO Association square neatly with the rebirth of active investors. Institutional investors delegate the job of being active monitors to agents best qualified to play the role. The LBO partnerships bond their performance by investing their own resources and reputations in the transaction and taking the bulk of their compensation as a share in the companies' increased value.

To be sure, this delegation is not without its tensions. The fact that LBO partnerships and divisional managers control the LBO Association's small equity base but hold little of the debt creates incentives for them to take high-risk management gambles. If their gambles succeed, they reap large rewards by increasing their equity value; if their gambles fail, creditors bear much of the cost. But the reputational consequences of such reckless behavior can be large. As long as creditors behave rationally, an LBO partnership that tries to profit at the expense of its creditors or walks away from a deal gone sour will not be able to raise funds for future investments.

To date, the performance of LBO Associations has been remarkable. Indeed, it is difficult to find any systematic losers in these transactions, and almost all of the gains appear to come from real increases in productivity. The best studies of LBO performance reach the following conclusions:

LBOs create large gains for shareholders. Studies estimate that the average total premium to public shareholders ranges from 40% to 56%.[12] Kaplan finds that in buyouts that go public again or are otherwise sold (which occurs on average 2.7 years after the original transaction), total shareholder value increases by an average of 235%, or nearly 100% above market-adjusted returns over the same period.[13] These returns are distributed about equally between prebuyout shareholders and the suppliers of debt and equity to the transaction. Prebuyout shareholders earn average market-adjusted premiums of 38%, while the total return to capital (debt plus equity) for buyout investors is 42%. This return to buyout investors is measured on the total purchase price of the LBO, not the buyout equity. Because equity returns are almost a pure risk premium, and therefore independent of the amount invested, they are very high. The median market-adjusted return on buyout equity is 785%, or 125% per year.

Value gains do not come at the expense of other financial constituencies. Some critics argue that buyout investors, especially managers, earn excessive returns by using inside information to exploit public shareholders. Managers do face severe conflicts of interest in these transactions; they cannot simultaneously act as buyer and agent for the seller. But equity-owning managers who are not part of postbuyout management teams systematically sell their shares into LBOs. This would be foolish if the buyout were significantly underpriced in light of inside information, assuming that these nonparticipating insiders have the same inside information as the continuing management team. Moreover, LBO auctions are becoming common; underpriced buyout proposals (including those initiated by management) quickly generate competing bids.

No doubt some bondholders have lost value through going-private transactions. By my estimate, RJR Nabisco's prebuyout bondholders lost almost $300 million through the downgrading of their claims on the newly leveraged company. This is a small sum in comparison to the $12 billion in total gains the transaction produced. As yet, there is no evidence that bondholders lose on average from LBOs. Evidence on LBOs completed through 1986 does show that holders of convertible bonds and preferred stock gain a statistically significant amount and that straight bondholders suffer no significant gains or losses.[14]

New data may document losses for bondholders in recent transactions. But the expropriation of wealth from bondholders should not be a continuing problem. The financial community is perfecting many techniques, including poison pills and repurchase provisions, to protect bondholders in the event of substantial restructurings. In fact, versions of these loss-prevention techniques have been available for some time. In the past, bondholders such as Metropolitan Life, which sued RJR Nabisco over the declining value of the company's bonds, chose not to pay the premium for protection.

LBOs increase operating efficiency without massive layoffs or big cuts in research and development. Kaplan finds that average operating earnings increase by 42% from the year prior to the buyout to the third year after the buyout. Cash flows increase by 96% over this same period. Other studies document significant improvements in profit margins, sales per employee, working capital, inventories, and receivables.[15] Those who doubt these findings might take a moment to scan the business press, which has chronicled the impressive postbuyout performance of companies such as Levi Strauss, A.O. Scott, Safeway, and Weirton Steel.

Importantly, employment does not fall systematically after buyouts, although it does not grow as quickly as in comparable companies. Median employment for all companies in the Kaplan study, including those engaged in substantial divestitures, increased by nearly 1%. Companies without significant divestitures increased employment by 5%.

Moreover, the great concern about the effect of buyouts on R&D and capital investment is unwarranted. The low-growth companies that make the best candidates for LBOs don't invest heavily in R&D to begin with. Of the 76 companies in the Kaplan study, only 7 spent more than 1% of sales on R&D before the buyout. Another recent study shows that R&D as a fraction of sales grows at the same rate in LBOs as in comparable public companies.[16] According to Kaplan's study, capital expenditures are 20% lower in LBOs than in comparable non-LBO companies. Because these cuts are taking place in low-growth or declining industries and are accompanied by a doubling of market-adjusted value, they appear to be coming from reductions in low-return projects rather than productive investments.

Taxpayers do not subsidize going-private transactions. Much has been made of the charge that large increases in debt virtually eliminate the tax obligations of an LBO. This argument overlooks five sources of additional tax revenues generated by buyouts: capital gains taxes paid by prebuyout shareholders; capital gains taxes paid on postbuyout asset sales; tax payments on the large increases in operating earnings generated by efficiency gains; tax payments by creditors who receive interest payments on the LBO debt; and taxes generated by more efficient use of the company's total capital.

Overall, the U.S. Treasury collects an estimated 230% more revenues in the year after a buyout than it would have otherwise and 61% more in long-term present value. The $12 billion gain associated with the RJR Nabisco buyout will generate net tax revenues of $3.3 billion in the first year of the buyout; the company paid $370 million in federal taxes in the year before the buyout. In the long term, the transaction will generate total taxes with an estimated present value of $3.8 billion.[17]

LBO sponsors do not have to take their companies public for them to succeed. Most LBO transactions are completed with a goal of returning the reconfigured company to the public market within three to five years. But recent evidence indicates that LBO sponsors are keeping their companies under private ownership. Huge efficiency gains and high-return asset sales produce enough cash to pay down debt and allow LBOs to generate handsome returns as going concerns. The very proliferation of these transactions has helped create a more efficient infrastructure and liquid market for buying and selling divisions and companies. Thus LBO investors can "cash out" in a secondary LBO or private sale without recourse to a public offering. One recent study finds that only 5% of the more than 1,300 LBOs between 1981 and 1986 have gone public again.[18]

Public companies can learn from LBO Associations and emulate many of their characteristics. But this requires major changes in corporate structure, philosophy, and focus. They can reduce the waste of free cash flow by borrowing to repurchase stock or pay large dividends. They can alter their charters to encourage large investors or experiment with alliances with active investors such as Lazard Frères' Corporate Partners fund. They can increase equity ownership by directors, managers, and employees. They can enhance incentives through pay-for-performance systems based on cash flow and value rather than accounting earnings. They can decentralize management by rethinking the role of corporate headquarters and shrinking their staffs.

Some corporations are experimenting with such changes—FMC, Holiday, and Owens-Corning—and the results have been impressive. But only a coordinated attack on the status quo will halt the eclipse of the public company. It is unlikely such an attack will proceed fast enough or go far enough.

Who can argue with a new model of enterprise that aligns the interests of owners and managers, improves efficiency and productivity, and unlocks hundreds of billions of dollars of shareholder value? Many people, it seems, mainly because these organizations rely so heavily on debt. As I've discussed, debt is crucial to management discipline and resolving the conflict over free cash flow. But critics, even some who concede the control function of debt, argue that the costs of leverage outweigh the benefits.

Wall Street economist Henry Kaufman, a prominent critic of the going-private trend, issued a typical warning earlier this year: "Any severe shock—a sharp increase in interest rates in response to Federal Reserve credit restraint, or an outright recession that makes the whole stock market vulnerable, or some breakdown in the ability of foreign firms to bid for pieces of U.S. companies— will drive debt-burdened companies to the government's doorstep to plead for special assistance."[19]

The relationship between debt and insolvency is perhaps the least understood aspect of this entire organizational evolution. New hedging techniques mean the risk associated with a given level of corporate debt is lower today than it was five years ago. Much of the bank debt associated with LBOs (which typically represents about half of the total debt) is done through floating-rate instruments. But few LBOs accept unlimited exposure to interest rate fluctuations. They purchase caps to set a ceiling on interest charges or use swaps to convert floating-rate debt into fixed-rate debt. In fact, most banks require such risk management techniques as a condition of lending.

Critics of leverage also fail to appreciate that insolvency in and of itself is not always something to avoid—and that the costs of becoming insolvent are likely to be much smaller in the new world of high leverage than in the old world of equity-dominated balance sheets. The proliferation of takeovers, LBOs, and other going-private transactions has inspired innovations in the reorganization and workout process. I refer to these innovations as "the privatization of bankruptcy." LBOs *do* get in financial trouble more frequently than public companies do. But few LBOs ever enter formal bankruptcy. They are reorganized quickly (a few months is common), often under new management, and at much lower costs than under a court-supervised process.

How can insolvency be less costly in a world of high leverage? Consider an oversimplified example. Companies A and B are identical in every respect except for their financial structures. Each has a going-concern value of $100 million (the discounted value of its expected future cash flows) and a liquidation or salvage value of $10 million. Company A has an equity-dominated balance sheet with a debt ratio of 20%, common for large public companies. Highly leveraged Company B has a debt ratio of 85%, common for LBOs (see Exhibit IV).

Now both companies experience business reversals. What happens? Company B will get in trouble with its creditors much sooner than Company A. After all, Company B's going-concern value doesn't have to shrink very much for it to be unable to meet its payments on $85 million of debt. But when it does run into trouble, its going-concern value will be nowhere near its liquidation value. If the going-concern value shrinks to $80 million, there remains $70 million of value to preserve by avoiding liquidation. So Company B's creditors have strong incentives to preserve the remaining value by quickly and efficiently reorganizing their claims outside the courtroom.

No such incentives operate on Company A. Its going-concern value can fall dramatically before creditors worry about their $20 million of debt. By the time creditors do intervene, Company A's going-concern value will have plummeted. And if Company A's value falls to under $20 million, it is much more likely than Company B to be worth less than its $10 million salvage value. Liqui-

Exhibit IV.

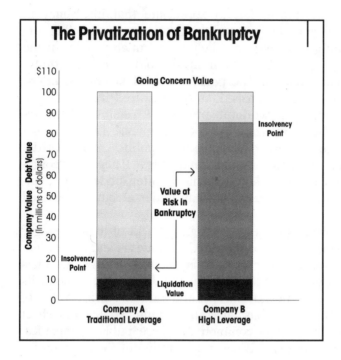

dation in this situation is the likely and rational outcome, with all its attendant conflicts, dislocations, and costs.

The evolving U.S. system of corporate governance and finance exhibits many characteristics of the postwar Japanese system. LBO partnerships act much like the main banks (the real power center) in Japan's keiretsu business groupings. The keiretsu make extensive use of leverage and intercorporate holdings of debt and equity. Banks commonly hold substantial equity in their client companies and have their own executives help them out of difficulty. (For years, Nissan has been run by an alumnus of the Industrial Bank of Japan, who became CEO as part of the bank's effort to keep the company out of bankruptcy.) Other personnel, including CFOs, move frequently between banks and companies as part of an ongoing relationship that involves training, consulting, and monitoring. Japanese banks allow companies to enter formal bankruptcy only when liquidation makes economic sense—that is, when a company is worth more dead than alive. Japanese corporate boards are composed almost exclusively of insiders.

Ironically, even as more U.S. companies come to resemble Japanese companies, Japan's public companies are becoming more like U.S. companies of 15 years ago. Japanese shareholders have seldom had any power. The banks' chief disciplinary tool, their power to withhold capital from high-growth, cash-starved companies, has been vastly reduced as a result of several factors. Japan's victories in world product markets have left its companies awash in profits. The development of domestic and international capital markets has created ready alternatives to bank loans, while deregulation has liberalized corporate access to these funds. Finally, new legal constraints prevent banks from holding more than 5% of the equity of any company, which reduces their incentive to engage in active monitoring.

Many of Japan's public companies are flooded with free cash flow far in excess of their opportunities to invest in profitable internal growth. In 1987, more than 40% of Japan's large public companies had no net bank borrowings—that is, cash balances larger than their short- and long-term borrowings. Toyota, with a cash hoard of $10.4 billion, more than 25% of its total assets, is commonly referred to as the Toyota Bank.[20]

In short, Japanese managers are increasingly unconstrained and unmonitored. They face no effective internal controls, little control from the product markets their companies already dominate, and fewer controls from the banking system because of self-financing, direct access to capital markets, and lower debt ratios. Unless shareholders and creditors discover ways to prohibit their managers from behaving like U.S. managers, Japanese companies will make uneconomic acquisitions and diversification moves, generate internal waste, and engage in other value-destroying activities. The long-term result will be the growth of bureaucracy and inefficiency and the demise of product quality and organizational responsiveness—until the waste becomes so severe it triggers a market for corporate control to remedy the excesses.

The Japanese remedy will reflect that country's unique legal system and cultural practices. But just as hostile takeovers, LBOs, and other control transactions went from unacceptable behavior in the United States to a driving force in corporate restructuring, so too will they take hold in Japan—once the potential returns outweigh the costs and risks of challenging the corporate status quo.

Meanwhile, in the United States, the organizational changes revitalizing the corporate sector will create more nimble enterprises and help reverse our losses in world product markets. As this profound innovation continues, however, people will make mistakes. To learn, we have to push new policies to the margin. It will be natural to see more failed deals.

There are already some worrisome structural issues. I look with discomfort on the dangerous tendency of LBO partnerships, bolstered by their success, to take more of their compensation in front-end fees rather than in back-end profits earned through increased equity value. As management fees and the fees for completing deals get larger, the incentives to do deals, rather than good deals, also increases. Institutional investors (and the economy as a whole) are best served when the LBO partnership is the last member of the LBO Association to get paid and when the LBO partnership gets paid as a fraction of the back-end value of the deals, including losses.

Moreover, we have yet to fully understand the limitations on the size of this new organizational form. LBO partnerships are understandably tempted to increase the reach of their talented monitors by reconfiguring divisions as acquisition vehicles. This will be difficult to accomplish successfully. It is likely to require bigger staffs, greater centralization of decision rights, and dilution of the high pay-for-performance sensitivity that is so crucial to success. As LBO Associations expand, they run the risk of recreating the bureaucratic waste of the diversified public corporation.

These and other problems should not cloud the remarkable benefits associated with the eclipse of the large public corporation. What surprises me is how few mistakes have occurred thus far in an organizational change as profound as any since World War II.

Notes

1. Equity values based on trends in the Wilshire Index. Private-placement data from IDD Information Services as published in Sarah Bartlett, "Private Market's Growing Edge," *New York Times,* June 20, 1989.

2. For more analysis of the oil industry, see my article, "The Takeover Controversy: Analysis and Evidence," in *Corporate Restruc-*

turing and Executive Compensation (Cambridge, Mass.: Ballinger, 1989).

3. Calculated from Standard & Poor's Compusat file.

4. Kevin J. Murphy, "Corporate and Managerial Remuneration," *Journal of Accounting and Economics* (1985), vol. 7, no. 1–3.

5. Federal Reserve Board, Balance Sheets of U.S. Economy.

6. G. Bennett Stewart III and David M. Glassman, "The Motives and Methods of Corporate Restructuring: Part II," *Journal of Applied Corporate Finance* (Summer 1988).

7. Stephen Phillips, "Revco: Anatomy of an LBO That Failed," *Business Week,* October 3, 1988.

8. "A Hollow Victory for Bob Mercer," *Industry Week,* February 23, 1987.

9. Jonathan P. Hicks, "The Importance of Being Biggest," *New York Times,* June 20, 1989.

10. Steven Kaplan, "The Effects of Management Buyouts on Operating Performance and Value," *Journal of Financial Economics* (1989), vol. 24, no. 2.

11. Michael C. Jensen and Kevin J. Murphy, "Performance Pay and Top Management Incentives," *Journal of Political Economy* (1990), vol. 98, no. 2.

12. Yakov Amihud, "Leveraged Management Buyouts and Shareholders' Wealth," in *Leveraged Management Buyouts: Causes and Consequences* (Homewood, Ill.: Dow Jones-Irwin, 1989).

13. That is, returns net of the returns that would normally be earned on these securities, given their level of systematic risk (beta) and general market returns.

14. L. Marais, K. Schipper, and A. Smith, "Wealth Effects of Going Private for Senior Securities," *Journal of Financial Economics* (1989), vol. 23, no. 1.

15. In addition to Kaplan, see Abbie Smith, "Corporate Ownership Structure and Performance," unpublished paper, University of Chicago, 1989. See also Frank R. Lichtenberg and Donald Siegel, "The Effects of Leveraged Buyouts on Productivity and Related Aspects of Firm Behavior," *National Bureau of Economic Research,* 1989.

16. Lichtenberg and Siegel, NBER, 1989.

17. Michael C. Jensen, Steven Kaplan, and Laura Stiglin, "Effects of LBOs on Tax Revenues of the U.S. Treasury," *Tax Notes,* February 6, 1989.

18. Chris Muscarella and Michael Vetsuypens, "Efficiency and Organizational Structure: A Study of Reverse LBOs," unpublished paper, Southern Methodist University, April 1989.

19. Henry Kaufman, "Bush's First Priority: Stopping the Buyout Mania," *Washington Post*, January 1, 1989.

20. Average (book value) debt ratios fell from 77% in 1976 to 68% in 1987. Given the 390% increase in stock prices over this period, market-value debt ratios fell even more dramatically. Figures calculated from the NEEDS Nikkei Financials file for all companies on the First Section of the Tokyo Stock Exchange.

2
Directors' Responsibility for Corporate Strategy

Kenneth R. Andrews

The strengthening of the corporate board of directors has not yet produced a clear or widely accepted conclusion about the board's role in formulating, ratifying, changing, or evaluating corporate strategy. Discussion of this subject among chief executive officers (who are often also board chairmen) does not thrive.

Previous articles in these pages—for instance, Samuel M. Felton's "Case of the Board and the Strategic Process"[1] and William W. Wommack's "The Board's Most Important Function"[2]—produced little response. Not much has been said elsewhere. Audit committees, compensation committees have all become commonplace, yet the pressures bringing them into being have only rarely produced strategy committees.

We do not have to look far to find out why. Many chief executive officers, rejecting the practicality of conscious strategy, preside over unstated, incremental, or intuitive strategies that have never been articulated or analyzed—and therefore could not be deliberated by the board. Others do not believe their outside directors know enough or have time enough to do more than assent to strategic recommendations. Still others may keep discussions of strategy within management to prevent board transgression onto management turf and consequent reduction of executives' power to shape by themselves the future of their companies.

Few chairmen whom I have encountered in my experience, research, or correspondence share the wish of Robert A. Charpie, president of Cabot Corporation, to "see a board 100% involved."[3] Able, amiable, and competent as they are, even fewer chairmen want to undertake the work and turmoil required to make such involvement useful.

But even if strategy were not such a sensitive topic, invoking latent tension between CEO and independent directors, it would require more time and sophistication than chairmen or outside directors, however willing, could easily summon to the task. At best, original contribution by outside directors is limited and infrequent. Nonetheless, the forces shaping corporate governance, including restlessness among independent directors, are pressing boards toward greater participation in determining the future direction and character of their companies.

I will make a careful statement now that, however harmless it looks, will certainly not win the commitment of most chief executives for some time:

A responsible and effective board should require of its management a unique and durable corporate strategy, review it periodically for its validity, use it as the reference point for all other board decisions, and share with management the risks associated with its adoption.

What Corporate Strategy Is

Virtually every word of so summary a statement requires definition before the statement can be fully understood. By the fashionable phrase, "corporate strategy," for example, I mean the pattern of company purposes and goals—and the major policies for achieving those goals—that defines the business or businesses the company is to be involved with and the kind of company it is to be.

A statement articulating corporate purpose differentiates the company in some way from all its competitors and stems from a perception of present and future market opportunities, distinctive competence, competitive advantage, available resources, and management's personal aspirations and values.

Corporate strategy reconciles what a company might do in terms of opportunity, what it can do in terms of its strengths, what its management wants it to do, and what it thinks is ethical, legal, and moral.

This concept of strategy thus involves economic, social, and personal purposes—not financial objectives alone. Although it evolves with the development of markets, company strengths, and institutional values, corporate strategy marks out a deliberately chosen direction and governs directly the investment decisions, organization structure, incentive systems, and indeed the essential character of the company. It embodies disciplined unity of purpose, a purpose which—to be powerful—must be clear and worthy of the commitment of energetic and intelligent people.[4]

Such a concept of strategy makes an important contribution to management. It forces continuous sensitivity to changes taking place in the company's environment and resources. It requires managers to lay conflicting personal agendas on the table and to look beyond immediate opportunities toward long-term growth and development. Such strategy summons up imagination, innovation, and a zest for risk; and it focuses the work of specialists as well.

The concept of corporate strategy has its shortcomings, as well, for it demands tough, high-risk commitment to a choice of direction. Because it means that a company must sometimes forgo immediate profits for long-term superiority, it can seem inconvenient. For instance, an acquisition that raises current earnings per share but has no future fit with either market development or distinctive competence will be ruled out. Corporate strategy demands that companies examine carefully the muted demands of the future and suppress the clamor of the present.

In both business and government, "muddling through" is the classic response to politically confused decisions about purpose. It has its proponents not only among practitioners but also among scholars. The coalition theory of R.M. Cyert and J.G. March substitutes internal bargaining among special interests for corporate strategy—on the assumption that organizations do not have purposes; only people do.[5] David Baybrooke and Charles E. Lindblom, without so much as a smile, call their view of purposeless organization "disjointed incrementalism."[6] And in 1967, H. Edward Wrapp published his beguiling but no less antistrategic "Good Managers Don't Make Policy Decisions."[7]

If a mangement group cannot decide on a loftier or more practical purpose than adapting to whatever comes, improvisation becomes its limited strategy and the planning horizon closes in. Should this occur, the board must look for an early breakout—even demanding new leadership if necessary—before its company flunks out of national and international competition.

Why Require a Corporate Strategy?

My argument thus far has been that it is better for corporate management to have a strategy than not. But why should a board concern itself with the strategy's content? I submit four principal reasons:

First, the board needs specific evidence that its management has a process for developing, considering, and choosing among strategic alternatives operating within the company.

Second, especially if they have no personal experience in the industry, independent directors need to understand the characteristics of their company's business. Knowledge of strategy makes intelligent overview feasible.

Third, knowing the company's strategy can give the board a reference point for separate decisions that come before it and insight into what matters should be presented to it. If their approval is to be more than routine assent, board members must be allowed to assess the impact of proposals—whether for capital appropriation, a new R&D facility, or an acquisition in an exchange of stock—on their company's strategy.

If management can answer the directors' questions about the strategic impact of a single proposal, the directors will be reassured not only about the soundness of that proposal but also about the continuing objectivity of management. Through a series of specific questions related to management's stated intentions, the board can prevent the company from straying off its strategic course, without resorting to overcautious conservatism.

The *fourth* reason for directors to insist not only that a company have an explicit strategy but also that it present the strategy to them is that evaluation of corporate strategy and of management's adherence to it allows continuous evaluation of management.

Short-term measures are unsatisfactory for evaluation. The best criterion for appraising the quality of management performance, in the absence of personal failures or unexpected breakdowns, is management's success over time in executing a demanding and approved strategy that is continually tested against opportunity and need. The combination of short-term return and long-term investment can only be evaluated over several years.

How to interpret windfall advantages and undeserved misfortune—and to judge skill against results—becomes straightforward when a board can observe executive performance against a consciously considered and explicitly stated corporate strategy. Discussion of strategic issues in the context of the company reveals executives' quality of mind and depth of judgment and gives directors a foundation for later interpretation of results.

Role in Strategy Development

How should the board participate in the development of strategy? This is a tough question to answer. A board does not formulate strategy; its function is *review*—a word as slippery in meaning as it is soft in sound.

If the review process leads the board to approve corporate actions, the board must stand behind its assent. This support entails sharing with the CEO the risks of the decisions it approves, and the board should not approve decisions until it is fully willing to accept those risks.

The review process, by which a management recommendation wins rather than coerces board approval, begins only after full-scale presentation of strategy to the board. The process resumes, as indicated earlier, whenever a capital appropriation, unexpected shortfall, or other strategically important matter comes before the board.

Review is principally discussion sparked by questions and answers. The rejected alternatives are discussed until the directors are satisfied that the process which produced the recommendation was thorough. Discussion concludes in consensus, either to approve or to support withdrawal of the recommendation. The degree to which the directors are convinced that the recommendation meets the strategic tests applied to it in advance affects their subsequent loyalty to the CEO if and when the project fails.

However, review of strategic recommendations goes beyond establishing the board's satisfaction with the strategic process. For example, a publishing house decided that, because of the progress of information technology, it should expand beyond a solely book-producing orientation. At a board meeting, the president proposed the acquisition of two small supplier companies involved in electronically accessible data bases. The entrepreneurial founders of the data base companies were present at the publisher's board meeting to discuss the synergy that would be made possible by the acquisition. An urbane, high-speed summary of the proposed acquisition, allegedly backed by extensive management inquiry, produced the board's expected affirmative vote—which was apparently justified strategically.

After the meeting, two of the outside directors (who had asked questions and received "answers") met at the elevator. Without speaking, they both shook their heads. Each had formed a negative opinion about the education, breadth, competence, and integrity of the entrepreneurs and about the future of the publishing company if these people became part of management. Subsequent to the acquisition, the two subsidiaries were eventually disbanded for reasons that appeared to justify—at least in the view of these skeptical directors—the wholly unexplored and uncertain distrust they had felt when the board made its original "strategic" decision.

Of course, the outcome might still have been the same, even had the consideration of these small acquisitions been more extensive. Perhaps the judgment, skill, and practice required for such a major decision were lacking among both management and the board.

Nonetheless, hindsight makes clear that the board's discussion should have led to further consideration of the proposal and to more skeptical appraisal of the two data base proprietors. The directors' questions, which could not have been wholly clear in the presence of the visitors, should have led management to realize that it needed better answers and that it needed to withdraw the proposal until it understood the import of the questions and had gotten those answers.

SPECIAL FULL-SCALE STRATEGY REVIEWS

A director cannot be incisive and influential unless he or she is familiar with the issues involved. Consideration of new strategies, complex annual reviews, and corporate updates are hard to fit into board meetings of ordinary length. A number of companies have undertaken a special two- or three-day strategy meeting at a location apart from the company, and sometimes with spouses invited for a partially separate program. Senior members of management and planning staff are included.

In such a setting, the systematic presentation of the past year's results compared to the year's plan (with analysis of discrepancies) is accompanied by the presentation of the following one- or two-year plan. The latter plan is then considered against the long-range plan.

More important, in informal sessions at the bar or at meals, the participants' concept of the company and its future is discussed without the usual constraints. Such discussion sometimes includes the board's role and how effectively it contributes to the strategy process.

Assigning more time to the formal consideration of the company's future does not of course guarantee useful contribution from the board, but it does contribute enormously to the board's education. Everyone is exposed to people they might not meet otherwise— directors, managers, staff members, and spouses—and this wider acquaintance leads to (1) greater knowledge of the company and its people, (2) greater trust in individuals' competence and goodwill, (3) understanding of the unevenness of management strength and the opportunity for management development, (4) relaxation of the tension between outside directors and chief executive officers, and (5) keener interest in future opportunities.

To prepare for and schedule a special full-scale strategy review meeting is a formidable undertaking. In fact, the time-consuming nature of the task lends support to Courtney Brown's arguments that the chief executive officer should not be chairman of the board.[8]

Although such a meeting need not culminate in a two- or three-day retreat every year, any effort to prepare a board to understand and play some part in the strategic decisions of a complex company requires more time than a CEO may be able to give it. A separate chairman to look after this and other board functions, or (as William Wommack suggests) a chief strategic officer in management ranks, or a massive delegation of operating responsibilities by the CEO may be necessary to allow time for strategic leadership.

But no matter how strategy sessions are arranged, good chairmanship—to provoke productive discussions or identification of the more debatable issues—is indispensable. At a minimum, careful reading of well-prepared staff reports, with discussion focused on issues that cannot yet be finally resolved, clarifies insight and informs subsequent judgment.

Corporate Strategy Committee

Especially since the collapse of Penn Central led to the proliferation of audit committees, organization by committee has been the board's means of coping with its increased workload. The audit committee performs the watchdog function by monitoring compliance with SEC regulations and the Foreign Corrupt Practices Act and by investigating problems of ethical conduct. The compensation and nominating committees often not only establish executive compensation and recommend new candidates for election but examine the qualifications and performance of senior management and of the board itself.

Organization by committee economizes the time of directors, puts the most qualified people in charge of given issues, educates directors, and provides a relatively private context for discussion of sensitive subjects.

The arguments against a strategy committee are the same arguments used against any form of board involvement in strategy. These arguments ignore powerful trends in corporate governance, minimize directors' potential contributions, and reduce the possibility of building a strong and able board. They will almost certainly fall on deaf ears with the onset of a new generation of chief executive officers, the developing awareness of responsibility among independent directors, and the possibility that conventional management practice tends to undermine productivity.

COMPOSITION AND FUNCTION

For a strategy committee to work, it should be composed of carefully chosen outside directors who have shown interest and talent in considering strategic questions brought to the board. New directors can be recruited expecially for this function.

In the few companies I know of in which a strategy committee has been established, the committee members started off slowly, hearing from one segment of a business at a time and acquainting themselves with the information as well as the managers presenting it. A second level of sophistication would be to have committee members prepare for meetings by reading staff studies that discuss future risks, possibilities, investments, and projects.

After it had become familiar with current strategy, the committee's function would be to assess the strategy's strengths and weaknesses and to consider what measures might improve the strategy. The committee would also discuss the issues being debated within management and consider key proposals before they reached the board. It would note whether other committees—like finance, investment, or pension management—had interest in a proposal.

One of the principal functions of the committee would be to encourage the strengthening of the strategic planning process within the company—to get to know the key participants and to appraise the context within which capital projects and new product ideas originate.

CHARACTER OF DISCUSSIONS

Participation in the strategy formulation process made possible by an active committee could become so intimate as to make CEOs very nervous. Putting information about many possibilities in the hands of outside directors who have become opinionated in their own success and self-esteem can lead to snap-judgment preferences hard to dislodge later.

In some boards where the strategy committee approach has been tried, the unwritten rules constraining discussion have been relaxed to the point that partisanship or bias has been avoided. Individual directors and the CEO challenge each other, and—their relationships strengthened by associations developed in such situations as off-site discussions—they explore things informally as well as more seriously. Directors too quick to substitute their opinions for those of management can be called for interference. Assured that the strategy committee members are not going to take a position prematurely or fault them for indecision, some CEOs have brought to the committee vexing problems, serious threats, and impending choices well before management was ready to make a formal recommendation to the board.

Besides encouraging directors to produce ideas, this strategy committee process could still the restlessness of directors who are uneasy at the yes or no choice given them when a new proposal arrives with a firm recommendation. The basis for saying yes is loyalty to management; the case for the proposal contains little basis for saying no. Prior discussion would let the directors be heard and might make them more understanding and less resentful if they were later overruled. The lines between management and board authority must remain clear, but the more communication across them the better.

The strategy committee would neither create nor dispose of problems of board-management relations. It would simply be a device to make practical the convergence of varied points of view and the dissipation of provincial, functional, or occupational bias. It would do what the board as a whole should but cannot do; it would segregate—like all effective committee structures—the appropriate problems, questions, and recommendations to those most interested and qualified. Like the other committees of the board, it would be shaped by its leadership, composition, and assigned function.

Contribution to Creative Strategy

No discussion of board involvement in strategy formulation, full-board strategy sessions, and corporate strategy committees should conclude without attempting to dispel the solemnity that usually descends on the subject. For individual directors, strategic participation means more work, more time, more thought, and probably at times more uncertainty, frustration, and concern.

Nonetheless, the most common response to exposure to central management issues is stimulation, excitement, satisfaction, greater confidence in being able to contribute, and ideas and knowledge to take back to one's own company. The opportunity to consider someone else's problems is usually exhilarating. The convergence of new points of view on long-standing problems previously viewed between one set of blinders sometimes produces dramatic and satisfying results.

The normal routine of assent to management proposals, based on general confidence in management as justified by past performance, is essentially boring. When participants have reason to wonder whether their confidence in past performance is a sound basis for expecting adequate future performance, they feel frustrated. If in their relationship the CEO is overly forceful and the board overly acquiescent, an unproductive, even dangerous, situation results.

Freer participation by the board in contributing to strategy formation would be of no great importance unless such participation produced better decisions by management. The heart of the strategic process is the generation of alternatives—combining in new ways market opportunity, customer needs, and company capabilities. If a company is to stand apart from its competitors with superior returns on its equity (and why not?), then it must nurture the kind of creativity that finds new applications and new definitions of its distinctive competence.

The current erosion of assets under inflation, the decline in productivity, the temporary collapse of our automobile industry, and the lessening of U.S. competitive capabilities all call for more boldness and imagination in the management of innovation and the undertaking of risk. The leaping innovation that is occasionally produced by imagination and creativity cannot be decreed or simulated. It is throttled by the fear of failure, the cracked voice of experience, the tyranny of plans mechanically requiring an arbitrary percentage growth rate quarter by quarter.

Nonetheless, imagination exists in all questing organizations and people; it can be released and encouraged. The articulated goal to be first in a chosen technology or market, supported by money and people focused on bold objectives, can produce a Wang or Intel at the expense of many a pedestrian competitor. Boards of directors do not themselves create or invent, but they can take into their overview the innovative processes of the company and support their strengthening.

Through its concern with its company's strategy, a board could emphasize and contribute to the search for new opportunity. "What's new?" is a question that should have an unending series of answers in the execution as well as formulation of strategy. Every qualified director has some special skill or experience that could be brought to bear without short-circuiting the authority of management.

Creativity can be served, in short, by realizing the potential for board contribution to corporate strategy. The variety of experience, points of view, technical and general knowledge and quality of judgment present in a full-put-together board can extend management's constrained view of the world and bring stimulation and new ideas to executives grooved by their company's experience to stereotyped policymaking and behavior.

This variety can be made fully effective only by involving boards in the most critical issues facing their chief executive officers—the identity and mission of their companies, the direction they are to maintain in a fast-changing world, and the innovative decisions that will make their strategies successful.

Notes

1. *Harvard Business Review* (July–August 1979), p. 20.
2. *Harvard Business Review* (September–October 1979), p. 48.
3. Quoted in *Harvard Business Review* (July–August 1979), p. 26.
4. For a fuller description, see my book, *The Concept of Corporate Strategy,* revised edition (Homewood, Ill.: Dow Jones-Irwin, 1980).
5. R.M. Cyert and J.G. March, *A Behavioral Theory of the Firm* (Englewood Cliffs, N.J.: Prentice-Hall, 1963).
6. David Baybrooke and Charles E. Lindblom, *A Strategy of Decision* (New York: The Free Press, 1963).
7. H. Edward Wrapp, "Good Managers Don't Make Policy Decisions," *Harvard Business Review* (September–October 1967), p. 91.
8. See Courtney C. Brown, *Putting the Corporate Board to Work* and *Beyond the Bottom Line* (New York: Macmillan, 1976 and 1979, respectively).

About the Contributors

Kenneth R. Andrews is Donald K. David Professor of Business Administration, Emeritus, at the Harvard Business School. He was editor-in-chief of the *Harvard Business Review* from 1979 to 1985, is author of *The Concept of Corporate Strategy*, and is editor of the HBR collection *Ethics in Practice: Managing the Moral Corporation*. He has served as consultant to, and director of, a number of major corporations.

Christopher A. Bartlett is a professor of general management at the Harvard Business School, where he is also chairman of the International Senior Management program. He is, with Sumantra Ghoshal, author of *Managing Across Borders: The Transnational Solution* (1989).

Donald J. Bowersox, the John H. McConnell University Professor at Michigan State University, is a well-known authority on logistics management. He was a founding member and the second president of the Council of Logistics Management. Before entering academic life, he was an executive with the E.F. MacDonald Company.

Andrew Campbell is a member of the Centre for Business Strategy at the London Business School. Previously he worked as a consultant for McKinsey & Company and as a loan officer for a British bank. He is co-author (with Michael Goold) of *Strategies and Style* (1988).

Alfred D. Chandler, Jr., is Straus Professor of Business History, Emeritus, at the Harvard Business School. The author of numerous

461

books, articles, and essays, he received both the 1978 Pulitzer and Bancroft Prizes for his book, *The Visible Hand*.

Gordon Donaldson is the Willard Prescott Smith Professor of Corporate Finance at the Harvard Business School. He is the author of *Strategy for Financial Mobility* (1969), *Basic Business Finance* with Hunt and Williams (1971), *Managing Corporate Wealth* (1984), and *Decision Making at the Top* with Jay Lorsch (1985).

Thomas L. Doorley is a founder and managing partner of Braxton Associates, an international strategy consulting firm.

Pankaj Ghemawat is associate professor of Business, Government, and Competition at the Harvard Business School, where he teaches courses on industry and competitive analysis. His research and consulting focus on competitive dynamics and strategic investments.

Sumantra Ghoshal is an associate professor who teaches business policy and international management at the European Institute of Business Administration (INSEAD) in Fontainebleau, France. He is co-author (with Christopher A. Bartlett) of *Managing Across Borders: The Transnational Solution* (1989).

Michael Goold was a vice president of the Boston Consulting Group and then joined the Centre for Business Strategy at the London Business School as a senior research fellow. He is co-author (with Andrew Campbell) of *Strategies and Style* (1988).

Gary Hamel is lecturer in business policy and management at the London Business School. One of the *Harvard Business Review* articles he co-authored with C.K. Prahalad, "Strategic Intent," won the 1989 McKinsey Award for excellence.

Robert H. Hayes is the Philip Caldwell Professor of Business Administration at the Harvard Business School and chairman of the production and operations management teaching area. His latest book (co-authored with Steven C. Wheelwright and Kim B. Clark) is *Dynamic Manufacturing: Creating the Learning Organization* (1988).

Bruce D. Henderson is the chairman emeritus of the Boston Consulting Group, which he founded in 1963, and which pioneered widely accepted approaches to the development of strategy. He has written extensively on business strategy and his latest book is *The Logic of Business Strategy* (1985). He is professor of management at Vanderbilt University's Owen Graduate School of Management.

Michael C. Jensen is the Edsel Bryant Ford Professor of Business Administration at the Harvard Business School and founding editor of the *Journal of Financial Economics*. His research and writing have figured prominently in the national debate over corporate governance and mergers and acquisitions, and have won many prizes.

Theodore Levitt is an internationally recognized expert in marketing and the Edward W. Carter Professor of Business Administration, Emeritus, at the Harvard Business School. He has taught for more than 30 years, has published numerous articles (he is a four-time winner of the *Harvard Business Review* McKinsey Award), as well as books, the latest of which is *Thinking about Management* (1990). He is a former editor of the *Harvard Business Review*.

F. Warren McFarlan is Ross Graham Walker Professor of Business Administration and director of research, Harvard Business School. He is co-author, with James I. Cash, Jr., and James L. McKenney, of *Corporate Information Systems Management: The Issues Facing Senior Executives* (1988). With James I. Cash, he is featured in a video program, *Competing through Information Technology*, which examines how information technology alters competitive conditions in industry.

Henry Mintzberg is the Bronfman Professor of Management at McGill University in Montreal, Canada. He revolutionized our understanding of what managers do in his landmark book, *The Nature of Managerial Work*. He runs popular seminars for executives; his latest book is *Mintzberg on Management: Inside Our Strange World of Organizations* (1989).

Cynthia A. Montgomery is a professor at the Harvard Business School, where she teaches competition and strategy. Her research centers on corporate strategy and the competitiveness of diversified firms. She has been extensively published in *Strategic Management Journal* (on whose editorial review board she sits), *The Academy of Management Journal*, *Management Science*, and other periodicals.

Kenichi Ohmae heads McKinsey's office in Tokyo. He is the author of *The Mind of the Strategist: The Art of Japanese Business* (1982), *Triad Power: The Coming Shape of Global Competition* (1985), and *Beyond National Borders* (1987).

Penny C. Paquette is research associate and director of the International University of Japan Program at the Tuck School of Management at Dartmouth.

Michael E. Porter teaches at the Harvard Business School, is an adviser to leading companies all over the world, and served on the President's Commission on Industrial Competitiveness. He is the author of *Competitive Strategy* (1980), *Competitive Advantage* (1985), and *The Competitive Advantage of Nations* (1990). He is featured in the Harvard Business School Videos Series program *Michael Porter on Competitive Strategy.*

C.K. Prahalad is professor of corporate strategy and international business at the University of Michigan. He is the co-author (with Yves Doz) of *The Multinational Mission: Balancing Local Demands and Vision* (1987) and author of many articles. One of those articles, "Strategic Intent," with Gary Hamel, won the 1989 McKinsey Award for excellence.

James Brian Quinn is the William and Josephine Buchanan Professor of Management at the Tuck School of Management at Dartmouth. He has contributed many articles to the *Harvard Business Review* as well as to other periodicals; he is the author of *Strategies for Change* (1980) and co-author of a textbook, *The Strategy Process* (1987).

Alfred Rappaport is the Leonard Spacek Professor of Accounting and Information Systems at Northwestern University's Kellogg Graduate School of Management and the author of *Creating Shareholder Value: The New Standard for Business Performance* (1986). He is also chairman of the Alcar Group Inc.

George Stalk, Jr., is a vice president and director of the Boston Consulting Group in Chicago, Illinois. He is co-author (with James C. Abegglen) of *Kaisha, the Japanese Corporation* (1985) and (with Thomas Hout) of *Competing Against Time* (1990).

Pierre Wack is retired head of the business environment division of the Royal Dutch/Shell Group. In the decade during which he headed the group, he developed the Shell system of scenario planning. He lectured on the subject at Harvard Business School and now consults and participates in scenario development with management teams around the world.

Steven C. Wheelwright is the first Class of 1949 Professor of Business Administration at the Harvard Business School. He has published widely in journals, has served as an associate editor of the *International Journal of Forecasting*, among others; and is the author or co-author of several books, the most recent of which was *Dynamic Manufacturing: Creating the Learning Organization* (1988).

INDEX